TRANSGENDER INTIMATE PARTNER VIOLENCE

Transgender Intimate Partner Violence

A Comprehensive Introduction

Edited by
Adam M. Messinger *and* Xavier L. Guadalupe-Diaz

NEW YORK UNIVERSITY PRESS
New York

NEW YORK UNIVERSITY PRESS
New York
www.nyupress.org

© 2020 by New York University
All rights reserved

References to internet websites (URLs) were accurate at the time of writing. Neither the authors nor New York University Press is responsible for URLs that may have expired or changed since the manuscript was prepared.

Library of Congress Cataloging-in-Publication Data
Names: Messinger, Adam M., 1982- editor. | Guadalupe-Diaz, Xavier L., editor.
Title: Transgender intimate partner violence : a comprehensive introduction / edited by Adam M. Messinger and Xavier L. Guadalupe-Diaz.
Description: New York : New York University Press, 2020. | Includes bibliographical references and index.
Identifiers: LCCN 2019041470 | ISBN 9781479830428 (cloth) | ISBN 9781479890316 (paperback) | ISBN 9781479829095 (ebook) | ISBN 9781479813483 (ebook)
Subjects: LCSH: Intimate partner violence. | Transgender people—Violence against.
Classification: LCC HV6626 .T73 2020 | DDC 362.82/92—dc23
LC record available at https://lccn.loc.gov/2019041470

New York University Press books are printed on acid-free paper, and their binding materials are chosen for strength and durability. We strive to use environmentally responsible suppliers and materials to the greatest extent possible in publishing our books.

Manufactured in the United States of America

10 9 8 7 6 5 4 3 2 1

Also available as an e-book

To the incredible scholars, service providers, and activists who contributed their expertise to this book, and to all those who pioneered and continue powering the movement to end transgender intimate partner violence—we owe you an immense debt of gratitude.

To our families: thank you for all that you do to make this a cozier, more loving world.

CONTENTS

Foreword   ix
   Connie Burk

PART I. INTRODUCTION AND OVERVIEW OF TRANSGENDER INTIMATE PARTNER VIOLENCE

1. The Intersection of Transphobia, Human Rights, and Transgender Intimate Partner Violence   3
   Adam M. Messinger and Xavier L. Guadalupe-Diaz

2. Tactics and Justifications of Abuse Involving Transgender Individuals   35
   Xavier Quinn

3. Undermining Transgender Survivors: Discrediting Identity Work in Intimate Relationships   62
   Amanda Koontz

PART II. TRANSGENDER IPV CONTEXT AND CAUSES

4. "Why Don't You Just Leave?": Transgender Resilience and Barriers to Escaping Abuse   91
   Rayna E. Momen and Walter S. DeKeseredy

5. Theorizing on the Roots of Transgender Intimate Partner Violence   110
   Adam M. Messinger

6. The Intersections of Race and Immigration   133
   Xavier L. Guadalupe-Diaz and Carolyn M. West

PART III. BEST PRACTICES IN TRANSGENDER IPV SERVICE PROVISION AND THE LAW

7. Providing Appropriate Health-Care Services to Transgender and Gender Nonconforming Survivors of IPV   169
   Shanna K. Kattari, Héctor Torres, Kim Fountain, and Ing Swenson

8. Best Practices in Shelter Provision   202
    Brian Tesch

9. Best Practices in Policing   224
    Kae Greenberg

10. Legal System Reform   258
    Leigh Goodmark

PART IV. FUTURE DIRECTIONS AND CONCLUSIONS

11. Beyond the Gender Binary: Trans/forming IPV Prevention Using a Public Health Framework   281
    Rebecca Howard, Sharyn J. Potter, Taylor Flagg, Mary M. Moynihan, and Zachary Ahmad-Kahloon

12. Training Service Providers to Identify and Overcome Service Barriers in Working with Transgender IPV Survivors   311
    michael munson and Loree Cook-Daniels

13. Overcoming Barriers to Knowledge Production in Transgender IPV Research   336
    Adam F. Yerke and Jennifer DeFeo

14. Working toward Transgender Inclusion in the Movement to Address Intimate Partner Violence   362
    Xavier L. Guadalupe-Diaz and Adam M. Messinger

About the Editors   379

About the Contributors   381

Index   387

FOREWORD

CONNIE BURK

On any given day, our social media feeds are filled with reports of the ongoing attacks on the humanity of transgender people in the United States and around the globe. The denials and delays start at the highest federal offices and wind their way down to even our local school boards. While attempts to delegitimize and criminalize transgender experience were reanimated in the US under the Trump administration, transgender people and transgender communities have been fighting against legislative and regulatory attacks at local, state, and federal levels for decades.

In the spring of 2016, I abandoned my cart of groceries to wade into a group of folks from the neighborhood gathered around a stack of citizen initiative petitions. "Please don't sign I-1515," I said, holding up my phone, a picture of my partner and kids glowing softly there. "This bill will hurt my family." This citizen initiative was one of over 175 local legislative attempts around the country that year to harm lesbian, gay, bisexual, transgender, and queer (LGBTQ) people, including 44 specifically targeting transgender people and those who do not conform to rigid expectations of gender identity and expression in the public square. Under transgender leadership working in coalition with transgender and non-transgender folks in the anti-violence movement, these discriminatory voter initiatives and so-called bathroom bills were defeated in my home of Washington State. In fact, even though their proponents often attempted to cloak themselves as sensitive to the experiences of sexual assault survivors, such bills targeting the basic human rights of LGBTQ people were nonetheless beaten back in states in every region of the country.

Across the nation, strategies to educate the public about how these policies hurt transgender people relied upon widespread solidarity from local and national anti-violence advocates and organizations. So, in addition to accosting people at my local grocery store, I was one of many leaders in the anti-violence field called upon to educate voters and policymakers about the actual needs of sexual assault survivors, including those experiencing intimate partner violence (IPV): that is, psychological, physical, or sexual abuse in a romantic or sexual relationship. Of particular import, transgender people experience some of the highest rates of sexual and intimate partner violence of any population in the United States.

This solidarity between the transgender rights and anti-violence movements was not a new phenomenon—in fact, the Violence Against Women Reauthorization Act of 2013 was among the first federal legislation of any kind to protect transgender people. Motivated by the simple rationale that our movements must protect all survivors of abuse and violence, anti-violence activists and advocates put their funding on the line and refused to accept a compromise that would eliminate gender identity and sexual orientation protections. Some in Congress threatened to scuttle the bill, but ultimately it passed with overwhelming support.

That solidarity was built on years upon decades upon generations of consciousness-raising, arguing, theorizing, research, and practice—often originating in anti-violence organizing among transgender and non-transgender people of color such as the Color of Violence conferences organized by INCITE!—that has resulted in the anti-violence movement being closely allied with transgender liberation.

The anti-violence movement, for all its flaws, is well suited to the task. Advocacy teaches us to consider an individual survivor in their social, political, and cultural context. Anti-violence advocates learn that each survivor's personal goals and desires exist in multiple, simultaneous contexts that present cooperating and competing interests in constant flux. Instead of demanding a survivor reduce reality to something simple, advocacy enjoins us to show up for all the messy realness in any given survivor's life. It teaches us to beware of binaries. To pay attention to the outliers—the experiences of abuse that do not map easily onto the stories we have become accustomed to hearing and telling. We cannot ignore what we learn in order to preserve outdated models. It is our obligation to recognize the unique experiences of transgender survivors of IPV, and, in doing so, enable better strategies and practices—of service, advocacy, activism, and research—to emerge.

Every day, we stand with survivors as they step away from everything their batterers and the world has told them they must do to earn their humanity, to deserve protection, or to buy or barter a moment of ease. Every day, we stand with survivors as they transform confusion into clarity, fear into action. We stand with survivors as they sort through the lies and misinformation, the gaslighting, and the tricks that were used to interrupt their relationships and to cause them to doubt themselves and delay action on their own behalf. We are there when survivors rearrange and repurpose everything in their reach to minimize harm and build the life they want to live.

The movement to end violence can expect no less from us.

Transgender Intimate Partner Violence: A Comprehensive Introduction provides an opportunity to amplify the commitment the anti-violence movement has made to transgender, nonbinary, and gender nonconforming survivors of IPV into concrete action and efficacious advocacy, research, and policy. It provides an opportunity to consider structural determinants and potential responses at the grassroots level, to synthesize contextual, experiential, and best research data into our emerging strategies.

Our movements put a stake in the ground: we will not relent on fighting for transgender survivors and transgender dignity. But that is not enough. We also must be willing to change our day-to-day practices in both simple and profound ways that will make advocacy and supportive services for and by transgender survivors possible.

We must examine our built environments and understand how the lack of privacy in our design of communal shelters exposes survivors to ongoing scrutiny and trauma. We must consider our hiring and retention practices, our pay scales and job requirements. Who can afford to do this work? How do our personnel practices shape the representation of survivors within our agencies and the field? We must ensure that assisting people with name changes, resolving documentation questions, and quashing nuisance arrests and convictions are part of routine direct service and advocacy work. We must improve how we organize our systems advocacy and demand concrete changes to protect the lives of transgender survivors in criminal-legal, medical, educational, and carceral institutions.

This book is an incredible trove of information and practical ideas grounded in a growing body of research, ready to be harnessed to move from aspiration to action in the commitment to transgender lives.

In this book, as is the case anytime we pay attention to the margins, we will encounter stories and analysis that resonate across identities and make sense for all survivors, transgender and cisgender alike. Acknowledging how this information can inform our work with all survivors of IPV is vital. However, we must resist the bad habit of simply taking the "aha moments" from our work with transgender survivors, applying those insights to our care of non-transgender people, and neglecting the transgender people whose lives and work made our new consciousness possible.

When you learn from the margins, you must give back to the margins. You must ensure that transgender people are represented in leadership and decision-making. Our movements are enriched by the knowledge held in the pages of this book; we must be willing to answer its call and fundamentally change our relationship to the many diverse transgender communities that made this book, and the research herein, possible.

The editors of this book have allowed for cross-cutting and divergent ideas. Unlike the trend toward groupthink embedded in our social media algorithms and siloed networks, this book offers perspectives from different vantage points that don't require homogeneity to harmonize. As feminist scholar and activist Loretta Ross has instructed us, a group of people moving in the same direction and saying the same thing is a cult, but a group of people moving in the same direction and saying different things just might be a movement.

Showing up is the first step toward solidarity. It's mandatory but not enough. This book is essential reading for those who have shown up and are asking, "What's next?" It's for policymakers, researchers, teachers and students, service providers and administrators, advocates and activists, survivors and allies, and more. This book is for everyone who suspects that the movement to end intimate partner violence and the movement for transgender liberation must work in solidarity if we are to foster loving and equitable relationships inside loving and just communities.

We need each other. We are each other. Let's pick up this book and get to work.

PART I

Introduction and Overview of
Transgender Intimate Partner Violence

1

The Intersection of Transphobia, Human Rights, and Transgender Intimate Partner Violence

ADAM M. MESSINGER AND XAVIER L. GUADALUPE-DIAZ

In many ways, Joe was a typical teenager. He lived at home with his mom. He loved plays. One day while working for a theatrical production, someone took a romantic interest in Joe. He rebuffed their advances at first. After all, Joe had never been in a "real" relationship. Soon, though, casual flirting became something more, and they started dating. "I'll just have a little fun and break it off," Joe thought.[1]

Unfortunately for Joe, abusers do not wear name tags. ("Hello, my name is: Batterer!" the sticker might warn.) If only we lived in such a world.

For Joe, what started off as young love slowly descended into a nightmare. His partner began telling Joe how to look and act. His partner insisted on certain sexual acts that made Joe uncomfortable. His partner raped Joe.

He wanted to call the police or ask for help. But Joe was all too familiar with the popular—yet false—myth that men can't get raped, and he feared he would not be believed.[2] On top of this, Joe's abuser was another man. In a world that so often takes same-gender abuse less seriously, Joe felt trapped.[3]

Like countless others, this is a familiar story of intimate partner violence (IPV)—psychological, physical, or sexual abuse in romantic and sexual relationships. However, Joe's experience is unique in one important way: unlike most men, Joe was assigned female at birth.

Unlike with cisgender people (those whose assigned biological sex at birth matches their current gender identity), IPV manifests in distinct ways with transgender people (those whose assigned sex at birth differs from their current gender identity, irrespective of whether or not they have engaged in medical interventions to alter their bodies—including those who were assigned male and identify as women, were assigned female and identify as men, or identify as agender, genderqueer, Two-Spirit, or another nonbinary gender). Importantly, the uniqueness of IPV among transgender people is largely due to two interrelated and pervasive norms in society: cisnormativity (the expectation that all people are cisgender, along with the privileging of cisgender experience and the pathologizing of transgender experience) and transphobia (a strong dislike of or fear of transgender people).

Cisnormativity and transphobia motivate and enable many abusers to shame and control their transgender partners. Consider Joe's relationship, where his abuser attempted to control and limit Joe's gender expression and transition. After he changed his legal name to Joe, his abuser showed a lack of respect for Joe's gender identity as a man, insisting on discovering Joe's given name and only reluctantly using his correct pronouns. When Joe considered undertaking certain gender-affirming medical interventions, his abuser worked to derail these plans: he explicitly told Joe that such procedures would be wrong, barred him from seeing medical healthcare professionals, coerced and forced Joe into vaginal sexual activities and then claimed "now we're really together," and threatened Joe with unwanted impregnation.[4] As Joe explained, "I do feel like it [being trans and transitioning] made me more vulnerable. I was in a really sensitive and kind of unstable place and I was trying to find my footing and I just, it's not a good; it's an ideal time for an abuser to strike. They take advantage of your fears or your uncertainty."[5]

Cisnormativity and transphobia also can hinder the ability of transgender people in abusive relationships to seek help. This was very much true for Joe. On top of concerns that police may not take a male-identified survivor as seriously, Joe feared that police might also be transphobic—a reasonable fear, according to research.[6] As Joe said, "I never did go to the police, I don't trust them because of my situation . . . I had just heard a lot of bad things, um it's a different situation someone who is um, trans, being abused by someone. . . . the whole 'you are a freak' . . ."[7] In addition to fearing a negative response, Joe also was concerned that police might even mislabel him as the abuser, perhaps drawing on the myth that transgender people are inherently violent. This too is a valid concern, according to Pooja Gehi, then an attorney with the transgender-focused Sylvia Rivera Law Project: "[W]hen my clients who are survivors of domestic violence call the police for assistance, they often end up getting arrested either instead of, or along with, their abuser.... Rather than investigate the situation, police officers tend to arrest based on assumptions..."[8] Finally, Joe had to weigh the potential ramifications of being intentionally or unintentionally outed in his efforts to seek help: "I was afraid of what other people would do if they found out," he reflected.[9] For many transgender people (11 percent, according to national estimates), their partners threaten to out them by exposing their transgender status to others, posing an additional deterrent to seeking help.[10]

The hurdles Joe encountered in escaping abuse are commonplace for transgender survivors. Since the inception of the modern international IPV prevention movement in the 1970s, policies and services have been constructed largely to address IPV between cisgender people—referred to in this volume as *cisgender IPV* (C-IPV). Such policies and services often presume that cisgender experiences of abuse are universally shared by everyone who experiences IPV, including transgender people. In doing so, they ignore the many unique causes, abusive tactics, and barriers to help seeking that characterize IPV involving either a transgender victim or perpetrator (regardless of whether their partner is transgender or cisgender)—referred to in this volume as *transgender IPV* (T-IPV).[11] In other instances, transgender survivors may be outright excluded by policies or services. For instance, since the 2013 reauthorization of the Violence Against Women Act (VAWA) and subsequent guidance by the Office for Civil Rights, survivor shelters in the United States are legally entitled to deny admission to transgender survivors of IPV if the stated rationale is to "ensure the victim's health and safety"[12] and it is deemed "necessary to the essential operation of a program."[13] Not surprisingly, research has found that shelters admit just 78 percent of transgender women and 55 percent of transgender men who seek help with victimization.[14] (Of note, although it incorporates the aforementioned problematic loophole, VAWA on its surface aimed to provide greater protections for transgender survivors—protections that are no longer in place as of the writing of this book. The US Congress permitted VAWA to expire on December 21, 2018, and has not yet reauthorized it.[15])

Beyond fueling abuse and limiting avenues of escape for transgender survivors, cisnormativity and transphobia also can limit awareness of the existence of T-IPV. After all, with public discourse, services, and policy largely focused on C-IPV, there are fewer opportunities in society to learn what constitutes healthy and unhealthy relationships among transgender people. Even as awareness of IPV in lesbian, gay, bisexual, transgender, and queer (LGBTQ) communities has continued to grow, research and service provision focused specifically on the *T* in the acronym has lagged behind.[16] Perhaps as a symptom of this knowledge gap, 27 percent of transgender people who experience IPV do not label these experiences as "abusive," which serves as a major barrier to seeking help.[17] Likewise, the limited extent of public awareness about T-IPV may hinder the ability of survivors to recognize IPV when perpetrated by a transgender partner.[18] Even among service providers specializing in aiding IPV survivors, by one estimate just half self-report being "at best, only minimally prepared" to serve transgender people.[19]

This invisible public health threat of IPV in transgender communities remains alarmingly prevalent. For instance, in the United States, national estimates have found that over half (54 percent) of transgender adults have experienced at least one form of IPV within their lifetimes.[20] If future policies and services are to be effective in decreasing T-IPV and its negative effects, these efforts must be evidence-based, informed by a deep research literature. It is for this reason that we are fortunate to live in a moment when scholarship on T-IPV is reaching a critical mass. Since the earliest empirical data on T-IPV were published in the late 1990s and early 2000s,[21] the rate of new empirical publications has dramatically accelerated. Studies also are becoming increasingly ambitious in scope. For instance, results from the first national-level study assessing T-IPV—albeit a study using nonrandom sampling—was published in just the past few years (US Transgender Survey),[22] and an ongoing, groundbreaking study will be the first in the transgender health literature to utilize a probability sample of transgender individuals (TransPop).[23] Thus, while knowledge gaps still exist, the emergent T-IPV literature is already quite diverse and robust.

With now two decades of empirical data studying the prevalence and nature of T-IPV, an important step toward improving future service provision, public policy, and research is to bring together in one go-to resource all that research can tell us about T-IPV. Unfortunately, just two books to date have reviewed substantial portions of the T-IPV literature, only one of which focused exclusively on transgender abuse.[24]

With this in mind, *Transgender Intimate Partner Violence: A Comprehensive Introduction* is the first-ever edited volume to comprehensively review the T-IPV research literature. It is written for expert and nonexpert audiences alike and is designed to be a resource for researchers, teachers, students, mental and medical health-care service providers, law enforcement agencies, IPV shelters and agencies, transgender rights groups and activists, survivors and allies, and anyone wishing to better understand T-IPV.

In this opening chapter, we review research on the prevalence and impact of T-IPV. Next, this chapter examines the links between IPV and the restriction of transgender human rights. As Joe's story illustrates, discrimination is part of the DNA of T-IPV, whether motivating abusers, enabling unique tactics to control survivors, or blocking passage to escape. Thus, to fully understand T-IPV, it is important to consider the extent of societal transphobia and its links with relationship abuse. Finally, this introductory chapter previews the thematic sections and chapters ahead.

Ultimately, it is our sincere hope that, by highlighting what is empirically known, this book offers not only a needed primer on T-IPV but also evidence-based tips for substantially improving future service provision, public policy, and scholarship. This book is about ensuring that Joe and the countless others like him live in a world where safety and justice are the rights of *all* people.

T-IPV Prevalence and Impact

Although research on intimate partner violence involving transgender individuals is still sorely needed, emerging literature repeatedly emphasizes two key facts: T-IPV is highly prevalent and its consequences for survivors are substantial.

T-IPV Prevalence

As compared to research on victimization, perpetration by transgender partners is substantially understudied. That said, one large study of youth ($N = 5,647$) that included a small transgender subsample ($n = 18$) found that high proportions of transgender youth had perpetrated psychological IPV (29.4 percent), physical IPV (58.8 percent), and technology-facilitated or "cyber" IPV (35.3 percent) in the past year. The same study found that transgender youth were more likely than cisgender youth (both women and men) to perpetrate physical and "cyber" IPV, and transgender youth were just as likely as cisgender young women and more likely than cisgender young men to perpetrate psychological IPV.[25]

A more robust literature on victimization finds that IPV is experienced at high rates among transgender individuals. In addition to prevalence studies examining victimization in the past six months[26] and the past year,[27] victimization through college graduation,[28] victimization by primary and casual partners,[29] and victimization among a subsample of those physically or sexually assaulted by anyone including strangers,[30] a number of studies have pointed to an alarming risk of IPV victimization across the full life span of transgender individuals. In particular, studies have shown that over their lifetimes, 44–57 percent of transgender people experience psychological IPV victimization such as verbal abuse and controlling behaviors,[31] 20–35 percent experience threats of physical violence[32] and 35–46 percent experience physical IPV victimization such as hitting or burning,[33] 8–47 percent experience sexual IPV victimization such as nonconsensual sexual touching or penetration,[34] and 27–73 percent experience anti-transgender "identity abuse" victimization (i.e., any IPV tactic that leverages a person's transgender status as a means of control).[35] (See figure 1.1.)

Of reports providing the prevalence of transgender people experiencing at least one form of IPV,[36] the 2015 US Transgender Survey is by far the largest and most generalizable study currently available in any nation. A study of 27,715 transgender people from across the United States and its territories, the US Transgender Survey found that 54 percent of transgender adults in the United States have experienced at least one form of IPV within their lifetimes.[37] Extrapolating from one conservative national estimate that 1.4 million Americans identify as transgender, at least 756,000 transgender people in the United States alone have experienced IPV in their lifetimes.[38] Conflicting studies have found that, relative to transgender men, transgender women are at greater risk of physical[39] and sexual IPV victimization,[40] similar risk of experiencing either physical or sexual IPV victimization,[41] and lower risk of experiencing at least one form of IPV victimization.[42] Considerably less research has examined IPV victimization prevalence among nonbinary individuals. One of the few such studies found that nonbinary

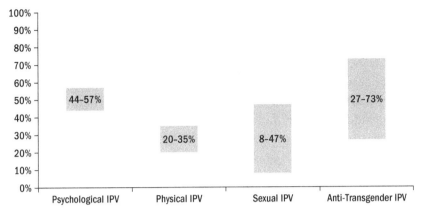

Figure 1.1. Range of Lifetime IPV Victimization Prevalence among Transgender Adults
Sources: James et al. 2016; Landers and Gilsanz 2009; National Coalition of Anti-Violence Programs 2017; Nemoto, Bödeker, and Iwamoto 2011; Pitts et al. 2006; Roch, Morton, and Ritchie 2010; Scottish Transgender Alliance 2008; Turell 2000; Woulfe and Goodman 2018.

and gender nonconforming participants in the sample were more likely to experience physical or sexual IPV victimization (60 percent) than transgender men (30 percent) and transgender women (44 percent), but the difference was not statistically significant.[43]

Among studies that have directly compared both groups, studies have generally shown transgender people to be at either similar or higher risk relative to cisgender people for all or at least some of the assessed forms of IPV victimization.[44] When turning to larger-scale studies, a cross-study comparison of the best available US national prevalence estimates for a transgender sample (the aforementioned 2015 US Transgender Survey) and a predominantly cisgender sample (the 2010 US National Intimate Partner and Sexual Violence Survey) reveals slightly higher lifetime physical IPV victimization rates for transgender people than for cisgender people (35 percent and 30 percent, respectively).[45]

T-IPV Impact

Just as with cisgender people,[46] IPV can have a host of negative effects on transgender people. For instance, transgender survivors often find that abuse exacts a heavy economic toll. Consider that many transgender survivors find that their ability to commute to work is impeded by the abuse (69.9 percent),[47] will continue to experience abuse at or near their workplace (69.6 percent),[48] find that IPV impacts their performance at work (95.7 percent),[49] and are forced to miss work or to stop looking for work due to the abuse (27 percent).[50] In addition, many transgender survivors suffer through constant fear (10–13 percent),[51] injury (16–42 percent),[52] and negative mental health consequences (76 percent)[53] such as depressive symptomology (65 percent).[54] Conflicting studies have found victimization for transgender people to be associated[55] and not associated[56] with substance abuse. Victimization among transgender people is also associated with engaging in sexual risk-taking behaviors such as unprotected sex.[57] With some exceptions,[58] studies have found that, among transgender people, experiencing IPV victimization is also associated with a greater risk of HIV,[59] although the cause-and-effect relationship between these factors is not yet clear. Studies of cisgender people indicate that IPV can at times directly cause exposure to HIV, such as when abusers refuse to use protection. At other times survivors who have left their abusers may engage in high-risk sexual behaviors with new partners as a means through which to regain a sense of personal control over their bodies following the disempowerment of victimization. At still other times abusers may be drawn to enter into relationships with people living with HIV if they believe that such partners will be more disempowered, dependent, and controllable.[60]

T-IPV and Discrimination

While T-IPV is both prevalent and impactful, it is not identical to C-IPV. As Joe's experience highlights, the causes, abusive tactics, and barriers to escape regarding T-IPV are fueled in part by the existence of discriminatory abusers, service providers, and policies. However, discriminatory attitudes are not biologically inevitable traits of a few bad apples. Rather, systemic bias against transgender people emerges when societies at large tacitly condone and even encourage discrimination, often buttressed by laws that restrict the basic human rights of transgender people. While ending transphobia may not end the existence of T-IPV, discrimination undeniably increases the vulnerability of transgender people to IPV and narrows their avenues of escape. In this sense, understanding why T-IPV takes its current forms necessitates recognizing the extent of discrimination against transgender people. This section explores (1) the current state of interpersonal transphobia in the world, (2) ongoing transgender human rights restrictions imbedded in law, and (3) how such discrimination ultimately impacts T-IPV.

Interpersonal Transphobia

In many societies today, transphobic attitudes are pervasive. Consider a recent study of sixteen countries drawn from every continent except Antarctica, which found that 23 percent of people in the world agree or strongly agree that transgender people have a mental illness, 30 percent worry about exposing children to transgender people, and 21 percent believe their society has "gone too far" in accommodating transgender people.[61] Of course, these mean average rates are even higher in some nations (e.g., in the United States, where these rates are 32 percent, 41 percent, and 36 percent, respectively). As researcher Julia Walker reflects, "trans people are possibly the most marginalized minority group in society; they are stigmatized in every culture across race, ethnicity, religion, and are even stigmatized by [lesbian, gay, and bisexual] movements and organizations."[62]

Not surprisingly, transphobic attitudes appear to translate into transphobic actions, with many transgender people reporting disturbing levels of discrimination and violence in their daily lives. (See table 1.1.) For instance, in the United States, discrimination extends from the family to school, employment, housing, and even public accommodations such as stores and restaurants. According to the nationally representative 2015 US Transgender Survey, among transgender people who were out about being transgender to the immediate family that they grew up with, 27 percent were not allowed by their family to wear clothing that matched their gender identity, 26 percent had a family member stop speaking with them because they were transgender, and 14 percent had been sent by their family to a professional in an attempt to stop them from being transgender. Of those who were out as transgender during their elementary, middle, and/or high school years, 54 percent were verbally bullied,

TABLE 1.1. Prevalence of Discrimination against Transgender People in the United States

Form of Discrimination	% of Transgender People
Family Discrimination (of those out about being transgender)	
Barred by family from wearing clothing matching gender identity	27%
Family member stopped speaking with them because they are transgender	26%
Sent by family to a professional to deter them from being transgender	14%
School Discrimination (during K–12 grades)	
Verbally bullied due to being transgender	54%
Physically attacked due to being transgender	24%
Sexually assaulted due to being transgender	13%
Employment Discrimination	
Verbally harassed in past year due to being transgender (of those employed)	14%
Fired, not promoted, or not hired in past year due to being transgender (of those employed or applying for a job)	27%
Housing Discrimination	
Kicked out of house by family (of those out about being transgender)	8%
Denied permission to buy or rent housing in past year due to being transgender	6%
Evicted from housing in past year	5%
Ever been homeless	30%
Public Accommodations Discrimination	
Verbally harassed in public accommodations in past year due to being transgender	24%
Denied equal treatment or services in public accommodations in past year due to being transgender	14%

Source: James et al. 2016.

24 percent were physically attacked, and 13 percent were sexually assaulted specifically because they were transgender.

In addition, 14 percent of respondents employed within the past year had been verbally harassed due to being transgender and, of those who were employed or had applied for a job in the past year, 27 percent reported being fired, not promoted, or not hired in the past year specifically due to being transgender. (In light of this extensive employment discrimination, it is unfortunately not surprising that the Center for American Progress recently found that transgender Americans are four times more likely to live in poverty than the general population.)[63] Regarding housing, 8 percent of respondents had been kicked out of their house by their family, in the past year 6 percent were denied permission to buy or rent and 5 percent were evicted from a home or apartment specifically due to being transgender, and 30 percent indicated they had been homeless at some point in their lives. In public accommodations such as restaurants and stores, 24 percent of respondents reported being verbally harassed and 14 percent were denied equal treatment or services in the past year specifically due to being transgender.[64] Perhaps the ultimate distillation of transphobic attitudes is violence. In addition to IPV, studies find that transgender people face alarming rates of hate crimes, physical and sexual assault, and homicide.[65]

Transgender Human Rights Restrictions

Scholar and transgender rights activist Paisley Currah argues that anti-transgender sentiment has only been growing in recent years, with this "new transgender panic" being used to justify ever-restrictive laws.[66] Indeed, in many parts of the world, transgender discrimination is codified in law.[67] Reflecting and reinforcing interpersonal transphobia, many societies use both existing laws and the absence of laws to restrict the basic human rights of transgender people, including the following: the rights to marriage and having children; the rights to freedom from discrimination in education, health care, employment, housing, credit and lending, public accommodations, and military service; and the fundamental right to exist.

Marriage can be particularly challenging for transgender people, particularly in nations that do not allow same-sex marriage, as courts have been known to deny or annul marriage licenses if both people have the same gender marker on their identity documents (regardless of their gender identity), if they appear to be the same gender (regardless of their legal gender markers), or if they have different legal gender markers but one of them had a different assigned sex at birth.[68] This potential barrier to marriage exists in the majority of the world, since, as of 2017, only twenty-four nations have legalized same-sex marriage.[69] Adding further complications is the fact that many nations make it difficult or impossible for gender markers to be changed on identity documents. For instance, only fifty-one nations permit a change in the gender listed on government documents such as birth certificates, driver's licenses, and passports; of these nations, twenty-nine require surgery, sterilization, or both before a name change is permitted, and only four permit a change to a third or nonbinary gender marker.[70] In the United States, gender-affirming surgery is required in order to change the gender marker on a birth certificate in nineteen states and on a driver's license in twelve states, despite the fact that many transgender people do not desire surgery.[71] Thus, whether due to court interpretations of transgender identity or laws inhibiting the change of gender markers on government documents, marriage is by no means a guaranteed right in the majority of the world. (It is important to note that an inability to change one's gender marker on identity documents poses additional challenges beyond marriage in any context requiring verification of identity, such as when voting in elections, signing contracts, using credit cards, seeking health care, filling medication prescriptions, pursuing education, boarding airplanes, and crossing police checkpoints.[72])

For transgender people wishing to expand their families by having children, additional legal barriers may be placed in their path. Consider the United States, where only three of fifty states have antidiscrimination state laws explicitly prohibiting discrimination against transgender people seeking to foster or jointly adopt children, and where nine states explicitly permit such discrimination by state-licensed child welfare agencies if religious beliefs are stated to be the justification.[73]

Beyond restricting the rights to marriage and children, many nations restrict the rights of transgender people to live free from discrimination in education. For instance, in the US, just thirteen of fifty states have antidiscrimination state laws explicitly prohibiting gender-based discrimination in education, and two states in fact prohibit the creation of gender-based antidiscrimination laws regarding education.[74] Following the path of six US states that prohibit the positive portrayal of "homosexual activity" in kindergarten through twelfth grade, several states have considered or are considering similar legislation to restrict education about transgender lives.[75] In addition, while the Obama administration directed public schools to interpret Title IX of the Education

Amendments Act of 1972 as prohibiting discrimination against transgender students, including but not limited to permitting them to access bathrooms corresponding with their gender identity, in February 2017 the US Departments of Justice and Education under the Trump administration withdrew that guidance, effectively legalizing discrimination against transgender students in education settings.[76]

Of course, educational settings have not been the only contexts in which policymakers have attempted to force transgender people to use public restrooms corresponding with their sex assigned at birth rather than their gender identity. For instance, in the US, North Carolina's Public Facilities Privacy and Security Act—passed into law in 2016 and repealed shortly thereafter in 2017—made it illegal not only in education but statewide for transgender people to use public facilities corresponding with their gender identity.[77] In defending the law, politicians erroneously painted transgender women as lying rapists, arguing without evidence that they are in fact cisgender men pretending to be women in an effort to sexually assault women inside women's restrooms.[78] Similar so-called bathroom bills were up for consideration in sixteen other states during the 2017 legislative session.[79]

Some nations also restrict the rights of transgender people to access health care free of discrimination. For instance, in the US, just thirteen of fifty states have antidiscrimination state laws explicitly prohibiting discrimination against transgender people in health care.[80] National estimates indicate that among transgender people in the US who have health insurance, 55 percent of those who have sought transition-related surgery in the past year and 25 percent of those who have sought transition-related hormone therapy in the past year have been denied coverage.[81] In addition, 23 percent of transgender people in the US reported that they avoided seeking needed health care in the past year due to concerns that they would be mistreated or disrespected—a valid concern given that 33 percent of transgender people who had seen a health-care provider in the past year reported having a negative experience with them related to being transgender.[82] Despite these realities, under current federal leadership the US Department of Health and Human Services created a new "Division of Conscience and Religious Freedom" to shield health-care workers who wish to deny treatment to patients on the basis of religious objection, including but not limited to transgender patients.[83]

Similar roadblocks to equal rights exist in other realms of society, including in employment, housing, credit and lending, public accommodations, and military service. For example, in the US, less than half of the fifty states have antidiscrimination state laws explicitly prohibiting discrimination on the basis of gender identity in employment (only twenty states have such protections), housing (twenty states), health care (thirteen states), public accommodations (nineteen states), and credit and lending (fourteen states).[84] The absence of national-level protections for transgender people in the US is deeply problematic for those living in the majority of states without laws prohibiting discrimination on the basis of gender identity. Lacking congressional support for a national antidiscrimination law, the Obama administration aimed to create the effect of such a law by interpreting Title VII of the Civil Rights Act of 1964 as indirectly prohibiting employment discrimination. However, administrative guidance does not carry the weight of law and can more readily be challenged in court, and, as has been the case under the Trump administration, such administrative guidance can be easily rescinded or reinterpreted when a new president takes office.[85] Given the need for nationwide antidiscrimination laws, it is troubling to note that, globally, only twenty-six nations have antidiscrimination laws specifically protecting transgender people, just twenty-one have laws prohibiting anti-transgender hate crimes, and only nineteen nations permit transgender individuals to serve in the military.[86]

Lastly, the fundamental right for transgender people to exist is under threat. In fifty-seven nations across the world being transgender is either criminalized or prosecuted, cross-dressing is criminalized in eight nations, and gender-affirming surgery is criminalized under certain circumstances in six nations.[87] For example, Human Rights Watch reports that nations such as Malaysia explicitly criminalize presenting as a different gender than one's sex assigned at birth, and the law permits incarcerating men who "pose" as women.[88] Moreover, only four nations in the world permit people to change their gender marker on government documents to one other than female or male, with the remaining governments of the world effectively denying the existence of nonbinary people.[89] Additionally, in late 2018 a memo by the US Department of Health and Human Services suggested that the Trump administration is considering legally redefining sex and gender under Title IX to effectively no longer recognize the existence of transgender people in the United States.[90] Ultimately, with the codification of transphobia in law, transgender people are often left with little or no legal recourse for experiences of discrimination and related violence.

T-IPV at the Nexus of Transphobia and Human Rights Restrictions

As noted above, transgender individuals face the risk of discrimination and legal barriers in a number of aspects of their lives, with respect to getting married, fostering and adopting children, going to school, maintaining employment, accessing credit and lending institutions, receiving health care, obtaining equal treatment and services in public accommodations, being permitted to serve in the military, and more. In turn, pervasive transphobia and transgender human rights restrictions each play integral roles in shaping and fueling T-IPV. In particular, interpersonal and law-based discrimination against transgender people may motivate some abusers, enable unique forms of abusive tactics, and increase barriers to escape for survivors.

DISCRIMINATION AND T-IPV MOTIVATIONS
Regarding motivations, that interpersonal transphobia is extensive in many societies no doubt increases the risk that individuals who are abusive to their transgender intimate partners will be transphobic. In turn, scholars theorize that those who internalize transphobic attitudes may be more likely to perpetrate IPV—whether because they view transgender survivors as subhuman and therefore deserving of abuse, or because some transgender abusers view IPV perpetration as a means to overcome transphobia-linked feelings of stress or disempowerment.[91] Qualitative studies suggest that some abusers do embrace discriminatory views of their transgender survivors,[92] and some transgender abusers verbally rationalize or excuse their behavior as inconsequential in comparison to their own experiences of societal transphobia.[93] The extent to which internalizing transphobic attitudes is associated with T-IPV perpetration has not yet been quantitatively assessed, although a similar association among sexual minorities has been found between internalized homophobia and IPV perpetration.[94]

DISCRIMINATION AND T-IPV TACTICS

Unique T-IPV tactics are made possible both by interpersonal transphobia and by transgender human rights restrictions. Consider first that transgender people who are out or public regarding being transgender risk extensive discrimination in society, in conjunction with fewer legal protections against such discrimination. It is therefore understandable why many transgender people choose not to share their gender identity or transgender status with everyone. Indeed, according to the US Transgender Survey, only 53 percent of transgender people in the US are out about being transgender to all of the immediate family members they grew up with, only 32 percent are out to all of their heterosexual and cisgender friends, and only 23 percent are out to all of their coworkers.[95] In turn, abusers of closeted transgender people gain a unique pressure point through which to gain control: as noted previously, one national estimate indicates that 11 percent of transgender people have at some point in their lifetime had a partner threaten to nonconsensually disclose the fact that they are transgender to others.[96]

In addition to threats of outing, other unique T-IPV tactics may be made possible by the uncertainty and shame that many transgender survivors feel about their identity or their inability to express their identity. Scholars emphasize that periods of gender transition and confirmation are sites of distinct vulnerability for transgender people.[97] For instance, during stages of identity affirmation, abusers may intentionally impede a transgender person's access to medical transition services and gendered clothing, refuse to use a transgender person's name and correct pronouns, demand a person remain closeted regarding the fact that they are transgender, verbally abuse a transgender person utilizing transphobic language, physically assault body parts that have particular gendered meaning, coerce a transgender person into sexual activities that feel particularly dissonant with their gender identity, and falsely rationalize abuse as being normal for or affirming of a person with the transgender person's gender identity.[98] As clinical psychologist and researcher Nicola Brown has noted, "perpetrators are acutely aware of the individual and institutional vulnerabilities faced by trans people and these vulnerabilities feature explicitly in the abuse tactics and harm done."[99] In societies where transgender lives are devalued by interpersonal and law-reinforced discrimination, transgender people are likely to continue to be particularly vulnerable to these forms of intimate partner identity abuse.

Some abusers may also threaten to prevent their transgender partner from accessing their children, should their partner seek help or leave. While not specifically unique to T-IPV,[100] threats regarding children may be especially credible for transgender survivors in nations where laws restrict the ability of transgender people to legally adopt or foster children. Not only do some legal systems weaken the ability of transgender people to gain parental rights, but attorneys may also use the fact that a parent is transgender to argue against their gaining custody.[101] In light of these concerns, it is perhaps not surprising that abusers use children as leverage over their transgender partners, with one study finding that transgender parents are more likely than cisgender parents to experience abusive tactics involving their children.[102]

DISCRIMINATION AND T-IPV HELP SEEKING

Pervasive interpersonal transphobia and transgender human rights restrictions also strengthen the many barriers transgender survivors face in seeking help and leaving their abusers. Kae Greenberg, attorney and legal scholar, refers to this as a form of social entrapment by which systems of stigmatization may work to isolate transgender survivors.[103]

The extent to which transphobia is embraced in many societies creates a realistic risk that potential sources of help may be dismissive or outright transphobic in their responses to a transgender person in an abusive relationship. For instance, when considering that a quarter of transgender people have had a family member stop talking with them specifically because they were transgender,[104] it is understandable that just 30 percent of transgender survivors ever disclose their victimization to family members.[105] Likewise, with research suggesting that some transgender survivors fear and experience a transphobic response by police and attorneys,[106] it is perhaps not surprising that only 12–18 percent of transgender survivors disclose the abuse to police and just 2 percent disclose to attorneys.[107] Concerns regarding police responses to T-IPV may be further exacerbated by broader fears that some in law enforcement will disregard any type of crime against transgender people, blame them for their victimization, and even participate in the victimization.[108] As one transgender survivor explained, "I didn't want to tell any service providers about the relationship problems as explaining the details would have required me to come out. . . . I was worried service providers would be ignorant of trans identities and potentially even quite prejudiced."[109] Likely exacerbating concerns that sources of help will be discriminatory is the fact that few agencies and organizations offer tailored services for transgender survivors.[110]

Moreover, some survivors are concerned that those they seek help from may intentionally out them as transgender.[111] Survivors also may risk being outed during court proceedings in jurisdictions that require using a person's legal name,[112] which is particularly an issue in the many nations that make it difficult or impossible to legally change one's gender marker and name on identity documents. As previously noted, interpersonal transphobia and the absence of antidiscrimination laws make it more difficult for transgender people to find employment, safe educational institutions, affirmative health care, and housing; therefore, the potential consequences of being outed are amplified for transgender survivors. Even for those who are not outed, survivors who leave an abuser with whom they cohabitated, shared financial resources, or shared medical insurance may fear future discrimination in seeking new housing, employment, and insurance coverage.

Finally, it is important to note that many IPV laws—such as those criminalizing IPV or providing no-contact orders to prevent abusers from seeking out those they have victimized—limit who can access these protections to those involved in certain legally recognized relationships, such as marital relationships and relationships between a man and a woman.[113] Such restrictive IPV laws can effectively bar many transgender survivors from their protections, whether because they are in a same-sex relationship or because their birth-assigned sex is misused in court to argue they are in a same-sex relationship.[114]

Implications and Next Steps

As this chapter has detailed, transgender people are subjected to interpersonal transphobia and discriminatory policies across the world, cultivating a hostile social environment for many transgender individuals. When considering the unique forms of motivations, abusive tactics, and barriers to escape for T-IPV, it is clear that understanding T-IPV necessitates recognizing the broader cultural patterns of discrimination that fuel vulnerability to violence.

Of course, the continued existence of IPV among cisgender people makes clear that T-IPV will not cease to exist simply by eradicating transphobic discrimination. At the same time, the undeniable interconnections between discrimination and T-IPV highlighted in this chapter indicate that, if nations did more to combat interpersonal transphobia and transgender human rights restrictions, transgender people may be substantially less likely to experience IPV and substantially more likely to seek and reach help when they do experience abuse. Thus, recommended policy shifts include the passage of nationwide antidiscrimination laws protecting transgender people in multiple realms of life, encouraging antidiscrimination education in both schools and the workplace, and revising IPV laws to explicitly cover transgender survivors.

Likewise, tailoring future efforts by service providers and policymakers to prevent and intervene in T-IPV must be deeply informed by the myriad ways in which discrimination shapes unique T-IPV causes, tactics, and barriers to escape. For instance, this may entail addressing unique T-IPV motivations in both IPV prevention programming and batterer intervention treatment, covering unique T-IPV tactics under IPV laws and including them as warning signs of abuse in prevention programs and victim service provision efforts, and enhancing access to victim support services through T-IPV knowledge training and antidiscrimination training for service providers, as well as developing more transgender-specific service advertising and organization branding.

Improving how societies assist T-IPV survivors is by no means a small task, and it must begin with knowledge. With this in mind, this book offers a deep dive into all that current research tells us about the nature of T-IPV and its intersections with discrimination. Building off this now two-decades-long knowledge base, this book proceeds to offer detailed and evidence-based recommendations for best practices in future service provision, public policy, and research. Armed with this knowledge, it is sincerely hoped that together we can spur an evolutionary leap forward in ensuring the safety and health of transgender communities.

Overview of This Book

This book is the first-ever edited collection of chapters on transgender intimate partner violence, written by leading research experts and victim service providers working on this pressing issue. In Part I, an introduction to T-IPV is offered. This opening chapter provided foundational terminology, an overview of T-IPV and its prevalence and outcomes, and an introduction to the ways in which T-IPV is uniquely shaped by discrimination and human rights restrictions. Chapter 2, "Tactics and Justifications of Abuse Involving Transgender Individuals" (Xavier Quinn), focuses on the rationalizations T-IPV abusers use to justify abuse and also details the ways in which T-IPV tactics can be similar to and also distinct from C-IPV tactics, with an emphasis on the relevance of societal transphobia. Chapter 3, "Undermining Transgender Survivors: Discrediting Identity Work in Intimate Relationships" (Amanda Koontz), extends the examination on patterns of abuse by highlighting the relevance of identity manipulation. While all humans actively construct identities, transgender identities are often structurally denigrated and interpersonally attacked. The chapter utilizes an identity work perspective to emphasize the ways in which abusers may attack certain aspects of the identity process in transgender survivors.

Part II examines the underlying context and causes of T-IPV. Chapter 4, "'Why Don't You Just Leave?': Transgender Resilience and Barriers to Escaping Abuse" (Rayna E. Momen and Walter S. DeKeseredy), addresses the ways in which T-IPV entraps survivors in ongoing patterns of abuse in intimate relationships. Themes of resiliency and coping mechanisms are addressed to contextualize help-seeking processes for transgender survivors. Chapter 5, "Theorizing on the Roots of Transgender Intimate Partner Violence" (Adam M. Messinger), reviews theories and existing empirical support regarding the causes of T-IPV, including those causes that are shared with C-IPV (e.g., techniques of neutralization, intergenerational socialization, victim vulnerabilities, etc.) and those that are distinct from C-IPV (e.g., disempowerment, minority stress, stigma power, etc.). Chapter 6, "The Intersections of Race and Immigration" (Xavier L. Guadalupe-Diaz and Carolyn M. West), focuses on relevant issues of race and immigration within the context of T-IPV. Drawing on both the T-IPV and C-IPV literatures, it becomes readily apparent that race and migration status create distinct realities for T-IPV survivors of color.

Part III applies both what is known about T-IPV and current societal efforts to address IPV to discuss best practices in T-IPV victim service provision and the law. Evidence-based tips are offered regarding avenues through which to improve mental and medical health-care provision, survivor shelter services, law enforcement procedures, and laws pertaining to T-IPV. Chapter 7, "Providing Appropriate Health-Care Services to Transgender and Gender Nonconforming Survivors of IPV" (Shanna Kattari, Héctor Torres, Kim Fountain, and Ing Swenson), examines best practices for mental and medical health-care provision for transgender survivors. As an often-medicalized community, transgender people rely on inclusive care while also often facing high levels of discrimination and bias from health-care providers. For transgender survivors, relevant issues of systemic prejudice and other barriers limit access to well-rounded care and well-being. Chapter 8, "Best Practices in Shelter Provision" (Brian P. Tesch), explores shelter accommodations and policies that have been historically geared toward cisgender women. The chapter identifies specific best practices that are either currently working for shelters or could be adapted by existing programs to improve services provided for transgender survivors. Chapter 9, "Best Practices in Policing" (Kae Greenberg), reviews strategies for ensuring affirming and effective law enforcement responses to T-IPV. Best practices are too rarely discussed in the literature or in application, which is unfortunate given that police are often first responders for IPV and can play a vital role as both help-seeking resources and safety enforcers. The chapter highlights some of the unique policing challenges in this area, with an emphasis on improving the response to transgender survivors. Chapter 10, "Legal System Reform" (Leigh Goodmark), examines legal structures and recourse for transgender survivors. Historically, IPV laws were not only focused on heterosexual survivors but were also cisnormative. While much of the law has evolved and improved over recent decades, this chapter emphasizes ways that the courts and legal system can continue working to improve responses to T-IPV.

Part IV, the final section of this book, contributes recommendations for future directions in addressing the problem of T-IPV, along with closing thoughts. Chapter 11, "Beyond the Gender Binary: Trans/forming

IPV Prevention Using a Public Health Framework" (Rebecca Howard, Sharyn J. Potter, Taylor Flagg, Mary M. Moynihan, and Zachary Ahmad-Kahloon), discusses new techniques and research in prevention education that are transgender-inclusive and centered. Past programs predominantly have been focused on cisgender and heterosexual people, with more recent expansions to include cisgender lesbian, gay, and bisexual people. Drawing on research-based knowledge of T-IPV, recommendations are provided for designing tailored prevention programs. Chapter 12, "Training Service Providers to Identify and Overcome Service Barriers in Working with Transgender IPV Survivors" (michael munson and Loree Cook-Daniels), reviews the potential for organizations to serve as training hubs for a multitude of IPV victim service agencies looking to improve services for transgender survivors. In particular, the chapter synthesizes what FORGE—a leader in transgender victim service provision—has learned about the barriers standing between transgender survivors and IPV victim service providers, and best practices in training approaches and techniques. Chapter 13, "Overcoming Barriers to Knowledge Production in Transgender IPV Research" (Adam F. Yerke and Jennifer DeFeo), addresses the overarching problems with conducting research on T-IPV within a subfield of scholarship that is often cisgender-focused. Working with a small, marginalized population presents a multitude of methodological challenges including those regarding sampling, inclusive survey measures, and more. Chapter 14, "Working toward Transgender Inclusion in the Movement to Address Intimate Partner Violence" (Xavier L. Guadalupe-Diaz and Adam M. Messinger), the final chapter of the book, reviews the core lessons of this book and each of its chapters and discusses how we might work to address key gaps in research, service provision, and the law—and, ultimately, how we can build toward a safer and more inclusive tomorrow.

NOTES

1 Guadalupe-Diaz 2013, 55.
2 Guadalupe-Diaz and Jasinski 2017, 784.
3 Basow and Thompson 2012; Blasko, Winek, and Bieschke 2007; Brown and Groscup 2009; Messinger, Birmingham, and DeKeseredy 2018; Seelau and Seelau 2005.
4 Guadalupe-Diaz 2013, 71; Guadalupe-Diaz and Anthony 2017; Guadalupe-Diaz and Jasinski 2017.
5 Guadalupe-Diaz and Anthony 2017, 8.

6 Amnesty International 2005.
7 Guadalupe-Diaz and Jasinski 2017, 784.
8 Goodmark 2013, 76.
9 Guadalupe-Diaz and Jasinski 2017, 784.
10 James et al. 2016.
11 Baker et al. 2013; Messinger 2017.
12 US Department of Justice 2014.
13 Violence Against Women Reauthorization Act of 2013, Pub. L. No. 113-4, 127 Stat. 54 (2013).
14 Hines and Douglas 2011.
15 Viebeck 2018.
16 See Messinger 2017.
17 Roch, Morton, and Ritchie 2010.
18 Brown 2007.
19 Ford et al. 2013.
20 James et al. 2016.
21 E.g., Clements, Katz, and Marx 1999; Turell 2000.
22 See James et al. 2016.
23 Meyer et al. 2018.
24 Guadalupe-Diaz 2019; Messinger 2017. The first book ever to be published on T-IPV (Guadalupe-Diaz 2019) follows the lives of numerous transgender survivors of IPV, offering a deeply informative, on-the-ground account of T-IPV.
25 Dank et al. 2014.
26 Reuter, Newcomb, Whitton, and Mustanski 2017.
27 Bachmann and Gooch 2018; Clements, Katz, and Marx 1999; Dank et al. 2014; Hoxmeier 2016; Hoxmeier and Madlem 2018; Valentine et al. 2017.
28 Griner et al. 2017.
29 Risser 2005.
30 Cense, de Haas, and Doorduin, 2017; Cook-Daniels and munson 2010; Murchison, Boyd, and Pachankis 2017; Testa et al. 2012; Xavier, Honnold, and Bradford 2007.
31 James et al., 2016; Turell 2000.
32 James et al., 2016; Landers and Gilsanz 2009.
33 James et al. 2016; Nemoto, Bödeker, and Iwamoto 2011; Pitts et al. 2006; Roch, Morton, and Ritchie 2010; Turell 2000.
34 James et al. 2016; Nemoto, Bödeker, and Iwamoto 2011; Pitts et al. 2006; Roch, Morton, and Ritchie 2010; Turell 2000.
35 James et al., 2016; National Coalition of Anti-Violence Programs 2017; Roch, Morton, and Ritchie 2010; Scottish Transgender Alliance 2008; Woulfe and Goodman 2018.
36 For example, Goldenberg, Jadwin-Cakmak, and Harper 2018; James et al. 2016; Keuroghlian et al. 2015; Langenderfer-Magruder, Walls, et al. 2016; Roch, Morton, and Ritchie 2010.

37 James et al. 2016.
38 Flores et al. 2016. Note that this analysis of the Behavioral Risk Factor Surveillance System almost certainly underestimates the US transgender population size because it excludes those who do not identify as transgender but nonetheless have a gender identity that differs from their birth sex. For instance, using a more inclusive—although still not comprehensive—definition of being transgender, Doan (2016) found that transgender people may represent upward of 2.9 percent of the US population—nearly five times the size of Flores and colleagues' (2016) estimate of 0.6 percent.
39 Clements, Katz, and Marx 1999; Valentine et al. 2017.
40 Valentine et al. 2017.
41 Goldenberg, Jadwin-Cakmak, and Harper 2018.
42 Pitts et al. 2006.
43 Goldenberg, Jadwin-Cakmak, and Harper 2018.
44 Dank et al. 2014; Griner et al. 2017; Hoxmeier 2016; Hoxmeier and Madlem 2018; Landers and Gilsanz 2009; Langenderfer-Magruder, Whitfield, et al. 2016; Pitts et al. 2006; Turell 2000; Valentine et al. 2017.
45 See James et al. 2016.
46 Black et al. 2011.
47 Wathen et al. 2018.
48 Wathen et al. 2018.
49 Wathen et al. 2018.
50 Roch, Morton, and Ritchie 2010.
51 Pitts et al. 2006.
52 Pitts et al. 2006; Roch, Morton, and Ritchie 2010.
53 Roch, Morton, and Ritchie 2010.
54 Goldenberg, Jadwin-Cakmak, and Harper, 2018.
55 Brennan et al. 2012; Keuroghlian et al. 2015; Parsons et al. 2018.
56 Goldenberg, Jadwin-Cakmak, and Harper 2018.
57 Brennan et al. 2012.
58 Goldenberg, Jadwin-Cakmak, and Harper 2018.
59 Brennan et al. 2012.
60 See Messinger 2017.
61 Ipsos Public Affairs 2018.
62 Walker 2015, 121.
63 Shoup 2013.
64 James et al. 2016.
65 Stotzer 2009.
66 Currah 2016.
67 Tellier 2017.
68 Sullivan 2015.
69 International Lesbian, Gay, Bisexual, Trans and Intersex Association 2017.
70 Trans Respect versus Transphobia Worldwide, n.d.

71 Movement Advancement Project 2018.
72 Global Action for Trans Equality 2018; Herman and Brown 2018.
73 Movement Advancement Project 2018.
74 Movement Advancement Project 2018.
75 Blad 2018; Moreau 2018; An Act to Prohibit Certain Gender Identity Instruction in Public Schools, S.B. 160, 93rd Leg., Reg. Sess. (S.D. 2018).
76 de Vogue, Mallonee, and Grinberg 2017.
77 Hanna, Park, and McLaughlin 2017.
78 Dastagir 2016; Kopan and Scott 2016.
79 National Conference of State Legislatures 2017.
80 Movement Advancement Project 2018.
81 James et al. 2016.
82 James et al. 2016.
83 Kodjak 2018.
84 Movement Advancement Project 2018.
85 Greenwood 2017; Taylor and Haider-Markel 2014.
86 LeBlanc 2017; Trans Respect versus Transphobia Worldwide, n.d.
87 Trans Respect versus Transphobia Worldwide, n.d.
88 Ghoshal and Knight 2016.
89 Trans Respect versus Transphobia Worldwide, n.d.
90 Green, Benner, and Pear 2018.
91 See Messinger 2017; Rogers 2017.
92 E.g., Guadalupe-Diaz and Anthony 2017; Singh and McKleroy 2011.
93 E.g., Brown 2007.
94 Balsam and Szymanski 2005; Bartholomew et al. 2008; Edwards and Sylaska 2013; Finneran et al. 2012; Finneran and Stephenson 2014; Kelley et al. 2014.
95 James et al. 2016.
96 James et al. 2016.
97 Guadalupe-Diaz and Anthony 2017; Roch, Morton, and Ritche 2010; Walker 2015; Woulfe and Goodman 2018.
98 Bornstein et al. 2006; Cook-Daniels 2015; FORGE 2013; Goodmark 2013; Roch, Morton, and Ritche 2010; Tesch and Bekerian 2015.
99 Brown 2011, 162.
100 Wallace and Roberson 2016.
101 Cooper 2013.
102 James et al. 2016.
103 Greenberg 2012.
104 James et al. 2016.
105 Kurdyla, Messinger, and Ramirez 2019.
106 Amnesty International 2005; Goodmark 2013.
107 Kurdyla, Messinger, and Ramirez, 2019; Langenderfer-Magruder, Whitfield, et al. 2016.
108 Dwyer 2015.

109 Roch, Morton, and Ritche 2010, 29.
110 See Messinger 2017.
111 E.g., Guadalupe-Diaz and Jasinski 2017.
112 Harada 2011.
113 Poirier 2007.
114 International Lesbian, Gay, Bisexual, Trans and Intersex Association 2017; Sullivan 2015.

REFERENCES

Amnesty International. 2005. *Stonewalled: Police Abuse and Misconduct against Lesbian, Gay, Bisexual and Transgender People in the US*. London: Amnesty International. www.amnesty.org.

Bachmann, Chaka L., and Becca Gooch. 2018. *LGBT in Britain: Trans Report*. London: Stonewall. www.stonewall.org.

Baker, Nancy L., Jessica D. Buick, Shari R. Kim, Sandy Moniz, and Khristina L. Nava. 2013. "Lessons from Examining Same-Sex Intimate Partner Violence." *Sex Roles* 69 (3–4): 182–192.

Balsam, Kimberly F., and Dawn M. Szymanski. 2005. "Relationship Quality and Domestic Violence in Women's Same-Sex Relationships: The Role of Minority Stress." *Psychology of Women Quarterly* 29 (3): 258–269.

Bartholomew, Kim, Katherine V. Regan, Doug Oram, and Monica A. White. 2008. "Correlates of Partner Abuse in Male Same-Sex Relationships." *Violence and Victims* 23 (3): 344–360.

Basow, Susan A., and Janelle Thompson. 2012. "Service Providers' Reactions to Intimate Partner Violence as a Function of Victim Sexual Orientation and Type of Abuse." *Journal of Interpersonal Violence* 27 (7): 1225–1241.

Black, Michele C., Kathleen C. Basile, Matthew J. Breiding, Sharon G. Smith, Mikel L. Walters, Melissa T. Merrick, and Mark R. Stevens. 2011. *The National Intimate Partner and Sexual Violence Survey: 2010 Summary Report*. Atlanta: National Center for Injury Prevention and Control, Centers for Disease Control and Prevention. www.cdc.gov.

Blad, Evie. 2018. "In a First, a State May Ban Its Schools from Teaching about Gender Identity." *Education Week*, February 8, 2018, http://blogs.edweek.org.

Blasko, Kelly A., Jon L. Winek, and Kathleen J. Bieschke. 2007. "Therapists' Prototypical Assessment of Domestic Violence Situations." *Journal of Marital and Family Therapy* 33 (2): 258–269.

Bornstein, Danica R., Jake Fawcett, Marianne Sullivan, Kirsten D. Senturia, and Sharyne Shiu-Thornton. 2006. "Understanding the Experiences of Lesbian, Bisexual and Trans Survivors of Domestic Violence: A Qualitative Study." *Journal of Homosexuality* 51 (1): 159–181.

Brennan, Julia, Lisa M. Kuhns, Amy K. Johnson, Marvin Belzer, Erin C. Wilson, and Robert Garofalo. 2012. "Syndemic Theory and HIV-Related Risk among Young Transgender Women: The Role of Multiple, Co-occurring Health Problems and Social Marginalization." *American Journal of Public Health* 102 (9): 1751–1757.

Brown, Michael J., and Jennifer Groscup. 2009. "Perceptions of Same-Sex Domestic Violence among Crisis Center Staff." *Journal of Family Violence* 24 (2): 87–93.

Brown, Nicola. 2007. "Stories from Outside the Frame: Intimate Partner Abuse in Sexual-Minority Women's Relationships with Transsexual Men." *Feminism and Psychology* 17 (3): 373–393.

Brown, Nicola. 2011. "Holding Tensions of Victimization and Perpetration: Partner Abuse in Trans Communities." In *Intimate Partner Violence in LGBTQ Lives*, edited by Janice L. Ristock, 153–168. New York: Routledge.

Cense, Marianne, Stans de Haas, and Tamar Doorduin. 2017. "Sexual Victimisation of Transgender People in the Netherlands: Prevalence, Risk Factors and Health Consequences." *Journal of Gender-Based Violence* 1 (2): 235–252.

Clements, Kristen, Mitchell Katz, and Rani Marx. 1999. *The Transgender Community Health Project: Descriptive Results*. San Francisco: San Francisco Department of Public Health. http://hivinsite.ucsf.edu.

Cook-Daniels, Loree. 2015. "Intimate Partner Violence in Transgender Couples: 'Power and Control' in a Specific Cultural Context." *Partner Abuse* 6 (1): 126–139.

Cook-Daniels, Loree, and michael munson. 2010. "Sexual Violence, Elder Abuse, and Sexuality of Transgender Adults, Age 50+: Results of Three Surveys." *Journal of GLBT Family Studies* 6 (2): 142–177.

Cooper, Leslie. 2013. *Protecting the Rights of Transgender Parents and Their Children: A Guide for Parents and Lawyers*. New York: American Civil Liberties Union and National Center for Transgender Equality. https://transequality.org.

Currah, Paisley. 2016. "The New Transgender Panic: Men in Women's Bathrooms." March 31, 2016. https://paisleycurrah.com.

Dank, Meredith, Pamela Lachman, Janine M. Zweig, and Jennifer Yahner. 2014. "Dating Violence Experiences of Lesbian, Gay, Bisexual, and Transgender Youth." *Journal of Youth and Adolescence* 43 (5): 846–857.

Dastagir, Alia E. 2016. "The Imaginary Predator in America's Transgender Bathroom War." *USA Today*, April 28, 2016. www.usatoday.com.

de Vogue, Ariane, Mary Kay Mallonee, and Emanuella Grinberg. 2017. "Trump Administration Withdraws Federal Protections for Transgender Students." *CNN*, February 23, 2017. www.cnn.com.

Doan, Petra L. 2016. "To Count or Not to Count: Queering Measurement and the Transgender Community." *Women's Studies Quarterly* 44 (3/4): 89–110.

Dwyer, Angela. 2015. "Teaching Young Queers a Lesson: How Police Teach Lessons about Nonheteronormativity in Public Spaces." *Sexuality & Culture* 19 (3): 493–512.

Edwards, Katie M., and Kateryna M. Sylaska. 2013. "The Perpetration of Intimate Partner Violence among LGBTQ College Youth: The Role of Minority Stress." *Journal of Youth and Adolescence* 42 (11): 1721–1731.

Finneran, Catherine, Anna Chard, Craig Sineath, Patrick Sullivan, and Rob Stephenson. 2012. "Intimate Partner Violence and Social Pressure among Gay Men in Six Countries." *Western Journal of Emergency Medicine* 13 (3): 260–271.

Finneran, Catherine, and Rob Stephenson. 2014. "Intimate Partner Violence, Minority Stress, and Sexual Risk-Taking among US Men Who Have Sex with Men." *Journal of Homosexuality* 61 (2): 288–306.

Flores, Andrew. R., Jody L. Herman, Gary J. Gates, and Taylor N. T. Brown. 2016. *How Many Adults Identify as Transgender in the United States?* Los Angeles: The Williams Institute. https://williamsinstitute.law.ucla.edu.

Ford, Chandra L., Terra Slavin, Karin L. Hilton, and Susan L. Holt. 2013. "Intimate Partner Violence Prevention Services and Resources in Los Angeles: Issues, Needs, and Challenges for Assisting Lesbian, Gay, Bisexual, and Transgender Clients." *Health Promotion Practice* 14 (6): 841–849.

FORGE. 2013. *Trans-Specific Power and Control Tactics*. Milwaukee: FORGE. http://forge-forward.org.

Ghoshal, Neela, and Kyle Knight. 2016. "Rights in Transition: Making Legal Recognition for Transgender People a Global Priority." *Human Rights Watch*, January 27, 2016. www.hrw.org.

Global Action for Trans Equality. 2018. *Gender Identity and Human Rights*. New York: Global Action for Trans Equality. http://transactivists.org.

Goldenberg, Tamar, Laura Jadwin-Cakmak, and Gary W. Harper. 2018. "Intimate Partner Violence among Transgender Youth: Associations with Intrapersonal and Structural Factors." *Violence and Gender* 5 (1): 19–25.

Goodmark, Leigh. 2013. "Transgender People, Intimate Partner Abuse, and the Legal System." *Harvard Civil Rights–Civil Liberties Law Review* 48 (1): 51–104.

Green, Erica L., Katie Benner, and Robert Pear. 2018. "'Transgender' Could Be Defined Out of Existence under Trump Administration." *New York Times*, October 21, 2018. www.nytimes.com.

Greenberg, Kae. 2012. "Still Hidden in the Closet: Trans Women and Domestic Violence." *Berkeley Journal of Gender, Law & Justice* 27 (2): 198–251.

Greenwood, Max. 2017. "Sessions Reverses DOJ Policy on Transgender Employee Protections." *The Hill*, October 5, 2017. http://thehill.com.

Griner, Stacey B., Cheryl A. Vamos, Erika L. Thompson, Rachel Logan, Coralia Vázquez-Otero, and Ellen M. Daley. 2017. "The Intersection of Gender Identity and Violence: Victimization Experienced by Transgender College Students." *Journal of Interpersonal Violence*. https://doi.org/10.1177/0886260517723743.

Guadalupe-Diaz, Xavier L. 2013. "Victims outside the Binary: Transgender Survivors of Intimate Partner Violence." PhD diss., University of Central Florida.

Guadalupe-Diaz, Xavier L. 2019. *Transgressed: Intimate Partner Violence in Transgender Lives*. New York: New York University Press.

Guadalupe-Diaz, Xavier L., and Amanda Koontz Anthony. 2017. "Discrediting Identity Work: Understandings of Intimate Partner Violence by Transgender Survivors." *Deviant Behavior* 38 (1): 1–16.

Guadalupe-Diaz, Xavier L., and Jana Jasinski. 2017. "'I Wasn't a Priority, I Wasn't a Victim': Challenges in Help Seeking for Transgender Survivors of Intimate Partner Violence." *Violence Against Women* 23 (6): 772–792.

Hanna, Jason, Madison Park, and Eliott C. McLaughlin. 2017. "North Carolina Repeals 'Bathroom Bill.'" *CNN*, March 30, 2017. www.cnn.com.

Harada, Satoko. 2011. "Comment: Additional Barriers to Breaking the Silence: Issues to Consider When Representing a Victim of Same-Sex Domestic Violence." *University of Baltimore Law Forum* 41 (2): 150–171.

Herman, Jody L., and Taylor N. T. Brown. 2018. *The Potential Impact of Voter Identification Laws on Transgender Voters in the 2018 General Election*. Los Angeles: The Williams Institute. https://williamsinstitute.law.ucla.edu.

Hines, Denise A., and Emily M. Douglas. 2011. "The Reported Availability of US Domestic Violence Services to Victims Who Vary by Age, Sexual Orientation, and Gender." *Partner Abuse* 2 (1): 3–30.

Hoxmeier, Jill C. 2016. "Sexual Assault and Relationship Abuse Victimization of Transgender Undergraduate Students in a National Sample." *Violence and Gender* 3 (4): 202–207.

Hoxmeier, Jill C., and Melody Madlem. 2018. "Discrimination and Interpersonal Violence: Reported Experiences of Trans* Undergraduate Students." *Violence and Gender* 5 (1): 12–18.

International Lesbian, Gay, Bisexual, Trans and Intersex Association. 2017. *Sexual Orientation Laws in the World—Overview*. Geneva: International Lesbian, Gay, Bisexual, Trans and Intersex Association. https://ilga.org.

Ipsos Public Affairs. 2018. *Global Attitudes toward Transgender People*. New York: Ipsos Public Affairs. www.ipsos.com.

James, Sandy E., Jody. L. Herman, Susan Rankin, Mara Keisling, Lisa Mottet, and Ma'ayan Anafi. 2016. *The Report of the 2015 U.S. Transgender Survey*. Washington, DC: National Center for Transgender Equality. www.ustranssurvey.org.

Kelley, Michelle L., Robert J. Milletich, Robin J. Lewis, Barbara A. Winstead, Cathy L. Barraco, Miguel A. Padilla, and Courtney Lynn. 2014. "Predictors of Perpetration of Men's Same-Sex Partner Violence." *Violence and Victims* 29 (5): 784–796.

Keuroghlian, Alex S., Sari L. Reisner, Jaclyn M. White, and Roger D. Weiss. 2015. "Substance Use and Treatment of Substance Use Disorders in a Community Sample of Transgender Adults." *Drug and Alcohol Dependence* 152:139–146.

Kodjak, Alison. 2018. "Trump Admin Will Protect Health Workers Who Refuse Services on Religious Grounds." *NPR*, January 18, 2018. www.npr.org.

Kopan, Tal, and Eugene Scott. 2016. "North Carolina Governor Signs Controversial Transgender Bill." *CNN*, March 23, 2016. www.cnn.com.

Kralik, Joellen, and Jennifer Palmer. 2017. "'Bathroom Bill' Legislative Tracking." National Conference of State Legislatures. www.ncsl.org.

Kurdyla, Victoria, Adam M. Messinger, and Milka Ramirez. 2019. "Transgender Intimate Partner Violence and Help-Seeking Patterns." *Journal of Interpersonal Violence*. https://doi.org/10.1177/0886260519880171.

Landers, Stewart J., and Paola Gilsanz. 2009. *The Health of Lesbian, Gay, Bisexual and Transgender (LGBT) Persons in Massachusetts: A Survey of Health Issues Comparing LGBT Persons with Their Heterosexual and Non-transgender Counterparts*. Boston: Massachusetts Department of Public Health. http://archives.lib.state.ma.us.

Langenderfer-Magruder, Lisa, N. Eugene Walls, Darren L. Whitfield, Samantha M. Brown, and Cory M. Barrett. 2016. "Partner Violence Victimization among Lesbian, Gay, Bisexual, Transgender, and Queer Youth: Associations among Risk Factors." *Child and Adolescent Social Work Journal* 33 (1): 55–68.

Langenderfer-Magruder, Lisa, Darren L. Whitfield, N. Eugene Walls, Shanna K. Kattari, and Daniel Ramos. 2016. "Experiences of Intimate Partner Violence and Subsequent Police Reporting among Lesbian, Gay, Bisexual, Transgender, and Queer Adults in Colorado: Comparing Rates of Cisgender and Transgender Victimization." *Journal of Interpersonal Violence* 31 (5): 855–871.

LeBlanc, Paul. 2017. "The Countries That Allow Transgender Troops to Serve in Their Armed Forces." *CNN*, July 27, 2017. www.cnn.com.

Messinger, Adam M. 2017. *LGBTQ Intimate Partner Violence: Lessons for Policy, Practice, and Research*. Oakland: University of California Press.

Messinger, Adam M., Rachel S. Birmingham, and Walter S. DeKeseredy. 2018. "Perceptions of Same-Gender and Different-Gender Intimate Partner Cyber-Monitoring." *Journal of Interpersonal Violence*. https://doi.org/10.1177/0886260518787814.

Meyer, Ilan H., Walter O. Bockting, Jody L. Herman, and Sari L. Reisner. n.d. TransPop: U.S. Transgender Population Health Survey. Accessed July 1, 2018. www.transpop.org.

Moreau, Julie. 2018. "Slew of State and Local Bills Are Targeting LGBTQ People." *NBC News*, February 21, 2018. www.nbcnews.com.

Movement Advancement Project. 2018. "Equality Maps." www.lgbtmap.org.

Murchison, Gabriel R., Melanie A. Boyd, and John E. Pachankis. 2017. "Minority Stress and the Risk of Unwanted Sexual Experiences in LGBQ Undergraduates." *Sex Roles* 77 (3–4): 221–238.

National Coalition of Anti-Violence Programs. 2017. *Lesbian, Gay, Bisexual, Transgender, Queer and HIV-Affected Intimate Partner Violence, 2016*. New York: National Coalition of Anti-Violence Programs. http://avp.org.

Nemoto, Tooru, Birte Bödeker, and Mariko Iwamoto. 2011. "Social Support, Exposure to Violence and Transphobia, and Correlates of Depression among Male-to-Female Transgender Women with a History of Sex Work." *American Journal of Public Health* 101 (10): 1980–1988.

Parsons, Jeffrey T., Nadav Antebi-Gruszka, Brett M. Millar, Demetria Cain, and Sitaji Gurung. 2018. "Syndemic Conditions, HIV Transmission Risk Behavior, and Transactional Sex among Transgender Women." *AIDS and Behavior* 22 (7): 1–12.

Pitts, Marian, Anthony Smith, Anne Mitchell, and Sunil Patel. 2006. *Private Lives: A Report on the Health and Wellbeing of GLBTI Australians*. Melbourne: Australian Research Centre in Sex, Health and Society, La Trobe University. www.glhv.org.au.

Poirier, Marc R. 2007. "Same-Sex Couples and the 'Exclusive Commitment': Untangling the Issues and Consequences: Piecemeal and Wholesale Approaches towards Marriage Equality in New Jersey; Is *Lewis v. Harris* a Dead End or Just a Detour?" *Rutgers Law Review* 59: 291–917.

Reuter, Tyson R., Michael E. Newcomb, Sarah W. Whitton, and Brian Mustanski. 2017. "Intimate Partner Violence Victimization in LGBT Young Adults: Demographic Differences and Associations with Health Behaviors." *Psychology of Violence* 7 (1): 101–109.

Risser, Jan M. H., Andrea Shelton, Sheryl McCurdy, John Atkinson, Paige Padgett, Bernardo Useche, Brenda Thomas, and Mark Williams. 2005. "Sex, Drugs, Violence, and HIV Status among Male-to-Female Transgender Persons in Houston, Texas." *International Journal of Transgenderism* 8 (2–3): 67–74.

Roch, Amy, James Morton, and Graham Ritchie. 2010. *Out of Sight, out of Mind? Transgender People's Experiences of Domestic Abuse*. Edinburgh: LGBT Youth Scotland and the Scottish Transgender Alliance. www.scottishtrans.org.

Rogers, Michaela. 2017. "Transphobic 'Honour'-Based Abuse: A Conceptual Tool." *Sociology* 51 (2): 225–240.

Scottish Transgender Alliance. 2008. *Transgender Experiences in Scotland: Research Summary*. Edinburgh: Equality Network. www.scottishtrans.org.

Seelau, Sheila M., and Eric P. Seelau. 2005. "Gender-Role Stereotypes and Perceptions of Heterosexual, Gay and Lesbian Domestic Violence." *Journal of Family Violence* 20 (6): 363–371.

Shoup, Anne. 2013. "Release: Transgender Workers at Greater Risk for Unemployment and Poverty." *Center for American Progress*, September 6, 2013. www.americanprogress.org.

Singh, Anneliese, and Vel S. McKleroy. 2011. "'Just Getting Out of Bed Is a Revolutionary Act': The Resilience of Transgender People of Color Who Have Survived Traumatic Life Events." *Traumatology* 17 (2): 34–44.

Stotzer, Rebecca L. 2009. "Violence against Transgender People: A Review of United States Data." *Aggression and Violent Behavior* 14 (3): 170–179.

Sullivan, J. Courtney. 2015. "What Marriage Equality Means for Transgender Rights." *New York Times*, July 16, 2015. www.nytimes.com.

Taylor, Jami K., and Donald P. Haider-Markel, eds. 2014. *Transgender Rights and Politics: Groups, Issue Framing, and Policy Adoption*. Ann Arbor: University of Michigan Press.

Tellier, Pierre-Paul. 2017. "The Impact on Mental and Physical Health of Human Rights as They Relate to Gender and Sexual Minority Adolescents and Emerging Adults." *International Journal of Human Rights in Healthcare* 10 (3): 213–220.

Tesch, Brian Peter, and Debra A. Bekerian. 2015. "Hidden in the Margins: A Qualitative Examination of What Professionals in the Domestic Violence Field Know about Transgender Domestic Violence." *Journal of Gay and Lesbian Social Services* 27 (4): 391–411.

Testa, Rylan J., Laura M. Sciacca, Florence Wang, Michael L. Hendricks, Peter Goldblum, Judith Bradford, and Bruce Bongar. 2012. "Effects of Violence on Transgender People." *Professional Psychology: Research and Practice* 43 (5): 452–459.

Trans Respect versus Transphobia Worldwide. n.d. "Legal and Social Mapping." Accessed July 1, 2018. https://transrespect.org.

Turell, Susan C. 2000. "A Descriptive Analysis of Same-Sex Relationship Violence for a Diverse Sample." *Journal of Family Violence* 15 (3): 281–293.

US Department of Justice. 2014. *Frequently Asked Questions: Nondiscrimination Grant Condition in the Violence Against Women Reauthorization Act of 2013*. Washington, DC: US Department of Justice. www.justice.gov.

Valentine, Sarah E., Sarah M. Peitzmeier, Dana S. King, Conall O'Cleirigh, Samantha M. Marquez, Cara Presley, and Jennifer Potter. 2017. "Disparities in Exposure to Intimate Partner Violence among Transgender/Gender Nonconforming and Sexual Minority Primary Care Patients." *LGBT Health* 4 (4): 260–267.

Viebeck, Elise. 2018. "Violence Against Women Act Expires with Government Shutdown." *Washington Post*, December 21, 2018. www.washingtonpost.com.

Walker, Julia K. 2015. "Investigating Trans People's Vulnerabilities to Intimate Partner Violence/Abuse." *Partner Abuse* 6 (1): 107–125.

Wallace, Paul Harvey, and Cliff Roberson. 2016. *Family Violence: Legal, Medical, and Social Perspectives*, 8th ed. New York: Routledge.

Wathen, C. Nadine, Jennifer C. D. MacGregor, Masako Tanaka, and Barbara J. MacQuarrie. 2018. "The Impact of Intimate Partner Violence on the Health and Work of Gender and Sexual Minorities in Canada." *International Journal of Public Health* 63 (8): 945–955.

Woulfe, Julie M., and Lisa A. Goodman. 2018. "Identity Abuse as a Tactic of Violence in LGBTQ Communities: Initial Validation of the Identity Abuse Measure." *Journal of Interpersonal Violence*. https://doi.org/10.1177/0886260518760018.

Xavier, Jessica, Julie A. Honnold, and Judith B. Bradford. 2007. *The Health, Health-Related Needs, and Lifecourse Experiences of Transgender Virginians*. Richmond: Virginia Department of Health.

2

Tactics and Justifications of Abuse Involving Transgender Individuals

XAVIER QUINN

Intimate partner violence (IPV) is a pattern of behaviors occurring in a romantic or sexual relationship when one partner uses tactics such as emotional abuse (i.e., verbal or controlling abuse), identity abuse, isolation tactics, financial abuse, physical abuse, or sexual abuse to gain power and control over their partner.[1] IPV can be hard for survivors to identify when it does not fit the dominant narrative of a man abusing a woman where both people are heterosexual and cisgender.[2] This narrative of who is a victim and who is an abuser of IPV arose during the feminist movement of the 1970s, a movement that demanded that the issue of IPV be addressed as a social problem.[3] In this framing of the issue, the cisgender man controls their partner through physical violence, threats, increased monetary power, enforcing gender stereotypes, and taking advantage of the social status awarded to men.[4] When transgender individuals are involved in IPV, whether as the abuser or the survivor, this dominant narrative is not expansive enough to fit our unique experiences.

While all survivors of IPV face a society that questions their experience of abuse,[5] there is often even more doubt for transgender survivors because their very existence is negated by the dominant culture. Research has definitively documented that transgender individuals face transphobic discrimination affecting their employment, housing, and physical safety.[6] In this sense, transphobia serves to cast doubt on the validity of our existence within most realms of public life.[7] We are told that we do not and cannot exist as transgender people and, by extension, our relationships are invisible and invalidated. With so much doubt and invisibility, how then can transgender individuals identify abuse in our relationships?

I am a transgender man and a survivor of IPV. I have worked with survivors of IPV for over ten years, with a focus on the needs of lesbian, gay, bisexual, queer, and transgender survivors. However, even with my knowledge of IPV and my background in the field, it took me years to move beyond my doubts and to acknowledge my partner's behavior as abusive. Part of the reason is because of the very nature of abuse itself: the isolation, the systematic destruction of a survivor's self-esteem, the lies, and crazy-making. Moving through what Lenore Walker termed the "cycle of abuse," my partner rocketed between the honeymoon stage where she was the person I fell in love with, the tension-building phase where I was walking on eggshells, and explosive incidents where she used tactics of abuse.[8] However, the dominant narrative of a heterosexual, cisgender man with more social and economic power controlling a cisgender woman with less social and economic power also contributed to my doubts. This is not what the dynamics looked like in my experience of IPV, and therefore I dismissed my partner's actions as not abusive. I am not alone in this: many survivors whose experiences of IPV do not fit the dominant narrative have also struggled to recognize their experience as abuse.[9] By some estimates, at least 27 percent of transgender survivors do not view themselves as IPV survivors.[10] To be clear, IPV exists when an abuser uses IPV tactics, regardless of whether or not the survivor labels the experience as IPV. Still, recognizing abuse in one's relationship is a vital step for survivors to understand their experiences, counteract a distorted sense of self-blame, and seek support and safety.

I share my experience in the hopes of helping both transgender survivors and those abused by transgender partners. By sharing the details of the tactics of abuse that were used against me, I hope to help others recognize and name the tactics of abuse they face. In the same way, I hope to expand the knowledge of advocates, researchers, counselors, and community members to better recognize and understand IPV when it involves transgender individuals. Because my experience is not universal, I will weave in what research tells us in order to present a more inclusive picture of IPV involving transgender individuals. Each section that follows will contain my own experiences of IPV as well as examples of tactics used against other transgender survivors. Because anyone—of any identity—can be abusive, I will also include tactics that an abusive transgender person might utilize to control their partner.

IPV exists in all communities regardless of race, gender, sex assigned at birth, sexual orientation, income, class, or ethnicity.[11] For this reason, some of the tactics I explore are shared across the experiences of many survivors. While there are IPV tactics that are specific to the experiences of transgender individuals, many tactics are remarkably similar across the experiences of all survivors.[12] To leave out these common experiences of abuse when speaking about transgender experiences with IPV would offer an incomplete understanding.

More often than not, IPV cannot be defined by a single incident; rather, it is a pattern of behaviors (i.e., multiple instances of an abuser using tactics of abuse) that an abuser employs to control their partner.[13] When a single incident is examined outside that broader context, it might be easy to wonder why the particular tactic the abuser used might have such a severe impact on the survivor. However, it is not the weight of one incident or one particular tactic but rather the combination of multiple incidents and often multiple tactics, along with confusing and contradictory messages from the abusive partner, that makes IPV so devastating. These contradictory messages can be observed in the cycle of abuse. After an explosive episode, when the survivor is most likely to leave the relationship, the abusive partner changes their behavior, using messages of love and sometimes messages that directly contradict those they communicated during the tension-building and explosive incident stages.[14] Along with these messages, the abusive partner also changes their behavior to persuade their partner to stay, perhaps being supportive, affectionate, offering concessions, apologizing, or making promises to change.[15] Throughout this cycle of abuse, the survivor may vacillate between love for their partner, fear of what their partner might do, self-blame, and hope that their partner will change.[16] This cycle is illustrated in the experience of Julie, a transgender woman and IPV survivor.[17] Her abuser's "oscillation—between acceptance and rejection"—of Julie's identity as a woman was one way in which the abuser maintained control.[18] Even when abusers indicate a repeated disrespect of transgender identities, abusers who intermix that transphobic disrespect with brief signs of accepting transgender identities may give survivors a false sense of hope that this time their abuser will change and love them for who they are. Along with this blend of turbulent emotions are other tactics of abuse, each acting as another bar in the cage that holds the survivor captive.

Although the impact of each tactic is impossible to separate from the overall experience of abuse, exploring the subtleties of the tactics can give us greater ability to identify IPV. Few tactics of abuse neatly fit under one classification, but separating the tactics into categories can aid in understanding the multifaceted nature of abuse. For instance, researchers often merge emotional, identity, isolation, and financial abuse under the catch-all label of "psychological abuse," but examining these forms of IPV separately helps illuminate key differences in their dynamics. In the pages that follow, tactics of abuse will be explored through the following categories: using vulnerabilities to justify abuse, emotional tactics, identity tactics, isolation, financial tactics, sexual tactics, and physical tactics.

My Story

In many ways, I had much more social power than my partner did. Though transgender and queer, I am also white, economically stable, gainfully employed, and a US citizen with a safety net of family in the region. She, on the other hand, although cisgender, was a gay woman of color and an immigrant with uncertain status. During our relationship, she was often unemployed or underemployed, had no family in the country, and had few friends. According to the dominant narrative of IPV, if anyone were to be abusive, it should have been me. I had more money, greater privileged status, more power as a US citizen, and more support. How then did it happen that she abused me?

The first, simple reason is that abuse is a choice; any person can be abusive, regardless of their identity.[19] The second reason is rooted in a particular dynamic of abuse that I have seen repeatedly, both in my own experience and through years of working with survivors of IPV. This type of abuse falls outside the dominant narrative that the person with more social power is the abuser. Naming it from the visceral level of my own experience, I call it *parasitic abuse*. In parasitic abuse, the abusive person is simultaneously dependent on the finances, labor, and support of the survivor and incredibly resentful and hostile about this dependency. The abuser relies on the survivor's empathy and loyalty as a means to control them, while contributing little in terms of labor, emotional support, or money. They maintain control over their partner in order to get their financial, emotional, and physical needs met. This bears similarities to what some IPV scholars term *disempowerment theory*, according to which abusers are motivated by a desire to regain a sense of control and power within a relationship or societal context in which they feel disempowered.[20]

Five years into a relationship where my partner was using tactics of parasitic abuse, I found myself working two jobs to support us both. Throughout our relationship, she had gone between unemployment and underemployment, often refusing to look for work. At times when I asked her to apply for jobs, she became enraged and screamed at me, accusing me of being unfair to her, and often stopped talking to me for days, creating a palpable feeling of tension in the silence. Although I paid for the food, bills, and rent and completed the majority of the housework, she relentlessly criticized my behavior, my personality, and my worldview. She constantly berated my choices, undermining my ability to trust myself and eroding my self-esteem. She consistently demanded that I take care of all her physical and emotional needs. Despite my well-meaning attempts to persuade her, she would not socialize with friends, go to a therapist, take care of her health, work out, go to a doctor, work, or leave the house. She expected me to provide for all her needs, and when she was unhappy—which she often was—she argued that I was the one to blame.

By this point, I was well aware of how miserable I was in the relationship, but I could not seem to end it. In order to end the relationship, she would have to move out, and she had no friends, resources, money, or support. Drawing a hard line would mean evicting her from our shared apartment and making her homeless. Whether or not this was a logistical possibility with her name on the lease, I could not bring myself to make the person I loved homeless. Even when the thought occurred, I doubted my motivations, reflecting on the social and economic power I had as a white, employed US citizen.

Using Vulnerabilities to Justify Abuse

Traditionally we think of an abuser exploiting the vulnerabilities of their partner in order to control them. However, another dynamic exists where the abusive partner uses their *own* vulnerabilities to control the survivor.²¹ In these cases, an abuser uses their vulnerabilities to justify tactics of abuse. For example, my abusive partner would use her mental health diagnosis as a justification for isolating us; we could not go out to shows, events, or parties. When we did go out, she also used her mental health diagnosis to deny responsibility for leaving an event in a rage and forcing me to leave with her. Similarly, my partner used her physical vulnerabilities as a justification for abuse. For example, she had chronic knee pain, and she would use this as an excuse to act belligerently. Absurdly, she would just yell "knees!" at me to end any conversation she did not like or to excuse her behavior.

As is consistently recorded with cisgender abusers,²² abusive transgender individuals use their vulnerabilities to justify IPV in similar ways.²³ For example, they may use occurrences of anti-transgender discrimination or transition as excuses for raging at their partner.²⁴ One survivor described her transmasculine partner using his experience of being called "she" as an excuse to justify "him going off on me for two hours."²⁵ An abusive transgender man or nonbinary person who is utilizing testosterone hormone therapy may use their increased testosterone levels as an (unjustified) excuse for physical violence and aggression.²⁶ Likewise, a transgender woman or nonbinary person utilizing estrogen hormone therapy may claim that they are unable to control their mood swings and may justify abuse in this manner. When confronted about their actions, a transgender abuser may claim that it is not possible for them to be abusive because of their marginalized identity.²⁷ For example, they may say, "I'm genderqueer, so I can't batter."²⁸

Some transgender abusers use their partner's cisgender privilege as grounds to demand concessions.²⁹ This behavior departs from the realm of reasonable requests (e.g., using the abuser's correct name and gender pronouns) to enter into the realm of abuse, where the survivor must follow arbitrary rules in order to avoid consequences.³⁰ This often coincides with the survivor being either unfamiliar with or disconnected from transgender communities. One survivor explained this dynamic by sharing, "I had to learn a whole new set of rules that I learned later were very specific to him . . . but because he was the first guy I was with and because of the nature of it he kind of spoke as if he defined trans experience."³¹

Abusers also commonly use their mental health vulnerabilities to manipulate and threaten their partners. For example, what my partner dismissed as "bipolar episodes" involved her yelling and crying for hours, stomping, destroying property, or physically acting out. She claimed she had no memory of these episodes and therefore would not apologize. Similarly, she consistently used self-harm and threats of suicide as a means of control. She would do so when I disagreed with her or tried to hold her accountable for her actions. On such occasions, she would enter into dramatic acts of self-harm, often while scowling at me. Whether it was punching a tree until her hand bled, violently stabbing her own arm with a spoon repeatedly, or slamming her head against the wall, these actions terrified me. They had the immediate impact of silencing me as I rushed to prevent her from hurting herself further. The long-term outcome was that I avoided the topics that would precede such acts of self-harm, such as by not asking her to stop yelling, not requesting that she contribute more financially, and not suggesting that we end our relationship. Contributing to my avoidance of these topics was her consistent matter-of-fact threats of suicide should we break up.

Transgender abusers may use similar threats of self-harm and suicide to control their partners.[32] In particular, transgender abusers may use the high rates of suicide among transgender people as a scare tactic to control their partner's behavior.[33] This could be to get their partner to comfort them rather than going out with friends, to end a discussion, or to persuade them to act according to their wishes in other ways. The implicit or sometimes explicit message from transgender abusers is, "If you don't take care of me, I will kill myself and it will be your fault." This message is emphasized even more when the abuser is socially isolated and reliant on their partner as their sole source of emotional support.

Emotional Abuse

Tactics of transgender intimate partner violence (T-IPV) can be categorized into six forms of abuse: emotional, identity, isolation, financial, physical, and sexual. (See table 2.1.) Each form of abuse can include tactics shared with cisgender IPV as well as tactics unique to T-IPV. Emotional abuse—often defined as a combination of verbal abuse and

TABLE 2.1. Forms of Transgender Intimate Partner Violence

T-IPV Form	Sample Tactics
Emotional Abuse	Name-calling, controlling routines, criticizing, lying, manipulation, blaming, changing history
Identity Abuse	Denigrating identity: using transphobic slurs, saying no one else will love the survivor because they are transgender, saying cisgender people are superior
	Denying identity: refusing to use correct name or pronouns, not accepting the survivor's identity, saying they are not a "real" man or woman
	Manipulating identity: controlling how the survivor transitions, offering compliments and criticism to control gender expression, compelling the survivor to act in stereotypically gendered ways
Isolation Abuse	Threatening to out the survivor as transgender
	Not allowing the survivor to participate in transgender communities
	Isolating the survivor from family, friends, or other supports
	Using fear of external transphobia as a justification for isolation
Financial Abuse	Demanding the survivor pay for transition-related expenses
	Forcing the survivor to support the abuser financially
	Not allowing the survivor to buy gender-related products
	Using finances to control the survivor
Physical Abuse	Targeting chest and genitals for physical violence
	Blocking transition-related care and recovery
	Not allowing the survivor to heal after surgery
	Threats to commit suicide or to kill the survivor
	Disrupting sleep
Sexual Abuse	Eroticizing the survivor's body without permission
	Intentionally calling body parts by the wrong names
	Coercing the survivor into sex
	Demanding sex as a way to affirm gender identity

controlling tactics—is one of the integral components of abuse.[34] Emotional abuse tactics include verbal abuse such as blaming, shaming, and name-calling, as well as extreme manipulative behaviors such as repeatedly lying, revising history, and attempting to control the survivor's behavior. In order to gain control, an abusive partner seeks to rob their partner of their autonomy, often by scrutinizing and subverting the survivor's daily routines.[35] This can manifest as the abuser controlling what the partner eats, when they sleep, what they wear, or when they go to the bathroom.[36] For me, these were some of the most difficult tactics to endure. My partner viciously attacked me for not adhering to her arbitrary rules about everything, from how to cook an egg to how to dry off after taking a shower. She scrutinized my every action and subjected me to long lectures about why her way was correct. This applied to the "proper" methods for replacing a toilet paper roll, hanging a dish towel, getting dressed, making the bed, or describing food. I found myself navigating a daily obstacle course to keep her from harassing me further.

This happened gradually. At first, I balked at the ridiculous notion that there was any "correct" way to do something, but after years of her needling me, lecturing me, and raging, I went along with her rules to preserve the few moments of peace that were available to me. She expected total obedience and strove to wear me down on every issue, no matter how miniscule. In fact, the more miniscule, the more she would press the issue—for weeks, months, or even years—until I was sorry I had ever refused her. Her constant criticism filled me with self-doubt, causing me to question my own intuition. She turned everything I revealed to her about my life against me, chiding me for being stupid, clumsy, overly trusting, or stubborn. Unfortunately, I am not alone in these experiences. Research suggests that 45 percent of transgender people have had a partner repeatedly put them down so that they feel worthless.[37]

Identity Abuse

Identity abuse—sometimes also termed cultural abuse—entails targeting a survivor's oppressed or marginalized identity.[38] This type of abuse manifests in several ways: directly denigrating the culture/identity of the survivor, telling the survivor that they are "too much" of a particular identity, using stereotypes about the survivor's identity to manipulate them, denying the survivor's identity, or telling them that they are "not enough" of their identity.[39] Abusers use these methods to attack a range of identities such as race, class, gender, sex at birth, ethnicity, sexual orientation, or religion. An example might be a white abusive partner attacking the ethnic or racial identity of their partner, or a heterosexual abusive partner attacking their partner's bisexuality. Identity attacks also can occur when both partners share an identity. For example, when both partners are Jewish, an abusive partner might accuse the other partner of being "too Jewish" or "not Jewish enough."

Because people's identities are complex and intersecting, identity abuse may be weaponized regardless of the privilege the survivor has in other areas. For example, although I am a US citizen and, at the time of the relationship, my former partner was not, and although I am white and she is Asian, she grew up with economic privilege that I did not have. She would regularly joke that I was from "peasant stock" and therefore was heartier at physical labor. She would also deride my purchases, saying that I chose low-quality products instead of more expensive brands.

As with other marginalized groups, transgender people may face attacks on their gender identity within a relationship where IPV is occurring. For example, an abuser may use identity abuse tactics in an attempt to control a transgender survivor's transition process.[40] Identity abuse of transgender people can often involve the following: (1) denigrating identities, (2) denying the existence of identities, and (3) manipulating the expression of identities.

Denigrating Identities

When an abuser denigrates a transgender survivor's gender identity directly, they might say that no one else will love them because they are transgender.[41] They may use derogatory and anti-transgender slurs,[42] such as one abuser who told their transgender partner, "You and your cronies are freaks, you're just all f-in freaks."[43] As one indication of the extensive damage created by denigrating transgender people's identities, research estimates that 52 percent of transgender people have at some point in life had a partner make them feel "ashamed, guilty, or wrong" about being transgender.[44]

Transgender abusers can similarly denigrate their partner's identity. For example, a transgender abuser may claim they are better at being a man or woman than their partner is.[45] A nonbinary abusive partner might chide their partner for having a binary gender or may assert that transgender people are superior.[46] Additionally, perhaps in order to distance himself from femininity—as a means of "doing gender"[47] and affirming his masculinity—an abusive transgender man may act in misogynistic ways toward a female partner.[48] One cisgender woman described her transgender partner acting in this way: "He would call girls flippant or stupid or make remarks about women's bodies. He was suspicious of women: women were definitely something other than what he was."[49] A transgender abuser might also enact identity abuse by demanding that their partner give up their identity as lesbian, gay, bisexual, transgender, or queer (LGBTQ).[50] For instance, an abuser who is a transgender woman may force her partner to stop identifying as gay in order to affirm her identity as a woman. When both partners are transgender, the abuser may accuse their partner of "not acting transgender enough" or being "too open" about being transgender.

Denying Identities

Instead of—or in addition to—denigrating a transgender survivor's identity, abusers may deny their transgender partner's identity altogether. This negation of gender identity is akin to "gaslighting," where abusers attempt to make survivors doubt themselves or their reality.[51] At times, gaslighting can occur through direct claims by an abuser. For instance, an abuser may tell a survivor that they are not transgender or not a "real" woman or man, a tactic experienced by 25 percent of transgender people in their lifetimes.[52] Gaslighting can also be more indirect, as when transgender survivors experience an abuser's continual refusal to use the correct name or pronouns.[53] One study indicated that 33 percent of transgender people experience this tactic at some point in their lifetimes.[54] Abusers may claim to "forget" or assert that they are exempt from using the correct pronouns based on their history with the survivor. This ongoing misgendering in public can lead others to mirror the wrong pronouns, further amplifying feelings of dysphoria and isolation in the transgender survivor.[55]

When my partner denied my gender identity, it was difficult for me to identify it as gaslighting because the rest of the world was consistently creating that same feeling inside me. I identified as genderqueer for fifteen years before medically transitioning to be recognized as a man. During those years, finding a pronoun that did not create a sense of disorientation and dysphoria inside me was difficult. At first, I asked some people to use the pronoun "he" for me while others continued to use "she." Eventually, I settled on "they" as a gender-neutral pronoun. I felt a profound feeling of disorientation and self-doubt after telling groups of people that my pronoun was "they" and then experiencing everyone continuing to use "she" for me, often after explicitly saying they supported my gender identity. Throughout our seven-year relationship, my partner exclusively used the pronoun "she" for me, despite intimate knowledge of my gender dysphoria and the pain that came with it. Nevertheless, this negation of my identity was less noticeable as a tactic since others in my life were doing the same thing.

Manipulating Gender Expression

Abusers may also attempt to control a transgender survivor's expression of their gender. This can be direct—such as when abusers critique survivors' expression of gendered norms. An abusive partner may justify such critiques of gender expression by drawing on gender stereotypes to narrowly define what it means to be a particular gender.[56] For example, an abuser may demand a transgender woman perform stereotypically feminine tasks such as cleaning and cooking, questioning her womanhood if she refuses. Likewise, an abuser may demand a transgender man pay for everything.[57] In the context of an abusive transgender man partnered with a woman, he might instruct his partner to act in stereotypical feminine ways in order to ease his gender dysphoria or to help him blend in.[58]

In addition to exerting direct control over a survivor's expression of gendered norms, abusers may also directly control how a survivor expresses their gendered appearance. A sadly typical example is the abuser destroying or hiding clothing, wigs, products, or prosthetics aligned with the survivor's gender.[59] Indeed, one study found that 30 percent of transgender people have had a partner prevent them from expressing their gender through their appearance (e.g., preferred clothing or makeup).[60] Research also suggests that 7 percent of transgender people have had a partner bar them from accessing gender-affirming medical treatment.[61]

While some abusers are overt in their attempts to control how a transgender survivor expresses their gender, many abusers are more like my partner in their subtlety. For instance, an abuser may object to the survivor's transition under the guise of "health concerns" or the impact that transition will have on their identity. Abusers may try to frighten transgender men or nonbinary people away from binding by raising associated health-related issues. With equal duplicity, an abuser may critique their partner's gender presentation under the auspices of providing "helpful feedback." One transgender woman shared her experience of her partner convincing her not to wear a dress out of the house by saying, "you're gonna be miserable and you know I think you look good but that's for home, baby—please, you look like a freak."[62] My partner would couch her criticism in similar ways, telling me that men's clothing was "unflattering" on my body or that short hair made me "look fat." The strategic use of appearance-related compliments and gifts also has the potential to coerce survivors into altering their gender expression. Fatima, a transgender woman, describes just such a situation:

> I started doing [wearing] some of the things he got, like, the better bras and silicone; I even did more on my face, like the lips and cheeks [referring to surgeries], that were just easy one day things. He would praise me for that . . . I started to just lose myself; I was just now this thing. This, like experiment or something, of his to use and "Doll Up." It only made me more depressed, which made him more angry, and then that's when he got colder, more distant, more angry and kind of like violent.[63]

Gifts in many societies are viewed as signs of affection and are impolite to refuse, and thus repeated appearance-related gifts have the potential to exert near-invisible control over a transgender survivor's gender expression.

As many abusers do, my partner offered occasional indulgences as a part of the honeymoon stage of the cycle of abuse and as a means of keeping me in the relationship. She occasionally affirmed my gender identity—just often enough that I would not give up on her completely. On one such occasion, I discussed wanting to medically transition, particularly with hormones and top surgery, and she initially was supportive. She knew I wanted kids, and she offered to get pregnant so I would not have to. It was a rare moment of acceptance and support around my gender that did not last. Later, she threatened to always resent me and our future child if she got pregnant. Because I wanted children, I delayed my medical transition in order to attempt to get pregnant.

Identity abuse ultimately serves to make transgender survivors more dependent on their abusers.[64] For instance, in an interview study of transgender survivors, one transgender woman recalled her abuser attacking her femininity, and that doing so "[took] away something that I was feeling good about and you know, how I was able to present myself as female, and learning how to look beautiful, and look pretty, and the way I dressed, and the way I see myself, and trying to turn that into a negative for me. It was taking away those things that I found self-fulfilling and trying to pull those away so that there would be a void there, that she could come in and fill it."[65] Another transgender woman shared that her abuser "was careful to tell me how beautiful I was *to her*. She was occasionally subtle and often not so subtle about using my trans status to tell me how no one could really love or accept me like her."[66]

Complicating matters further is the fact that transgender survivors have a myriad of other identities revolving around race, class, sexual orientation, and more. Any one or a combination of these identities can be targeted in a similar fashion, with the use of derogatory comments, stereotypes, denial of identity, and assertions that a survivor is "too much" or "not enough" of their identity. One transgender survivor spoke to how hir partner targeted hir disability, explaining, "First, I didn't take it up as abuse because it was directed towards my health. . . . When she first started, it was just about 'Oh this is so stupid. I hate that we have to come to the emergency room. I don't understand why you're so fucked up.'"[67]

Isolation Abuse

Abuse is more effective when a survivor is isolated from any worldview other than their abusive partner's.[68] The less variety of perspectives the survivor has access to, the more the abuser can enforce their own, enabling them to have more power and control over the survivor. When the abuser is a transgender survivor's primary connection to transgender communities, the abuser might only continue to provide access to these communities if the survivor follows the abuser's rules.[69] Moreover, isolation from one's traditional social support network—friends and family—decreases avenues for coping and escape.[70] Abusers often use isolation tactics in the context of IPV for these reasons.

My partner was no different. She attempted to isolate me from friends, family, our spiritual community, and allies at work. She was selfish with my attention and became jealous when I directed it toward others. After talking with family members on the phone, I would face her hostility. She would listen in on my conversations and chide me afterward for talking about her incorrectly. When I went out with friends, she would get jealous, regularly starting fights with me when I got home.

Because abusers often isolate survivors from their unique communities of support,[71] abusers may explicitly deny transgender survivors the right to attend LGBTQ or transgender-specific events. Research suggests that 15 percent of transgender people have at some point in their lives had a partner prevent them from socializing with other transgender people or from attending transgender social groups or support groups.[72] Such isolation efforts may take the guise of criticizing a local transgender or LGBTQ community in order to persuade survivors to avoid it, or abusers causing unpleasant consequences if survivors attend events.[73] Conversely, an abusive partner may attend LGBTQ events with the transgender survivor in order to monitor them or prevent them from interacting with others.

This latter isolation strategy—of working to break a survivor away from a potential social support network by joining the same network—was repeatedly used by my abuser. At the beginning of our relationship, my partner pressured me heavily into joining her religious community. Her constant demanding finally wore away at me and I joined. Soon I embraced it, as it was one of the few social spaces my partner would allow me to access. Once I was more fully involved and became a leader in the community, she decided we needed to leave it. She punctuated this by yelling her criticisms publicly at a community event, storming out, and stating we would not return. Things went dramatically downhill after that. We became extremely socially isolated, and she became extremely angry and hostile at the mere mention of our previous religious community.

A similar pattern of undoing my support networks from within occurred at work. With my world getting smaller, work remained one of my few refuges. At my job, people used the correct pronouns for me and were supportive of my transgender identity. My partner was aware of this and did everything she could to drive a wedge between those supportive allies and me. She would vacillate between saying she was supportive of my organization and criticizing it relentlessly. She attacked my organization's values and the personalities of my coworkers and the way they approached their work. In a seemingly nonsensical U-turn, she eventually decided to volunteer at my office. Once she infiltrated this space, she found more detailed ways to tear the agency apart with her criticism, all the while acting as if she was supporting them. Not long after, she began threatening to tell my coworkers that *I* was abusive.

In the context of T-IPV, abusers frequently verbalize two related rationalizations for isolating survivors: (1) the outside world may be hostile to the survivor and (2) the outside world may be hostile to the abuser. Regarding the first rationalization, abusive partners may paint the outside world as dangerous for transgender survivors, highlighting transphobia as a means of keeping the survivor away from others.[74] Abusers may use this information to increase a transgender survivor's fear of reaching out to service providers or community members. Similarly, they may use the perception or reality that transgender people are marginalized in LGBTQ communities as a way of discouraging their partner from attending events.[75] Abusive partners may encourage a transgender partner to avoid transphobia by hiding their identity—even demanding they get rid of any items such as books, clothing, or movies that are associated with transgender people.[76] They may tell a transgender survivor that no one will help them because they are transgender.[77] An abuser also may threaten to tell others that the survivor is transgender, knowing that this may put the survivor's relationships, job, or safety at risk.[78] As a means of persuading the survivor not to transition, an abuser may threaten to seek sole custody of shared children, a threat reinforced by historical anti-transgender bias in the legal system.[79] Thus, by instilling fear in a transgender survivor over transphobia in society, abusers gain leverage with which to isolate transgender survivors.

Regarding the second rationalization, transgender abusers may justify isolating not only themselves but also the survivor from society as a means by which to protect the abuser from transphobia in the outside world. Of course, these two rationalizations for isolation—fear of how societal transphobia will affect transgender survivors and fear of how it will affect transgender abusers—have the potential for an even greater impact when both partners are transgender. In such relationships, the abuser can encourage an "us against the world" mentality to keep their partner isolated and fearful to trust others. Perhaps out of fear that others will conclude that the abuser is transgender if their partner is also transgender, transgender abusers often demand that a transgender survivor not participate in LGBTQ communities or remain closeted altogether.[80] Indeed, one study found that as many as 30 percent of transgender people have had a partner stop them from telling other people about their transgender background or identity.[81]

Financial Abuse

Financial tactics of abuse generally fall under one of two extremes. At one extreme, the abusive partner utilizes the survivor's economic resources by demanding they pay for the majority of expenses.[82] At the other, the abuser uses their economic power to dictate decisions, coerce or guilt their partner, or deny access to basic needs such as housing, transportation, food, or clothing.[83]

Regarding the first form of financial abuse, a transgender abuser may demand that their partner support them economically. Since many transgender individuals face economic barriers due to anti-transgender discrimination in the workplace and elsewhere, they may use this vulnerability to justify their partner supporting them economically.[84] They may demand money for clothing or surgeries, claiming that the survivor is putting them at risk of transphobic violence by denying them money.[85] One cisgender woman described just such an experience: "I spent so much time paying for his blood work and his testosterone, which he needed and if I didn't pay for [it] . . . I was a bad girlfriend, I wasn't supportive of him, and then I became 'anti-trans.'"[86] In the same way, an abuser may insist that money be prioritized for surgeries above other basic needs such as rent, or may pressure the survivor to take an extra job to pay for transition-related expenses.[87]

Similarly, my abusive partner demanded that I support them economically. All the credit cards were in my name, and she would run up the bills. She worked fewer than fifteen hours a week, but despite my begging, pleading, or getting angry, she would not take on more hours. She even turned down jobs she felt were inconvenient or "beneath" her. Meanwhile, I was supporting two adults in an expensive city on a small salary and was plunging into debt. No matter how many times I tried to explain my financial situation to her, she insisted that I could get rich if I would only buy a condo and flip it, berating me for not doing so. Likewise, she would spend hours trying to convince me to buy her luxury items that I could not afford, such as thousand-dollar kayaks and specialized bicycles.

Conversely, regarding the second form of financial abuse, abusers of transgender survivors may use their greater economic power to control their partner's actions. Research suggests that 18 percent of transgender people have had a partner either block them from accessing their fair share of financial resources or take money from them.[88] Restricting access to funds—or threatening to do so—can be used by abusers as a means through which to gain power. For instance, the abuser may provide room and board with the caveat that the survivor must follow extensive rules. They may refuse to let the survivor buy clothing that fits their gender identity or not allow money for transition-related medical expenses like hormones or surgery.[89] An abuser may deny the transgender survivor access to a vehicle as a punishment for behavior the abuser does not like, further isolating them and making it difficult for the survivor to retain employment.[90] Transgender survivors who are more economically stable might find their partner threatening to out them as being transgender to their workplace, knowing that it will put their job in jeopardy.[91] Similarly, they may out the survivor at school or to a relative who may be helping with tuition, knowing that this could lead to the survivor losing financial support.[92]

Physical Abuse

Physical abuse does not occur in all instances of T-IPV. When it is present, physical abuse can include both threats of and acts of pushing, hitting, punching, burning, throwing objects at the survivor, strangulation, and murder. Julie, a transgender survivor, shared her experience of physical abuse at the hands of her partner: "[S]he used everything short of killing me . . . and that lasted most of our married life from when I was 22 to when we split up when I was 50."[93] Similarly, a transgender man shared, "When I tried to break up with her one time, she put a revolver in my face because she was threatening suicide. Then she was like, 'Well I'll just take you with me.'"[94] Unique to transgender survivor experiences, the abuser may target a survivor's gendered body parts during violent attacks, particularly the chest and genitals.[95] One survivor recounted a violent episode after surgery: "He slapped me and pushed on my chest and pushed on my surgical scars and made them bleed."[96] In the wake of such violence, transgender survivors may be reluctant to get medical care due to the potential discrimination they may face in health-care settings.[97] Their abusive partner may remind them of this as a means to keep them from seeking help after a violent episode.[98]

Physical abuse also can involve less noticeably violent tactics that either generate fear of imminent violence—such as threatening looks and gestures, breaking things, and driving dangerously—or have a deleterious physical impact, such as taking mobility aides or prosthetics, restricting medical access, controlling food, denying sleep, or locking the survivor in or out of the house.[99] An abusive partner may disrupt a transgender survivor's transition-related medical care. Withholding hormones from the survivor may cause unwanted changes in characteristics such as location of fat, body hair, and mood.[100] This can worsen gender dysphoria and contribute to the survivor being more conspicuously identifiable as transgender, potentially putting the survivor at greater risk of harassment or discrimination.[101] An abuser also may prevent the survivor from recovering after a transition-related surgery by forcing them to work more than they are physically capable or not letting them rest.[102]

Disrupting sleep is a tactic of physical abuse that has a profound impact. My abusive partner often disrupted my sleep by kicking and punching me, or elbowing me in the head, claiming that she did this unconsciously. She became angry if I went to sleep before she did, which occurred nearly every weeknight because of my work schedule. Just as I was falling asleep, I would often wake to her face hovering over mine, saying, "No!" As a result, I was chronically exhausted and my mental health symptoms worsened considerably. Sleep deprivation can have deleterious physical, mental health, and economic effects on survivors, as the experience of another transgender survivor illustrates: "I was literally getting 4–5 hours of sleep per night. I'm failing everything. Even with my job, I wasn't falling asleep at my job, but I was making careless mistakes like burning myself on the grill. Every aspect of her controlling me, and no sleep, and the stress of life, and literally breaking down and crying every single day—it had so much of an impact on my life. It affected how I functioned."[103]

Sexual Abuse

Sexual tactics of abuse are often shrouded in secrecy because of the deep feelings of shame and disgust they create within the survivor. Sexual tactics can include forcing sexual acts, not respecting sexual boundaries, forcing the survivor to practice polyamory or monogamy, intentionally exposing the survivor to sexually transmitted infections, forcing pregnancy, or forcing sex work.[104] Early in our relationship, I had made my partner aware that certain sexual acts would trigger memories of past sexual assaults and set them as off limit. However, she would consistently violate the boundaries I had set. These were some of the worst moments of abuse. She often would ignore our safe word until I was in tears. Regardless of how many times I tried to explain the impact of her actions, she refused to stop this behavior. She was practically reenacting my past sexual assaults regularly, which kept my past trauma in the forefront, dramatically exacerbating my post-traumatic stress disorder symptoms.

Aside from violating boundaries and forcing sex acts, an abuser may refuse to appropriately refer to the transgender survivor's body parts, causing increased feelings of dysphoria.[105] Likewise, an abuser might ridicule a transgender person's body and claim that no one else would want to have sex with them.[106] Conversely, they may eroticize their body without consent, fetishizing their anatomy to the point of sexual harassment.[107]

Transgender individuals have a range of sexual identities and sexual activities they are comfortable with that abusers often disregard. Abusers may insist on sex acts that go against transgender survivors' understandings of themselves.[108] For example, an abusive partner may focus on parts of a transgender woman's anatomy that she feels uncomfortable with.[109] Similarly, the abusive partner of a nonbinary person may use gender-based terminology during sex, causing their partner to feel disrespected or dysphoric. An abuser may coerce a transgender man into sex he does not want, stating he should always be receptive to sex in order to be masculine.[110]

Transgender abusers may use a variety of transgender-specific justifications for sexual abuse. A transgender abuser may demand particular sex acts from their partner in order to affirm their gender identity.[111] One survivor explained, "His abusers had been female, and as a non-trans person and non-survivor I 'owed' him sexually. It was my duty to provide for his pleasure, any needs and boundaries of my own were supposedly abusive."[112] Abusers may tell survivors that there is no way to have safe sex with transgender bodies and use that as an excuse to have unprotected sex.[113] An abusive transgender person taking testosterone may use their increased libido as an excuse to coerce or pressure their partner into sex.[114]

Healing from Abuse

It is important to recognize that IPV is not limited to an ongoing relationship but can extend into—and at times escalate during—the separation process, as well as long after a relationship officially ends. Leaving any relationship is hard, but leaving an abusive partner is harder. Often the abusive partner will not "let" the survivor break up with them. This was the case with me. I had tried unsuccessfully to end our relationship many times. In the end, my partner left me. It happened at a time when I was getting stronger, and she started using threats of breaking up with me to try to regain control. When she threatened to move in with a new friend, I seized hold of the opportunity to get her out of the apartment. Once out, she tried several times to convince me to let her move back in, but with the help of my friends I was able to stay strong and keep her out.

The abuse continued, but from a distance. The distance made a world of difference and gave me a chance to start to heal. Every time I had to call her for something, she turned ugly. When I asked her for money she owed me, she would threaten suicide in order to "pay me with life insurance." When she was hospitalized for suicidality, it was hard for me not to feel responsible. It took nearly a year to fully untangle her from my life, legally and financially. During that time, I was overwhelmed by an enormous wave of grief as I came to terms with the fact that the person I loved had abused me. She had made me question the very nature of my being, and I felt like I had no sense of self once she was gone, just a list of things she liked and did not like. It felt so shameful to admit that someone had that much control over me.

Working with an IPV survivor advocate helped considerably; I was able to name all the secrets, the shame, and the confusion. She helped me untangle all the lies and manipulation; she pointed out the patterns and the crazy-making. I worked hard to reject my ex-partner's beliefs that people are evil, selfish, and dangerous. I struggled to not internalize her messages that I was clumsy, stupid, fat, ugly, grotesque, too loud, too inappropriate, too analytical, too old, and too emotional. I kept striving to connect with people, to break my isolation, and to be brave enough to be myself. I was finally able to take the steps I had wanted to take for so long to physically transition and legally change my name.

Healing for me came from meeting with an advocate who understood transgender issues and could help me understand the ways in which my partner used transphobia as a weapon against me. Transgender survivors need and deserve advocates and counselors who are welcoming and who understand the nuances of their experiences. Partners of transgender abusers also need this type of culturally competent provider to help them sort through the manipulation, particularly when it revolves around their abusive partner's identity as a transgender person. Furthermore, those who work in batterer intervention programs need to become knowledgeable in working with transgender abusers. Understanding the specific tactics that abusers utilize in intimate partner violence involving transgender individuals is an essential part of providing these much-needed services.

NOTES

1. The Network/La Red 2010.
2. Messinger 2017.
3. Barnett, Miller-Perrin, and Perrin 2011; Kurdyla 2017; Loseke 2001.
4. Brown 2011; J. Walker 2015.
5. Roberson and Wallace 2016.
6. Grant et al. 2011.
7. Grant et al. 2011.
8. L. Walker 1979. See also Santiago 2016.
9. Messinger 2017.
10. Roch, Morton, and Ritchie 2010.
11. Quinn 2010.
12. Cook-Daniels 2015.
13. Quinn 2010; Santiago 2016.
14. Herman 1992; Roberson and Wallace 2016; Santiago 2016.
15. Roberson and Wallace 2016; Santiago 2016.
16. Roberson and Wallace 2016; Santiago 2016.
17. Rogers 2017.
18. Rogers 2017.
19. Santiago 2016.
20. McKenry et al. 2006.
21. Brown 2011.

22 Scott and Straus 2007.
23 Brown 2007, 2011.
24 Brown 2011.
25 Brown 2007.
26 Brown 2011.
27 Brown 2011; Messinger 2017.
28 Messinger 2017.
29 Brown 2011; Cook-Daniels 2015.
30 Brown 2007.
31 Brown 2007, 377.
32 Cook-Daniels 2015.
33 Cook-Daniels 2015.
34 Zavala and Guadalupe-Diaz, 2018.
35 Herman 1992.
36 Stark 2009.
37 Roch, Morton, and Ritchie 2010.
38 Woulfe and Goodman 2018.
39 Cook-Daniels 2015; Quinn 2010.
40 Guadalupe-Diaz and Anthony 2017.
41 Cook-Daniels 2015; Greenberg 2012.
42 Cook-Daniels 2015; Greenburg 2012.
43 Roch, Morton, and Ritchie 2010, 17.
44 Roch, Morton, and Ritchie 2010.
45 Cook-Daniels 2015.
46 Cook-Daniels 2015.
47 Anderson 2005.
48 Brown 2011.
49 Brown 2007.
50 Cook-Daniels 2015.
51 Herman 1992; Kurdyla 2017; Whiting, Oka, and Fife 2012.
52 Anderson 2005; Bornstein et al. 2006; Cook-Daniels 2015; Goodmark 2013; James et al. 2016.
53 Cook-Daniels 2015.
54 Roch, Morton, and Ritchie 2010.
55 Quinn 2010.
56 Guadalupe-Diaz and Anthony 2017.
57 Quinn 2010.
58 Brown 2011.
59 Cook-Daniels 2015; Guadalupe-Diaz and Anthony 2017; Rogers 2017.
60 Roch, Morton, and Ritchie 2010.
61 Cook-Daniels 2015; Goodmark 2013; Roch, Morton, and Ritchie 2010.
62 Guadalupe-Diaz and Anthony 2017, 10.
63 Guadalupe-Diaz and Anthony 2017, 11.

64 Guadalupe-Diaz and Anthony 2017.
65 Guadalupe-Diaz and Anthony 2017, 9.
66 Greenberg 2012, 217.
67 Kurdyla 2017, 85.
68 Messinger 2017.
69 Brown 2011.
70 Greenberg 2012.
71 Stark 2009.
72 Roch, Morton, and Ritchie 2010.
73 Quinn 2010.
74 Greenberg 2012.
75 Bornstein et al. 2006.
76 Roch, Morton, and Ritchie 2010.
77 Greenberg 2012.
78 Cook-Daniels 2015; Greenberg 2012.
79 Cooper 2013.
80 Cook-Daniels 2015; Roch, Morton, and Ritchie 2010.
81 Roch, Morton, and Ritchie 2010.
82 Messinger 2017.
83 Messinger 2017.
84 Grant et al. 2011.
85 munson and Cook-Daniels 2016.
86 Brown 2007, 380.
87 munson and Cook-Daniels 2016.
88 Roch, Morton, and Ritchie 2010.
89 Yerke and DeFeo 2016.
90 Rogers 2017.
91 Greenberg 2012.
92 Quinn 2010.
93 Rogers 2017, 18.
94 Kurdyla 2017, 70.
95 Yerke and DeFeo 2016.
96 Guadalupe-Diaz 2013.
97 Grant et al. 2011.
98 Greenberg 2012.
99 Quinn 2010.
100 Quinn 2010.
101 Quinn 2010.
102 Quinn 2010.
103 Kurdyla 2017, 71.
104 Quinn 2010.
105 Greenberg 2012.
106 Cook-Daniels 2015.

107 Cook-Daniels 2015.
108 Cook-Daniels 2015; Greenberg 2012.
109 Greenberg 2012.
110 Quinn 2010.
111 munson and Cook-Daniels 2016.
112 munson and Cook-Daniels 2016.
113 munson and Cook-Daniels 2016.
114 Brown 2011.

REFERENCES

Anderson, Kristin L. 2005. "Theorizing Gender in Intimate Partner Violence Research." *Sex Roles* 52 (11–12): 853–865.

Baker, Nancy L., Jessica D. Buick, Shari R. Kim, Sandy Moniz, and Khristiana L. Nava. 2013. "Lessons from Examining Same Sex Intimate Partner Violence." *Sex Roles* 69 (3–4): 182–192.

Barnett, Ola W., Cindy L. Miller-Perrin, and Robin D. Perrin. 2011. *Family Violence across the Lifespan: An Introduction*. Los Angeles, CA: Sage.

Bornstein, Danica R., Jake Fawcett, Marianne Sullivan, Kirsten D. Senturia, and Sharyne Shiu-Thornton. 2006. "Understanding the Experiences of Lesbian, Bisexual and Trans Survivors of Domestic Violence: A Qualitative Study." *Journal of Homosexuality* 51 (1): 159–181.

Brown, Nicola. 2007. "Stories from Outside the Frame: Intimate Partner Abuse in Sexual-Minority Women's Relationships with Transsexual Men." *Feminism and Psychology* 17 (3): 373–393.

Brown, Nicola. 2011. "Holding Tensions of Victimization and Perpetration: Partner Abuse in Trans Communities." In *Intimate Partner Violence in LGBTQ Lives*, edited by Janice L. Ristock, 153–168. New York: Routledge.

Cook-Daniels, Loree. 2015. "Intimate Partner Violence in Transgender Couples: 'Power and Control' in a Specific Cultural Context." *Partner Abuse* 6 (1): 126–139.

Cooper, Leslie. 2013. *Protecting the Rights of Transgender Parents and Their Children: A Guide for Parents and Lawyers*. New York: American Civil Liberties Union, and Washington, DC: National Center for Transgender Equality. https://transequality.org.

Goodmark, Leigh. 2013. "Transgender People, Intimate Partner Abuse, and the Legal System." *Harvard Civil Rights–Civil Liberties Law Review* 48 (1): 51–104.

Grant, Jaime M., Lisa A. Mottet, Justin Tanis, Jack Harrison, Jody L. Herman, and Mara Keisling. 2011. *Injustice at Every Turn: A Report of the National Transgender Discrimination Survey*. Washington, DC: National Center for Transgender Equality and National Gay and Lesbian Task Force. www.transequality.org.

Greenberg, Kae. 2012. "Still Hidden in the Closet: Trans Women and Domestic Violence." *Berkeley Journal of Gender, Law & Justice* 27 (2): 198–251.

Guadalupe-Diaz, Xavier L. 2013. "An Exploration of Differences in the Help-Seeking of LGBQ Victims of Violence by Race, Economic Class and Gender." *Gay & Lesbian Issues and Psychology Review* 9 (1): 15–33.

Guadalupe-Diaz, Xavier L., and Amanda Koontz Anthony. 2017. "Discrediting Identity Work: Understandings of Intimate Partner Violence by Transgender Survivors." *Deviant Behavior* 8 (1): 1–16.

Herman, Judith. 1992. *Trauma and Recovery*. New York: Basic.

James, Sandy E., Jody L. Herman, Susan Rankin, Mara Keisling, Lisa Mottet, and Ma'ayan Anafi. 2016. *The Report of the 2015 U.S. Transgender Survey*. Washington, DC: National Center for Transgender Equality. www.ustranssurvey.org.

Kurdyla, Victoria A. 2017. "Exploring Experiences of Disclosure for Transgender and Nonbinary Survivors of Abuse." Master's thesis, the University of North Carolina at Greensboro.

Loseke, Donileen R. 2001. "Lived Realties and Formula Stories of 'Battered Women.'" In *Institutional Selves: Troubled Identities in a Postmodern World*, edited by Jaber F. Gubrium and James A. Holstein, 107–126. Oxford: Oxford University Press.

McKenry, Patrick C., Julianne M. Serovich, Tina L. Mason, and Katie Mosack. 2006. "Perpetration of Gay and Lesbian Partner Violence: A Disempowerment Perspective." *Journal of Family Violence* 21 (4): 233–243.

Messinger, Adam M. 2017. *LGBTQ Intimate Partner Violence: Lessons for Policy, Practice, and Research*. Oakland: University of California Press.

munson, michael, and Loree Cook-Daniels. 2016. *A Guide for Partners and Loved Ones of Transgender Sexual Violence Survivors*. Milwaukee, WI: FORGE. http://forge-forward.org.

Network/La Red, The. 2010. Information for Domestic Violence Providers about LGBTQ Partner Abuse. Boston: The Network/La Red. www.lgbtagingcenter.org.

Quinn, M.-E. 2010. *Open Minds Open Doors: Transforming Domestic Violence Programs to Include LGBTQ Survivors*. Boston: The Network/La Red. www.ncdsv.org.

Roberson, Cliff, and Paul Harvey Wallace. 2016. *Family Violence: Legal, Medical, and Social Perspectives*. New York: Routledge.

Roch, Amy, James Morton, and Graham Ritchie. 2010. *Out of Sight, out of Mind? Transgender People's Experiences of Domestic Abuse*. Edinburgh: LGBT Youth Scotland and the Scottish Transgender Alliance. www.scottishtrans.org.

Rogers, Michaela. 2017. "Challenging Cisgenderism through Trans People's Narratives of Domestic Violence and Abuse." *Sexualities*. https://doi.org/10.1177/1363460716681475.

Santiago, Sabrina. 2016. *Power With Power For*. Boston: The Network/La Red. http://tnlr.org.

Scott, Katreena, and Murray Straus. 2007. "Denial, Minimization, Partner Blaming, and Intimate Aggression in Dating Partners." *Journal of Interpersonal Violence* 22 (7): 851–871.

Stark, Evan. 2009. *Coercive Control: The Entrapment of Women in Personal Life*. New York: Oxford University Press.

Walker, Julia K. 2015. "Investigating Trans People's Vulnerabilities to Intimate Partner Violence/Abuse." *Partner Abuse* 6 (1): 107–125.

Walker, Lenore E. 1979. *The Battered Woman*. New York: Harper Perennial.

Whiting, Jason B., Megan Oka, and Stephen T. Fife. 2012. "Appraisal Distortions and Intimate Partner Violence: Gender, Power, and Interaction." *Journal of Marital and Family Therapy* 38:133–149.

Woulfe, Julie M., and Lisa A. Goodman. 2018. "Identity Abuse as a Tactic of Violence in LGBTQ Communities: Initial Validation of the Identity Abuse Measure." *Journal of Interpersonal Violence*. https://doi.org/10.1177/0886260518760018.

Yerke, Adam, and Jennifer DeFeo. 2016. "Redefining Intimate Partner Violence beyond the Binary to Include Transgender People." *Journal of Family Violence* 31:975–979.

Zavala, Egbert, and Xavier L. Guadalupe-Diaz. 2018. "Assessing Emotional Abuse Victimization and Perpetration: A Multi-Theoretical Examination." *Deviant Behavior* 39 (11): 1515–1532.

3

Undermining Transgender Survivors

Discrediting Identity Work in Intimate Relationships

AMANDA KOONTZ

How do we come to gain a sense of self? While we may generally think of the self-concept as emerging from within, sociologists consider there to be multiple influences on how we think about ourselves. Rather than just one inherent "self," the self-concept can better be understood as a set of beliefs about our essential character or nature, idealized images of who we want to be and how we want to be seen, and understandings of how others categorize us. A related practice, defined by sociologists as *identity work*, refers to a process of constructing ourselves through signifiers. Signifiers are "physical, symbolic, verbal, textual, and behavioral" cues that, taken together, create an image of who we are as people.[1] These signs only gain meaning through interactions and others' reactions to them, with both the signs and others' reactions then coming to influence our identities.[2] Therefore, identity work involves performances, yet others in our lives can accept, reject, or even ignore the ways that we try to identify and express ourselves. In turn, we can have fears of others rejecting us or our desired identities, so that the universal need to uphold our self-worth can be a powerful incentive for us to alter our development and signification of self-concepts.[3] Accordingly, sociologists David Snow and Leon Anderson argue that identity work—and its connections with self-realization and categorizations—is just as essential to our existence as our physiological needs for basic subsistence.[4] Though identity work processes influence almost all parts of our lives, this chapter specifically examines how some abusers manipulate the identity work of transgender partners as a means of exerting control and, ultimately, as an underexplored tactic of transgender intimate partner violence (T-IPV).

To date, the role of identity work in T-IPV has largely been subsumed by and obscured within the emerging research literature on identity abuse.[5] Psychologists Julie Woulfe and Lisa Goodman define identity abuse as "abuse tactics within an intimate partnership that leverage systemic oppression such as ableism, sexism, and racism to harm an individual," noting that this type of IPV "has received little empirical attention despite its apparent salience for LGBTQ communities."[6] (See chapter 2 for more on tactics of abuse.) In helping to move the literature forward by integrating an identity work approach, sociologist Xavier Guadalupe-Diaz and I aimed to illuminate one key instrument of what has now been labeled as identity abuse when we introduced the concept of *discrediting identity work*, defined as "an individual's engagement in activities that direct another's identity construction away from desired identity signification."[7]

Through drawing on research literature and analyzing data collected from qualitative interviews with eighteen transgender survivors of IPV, I look to further develop the concept of discrediting identity work by defining two sub-strategies: *retroverting* and *maneuverting*. I will also consider ways in which discrediting identity work can offer insight into why transgender survivors stay in abusive relationships, as related to the societal context and manipulation of identity work that contributes to constricting transgender people's self-concepts. Before reviewing the specific findings from this qualitative study, I will first delve further into the research literature, including three primary points that provide the necessary background from which to understand how romantic love narratives, issues of stability, and manipulation can play a role in T-IPV.

Romantic Love Narratives and Constructing the Self

Popularly circulated Western storylines of romantic love perpetuate a dominant ideal in which intimate relationships are, as explained by sociologists Amanda Koontz, Lauren Norman, and Sara Okorie, perceived as "based in the search for self-knowledge and identity development," so that "love is thus looked upon for both stability and flexibility as partners strive to achieve authentic self-realization."[8] Research, predominately based on cisgender women in the United States, emphasizes that the romantic love narrative is especially influential in people's life planning and is "interwoven into the construction of self."[9] For instance, psychologist Terri Conley and colleagues note that people perceive relationships as conferring happiness and societal acceptance. In particular, they suggest that dominant "romantic relationship ideals encourage coupling to promote happiness and espouse long-term monogamous relationships as standard and normal."[10] As such, monogamous relationships can be perceived as a cornerstone for life planning, which in turn enables partners to define and fulfill their potential even beyond the context of the relationship.[11]

Accordingly, perhaps it is not surprising that romantic relationships hold substantial influence in transgender people's lives, in part because of the expected benefits they can offer to intimate partners. In fact, sociologist Douglas Mason-Schrock's research reveals that transgender individuals' construction of a "new 'true self'—one almost antithetical to the old," yet reflective of a self that they feel has been there all along—entails fitting their self-narratives into a storyline of "falling in love that circulates in Western culture."[12] The romantic love narrative can be understood as critical in constructing the true self for two interrelated reasons: the construction of a desired identity can be so comprehensive and transformative that an intimate support system is needed, and individuals can perceive a romantic partner as providing all of the social support needed for realizing desired life goals. However, as revealed through discussions by Mason-Schrock, along with Guadalupe-Diaz and Anthony, this romantic love storyline can offer additional benefits to transgender individuals, such as buffering societal discrimination and offering a safe space for identity work.[13] As such, recognizing abuse and leaving an abuser may be especially complex for transgender survivors of IPV.

Identity Work and (In)stability

Young adults often view stable relationships as catalysts for obtaining such markers of successful adulthood as self-sufficiency, financial independence, and other lifelong dreams embellished by sayings of "happily ever after."[14] Particular emphasis may be placed on having a stable (i.e., supportive, long-term, consistent) relationship. Individuals can perceive this relationship as laying the groundwork for developing other areas of their lives, and they may perceive their partner to be the needed guide for navigating these major life changes.[15] Stable relationships, therefore, can be seen as a counter to the instability that often accompanies major life changes and transitions. In relation to transitions, the term *work* is especially fitting because transgender individuals often consciously work on learning how to signify the gender identities that fit and embody their true selves. As sociologists Kristen Schilt and Danya Lagos noted in their literature review, much research has focused on the "gendered appearance cues" and "bodywork" entailed in gender transitions, as the desired expression of gender identities predominately does not match the roles that transgender individuals were socialized into as children.[16] Transgender individuals must negotiate not only a more conscious secondary process of socialization, which typically requires breaking old habits in order to learn new ones, but also institutional and interpersonal constraints.[17]

The process of transitioning, therefore, can create an extended state of liminality. Liminality—experiences of ambiguities and discontinuities during transition processes—can lead some transgender individuals to feel the need to distance themselves from others, leaving them feeling isolated when they have left their original state but have yet to feel affiliated with their new identity.[18] The identity work that enables transgender individuals to present what they define as their true selves can entail the ending of a former identity; to others around a transgender person, this can involve a time of adjustment in learning how to accept and interact with what is a "new identity" for them. This adjustment period can create major changes not only in friendships and familial relationships but also oftentimes jobs (e.g., requiring greater support from coworkers during a gender transition process or requesting to delay the start of a new position until later in a transition process).[19]

Intimate relationships may thus be considered safe havens for transgender people, in which to be understood and accepted. The sustenance of an intimate relationship also can potentially be seen as both a support system for an individual's identity work and reflective of successful identity work in being able to maintain a relationship. This is because, in part, transgender individuals regularly face societal discrimination in everyday life.[20] However, the romantic love storyline—that is, societal standards for the often-unachievable, perfect romantic relationship[21]—is not only heteronormative (presuming mutually attracted male and female partners) but also cisnormative (presuming cisgender partners, whose gender identity aligns with their assigned sex). Consequently, normalized interactions and systemic regulations in transphobic societies can marginalize and devalue transgender identities, which in turn marginalize transgender identities in the context of romantic relationships, creating even more acute obstacles for transgender individuals entering into and maintaining intimate relationships.

The aforementioned significance of romantic relationships in many transgender people's lives is also vital to understanding the challenges transgender individuals face in identifying and escaping IPV. In the cisgender IPV literature, research has found that people may overlook cues of IPV early in a relationship due to their dedication to realizing the romantic love storyline through their intimate relationships. For example, Charmaine Power and fellow nursing scholars explored how women negotiated their identities in relation to femininity and the storyline of romantic love.[22] They found that women did not recognize cues of IPV early in their relationships because of pressure from expectations to "establish and invest" in the relationship.[23] Their findings uphold established contemporary ideologies of love, in which sociologists argue that partners in intimate relationships adopt a "romantic work ethic"; in ways similar to a construction project, this approach to romantic relationships involves a form of costs/benefits analysis and the related investment of time, effort, and resources.[24] Power and colleagues further explained that "romantic love may be desirable for the sharing of warmth, safety and protection, and yet can mask behaviours that are cues for domestic violence."[25] With the desirability and stability propagated by romantic love narratives, transgender individuals may be even more invested in making relationships succeed.

Unfortunately, abusers can take advantage of and gain leverage from the desired support and extreme instability transgender people can face as they work toward their desired identities. The above-mentioned transitions can create greater openings for manipulation by intimate partners due to the particularly active and explicit nature of identity work, which may entail a greater reliance on props (i.e., tools that help express a desired identity, which can range from accessories like jewelry and makeup to furniture[26]). Bringing each of these points together helps to contextualize T-IPV from a new perspective on identity, grounded in the contemporary sociocultural context. Both partners (individuals who become defined as the victim and the abuser) enter into intimate relationships (a) within the context of romantic love narratives and (b) engaging in ongoing identity work, where significant others are taken into especial account in feedback on constructing self-identities. This creates greater openings for others to interject and influence victims' identity work.

Discrediting Identity Work through Altercasting

The findings of Guadalupe-Diaz and Anthony helped to reveal how abusers could take advantage of these openings in relation to *altercasting*, a concept that had been applied to everyday manipulations of interactions.[27] In order for interactions to go smoothly, and for people to act in appropriate ways that fit different settings, social psychological perspectives put forth that individuals must define the situation. The "definition of the situation" involves individuals taking into account social norms and practices, helping to determine how they can act in order to produce desired reactions from others.[28] The definition of the situation is now the basis for numerous social psychological perspectives, as the subjective expectations brought into a situation and the interpretations deriving from interactions can have very real consequences for the participants. Accordingly, if individuals can manipulate the definition of the situation, they then also can direct another's identity work by limiting the options for successful signification.

In altercasting, Individual A can "cast" Individual B (the "alter," or other) into a specific identity of Individual A's choosing.[29] Extending the concept of altercasting to abuse can offer insight into how abusers can reframe a situation in ways that have negative consequences for survivors' identity work. For instance, defining the situation can be related to restricting the ways that survivors respond, which could include: limiting what actions and behaviors seem to be acceptable, the perceived options for how the survivor can act out desired identities, or what identities even seem achievable for survivors. An everyday example could be "guilt-tripping," in that this is a way to frame and manipulate how another person views the situation, to foster a negative emotion (guilt) in that other person, and in turn to influence their personal identity.

Altercasting therefore offers insight into potential entry points by which forms of manipulation can enter into relationships through others' interactional control.

Research by Guadalupe-Diaz and Anthony further identified two strategies of altercasting used by abusers: redefining the situation to focus on survivor-defined insecurities, and targeting sign-vehicles.[30] As "sign" relates to "signifying," we can rather literally understand sign-vehicles as tools for relaying what we are trying to signify.[31] (*Sign-vehicles* is a more inclusive term than *props*, as props are often confined to physical tools that help to express oneself.) In that original study, we classified under targeting of sign-vehicles such processes as regulating gender transition treatments and controlling through props.[32]

While research highlights the place of others in the identity work process, including the possibility for when others question or misinterpret an individual's identity work, this chapter takes the opportunity to further extrapolate on the original two strategies to further examine the generic processes central to controlling another's identity work. In particular, the active negation of individuals' attempts toward self-realization or prevention of self-expression by others is a critical component of identity work that needs further theoretical development.

Study Background

This chapter presents an alternative analysis of the data previously published in research from Guadalupe-Diaz and Anthony on transgender survivors of IPV and identity work.[33] In that study, Guadalupe-Diaz collected data through interviews conducted by telephone and online instant messages with thirteen transgender participants. Five additional participants completed an online open-ended questionnaire, equaling a total of eighteen transgender respondents (see table 3.1 for respondent traits). The group was diverse in terms of gender identities, with roughly seven transgender women (with identities including transwoman, MTF [male to female] transgender, and transfemale), seven transgender men (with identities including transman, FTM [female to male] transgender, transmale, transgender male, and transsexual man), and four nonbinary people (with identities including transmasculine, transfeminine, genderqueer, and transgender stone butch). As a group,

TABLE 3.1. Participant Characteristics

Pseudonym	Gender Identity	Race/Ethnicity	Age
Todd	Transmasculine / Genderqueer	White	22
Jessica	Transwoman	White	49
Brittany	Transwoman	White	34
Anna	MTF Transgender	Latina	30
Laura	Transwoman	Black	33
Tom	Transman	Black	24
David	FTM Transgender	White	23
Joe	Transgender Male	White/Latino	18
Rebecca	Transwoman	Black	38
Chris	Transfeminine / Genderqueer	White	22
John	FTM, Transmale	Multiracial/Latino	29
Fatima	Transwoman	Latina	30
Audrey	Transfemale	White	42
Jim	FTM Transgender	White	21
Sam	Transgender Stone Butch	White	38
Casey	Genderqueer	White	32
William	Male, Transmale	White	35
Owen	Transsexual man	Latino	19

all participants were either early into their transitions or coming out processes or just a few years into their transition. All participants had experienced victimization in an abusive relationship (one participant had experienced victimization in more than one relationship), and all had left their abusive partners by the time of the study.

As the only difference found between interviews and questionnaire responses was that the interviews were more detailed, all data were analyzed together. Modified grounded theory was used to analyze the data. The original study and the following analysis were both informed by the interactionist approach of "generic social processes."[34] Rather than looking at what may be unique to a population, this approach encourages looking at what actions and consequences can be held in common within and beyond groups of people. The study therefore adopted one goal of the generic social processes approach, which is to understand the occurrence of tactics for abusively influencing identity work "more generally."[35] While still influenced by context, we can, as Schwalbe et al. state, find the "common analytic ground" across "multiple contexts wherein social actors face similar or analogous problems."[36]

Love and Altercasting in a Sample of Transgender Survivors

In this section I review three key themes identified in our study. First I begin with the role of romantic love narratives in increasing the vulnerability of transgender study participants to IPV victimization. By examining participants' own explanations of their vulnerability, these quotes can be considered accounts for why they stayed in the relationship even when there were cues of an abusive relationship, as related to defining the situation and the importance of stability.

The second and third thematic findings relate to the role of two sub-strategies of altercasting used by IPV abusers to discredit identity work: retroverting and maneuverting. The root word of these labels (*vert*) refers to "versus" or "to turn," in reference to the abuser's (re)direction and manipulation of the victim's identity work.

Retroverting is a strategy by which abusers reference back to a survivor's past undesired identity or perceived identity, therefore redirecting the survivor's current identity work away from constructing a desired identity. They instead direct the survivor's identity work toward reinforcing a past undesired identity and/or force survivors to work against allowing a reemergence of their "old" self. From a sociological, social constructionist identity perspective, a "true" identity does not necessarily "exist," even though it can be perceived. In following that theoretical approach, one's "desired identity" can therefore be defined as one that an individual perceives as matching their true self—although perceptions of one's true self and desired identity can continue to grow and change over time. This approach, then, views identity development—for both transgender individuals and cisgender individuals—as an ongoing process rather than having a singular goal that can be achieved, which can also leave room for fluidity and ongoing identity development.

Conversely, the strategy of *maneuverting* entails abusers holding abstract, idealized traits or physical props over the survivor, making the survivor's desired identity appear unachievable. While retroverting redirects attention from the progressive realization of a desired identity by creating a focus on an undesired past, maneuvering reframes the desired identity as unobtainable. Abusers of transgender people oftentimes do so by, for instance, framing a desired masculine identity as only achievable if one is stereotypically "tough" (i.e., according to a cisnormative, dominant ideal standard), or by destroying needed props (e.g., cologne, chest binders, etc.) in a strategic manner to make control over the props all but out of the survivor's reach.

Each of these forms of discrediting identity work can create a sense of futility in survivors' work toward their desired identities and lead to survivors internalizing abusers' efforts to discredit their identity work. This, in turn, contributes to the power of abusers' manipulation because, as survivors negotiate the discrediting of identity work, they in turn can progressively integrate the associated negative traits as their own. In time, a survivor's self-concept can shift in ways that match the traits put forth by the abuser, so that their identity work incorporates that of the abusers' discrediting identity work, reinforcing undesired identities.

Romantic Love Accounts

Current romantic love ideologies consist of a convergence of ideal and realist love, in which story-patterns still include the concept of "one true love" and a magical connection that can overcome all obstacles, yet also a rationalized romantic ethic that one must work to create and uphold the relationship. Cues of potential abuse may be at first discredited, due in part to a misconstruing of how much "cost" (sacrifices) survivors are supposed to endure in order to achieve the benefits of relationships and achieve dominant ideals of intimate relationships, including stability. Abusers' discrediting identity work can "cast" their partners into roles (i.e., lead their partners to perceive themselves as being in roles) in which survivors are the cause of—and therefore solely responsible for the solution to—the problems of the relationship. This redirects attention away from the abusers and reframes their abuse as simply issues within a relationship that can or should be "fixed" by the survivor.

Current ideologies promote the idea that individuals must "work" on a relationship like it is a construction project, which entails concerted effort and working through their partners' imperfections. As related to the sense of the romantic relationship as a work project, discrediting identity work can entail abusers defining the situation so that survivors feel they are the ones who need to change and be responsible for "fixing" any problems they perceive in the relationship. For instance, John, a twenty-nine-year-old FTM transmale, explained why he stayed in the relationship longer, with a romantic love work ethic integrated into his reasoning.

> I didn't really think it would ever get like this and also, I was in love and I had it good so I just thought, I don't know. I had been single for 2 years because my long term girlfriend left me after coming out trans. So maybe I thought this was like a rare thing that I should try to fix. I had other trans friends and they all didn't have relationships or couldn't keep one so maybe I was trying to be like the one that had a success.

The dominant romantic love storyline offers a plot for people to follow as they enter into or plan relationships, and therefore also offers a resource that people can draw from to understand why they stayed in a relationship even through what they came to understand as abuse.

Even though neoliberal ideologies state that individuals will only stay in a relationship as long as it serves both partners, a traditional romantic storyline upholds the need to "sacrifice" for the betterment of the relationship and that, since it is work, it will not be easy. For instance, Rebecca, a thirty-eight-year-old transwoman, described an opening for abuse based in a desire for the support implied in stable relationships: "It's easy for that person to just look from the outside and say 'just leave,' but when I've literally lost so much over the years; it's hard to 'just leave.' I wanted so badly to have stability that I just made myself put up with him. I thought it was a small price to pay for the stable home." Rebecca exemplifies how abuse can be diminished (i.e., "a small price to pay") when framed through storylines that emphasize the importance of relationships to stability and the idea that individuals can control the success of a relationship. Contemporary ideologies, as also explained through participants' own words, help to contextualize the IPV experiences of transgender individuals and the vulnerabilities that abusers can manipulate in the process of discrediting identity work.

Retroverting

Retroverting occurs through abusers' taking advantage of survivors' insecurities to direct their identity work back toward self-described insecure and former identities. Study participants' stories suggest how discrediting identity work can influence self-concepts, as participants described not only their lines of action shifting over time but also how they viewed themselves. Extending from the perspective of altercasting, abusers' manipulation of identity work and survivors' own identity work can intersect when survivors sense they need the abusers' help, comfort, or support.[37] In retroverting, abusers can take advantage of transgender survivors' desire for relationship-based stability and fears associated with transitioning. Accordingly, these vulnerabilities faced by transgender individuals can create a basis through which abusers direct identity work toward former, insecure identities—also perpetuating positions in which survivors feel they need greater external support.

Abusers accordingly can take advantage of insecurities and influence survivors' decision-making through directing their identity work toward positions in which they feel a continued need for their abusers' support. For instance, Audrey, a forty-two-year-old transfemale, described ways in which her abuser created a void that she could take advantage of by discrediting and redirecting Audrey's identity work:

> [H]er attacks on my passability [sic] as a woman . . . it was an attempt to manipulate me. To take away something that I was feeling good about and you know, how I was able to present myself as female, and learning how to look beautiful, and look pretty, and the way I dressed, and the way I see myself, and trying to turn that into a negative for me. It was taking away those things that I found self-fulfilling and trying to pull those away so that there would be a void there, that she could come in and fill it.

Through the perspective of altercasting, an abuser takes a "proactive stance," in which the abuser controls the interactions to create a situation, rather than responding after changes have occurred.[38] In other words, for the specific example above, the abuser actively made negative attacks on Audrey's passability—or ability to be perceived by others as a woman—directing focus to her looks—a point of insecurity—in such a way that prevented her from creating a positive self-identification as "beautiful" or "pretty." The abuser's attacks revolved around the way Audrey saw herself, preventing her desired identity work toward positively presenting as female and reverting progress on self-realization through "taking away those things" that Audrey "found self-fulfilling."

Through the strategy of retroverting, abusers strategically direct identity work to keep transgender survivors in a state of liminality in their transition, preventing progress on their path to a desired identity. For example, Joe, an eighteen-year-old transgender male, a participant early in his transition process, stated:

> I do feel like it [being trans and transitioning] made me more vulnerable. I was in a really sensitive and kind of unstable place and I was trying to find my footing and I just, it's not a good; it's an ideal time for an abuser to strike. They take advantage of your fears or your uncertainty. . . . I remember, like, I was actually changing my name legally and I changed it on my own and he wanted to know my birth name um, and I refused to tell him . . . [explaining] "That's not your business; that's not what I go by," and he got really angry and that was the first time he got really angry at me . . . from the start, he wanted to control the entire process in some form.

Here, Joe offers explanations of how he was taking steps to control processes of identity work in the way he desired, yet his abuser targeted relevant identity-related changes to control and redirect Joe's focus back to points of instability. For transgender individuals, the selection of a name often encompasses the active construction of a new identity.[39] By seemingly forcing Joe to refocus on his birth name, for instance, his abuser prevented Joe from moving forward into his desired identity. Retroverting does not involve abusers directing survivors' identity work toward the construction of new identities—positive or negative—but instead entails taking advantage of current or former insecurities. One component of retroverting, therefore, can be defined as a form of stalling or regression, forcing survivors to continue negotiating negative identity traits or negative self-conceptualizations.

Additional examples, such as Rebecca's following description, reveal how partners take advantage of insecurities:

I always had a good sense of self, like since I transitioned years ago before him, I really came to be myself—who I was—but he just had this way of pulling out old insecurities, ones that I had put behind me, like he just knew where I was vulnerable and he knew what to attack. I got really down on myself and preoccupied with my looks since he went after that a lot. . . . After a while, I felt just defeated, I was now just basically back to what I had been feeling like years ago, I was self-conscious, timid, I started isolating myself from everyone.

Those who have undergone, or are in the process of undergoing, a significant identity transformation may be particularly vulnerable to the strategy of retroverting because there is a former "identity" for the abuser to augment and direct the survivor's identity work back toward. John also described what he termed as a "power play" by his abuser, as John described a sense of reverting to a place of insecurity. John's description also offers insight into the power of verbal manipulations:

I was so proud of myself and everything that I had accomplished and I had done it all on my own, and I been out as trans, I got the things that I needed to do it, I went through it and had to deal with so much loss [i.e. jobs, family] but then, on top of all of that shit, all that I had to deal with before, she came in and had to do that [abuse] to me. It was just such a power play for her. . . . I didn't think of myself as like, a soft, like you know—I'm a tough man, I really am, but I would've never thought that words could just bring someone down like she did. All those insecurities and all that, she got into it.

Participants' descriptions reveal that even after coming out as transgender, trans individuals can remain in what can be a precarious position for multiple reasons, such as the losses described by John. Experiencing such precariousness can influence survivors clinging to relationships or misconstruing notions of romantic love. Precariousness or liminality creates greater openings for an abuser to restrict their partner's identity work in signifying their desired gender identity. In part, contemporary social ideologies emphasizing individualized responsibility for successes and failures, both generally and within intimate relationships, can undergird abusers' discrediting identity work to create an especially conducive set of circumstances for manipulation. The abuser can successfully discredit identity work due to the combination of current social ideologies emphasizing self-realization, individualized responsibility for successes and failures, and the sense that ongoing work is required to keep a relationship going. This can create fertile ground for manipulation.

Taking the romantic love narrative into account, the abuser can gain power as the survivor may feel responsible for putting in the work to keep the relationship going. The abuser can then recognize or foster the survivor's sense of failure in upholding the relationship. In so doing, they can manipulate the survivor's self-categorization by allowing or encouraging them to feel like "a failure." This, however, can keep the survivor confined to the relationship because the survivor can then feel they must put in *more* effort and work, forgive the abuser because the abuser is also trying to grow and be there for them, and remain dedicated to their "true" partner. Self-realization, or the push toward realizing one's full potential and true self, is a dominant contemporary ideology; popular representations and self-help rhetoric promote finding one's "true self." In combination with romantic love narratives, the contemporary context can promote sacrificing and working through issues to experience success and growth toward a desired identity. Although these ideologies have positive potential, when in the hands of a manipulative abuser these ideologies can be twisted to promote an individual staying in an abusive relationship because the survivor "should" be appreciative of the stability and sacrifice to make the relationship work.

Maneuverting

A second generic strategy, maneuverting, again involves altercasting, yet through the dimension of limiting the "degree of freedom allowed."[40] Retroverting targets identities that survivors want to move away from, with abusers perpetuating a focus on the (re)construction of a former, negative identity. Alternatively, maneuverting is a strategy that targets identities that survivors want to develop, with abusers narrowing the range of possibilities for survivors to achieve their desired identity. Maneuverting can involve preventing survivors from utilizing or accomplishing certain forms of identity work, such as through controlling props, or directing identity work by delimiting traits deemed as acceptable or representative of the survivor's desired gender identity.

Abusers can undermine survivors' identity work, making survivors question their ability to achieve their desired identity, by directing their identity work toward a limited identity redefined by the abuser. For instance, Todd, a twenty-two-year-old transmasculine genderqueer individual, described his partner holding "traditionally masculine characteristics over me like, 'If you were more of a man, you would do x, y and z,' or 'If you had more honor and integrity you wouldn't be acting like this,' or 'Why can't you just talk to me face-to-face like a man?' that were specifically gendered—that were supposed to be used as threats against my character or my transition." Todd's examples help to show how abusers discredit identity work by creating new stories for survivors, developing new meanings for survivors' actions. The abuser shifts the intent behind the survivor's actions, which can make the survivor second-guess their own agency, decision-making, or self-expression. At times, survivors may still act in such a way that is more fulfilling of their desired identity, but in these cases abusers can still undermine such actions by creating a new narrative or account for why survivors acted in such a way.

Although a survivor may feel as though they successfully signified or are in the process of successfully signifying a desired identity, the abuser creates a new story. One such tactic might entail an abuser claiming a survivor acted in a particular way just for attention, rather than for another more benign or benevolent reason. For example, Rebecca told a story of her abuser targeting the props that help Rebecca to present a desired identity, with the abuser undermining the reason that she used the props:

> He shattered my favorite perfume. . . . We weren't even fighting over perfume but he quickly tried to justify it like, he said, "You only wear that perfume for everyone else you don't wear that for me, you just trying to get other men"; blah blah and he said, "If you ain't gonna look like a real woman you might as well smell like one right?" He would just say mean things like that to attack me. He'd start trying to put me down all the time and making [me] feel bad.

An abuser therefore can reframe choices, so that rather than acknowledging that their partner's fashion style expresses their free-spirited nature or creativity, for instance, they might instead declare that the way their partner dresses makes them seem promiscuous or like a show-off. Transgender individuals' identity work can be particularly beholden to and reliant on external props in order to support physical transition or the expression of their desired gender identity. Maneuverting therefore can entail the controlling of props, which prevents survivors from presenting their desired identities or causes survivors to question their ability to fulfill their desired identities.

Although a story shared by Laura, a thirty-three-year-old transwoman, explained how she was physically injured, her story clarified the dress as the abuser's target: "He started to rip up my clothes. It was a nice outfit, I loved that dress; I went out just grocery shopping in it but I loved it and I always got compliments on it. He ripped it up; he took a knife off the table and ripped it close to my skin and he cut me. He cut me while ripping it up and yelling things and he said, 'You wanna be a woman so bad.' And he kept ripping up my dress and turned me around." By targeting a uniquely special dress, in that it was one of Laura's favorites and garnered compliments, her abuser showed control by treating nothing as sacred. The targeting of this prop reflects how abusers can strategically make survivors question their core identity by attaching their identity to a prop (i.e., targeting the dress while verbally connecting it to "being a woman"). As the prop is external to the survivor, it increases the ability of the abuser to control their partner's gender signification. Abusers can use sign-vehicles against survivors because of the importance of these props to signification of one's desired gender identity.

Maneuverting creates a sense of instability in how the survivor's identity work will be received by their significant other. The uncertainty in how an abuser will react keeps a survivor tethered to the abuser because they must pay close attention and be alert to potential cues as to how the abuser will act. In and of itself, the survivor's attention to the abuser influences the survivor's identity work to include preparing for possible unpredictable and potentially dangerous reactions (physically or emotionally). Negotiating this uncertainty can keep a survivor in a state of liminality, in that their partner can at times actively support their desired identity work and then, at any unforeseen point in time, actively go against their desired identity work. For example, Jessica, a forty-nine-year-old transwoman, explained that her partner "could often do anything she wanted you know? She simply just had to pick up lipstick or you know, a pair of nylons for me and throw me a bone like 'here I got you something' that was supposed to forgive anything she chose to do and I really felt like she was manipulating me." Due to the particular reliance on props, maneuverting can thus occur through gifting and compensation for abusive actions, which helps to keep survivors in an abusive cycle of questioning their place with and reliance on the abuser. Tom, a twenty-four-year-old transman, also spoke to this tactic, explaining, "Sometimes she would hide my chest binder just to ruin my day, knowing I couldn't go outside without it." Abusers maintain a place of power by controlling props needed by survivors to construct desired identities that are recognized by others, both taking props away and providing them.

Maneuverting can therefore have broad identity work consequences. A sense of uncertainty can again influence survivors' future signification, as they may suppress expressing an emotion or acting in a certain way due to fear of rejection or violent reactions, which in turn deters potential actions out of concern that the action will put them at risk. The abuser can then offer the survivor an outlet for presenting their desired identity, elevating their presentation of self in such a way that can make the abuser's undermining of the next signification even more detrimental to the survivor's sense of self. An abuser's denial or denouncement of a survivor's critical identity signification can be emotionally draining and morally defeating, further deterring desired identity work.

In relation to controlling props, an abuser can additionally objectify a survivor, which inhibits the survivor's ability to embody and live out their desired identity. Such objectification, in the extreme, can turn survivors into a "prop" themselves, to be manipulated through abusers' directives. The control of the body as an object can be seen in the story of Sam, a thirty-eight-year-old transgender stone butch, who explained: "I was genderfluid at the time [while dating]. I was told I could not transition before him, and was often not allowed to present in masculine ways. I was ordered to embody particular genders by him and the people he traded me to for goods/services." This example also helps to reveal how maneuverting can direct a survivor's identity work toward the construction of an identity desired by the abuser, rather than an identity desired by the survivor. In relation to physical alterations and treating the body as an object, Joe explained: "He would say 'I can handle you physically modifying the upper half of your body but if you change the lower half of your body it's wrong' that you have to keep what you have you have to use it you have to get over it and make a baby with me." In these ways, the body can be objectified according to cisnormative expectations of reproduction. A survivor may never desire a heteronormative or cisnormative ideal, but the survivor's actions and the related consequences reflect the abuser's control over the survivor's transition process and associated identity work.

Abusers can regulate the embodiment of gender through the reinforcement of cisnormative, dominant ideals, crafting connections between the body, sexuality, and social practice to regulate the construction of the survivor's identity, or who the survivor is.[41] For instance, the account of Fatima, a thirty-year-old transwoman, exemplifies how stereotypical femininity (or what sociologist R. W. Connell terms "emphasized femininity"[42]) was expected and regulated by her abuser:

> I started doing [wearing] some of the things he got, like, the better bras and silicone; I even did more on my face, like the lips and cheeks [referring to surgeries], that were just easy one day things. He would praise me for that and then do stuff for me, like things that I had been asking to do; like just more public things. I started to just lose myself; I was just now this thing. This, like experiment or something, of his to use and "Doll Up." It only made me more depressed, which made him more angry, and then that's when he got colder, more distant, more angry and kind of like violent.

Abusers take advantage of and manipulate desired props and sign-vehicles, shifting the control of identity work away from survivors and into the abusers' hands. An abuser's control of a survivor's outward presentation of self in turn contributes to their control of the survivor's self-identity, as the outer signifiers hold personal symbolic meaning for the survivor too. To lose control of those symbolic representations of self is, arguably, to lose control of one's self-expression.

Abusers can prevent survivors' desired identity work not only through physical force but also through shifting survivors' perceptions as to how others will receive their identity work. Survivors can then integrate these shifts in perception into their self-identity, so that the new and negative perspectives become a part of how survivors view themselves. For instance, Laura described how her abuser targeted her hormone treatment right when Laura had finally started feeling confident enough to wear a dress for a dinner date. Laura explained,

> I said [to her partner], "But I thought you said the hormones were working and I feel like my voice is better." And I had gotten this new bra that had the breasts in it and I looked real good. He said, "Please don't do this to me right now, I can't." . . . He just was like "No, this is gonna be a problem baby . . . you're gonna be miserable and you know I think you look good but that's for home, baby—please, you look like a freak."

Abusers can compare or contrast survivors with a cisnormative standard or dominant ideal—for instance, emphasizing masculinity or a lack thereof. Even if survivors feel they are making progress toward achieving traits of their desired identities, abusers can discredit their identity work by claiming they are, in fact, failing to fulfill their desired identity by redefining what expression of the desired identity actually entails. Abusers can additionally undermine identity work by determining that survivors' desired identity work will, in the words of Laura's abuser, make them "miserable" or "a freak."

Maneuverting can therefore redirect survivors' future interpretations, perpetuating the discrediting of identity work. Rather than interpreting their actions through their own lenses, survivors can adopt the discrediting perspective of their abusers. Abusers can take advantage of such identity work to develop their own identities, in that the concerns for survivors reflect back onto the abusers' identities.

Conclusion

Retroverting and maneuverting show how the power of identity abuse, in particular discrediting identity work, derives from the fact that abusers are directing survivors' identity work in ways that influence what identities the survivors construct as their own. Discrediting identity work influences a range of issues related to self-conceptualization, including the perpetuation of insecurities and fears, thought processes leading up to identity signification, the ability to publicly signify a desired identity, and the internalization of the identity that one can and should signify. It therefore cuts across the emotional, mental, and physical components of identity construction. Over the course of time, discrediting identity work can implant in survivors' minds alternative ways of envisioning the process of identity signification. These alternative processes of identity signification reflect abusers' perspectives and intentions, rather than contributing to the development of survivors' desired self-realization (a process akin to gaslighting[43]). Discrediting identity work can, in turn, lead to a physical presentation of self that differs from the desired identity. Relatedly, discrediting identity work can result in both immediate and long-term influences on survivors' identity work.

The insight gained from examining discrediting identity work can therefore also contribute to our understanding of why survivors remain in abusive relationships. In part, this chapter demonstrates how the combination of romantic love narratives and ideologies of self-realization can, in an abusive relationship, contribute to survivors feeling that they need to stay in and work on the relationship. Beyond this, discrediting identity work can lead to survivors taking on their abusers' perspectives, leading to an internalization of themselves as failures, as weak, or as having other negative traits. Arguably, this could contribute to survivors staying because they start to feel that they are "deserving" of abuse, that abusive treatment is "normal," or that the abuser is "right" in the way they frame the survivor or situation (e.g., that the survivor is actually "ugly" or that others will see them as a "freak"). Trying to predict the abuser's reactions, whether to avoid potentially violent behavior or to avoid demeaning treatment, can still perpetuate the survivor integrating the abuser's perspectives into their identity work. Taken together, in addition to offering insight into why survivors stay, the details surrounding and consequences of discrediting identity work also suggest the importance of survivors' intensive efforts focused on redefining themselves (on top of the resocialization processes accompanying transitions) when they are able to leave abusive relationships.

While the abusive tactic of discrediting identity work may occur in other populations, findings from the present study support the conclusion that transgender individuals are especially susceptible due to stages of liminality related to gender transition. More specifically, transgender survivors may be especially vulnerable to discrediting identity work due to the combination of perceived instability, a sense of isolation and incongruity, a greater reliance on props, and a desire (need) for support and acceptance in often-hostile social contexts. All of this is contextualized by larger sociocultural ideologies that perpetuate limited ideals for romantic relationships: a cisnormative framework where one is supposed to only be a "man" or "woman," to find and overcome all obstacles to obtain true love, and to sacrifice in order to achieve one's desires. Transgender individuals must work within a system that can be interpreted as more rigged against them than cisgender individuals, so that finding a hint of support and stability can mean even more, thus contributing to an increased vulnerability to identity abuse.

An identity work perspective thus offers insight into how even seemingly everyday interactions can be a part of abusers' manipulation of transgender survivors of IPV. Retroverting and maneuverting can include verbal and emotional abuse that can even lead to survivors adopting their abusers' perspectives. With such knowledge of discrediting identity work, however, we can work to further examine these forms of identity abuse in order to better hold abusers accountable, along with better supporting transgender survivors of intimate partner violence in their ability to recognize, leave, and heal from abusive relationships.

NOTES

1 Beech 2008, 52; Guadalupe-Diaz and Anthony 2017; Schwalbe and Mason-Schrock 1996.
2 Schwalbe and Mason-Schrock 1996; Snow and Anderson 1987.
3 Anthony and McCabe 2015; Cerulo 1997.
4 Snow and Anderson 1987.
5 Scheer, Woulfe, and Goodman 2019; Woulfe and Goodman 2018.
6 Woulfe and Goodman 2018, 2.
7 Guadalupe-Diaz and Anthony 2017, 1.
8 Koontz, Norman, and Okorie 2017, 3.
9 Bellah et al. 2008; Cancian 1987; Giddens 1993; Koontz, Norman, and Okorie 2017, 18; Swidler 2001.
10 Conley et al. 2013, 4; Conley et al. 2017.

11 Arnett 2000, 2001; Giddens 1993; Pyysiäinen, Halpin, and Guilfoyle 2017; Shafer, Jensen, and Larson 2014; Swidler 2001.
12 Mason-Schrock 1996, 177–178.
13 Guadalupe-Diaz and Anthony 2017; Mason-Shrock 1996.
14 Arnett 2001; Koontz and Norman 2019.
15 Brown 2011; Guadalupe-Diaz and Anthony 2017.
16 Schilt and Lagos 2017, 432.
17 Schilt and Lagos 2017, 432–433.
18 Turner 1987.
19 Schilt and Lagos 2017.
20 James et al. 2016.
21 Conley et al. 2013; Conley et al. 2017; Koontz, Norman, and Okorie 2017.
22 Power et al. 2006.
23 Power et al. 2006, 174.
24 Power et al. 2006, 174.
25 Power et al. 2006.
26 Goffman 1959.
27 Guadalupe-Diaz and Anthony 2017.
28 Weinstein and Deutschberger 1963, 455.
29 McCall and Simmons 1978; Weinstein and Deutschberger 1963.
30 Guadalupe-Diaz and Anthony 2017.
31 Schwalbe and Mason-Schrock 1996, 119.
32 Guadalupe-Diaz and Anthony 2017, 2.
33 Guadalupe-Diaz and Anthony 2017.
34 Schwalbe et al. 2000, 420–421.
35 Schwalbe et al. 2000, 421.
36 Schwalbe et al. 2000, 421.
37 Weinstein and Deutschberger 1963.
38 Valenta 2009, 366.
39 Gagné, Tewksbury, and McGaughey 1997.
40 Weinstein and Deutschberger 1963, 458.
41 Connell and Messerschmidt 2005.
42 Connell 1987, 186.
43 Abramson 2014.

REFERENCES

Abramson, Kate. 2014. "Turning Up the Lights on Gaslighting." *Philosophical Perspectives* 28 (1): 1–30.

Anthony, Amanda Koontz, and Janice McCabe. 2015. "Friendship Talk as Identity Work: Defining the Self Through Friend Relationships." *Symbolic Interaction* 38 (1): 64–82.

Arnett, Jefferey Jensen. 2000. "Emerging Adulthood: A Theory of Development from the Late Teens through the Twenties." *American Psychologist* 55 (5): 469–480.

Arnett, Jefferey Jensen. 2001. "Conceptions of the Transition to Adulthood: Perspectives from Adolescence through Midlife." *Journal of Adult Development* 8 (2): 133–143.
Beech, Nic. 2008. "On the Nature of Dialogic Identity Work." *Organization* 15 (1): 51–74.
Bellah, Robert N., Richard Madsen, William M. Sullivan, Ann Swidler, and Steven M. Tipton. 2008. *Habits of the Heart: Individualism and Commitment in American Life*. Berkeley: University of California Press.
Brown, Nicola. 2011. "Holding Tensions of Victimization and Perpetration: Partner Abuse in Trans Communities." In *Intimate Partner Violence in LGBTQ Lives*, edited by Janice L. Ristock, 153–168. New York: Routledge.
Cancian, Francesca M. 1987. *Love in America: Gender and Self-development*. Cambridge, England: Cambridge University Press.
Cerulo, Karen A. 1997. "Identity Construction: New Issues, New Directions." *Annual Review of Sociology* 23:385–409.
Conley, Terri D., Jes L. Matsick, Amy C. Moors, and Ali Ziegler. 2017. "Investigation of Consensually Nonmonogamous Relationships: Theories, Methods, and New Directions." *Perspectives on Psychological Science* 12:205–232.
Conley, Terri D., Amy C. Moors, Jes L. Matsick, and Ali Ziegler. 2013. "The Fewer the Merrier? Assessing Stigma Surrounding Consensually Nonmonogamous Romantic Relationships." *Analyses of Social Issues and Public Policy* 13 (1): 1–30.
Connell, R. W. 1987. *Gender and Power: Society, the Person and Sexual Politics*. Stanford, CA: Stanford University Press.
Connell, R. W., and James W. Messerschmidt. 2005. "Hegemonic Masculinity: Rethinking the Concept." *Gender & Society* 19 (6): 829–859.
Gagné, Patricia, Richard Tewksbury, and Deanna McGaughey. 1997. "Coming Out and Crossing Over: Identity Formation and Proclamation in a Transgender Community." *Gender & Society* 11 (4): 478–508.
Giddens, Anthony. 1993. *The Transformation of Intimacy: Sexuality, Love and Eroticism in Modern Societies*. Oxford: Polity Press.
Goffman, Erving. 1959. *The Presentation of Self in Everyday Life*. New York: Doubleday.
Guadalupe-Diaz, Xavier L., and Amanda Koontz Anthony. 2017. "Discrediting Identity Work: Understandings of Intimate Partner Violence by Transgender Survivors." *Deviant Behavior* 38 (1): 1–16.
James, Sandy E., Jody. L. Herman, Susan Rankin, Mara Keisling, Lisa Mottet, and Ma'ayan Anafi. 2016. *The Report of the 2015 U.S. Transgender Survey*. Washington, DC: The National Center for Transgender Equality. www.ustranssurvey.org.
Koontz, Amanda, and Lauren Norman. 2019. "Happily Ever After? Exploring U.S. Collegiate Women's Understandings of Love as Impermanent and Timeless in the Age of Capitalism." *Sociological Perspectives* 62 (2): 167–185.
Koontz, Amanda, Lauren Norman, and Sarah Okorie. 2017. "Realistic Love: Contemporary College Women's Negotiations of Princess Culture and the 'Reality' of Romantic Relationships." *Journal of Personal and Social Relationships*. https://doi.org/10.1177/0265407517735694

Leisenring, Amy. 2006. "Confronting "Victim" Discourses: The Identity Work of Battered Women." *Symbolic Interaction* 29 (3): 307–330.
Loseke, Donileen R. 1987. "Lived Realities and the Construction of Social Problems: The Case of Wife Abuse." *Symbolic Interaction* 10 (2): 229–243.
Mason-Schrock, Douglas. 1996. "Transsexuals' Narrative Construction of the 'True Self.'" *Social Psychology Quarterly* 59 (3): 176–192.
McCall, George J., and J. L. Simmons. 1978. *Identities and Interactions*. Chicago: University of Chicago Press.
Power, Charmaine, Tina Koch, Debbie Kralik, and Debra Jackson. 2006. "Lovestruck: Women, Romantic Love and Intimate Partner Violence." *Contemporary Nurse* 21 (2): 174–185.
Pyysiäinen, Jarkko, Darren Halpin, and Andrew Guilfoyle. 2017. "Neoliberal Governance and 'Responsibilization' of Agents: Reassessing the Mechanisms of Responsibility-Shift in Neoliberal Discursive Environments." *Distinktion: Journal of Social Theory* 18 (2): 215–235.
Roch, Amy, James Morton, and Graham Ritchie. 2010. *Out of Sight, out of Mind? Transgender People's Experiences of Domestic Abuse*. Edinburgh: LGBT Youth Scotland and the Scottish Transgender Alliance. www.scottishtrans.org.
Scheer, Jillian R., Julie M. Woulfe, and Lisa A. Goodman. 2019. "Psychometric Validation of the Identity Abuse Scale among LGBTQ Individuals." *Journal of Community Psychology* 47(2): 371–384.
Schilt, Kristin, and Danya Lagos. 2017. "The Development of Transgender Studies in Sociology." *Annual Review of Sociology* 43:425–443.
Schwalbe, Michael, Daphne Holden, Douglas Schrock, Sandra Godwin, Shealy Thompson, and Michele Wolkomir. 2000. "Generic Processes in the Reproduction of Inequality: An Interactionist Analysis." *Social Forces* 79 (2): 419–452.
Schwalbe, Michael L., and Douglas Mason-Schrock. 1996. "Identity Work as Group Process." In *Advances in Group Processes*, vol. 13, edited by Barry Markovsky, Michael J. Lovaglia, and Robin Simon, 113–147. Greenwich, CT: JAI Press.
Shafer, Kevin, Todd M. Jensen, and Jeffry H. Larson. 2014. "Relationship Effort, Satisfaction, and Stability: Differences across Union Type." *Journal of Marital & Family Therapy* 40 (1): 212–232.
Snow, David A., and Leon Anderson. 1987. "Identity Work among the Homeless: The Verbal Construction and Avowal of Personal Identities." *American Journal of Sociology* 92 (6): 1336–1371.
Swidler, Anne. 2001. *Talk of Love: How Culture Matters*. Chicago: University of Chicago Press.
Taylor, Stephanie. 2015. "Identity Construction." In *International Encyclopedia of Language and Social Interaction*, edited by Karen Tracy, 1–9. Hoboken, NJ: John Wiley & Sons.
Turner, Victor. 1987. "Betwixt and Between: The Liminal Period in Rites of Passage." In *Betwixt and Between: Patterns of Masculine and Feminine Initiation*, edited by

Louise Carus Mahdi, Steven Foster, and Meredith Little, 3–19. La Salle, IL: Open Court Publishing.

Valenta, Marko. 2009. "Immigrants' Identity Negotiations and Coping with Stigma in Different Relational Frames." *Symbolic Interaction* 32 (4): 351–371.

Weinstein, Eugene A., and Paul Deutschberger. 1963. "Some Dimensions of Altercasting." *Sociometry* 26 (4): 454–466.

Woulfe, Julie M., and Lisa A. Goodman. 2018. "Identity Abuse as a Tactic of Violence in LGBTQ Communities: Initial Validation of the Identity Abuse Measure." *Journal of Interpersonal Violence*. https://doi.org/10.1177/10.1177/0886260518760018.

PART II

Transgender IPV Context and Causes

4

"Why Don't You Just Leave?"

Transgender Resilience and Barriers to Escaping Abuse

RAYNA E. MOMEN AND WALTER S. DEKESEREDY

Transgender intimate partner violence (T-IPV) is multidimensional in nature. Following sociologists Walter DeKeseredy and Amanda Hall-Sanchez, IPV is conceptualized here as the misuse of power by a current or former intimate partner, resulting in a loss of dignity, control, and safety as well as a feeling of powerlessness and entrapment experienced by the person who is the direct target of ongoing or repeated physical, psychological, economic, sexual, verbal, and/or spiritual abuse.[1] Additionally, IPV can include persistent threats or forcing people to witness violence against their children, other relatives, friends, pets, and/or cherished possessions by their current or ex-partners. Leaving an abusive partner can be quite complex. Taking into account an array of potential benefits and risks, many transgender survivors remain with abusers, while at the same time taking active steps to cope with and resist abuse. To this end, this chapter focuses on the complexity of factors that often deter transgender survivors from leaving their abusive partners, and the resilience and coping strategies they employ. We conclude by suggesting some new and theoretical directions in studying help seeking, resilience, and coping among transgender survivors.

Defining Help Seeking, Resilience, and Coping

Before delving into T-IPV, we begin with an overview of the three organizing concepts of this chapter: help seeking, resilience, and coping. To begin, examining the barriers transgender survivors face when attempting to escape their abusers necessitates a focus on help seeking. In this context, we follow sociologists Xavier Guadalupe-Diaz and Jana Jasinksi's conception of help seeking as being "the process by which victims of IPV first identify their situation as problematic, which may be followed by a need for external assistance that could involve navigating formal or informal avenues in an attempt to remedy the situation or leave an abuser."[2] Formal avenues may include seeking protective orders and reporting abuse to the police, while informal ones may include seeking support from family or friends.

There are many definitions of resilience, with some focused on personal characteristics that enable people to cope with adverse circumstances while others emphasize the capacity of individuals to actively engage with and adapt to difficult situations.[3] For the purpose of this chapter, we conceptualize resilience along the same lines as marriage and family therapists Ronald Werner-Wilson, Toni Schindler Zimmerman, and Dorothy Whalen.[4] They argue that resilience consists of the interaction between personal traits and systemic components, manifesting three behavioral elements: the ability to change or adapt to harsh circumstances; the capacity to "bounce back" and succeed in the face of negative outcome expectances; and the capacity for a determined engagement, rather than avoidance, with the risk factor in question. Research suggests that these capacities are linked to IPV survivors' improved physical and mental health status, as well as to expanded social support.[5] Thus, an understanding of the role of resilience is important because it can help service providers build practical strategies, skills, or competencies for survivors to exit or survive abusive relationships.[6] (See chapter 12 for more on training service providers.)

The broader literature conceptualizes coping as the actions and thoughts individuals employ as a means of handling the expectations that come with circumstances deemed as stressful.[7] Applying the concepts of help seeking, resilience, and coping to transgender survivors is further complicated by transgender people's realities, as the stigmas attached to this group create barriers for those who attempt to escape abusive partners and seek help for the harm that has been caused. Such barriers inform why some transgender individuals remain with abusive partners, although the strategies used to cope with their circumstances and be resilient in the face of victimization may be used during and after the abuse.

The next sections detail the ways in which stigma can uniquely shape transgender survivors' responses to IPV. We begin by examining help seeking and barriers to escape in the context of T-IPV. Then we review the significance of resilience and coping in better understanding T-IPV victimization.

Barriers to Escaping T-IPV

Despite limited literature on T-IPV victimization more broadly,[8] and on survivors' resilience and coping strategies in particular, existing research reveals greater insight into the multitude of reasons why many stay with abusers, dispelling the myth of the willing transgender victim. Some barriers to escaping IPV, such as concerns about retaliation,[9] lack of resources for leaving abusive partners,[10] inadequate response from law enforcement,[11] self-doubt,[12] rural isolation,[13] being stigmatized as victims,[14] and awareness that many service providers prioritize separation from abusers in a way that may not reflect the survivor's reality,[15] are common to both cisgender and transgender survivors. Child custody issues also create barriers to leaving.[16] As with cisgender survivors, when transgender survivors with children contemplate exiting, they may be hesitant, anticipating that the legal system will unfairly discriminate against them and award custody to the abusive parent.[17] Likewise, as with cisgender survivors, transgender survivors with undocumented immigrant status face additional help-seeking barriers.[18] For instance, choosing to pursue formal avenues for support may put them at risk of deportation. (See chapter 6 for more on T-IPV, race, and immigration.)

However, the many barriers transgender survivors face when seeking to end such abuse are also shaped by transphobia and the unique manifestations of T-IPV,[19] and increase the likelihood that they will suffer in silence. We address the following barriers: (1) the notion of choice and awareness of victimization, (2) self-blame and shame, (3) knowledge deficiencies among service providers,[20] (4) gender-segregated services, (5) fear of being outed,[21] (6) transphobia-enhanced financial dependence on abusers, (7) transphobia-fueled isolation and need for the emotional stability that relationships can symbolically represent, and (8) fear of further stigmatizing transgender communities. These barriers are reviewed in figure 4.1.

Figure 4.1. Unique Barriers to Escaping Transgender IPV

1. Low Awareness of T-IPV in Society and in One's Relationship
2. Stigma-Related Self-Blame and Shame
3. Inadequately Trained Service Providers
4. Inaccessible Gender-Segregated Services
5. Fear of Being Outed as Transgender
6. Transphobia-Fueled Financial Dependence on Abusers
7. Transphobia-Fueled Isolation and Enhanced Emotional Dependence
8. Fear of Further Stigmatizing Transgender Communities

The first barrier to help seeking that we review is a lack of awareness that one is experiencing abuse. Leaving abusive partners implies an element of choice. On the one hand, it assumes that survivors are aware of their victimization, a process that is critical to the decision to seek help.[22] However, transgender survivors often fail to perceive their victimization as abuse, for reasons such as the dearth of publicly available information on IPV that is inclusive of transgender people and the gendered way victim status has been constructed, which portrays victims as feminine and submissive.[23] Some transgender survivors fail to view themselves as deserving of help due to negative self-perceptions that result from a stigmatized status.[24]

A second barrier to help seeking is self-blame and shame, which collectively serve to deter some transgender survivors from seeking help. Self-blame and shame can result from violating traditional gender norms and internalizing transphobic attitudes. Many transgender people experience shame surrounding their gender identity, having received messages throughout their lives that they should deny who they are and attempt to conform. Though there are multiple masculinities, *hegemonic masculinity* is the most dominant, culturally accepted, and privileged form.[25] The basic components of such a masculinity are that men should avoid all things feminine, restrict their emotions severely, show toughness and aggression, exhibit self-reliance, strive for achievement and status, exhibit nonrelational attitudes toward sexuality, and actively engage in homophobia.[26] Transgender men who are shamed for failing to be masculine enough, according to society's notions of what a man should be, may internalize the oppression or experience guilt for not striving to adhere to the norms of hegemonic masculinity and successfully resisting abuse.[27] Society continues to punish individuals who disrupt the gender binary, and over time the consequences can be both lasting and normalized. This "othering" process has been identified as a barrier to accessing social care for transgender survivors because the experience of being treated as essentially different from cisgender people can be internalized to the extent that transgender survivors come to believe they are undeserving of assistance.[28] According to T-IPV experts Diana Courvant and Loree Cook-Daniels, "this early punishment for simply expressing gender identity leaves many scars, but the experiences that lead trans and intersexual domestic violence survivors to believe that it's normal for 'people like me' to live with abuse only increase in magnitude as the trans or intersex survivor matures."[29]

A third barrier to help seeking rests with perceived and actual inadequate knowledge of some service providers regarding T-IPV. The myth of the willing transgender victim rests in part on the assumption that survivors have accessible to them the resources needed to escape, and that these resources will not only admit them but are also transgender-inclusive in the content of their services. Accepting transgender clients is one dimension, while understanding the unique needs of transgender survivors is quite another.[30] Knowledge deficiencies are common among many practitioners, and without adequate transgender-specific training they may either discriminate against or unintentionally provide poorly fitting services for transgender people seeking help.[31] Parallels can be drawn from the literature on IPV among lesbian, gay, bisexual, transgender, and queer (LGBTQ) people more broadly. For instance, public health specialist Anthony DiStefano found that officially reporting abuse or seeking medical treatment was virtually unheard of among lesbian, gay, bisexual, transgender, and intersex IPV survivors in Japan, with participants believing that doing so carried little weight.[32] Limited availability of transgender-inclusive IPV services, coupled with the perception that some services will be discriminatory in response to transgender survivors, contributes to staying in abusive relationships and exposure to ongoing abuse. Such barriers have been experienced at the micro, meso, and macro levels, adding to their complexity.[33] As psychologist Julia Walker observes, "one of the main barriers to seeking help for trans people is the lack of resources."[34] Internationally, many transgender people discover that there are few, if any, available transgender-specific services.[35] Where such organizations exist, they often rely on volunteers and charitable donations, contributing to the limited availability of services in proximity to transgender survivors.[36]

Gendered spaces, in the context of shelters for IPV survivors, present a significant, fourth barrier to help seeking that can be difficult to navigate for transgender survivors.[37] Despite IPV survivor agencies often being designated for female survivors only, transgender women frequently experience exclusion because their womanness or femaleness is questioned.[38] Transgender men of course often also are unable to access women-only shelters without compromising their gender identity, and gaining access is not itself without problems, as shelters are often set up to support cisgender women whose abusers are cisgender men.[39] Even when male-centered services are available, transgender men who are IPV survivors may avoid seeking help out of fear that their transgender status will be revealed, or that cisgender male survivors will further stigmatize them.[40] Relatedly, nonbinary survivors frequently find themselves with even fewer gender-segregated spaces that will admit them. Gender-segregated services ultimately render many transgender survivors uncertain of their eligibility for assistance and the stipulations that may apply.[41]

A fifth barrier to help seeking is rooted in fears of being outed. Due to their invisibility and lack of access to human rights, transgender survivors are uniquely vulnerable when attempting to escape abuse. Being outed as transgender can lead to loss of employment, housing, family, and friends.[42] Whether perpetrated by a partner or another individual, being outed is a legitimate fear with real-world consequences.[43] As psychologist Nicola Brown reminds us, "perpetrators are actually aware of the individual and institutional vulnerabilities faced by trans people and these vulnerabilities feature explicitly in the abuse tactics and harm done."[44] Perpetrators also often attempt to exploit transgender survivors' insecurities and fears, factoring into why some survivors choose to stay.

A sixth barrier to help seeking pertains to financial dependence on abusers. Due to discrimination and lack of adequate labor laws, many transgender people experience obstacles to obtaining legitimate employment and are often forced into the underground economy, such as doing sex work, to earn income.[45] As such, these individuals may rely heavily on their partners to meet their basic needs, lacking the economic resources to escape.[46] The abusive partner may also financially control their gender transition process, making it even more difficult for transgender survivors to separate.[47] What is more, transgender people who exit abusive relationships are at high risk of homelessness because of limited housing and shelter options.[48] Transgender people are at a heightened risk for homelessness compared to the average US citizen, and transgender youth experience homelessness at particularly disproportionate rates.[49] Due to the gender-segregated nature of many IPV shelters, some transgender survivors seek out homeless shelters for refuge, which are not equipped to address the specific needs of IPV survivors.[50] (See chapter 8 for more on shelters.)

Transphobia-fueled isolation and a need for emotional stability in a transphobic society can together pose a seventh barrier to help seeking. Since transgender individuals often live in isolation due to their marginalized status, many transgender survivors share social networks with their abusers. Walker observes: "[E]ven if terminating a relationship is their preferred solution, trans people's geographical space is often limited. Segregated from the rest of society because of their marginalized status, trans people form their own communities which ideally offer them a sense of safety and belonging; as a result, escaping an abusive partner is difficult because of their shared social spaces."[51] Coupled with the belief that a stigmatized gender identity translates to fewer opportunities for meaningful relationships, many transgender people believe that any partner is better than none.[52] Survivors also report staying with abusers because the ability to maintain long-term relationships translates to feelings of stability.[53]

An eighth reason some transgender survivors remain with abusive partners is the fear of adding to the already prevailing stigmas associated with transgender communities. By seeking help to leave an abusive relationship, many transgender survivors worry that their experiences will reinforce negative perceptions of the community to which they belong.[54] Taken together, T-IPV may be an underreported phenomenon, reinforcing the myth that its occurrence is rare. As Walker puts it, "The lack of reporting within trans populations . . . is maintaining perceptions that intimate partner violence/abuse (IPV/A) does not occur outside of heteronormative relationships."[55]

Resilience and Coping in T-IPV

Faced with barriers to help seeking and the challenges of finding safe and supportive housing, some transgender survivors remain with their abusers. Others succeed in exiting harmful relationships. Although more research is still needed, evidence suggests that transgender survivors employ various coping strategies as acts of resistance. We recognize transgender survivors as resilient whether they remain with their abusers or successfully exit abusive relationships, as strategies to resist and cope can be utilized during and after abusive occurrences.

As one indicator of resilience, research suggests that 76–78 percent of transgender survivors seek help from someone.[56] As to whom survivors seek help from, a number of studies with small transgender subsamples have begun to examine this question.[57] For instance, psychologist Susan Turell and anthropologist La Vonne Cornell-Swanson found that transgender survivors were more likely than their cisgender survivor counterparts to seek support from members of the clergy, and this finding was statistically significant.[58] It is important to note, however, that only 1 percent of their sample identified as transgender. Only a handful of quantitative studies with more substantial transgender representation in their samples have examined the entities transgender survivors are most likely to seek help from, including one study on seeking help from police in the US[59] and two studies on seeking help from a broad range of resources in the US[60] and Scotland,[61] respectively. Taken together, these studies indicate that transgender survivors are most likely to seek help from informal support resources, including friends (from whom 77 percent of transgender survivors seek help) and relatives (30 percent).[62] By far the most commonly sought-out formal source of help is a mental health-care professional such as a therapist (40 percent), followed more distantly by a medical doctor (21 percent), an organization dedicated to serving LGBTQ communities (14–20 percent), and police (12–18 percent).[63] Least likely to be sought out are IPV survivor agencies and shelters (2–7 percent) and attorneys (2 percent).[64] It is likely that these help-seeking patterns are reflective of a broader distrust of formal resources, which are often perceived by transgender survivors to be more transphobic than friends and family.[65] Of course, one negative consequence of these help-seeking preferences is that those who are potentially best equipped (in terms of both training and access to resources) to assist transgender survivors—such as IPV survivor agencies, survivor shelters, and police—cannot help those who are unwilling to seek them out. Clearly, improvements are needed with respect to the transgender inclusivity and cultural competence of the advertising and services provided by formal resources, with the ultimate goal of improving T-IPV help-seeking rates and access to much-needed assistance.

Psychologist Anneliese Singh and public health specialist Vel McKleroy[66] examined resilience among eleven transgender people of color in response to trauma, five of whom identified as IPV survivors.[67] This study is unique because, as Singh and McKleroy correctly point out, "[L]iterature on resilience of trauma survivors tends to use a distinctly Western, White approach to research and practice—focusing on individual as opposed to relational processes of resilience."[68] Emerging from their interviews were six factors that promoted resilience to trauma: "(a) pride in one's gender and ethnic/racial identity, (b) recognizing and negotiating gender and racial/ethnic oppression, (c) navigating relationships with family, (d) accessing health care and financial resources, (e) connecting with an activist transgender community of color, and (f) cultivating spirituality and hope for the future."[69]

Regarding the first of these six factors, for participants in Singh and McKleroy's study, developing pride in their identities entailed a process of working through negative societal responses to being both transgender and a person of color. (See chapter 6 for more on race and T-IPV.) Overcoming these barriers led to feelings of empowerment that helped participants navigate traumatic experiences. Additionally, regarding the second factor, learning to recognize and negotiate gender and racial/ethnic oppression allowed them to gain the language and voice necessary to establish and maintain relationship boundaries, which included leaving abusive partners when violence was experienced. As for the third factor, when family members perceive transgender people's gender identity as unhealthy, this can be a barrier to help seeking. On the other hand, family acceptance—whether early on or later in life—translates to feelings of protection when dealing with life challenges. Regarding the fourth factor, access to transgender-positive health care and adequate financial resources also greatly contributed to participants' self-esteem, increasing their ability to cope with traumatic life experiences in healthy ways.[70]

Several of Singh and McKleroy's participants stated that employment discrimination was inextricably linked to lower socioeconomic status, as well as unhealthy, abusive relationships. Financial stability, though, often translated to the ability to afford the resources necessary for gender transition, leading to feeling more comfortable in their bodies and, in some cases, to better jobs and less employment discrimination. Turning to the fifth factor, establishing connections with activist communities of transgender people of color is challenging due to limited resources and existing support groups. Yet such connections are crucial for becoming resilient, developing more positive coping mechanisms in response to trauma, and affording access to transgender-affirming legal avenues, law enforcement officials, and others who work to improve the safety and life chances for transgender people of color. Sixth and lastly, regardless of whether participants had negative or positive experiences with religion or spirituality in their upbringings, most reported that some form of spirituality constituted a means of resilience and an avenue to realizing a promising future.[71]

Research on other marginalized populations suggests that resiliency may be more successful outside the context of an ongoing violent incident. For example, some of the participants in DiStefano's study, some of whom were transgender, reported leaving abusive relationships, but not during violent acts.[72] Those who attempted to fight back or escape during violent incidents were largely unsuccessful. However, because the gendered discourse implies that survivors do not attempt to fight back, rejecting the label "survivor" is one important way many such individuals distinguish themselves.[73] A shared experience among survivors of both sexual and physical IPV was that they were unsuccessful in fighting off their abusers because they were physically dominated. For others, not resisting was a choice made "in order to avoid hurting their abusive partner's pride."[74]

Conclusion

The bulk of the social scientific literature on IPV survivors' resilience and coping strategies is both heteronormative and cisnormative. The same can be said about the literature on violence during and after the process of leaving an intimate relationship.[75] Violence that occurs as part of exiting or attempting to exit a relationship is certainly not purely a heterosexual or cisgender phenomenon, and future research is needed to continue filling in this major research gap on help seeking, coping, and resilience among transgender survivors of IPV.

Due to variance in identities that fall under the transgender umbrella, future empirical and theoretical work should acknowledge such heterogeneity.[76] The importance of intersectionality is also critical, particularly with regard to transgender survivors of color. As Singh and McKleroy assert, "[M]ultiple identities intersect and influence the well-being of transgender people of color's experiences of traumatic life events."[77] Intersectionality involves addressing "the manner in which racism, patriarchy, class oppression, and other discriminatory systems created background inequalities that structure the relative positions of women, races, ethnicities, classes" and members of LGBTQ communities.[78] Intersectionality is front and center in the North American feminist criminological literature on the lives of inner-city African American girls and women, with two prime examples being the writings of sociologists Nikki Jones and Hillary Potter.[79] Yet application of an intersectional lens needs to gain greater momentum in T-IPV research.[80]

Some scholars hypothesize that LGBTQ people are more vulnerable to discrimination and violence in rural places because of greater isolation in less dense populations, fewer support services in close proximity, significantly higher rates of gun ownership, and a higher proportion of conservative residents.[81] Yet we do not actually know if rural transgender people are at higher risk of being abused than are those living in urban and suburban places. Are transgender survivors' resilience strategies and barriers to escaping abusive relationships different or similar across urban, suburban, and rural areas? This question, as well, has yet to be answered empirically or theoretically. As sociologist Adam Messinger puts it, intimate violence against LGTBQ people living in rural places is "greatly understudied."[82] Perhaps this is because researchers incorrectly assume that LGBTQ people are more comfortable in urban settings and thus believe that it would be difficult, if not impossible, to generate a reasonable sample size. Recent research on the lives of rural LGBTQ people may be limited, but what does exist shows that many LGBTQ people live in rural areas and enjoy doing so.[83] Hence, as Johnson, Gilley, and Gray put it, "we need to think twice ... before acceding to the notion that rural life necessarily involves isolation from broader national and international trends."[84]

If there is a dearth of research on rural T-IPV in the Global North, there is even less T-IPV research overall in the Global South.[85] Following Kerry Carrington, Russell Hogg, and Maximo Sozzo, a key difference between the Global North and the Global South is "the divide between the metropolitan states of Western Europe and North America, on the one hand, and the countries of Latin America, Africa, Asia, and Oceania, on the other."[86] Perhaps, then, T-IPV researchers should follow in the footsteps of those studying lesbian battering in the Global South by breaking away from the canons of mainstream research to do case studies, collect stories and narratives, and obtain visual representations.[87] It should also be noted that some African lesbian activists are working to prevent violence in lesbian relationships and are developing initiatives to prevent homophobic and transphobic violence.[88]

The data-gathering techniques recommended for use in the Global South are also appropriate for studies of transgender people's violent experiences in the Global North. DeKeseredy contends that some rural Northern communities are likely to be more transphobic than others, so the methods suggested above help researchers deal with the challenges of "silence, repression, and uncertainty."[89]

Research on the prevalence and scope of cyber T-IPV is also warranted, due to society's increasing reliance on social media and the internet for sharing information about individuals and groups. Considering the limited scholarship on T-IPV resilience, coping, and help seeking, even less is known about such issues regarding survivor responses to cyber T-IPV. Until recently, research on IPV in any type of adult relationship either ignored or overlooked the fact that various new technologies are now tools used by people to exert control and power over their current or former intimate partners.[90] Research on this problem among cisgender people is now mushrooming, but empirical and theoretical work on transgender people's experiences with image-based sexual abuse and other electronic means of IPV (e.g., stalking) is in short supply. Consider that only one study addressing cyber assaults on transgender people is cited in Messinger's comprehensive book on the LGBTQ intimate partner violence research literature.[91] It is likely that more such studies have since been conducted, but the number is still likely to pale in comparison with the amount of studies of cisgender populations done after the one reviewed by Messinger.

Joseph F. Donnermeyer recently stated, "There are simply too many rural issues to squeeze into a single journal article about a global criminology of the South and rural criminology."[92] Likewise, there are too many issues to squeeze into a single chapter that reviews the extant literature on transgender survivors' resilience and coping strategies, and barriers to social support. Moreover, the new directions in empirical and theoretical work suggested here constitute just the tip of the iceberg. While more research on transgender survivors' concerns is necessary, the good news is that more people, such as the contributors to this anthology, are joining to respond to this call. Hopefully, our colleagues will take the next steps suggested here and answer the question, "What is to be done about T-IPV?" In the words of Courvant and Cook-Daniels, "We owe these survivors much more thought and effort to ensure that we do not either force them to stay in the hands of their abusers or revictimize them once they take that first step away."[93]

NOTES
1 DeKeseredy and Hall-Sanchez 2018.
2 Guadalupe-Diaz and Jasinski 2017, 773; see also Dunbar 2006; Liang et al. 2005.
3 Alvi, Clow, and DeKeseredy 2008.
4 Werner-Wilson, Schindler Zimmerman, and Whalen 2000.
5 Alvi, Clow, and DeKeseredy 2008; Miller 2018.
6 Humphreys 2003.
7 Folkman and Moskowitz 2004; Zink et al. 2006.
8 Guadalupe-Diaz and Jasinski 2017; White and Goldberg 2006.
9 Anderson et al. 2003; Singh and McKleroy 2011.
10 Anderson et al. 2003; Guadalupe-Diaz and Jasinski 2017.
11 Guadalupe-Diaz and Jasinski 2007; Logan et al. 2005.
12 Courvant and Cook-Daniels 2003.
13 Krishnan, Hilbert, and VanLeeuwen 2001; Ristock and Timbang 2005.
14 Anderson et al. 2003; Walker 2015.
15 Goodmark 2013.
16 Courvant and Cook-Daniels 2003; White and Goldberg 2006.
17 Cooper 2013; Courvant and Cook-Daniels 2003; Kurdyla 2017.
18 Mendez 1996; Ristock and Timbang 2005.
19 Calton, Cattaneo, and Gebhard 2015; Cruz 2003; FORGE 2011; Renzetti 2001; Ristock and Timbang 2005; White and Goldberg 2006; Yerke and DeFeo 2016.

20 Rogers 2016.
21 Rogers 2016; White and Goldberg 2006.
22 Guadalupe-Diaz and Jasinksi 2017.
23 Guadalupe-Diaz and Jasinski 2017; Langenderfer-Magruder et al. 2016; Walker 2015.
24 Rogers 2016.
25 Connell 1995.
26 Brannon and David 1976; Schwartz and DeKeseredy 1997.
27 Courvant and Cook-Daniels 2003.
28 Rogers 2016.
29 Courvant and Cook-Daniels 2003, 2.
30 White and Goldberg 2006.
31 Guadalupe-Diaz 2015.
32 DiStefano 2009.
33 Rogers 2016.
34 Walker 2015, 118.
35 DiStefano 2009; Halverson 2017.
36 Walker 2015.
37 Rogers 2016.
38 Guadalupe-Diaz 2015.
39 Brown 2011; Courvant and Cook-Daniels 2003, 3; Ristock and Timbang 2005, 11.
40 Courvant and Cook-Daniels 2003.
41 Rogers 2016; White and Goldberg 2006.
42 Courvant and Cook-Daniels 2003; Walker 2015.
43 Calton, Cattaneo, and Gebhard 2015; DiStefano 2009; Grant et al. 2011; Kurdyla 2017.
44 Brown 2011, 162.
45 Clements-Nolle et al. 2001; Guadalupe-Diaz 2015.
46 Walker 2015.
47 FORGE 2011; White and Goldberg 2006; Yerke and DeFeo 2016.
48 ACON 2004; Ristock and Timbang 2005.
49 National Center for Transgender Equality 2018; Singh and McKleroy 2011.
50 DiStefano 2009.
51 Walker 2015, 119.
52 Courvant and Cook-Daniels 2003; Guadalupe-Diaz 2015.
53 Guadalupe-Diaz and Anthony 2017.
54 Ristock and Timbang 2005.
55 Walker 2015, 114.
56 Guadalupe-Diaz and Jasinski 2017; Roch, Morton, and Ritchie 2010.
57 E.g., Farrell and Cerise 2006; Guadalupe-Diaz and Jasinski 2017; Kurdyla 2017; Turell and Cornell-Swanson 2005.
58 Turell and Cornell-Swanson 2005.
59 Langenderfer-Magruder et al. 2016.

60 Kurdyla, Messinger, and Ramirez 2019.
61 Roch et al. 2010.
62 Kurdyla et al. 2019.
63 Kurdyla et al. 2019; Langenderfer-Magruder et al. 2016; Roch, Morton, and Ritchie 2010.
64 Kurdyla et al. 2019; Roch, Morton, and Ritchie 2010.
65 See Kurdyla 2017; Messinger 2017.
66 Singh and McKleroy 2011.
67 Singh and McKleroy 2011.
68 Singh and McKleroy 2011, 35.
69 Singh and McKleroy 2011, 38.
70 Ristock and Timbang 2005.
71 Singh and McKleroy 2011, 38.
72 DiStefano 2009.
73 Guadalupe-Diaz and Jasinksi 2017.
74 DiStefano 2009, 135.
75 DeKeseredy, Dragiewicz, and Schwartz 2017.
76 Walker 2015.
77 Singh and McKleroy 2011, 40.
78 Crenshaw Williams 2000, 8.
79 Jones 2010; Potter 2015.
80 Ristock and Timbang 2005.
81 ACON 2004; Mahoney, Williams, and West 2001; Ristock and Timbang 2005.
82 Messinger 2017, 57.
83 Baker 2016.
84 Johnson, Gilley, and Gray 2016, 3.
85 DeKeseredy and Hall-Sanchez 2018.
86 Carrington, Hogg, and Sozzo 2016, 2.
87 Currier and Migraine-George 2016; DeKeseredy 2018; Morgan and Wieringa 2005.
88 Currier 2012; Matebeni 2009; Theron 2013.
89 Currier and Migraine-George 2016, 1; DeKeseredy 2018.
90 DeKeseredy, Dragiewicz, and Schwartz 2017; Southworth et al. 2005.
91 Dank et al. 2014; Messinger 2017.
92 Donnermeyer 2017, 129.
93 Courvant and Cook-Daniels 2003, 6.

REFERENCES

ACON. 2004. *Homelessness and Same Sex Domestic Violence in the Supported Accommodation Assistance Program*. Sydney: ACON.

Alter, Charlotte. 2017. "Transgender Men See Sexism from Both Sides." *Time*, March 13, 2017. http://time.com.

Alvi, Shahid, Kimberley A. Clow, and Walter S. DeKeseredy. 2008. "Woman Abuse and Resilience in a Sample of Minority Low-Income Women." *Women's Health* 7:51–67.

Anderson, Michael A., Paulette M. Gillig, Marilyn Sitaker, Kathy McCloskey, Kathleen Malloy, and Nancy Grigsby. 2003. "'Why Doesn't She Just Leave?': A Descriptive Study of Victim Reported Impediments to Her Safety." *Journal of Family Violence* 16 (3): 151–155.

Baker, Kelly. 2016. "Out Back Home: An Exploration of LGBT Identities and Community in Rural Nova Scotia, Canada." In *Queering the Countryside: New Frontiers in Rural Queer Studies*, edited by Mary L. Gray, Colin R. Johnson, and Brian J. Gilley, 25–48. New York: New York University Press.

Brannon, Robert, and Deborah David. 1976. "The Male Sex Role: Our Culture's Blueprint of Manhood, and What It's Done for Us Lately." In *The Forty-Nine Percent Majority: The Male Sex Role*, 1–48. Reading, MA: Addison-Wesley.

Brown, Nicola. 2011. "Holding Tensions of Victimization and Perpetration: Partner Abuse in Trans Communities." In *Intimate Partner Violence in LGBTQ Lives*, edited by Janice L. Ristock, 153–168. New York: Routledge.

Calton, Jenna M., Lauren Bennett Cattaneo, and Kris T. Gebhard. 2015. "Barriers to Help Seeking for Lesbian, Gay, Bisexual, Transgender, and Queer Survivors of Intimate Partner Violence." *Trauma, Violence and Abuse* 17 (5): 585–600.

Carrington, Kerry, Russell Hogg, and Maximo Sozzo. 2016. "Southern Criminology." *British Journal of Criminology* 56 (1): 1–20.

Clements-Nolle, Kristen R., Marx, Robert Guzman, and Mitchell Katz. 2001. "HIV Prevalence, Risk Behaviors, Health Care Use, and Mental Health Status of Transgender Persons: Implications for Public Health Intervention." *American Journal of Public Health* 91 (6): 915–921.

Connell, Robert W. 1995. *Masculinities*. Berkeley: University of California Press.

Cooper, Leslie. 2013. *Protecting the Rights of Transgender Parents and Their Children: A Guide for Parents and Lawyers*. New York: American Civil Liberties Union, and Washington, DC: National Center for Transgender Equality. https://transequality.org.

Courvant, Diana, and Loree Cook-Daniels. 2003. *Trans and Intersex Survivors of Domestic Violence: Defining Terms, Barriers and Responsibilities*. National Coalition Against Domestic Violence. www.survivorproject.org.

Crenshaw Williams, Kimberlé. 2000. "The Intersectionality of Race and Gender Discrimination." Background Paper, Expert Group Meeting on Gender and Race Discrimination, Zagreb, Croatia, November 21–24.

Cruz, J. Michael. 2003. "'Why Doesn't He Just Leave?' Gay Male Domestic Violence and the Reasons Victims Stay." *Journal of Men's Studies* 11 (3): 309–324.

Currier, Ashley. 2012. *Out in Africa: LGBT Organizing in Namibia and South Africa*. Minneapolis: University of Minnesota Press.

Currier, Ashley, and Thérèse Migraine-George. 2016. "'Lesbian'/Female Same-Sex Sexualities in Africa." *Journal of Lesbian Studies* 21 (2): 133–150.

Dank, Meredith, Pamela Lachman, Janine M. Zweig, and Jennifer Yahner. 2014. "Dating Violence Experiences of Lesbian, Gay, Bisexual, and Transgender Youth." *Journal of Youth and Adolescence* 43: 846–857.

DeKeseredy, Walter S. 2018. "Intimate Violence against Rural Women: The Current State of Sociological Knowledge." *International Journal of Rural Criminology* 4 (2): 134–144.

DeKeseredy, Walter S., Molly Dragiewicz, and Martin D. Schwartz. 2017. *Abusive Endings: Separation and Divorce Violence against Women*. Oakland: University of California Press.

DeKeseredy, Walter S., and Amanda Hall-Sanchez. 2018. "Male Violence against Women in the Global South: What We Know and What We Don't Know." In *The Palgrave Handbook of Criminology and the Global South*, edited by Kerry Carrington, Russell Hogg, John Scott, and Maximo Sozzo, 883–900. New York: Palgrave Macmillan.

DiStefano, Anthony S. 2009. "Intimate Partner Violence among Sexual Minorities in Japan: Exploring Perceptions and Experiences." *Journal of Homosexuality* 56 (2): 121–146.

Donnermeyer, Joseph F. 2017. "The Place of Rural in a Southern Criminology." *International Journal for Crime, Justice and Social Democracy* 6 (1): 120–134.

Dunbar, Edward. 2006. "Race, Gender, and Sexual Orientation in Hate Crime Victimization: Identity Politics or Identity Risk?" *Violence and Victims* 21 (3): 323–337.

Farrell, Janine, and Somali Cerise. 2006. *Fair's Fair: A Snapshot of Violence and Abuse in Sydney LGBT Relationships*. Sydney: AIDS Council of NSW and the Same Sex Domestic Violence Interagency and Working Group, 2006. http://static1.1.sqspcdn.com/static/f/471667/8241404/1282546269423/SSDV_A4Report.pdf.

Folkman, Susan, and Judith Moskowitz. 2004. "Coping Pitfalls and Promise." *Annual Reviews of Psychology* 55:745–774.

FORGE. 2011. *Transgender Domestic Violence and Sexual Assault Resource Sheet*. Milwaukee, WI: FORGE. https://avp.org.

Goodmark, Leigh. 2013. "Transgender People, Intimate Partner Abuse, and the Legal System." *Harvard Civil Rights–Civil Liberties Law Review* 48 (1): 51–104.

Grant, Jamie M., Lisa A. Mottet, Justin Tanis, Jack Harrison, Jody L. Herman, and Mara Keisling. 2011. *Injustice at Every Turn: A Report of the National Transgender Discrimination Survey*. Washington, DC: National Center for Transgender Equality and National Gay and Lesbian Task Force. www.transequality.org.

Guadalupe-Diaz, Xavier. 2015. "Same-Sex Victimization and the LGBTQ Community." In *Sexual Victimization: Then and Now*, edited by Tara N. Richards and Catherine D. Marcum, 173–192. Thousand Oaks, CA: Sage.

Guadalupe-Diaz, Xavier L., and Amanda Koontz Anthony. 2017. "Discrediting Identity Work: Understandings of Intimate Partner Violence by Transgender Survivors." *Deviant Behavior* 38(1): 1–16.

Guadalupe-Diaz, Xavier L., and Jana Jasinski. 2017. "'I Wasn't a Priority, I Wasn't a Victim': Challenges in Help Seeking for Transgender Survivors of Intimate Partner Violence." *Violence against Women* 23 (6): 772–792.

Halverson, Ashley M. 2017. "Intimate Partner Victimization of Transgender People and Access to Social Services." PhD diss., San Diego State University.

Humphreys, Janice. 2003. "Resilience in Sheltered Battered Women." *Issues in Mental Health Nursing* 24 (2): 137–152.

Johnson, Colin R., Brian J. Gilley, and Mary L. Gray. 2016. "Introduction." In *Queering the Countryside: New Frontiers in Rural Queer Studies*, edited by Mary L. Gray, Colin R. Johnson, and Brian J. Gilley, 1–21. New York: New York University Press.

Jones, Nikki. 2010. *Between Good and Ghetto: African American Girls and Inner-City Violence*. New Brunswick, NJ: Rutgers University Press.

Krishnan, Satya P., Judith C. Hilbert, and Dawn VanLeeuwen. 2001. "Domestic Violence and Help-Seeking Behaviors among Rural Women: Results from a Shelter-Based Study." *Family & Community Health* 24 (1): 28–38.

Kurdyla, Victoria A. 2017. "Exploring Experiences of Disclosure for Transgender and Nonbinary Survivors of Abuse." Master's thesis, the University of North Carolina at Greensboro.

Kurdyla, Victoria A., Adam M. Messinger, and Milka Ramirez. 2019. "Transgender Intimate Partner Violence and Help-Seeking Patterns." *Journal of Interpersonal Violence*. https://doi.org/10.1177/0886260519880171.

Langenderfer-Magruder, Lisa, Darren L. Whitfield, N. Eugene Walls, Shanna K. Kattari, and Daniel Ramos. 2016. "Experiences of Intimate Partner Violence and Subsequent Police Reporting among Lesbian, Gay, Bisexual, Transgender, and Queer Adults in Colorado: Comparing Rates of Cisgender and Transgender Victimization." *Journal of Interpersonal Violence* 31 (5): 855–871.

Liang, Belle, Lisa Goodman, Pratyusha Tummala-Narra, and Sarah Weintraub. 2005. "A Theoretical Framework for Understanding Help-Seeking Processes among Survivors of Intimate Partner Violence." *American Journal of Community Psychology* 36 (1–2): 71–84.

Logan, T. K., Lucy Evans, Erin Stevenson, and Carol E. Jordan. 2005. "Barriers to Services for Rural and Urban Survivors of Rape." *Journal of Interpersonal Violence* 20 (5): 591–616.

Mahoney, Patricia, Linda Williams, and Carolyn West. 2001. "Violence against Women by Intimate Relationship Partners." In *Sourcebook on Violence against Women*, edited by Claire M. Renzetti, Jeffrey Edelson, and Raquel K. Bergen, 143–178. Thousand Oaks, CA: Sage.

Matebeni, Zethu. 2009. "Feminizing Lesbians, Degendering Transgender Men: A Model for Building Lesbian Feminist Thinkers and Leaders in Africa." *Souls* 11 (9): 347–354.

Mendez, Jorge M. 1996. "Serving Gay and Lesbians of Color Who Are Survivors of Domestic Violence." In *Violence in Gay and Lesbian Domestic Partnerships*, edited by Claire M. Renzetti and Charles H. Miley, 23–33. New York: Harrington Park Press.

Messinger, Adam M. 2017. *Intimate Partner Violence: Lessons for Policy, Practice, and Research*. Oakland: University of California Press.

Miller, Susan L. 2018. *Journeys: Resilience and Growth for Survivors of Intimate Partner Abuse*. Oakland: University of California Press.

Morgan, Ruth, and Saskia Wieringa. 2005. *Tommy Boys, Lesbian Men and Ancestral Wives: Female Same-Sex Practices in Africa.* Johannesburg: Jacana Media.
National Center for Transgender Equality. 2018. "Housing and Homelessness." https://transequality.org.
Potter, Hillary. 2015. *Intersectionality and Criminology: Disrupting and Revolutionizing Studies of Crime.* London: Routledge.
Renzetti, Claire M. 2001. "Violence in Lesbian and Gay Relationships." In *Sourcebook on Violence against Women*, edited by Claire M. Renzetti, Jeffery Edelson, and Raquel K. Bergen, 285–293. Thousand Oaks, CA: Sage.
Ristock, Janice, and Norma Timbang. 2005. "Relationship Violence in Lesbian/Gay/Bisexual/Transgender/Queer [LGBTQ] Communities: Moving beyond a Gender-Based Framework." *Violence Against Women Online Resources.* https://vawnet.org.
Roch, Amy, James Morton, and Graham Ritchie. 2010. *Out of Sight, out of Mind? Transgender People's Experiences of Domestic Abuse.* Edinburgh: LGBT Youth Scotland and the Scottish Transgender Alliance. www.scottishtrans.org.
Rogers, Michaela. 2016. "Breaking Down Barriers: Exploring the Potential for Social Care Practice with Trans Survivors of Domestic Abuse." *Health & Social Care in the Community* 24 (1): 68–76.
Schwartz, Martin D., and Walter S. DeKeseredy. 1997. *Sexual Assault on the College Campus: The Role of Male Peer Support.* Thousand Oaks, CA: Sage.
Singh, Anneliese A., and Vel S. McKleroy. 2011. "'Just Getting Out of Bed is a Revolutionary Act': The Resilience of Transgender People of Color Who Have Survived Traumatic Life Events." *Traumatology* 17 (2): 34–44.
Southworth, Cindy, Shawndell Dawson, Cynthia Fraser, and Sarah Tucker. 2005. "A High-Tech Twist on Abuse: Technology, Intimate Partner Stalking, and Advocacy." *Violence Against Women Online Resources.* https://vawnet.org.
Theron, Liesel. 2013. "Does the Label Fit?" In *Queer African Reader*, edited by Sokari Ekine and Hakima Abbas, 316–327. Dakar, Senegal: Pambazuka.
Turell, Susan C., and La Vonne Cornell-Swanson. 2005. "Not All Alike: Within-Group Differences in Seeking Help for Same-Sex Relationship Abuses." *Journal of Gay & Lesbian Social Services* 18 (1): 71–88.
Walker, Julia K. 2015. "Investigating Trans People's Vulnerabilities to Intimate Partner Violence/Abuse." *Partner Abuse* 6 (1): 107–125.
Werner-Wilson, Ronald J., Toni Schindler Zimmerman, and Dorothy Whalen. 2000. "Resilient Response to Battering." *Contemporary Family Therapy* 22 (2): 161–188.
White, Caroline, and Joshua Goldberg. 2006. "Expanding Our Understanding of Gendered Violence: Violence against Trans People and Their Loved Ones." *Canadian Women's Studies* 25 (1–2): 124–127.
Yerke, Adam F., and Jennifer DeFeo. 2016. "Redefining Intimate Partner Violence beyond the Binary to Include Transgender People." *Journal of Family Violence* 31 (8): 975–979.
Zink, Therese, C. Jeff Jacobson Jr., Stephanie Pabst, Saundra Regan, and Bonnie S. Fisher. 2006. "A Lifetime of Intimate Partner Violence: Coping Strategies of Older Women." *Journal of Interpersonal Violence* 21 (5): 634–651.

5

Theorizing on the Roots of Transgender Intimate Partner Violence

ADAM M. MESSINGER

Successful efforts to prevent, intervene in, and address the negative effects of intimate partner violence (IPV) require understanding not merely what IPV is but particularly why it happens. For instance, research in the United States finds that most IPV prevention education programs,[1] most court-mandated batterer intervention programs,[2] and, to a lesser extent, some victim mental health treatment modalities[3] operate under two interrelated assumptions: (1) many abusers are in part motivated by patriarchal attitudes encouraging cisgender men to feel entitled to control over cisgender women and, therefore, (2) undermining an individual's acceptance of these same patriarchal attitudes is key to preventing cisgender men from ever becoming abusive, rehabilitating cisgender men who have already engaged in abuse, and helping cisgender female survivors cope with the negative effects of abuse. This approach has shown limited success in addressing IPV among heterosexual, cisgender people.[4] However, it is unclear whether the same strategy is effective at all in addressing IPV involving transgender perpetrators or survivors (i.e., transgender IPV, or T-IPV), since studies have yet to evaluate the efficacy of existing IPV prevention programs, batterer intervention programs, and IPV victim mental health treatments when applied to transgender populations.[5] Moreover, current efforts to address IPV are largely cisnormative, addressing only the causes of IPV between two cisgender partners (i.e., cisgender IPV, or C-IPV) while presuming the causes of T-IPV to be identical.[6] If ultimately research bears out that T-IPV and C-IPV do not have identical risk factors, serious doubt will be cast on whether the cisnormative strategies currently in use by many prevention educators and service providers will be adequate to successfully combat abuse in transgender communities.

Thus, in a very real way, the path toward curbing the future prevalence and fallout of T-IPV must begin with increasing our understanding of why T-IPV occurs, including examining not only risk factors for perpetration but also victimization. Importantly, T-IPV research is overwhelmingly cross-sectional, involving data collection at one rather than multiple points in time. (See chapter 13 for more on methodological challenges in T-IPV research.) Unfortunately, with the exception of risk factors that clearly precede the occurrence of adult IPV (e.g., child abuse victimization), cross-sectional research inevitably inhibits a deeper understanding of whether IPV risk factors are always causes of IPV or whether they are at times instead outcomes of IPV.[7] That said, identifying T-IPV covariates even in cross-sectional research is a critical first step to the future design of longitudinal studies and retrospective qualitative studies that will help disentangle causes from outcomes. Moreover, even in the absence of a clearer understanding of event sequencing, identified covariates of T-IPV can be utilized by providers as potential red flags to screen for in identifying IPV perpetrators and survivors, and IPV covariates may themselves represent comorbid health issues that also need to be treated.

With this in mind, the present chapter reviews theories, supporting evidence, and gaps in our knowledge of T-IPV perpetration causes and victim vulnerability, highlighting likely causal pathways that are shared by T-IPV and C-IPV as well as pathways unique to T-IPV. While additional theories and risk factors undoubtedly will be examined by researchers in the future, this chapter focuses primarily on explanations of T-IPV for which currently there is at least preliminary empirical support.

Causal Pathways Shared by T-IPV and C-IPV

The literature provides preliminary empirical support for a number of causal pathways that are similar across T-IPV and C-IPV. These shared pathways are theorized to include (1) the use of rationalizations by abusers to neutralize potential guilt over hurting their partners, (2) the socialization of survivors into IPV-condoning attitudes, and (3) vulnerabilities of survivors that assist abusers in controlling and trapping them. Each theory is supported by varying degrees of empirical evidence, reviewed below.

Use of Rationalizations by Abusers

In large part due to the dearth of research on transgender abusers, few theories of why transgender people might abuse their partners have been empirically tested. One of the few C-IPV perpetration theories to find limited support in the T-IPV literature is what criminologists refer to as a theory of "techniques of neutralization."[8] Applied to the context of IPV, this theory suggests that abusers are in part able to be abusive because they often internalize and vocalize rationalizations for their abuse, thereby relieving any potential guilt they may have felt for their actions.[9] Some abusers may attempt to reframe IPV as justified under particular circumstances, or they may aim to deflect attention away from the abuse toward other issues in their lives, in either event reducing any potential responsibility they may have otherwise felt. Empirical support for this theory has been found in the C-IPV literature.[10]

In the T-IPV literature, limited evidence indicates that these rationalizations by abusers can take several forms. For instance, anecdotal evidence suggests that abusers may justify their abuse—and encourage survivors to justify being abused—as an acceptable validation of their gender identities. As one transgender woman survivor reflected, "Being beaten made me feel more like a woman."[11] Similarly, abusers may physically assault transgender men under the justification of making them more "manly."[12] In a related vein, abusers may justify sexual violence by telling transgender survivors that "real" women or men like "rough sex."[13] Some abusers may also mask sexual violence under the guise of seemingly consensual BDSM. As one transgender survivor explained, "My partner took advantage of the fact that it was my first experience of [BDSM]. . . . I believed that I had to consent to anything or could not withhold consent, and the abuse was couched as 'play.'"[14] Thus, by reframing abuse as a desirable form of gender performance or sexual play, some abusers may avoid guilt and responsibility for hurting their partners.

Another type of rationalization entails some transgender abusers deflecting responsibility for their abusiveness by framing themselves as the actual victims of a transphobic society. Sherisse, a cisgender woman, explains how this rationalization limited her ability to recognize her partner, a transgender man, as abusive:

I'd feel like being on the receiving end of emotional abuse that I believed I never would have taken from a non-trans man and I never would have taken from a woman. . . . I spent a lot of time . . . educating myself on his oppression and [thinking of him as] so powerless in a societal sense that there would be no way he could have enough power to be abusive, so I didn't recognize it in a way that I would have otherwise . . . but I know that he used his various identities—trans included—to reinforce that myth for me.[15]

Relatedly, some transgender abusers may refer to the stigma and anxieties associated with transitioning in efforts to deflect blame for their abuse. When Serena, a cisgender woman, confronted her abuser, a transgender man, he implied that she should care more about his struggles than her own IPV victimization: "This is not about you, it's about me. I'm transitioning, not you," she recalled her abuser saying.[16] A service provider at the NW Network, a US community organization working to end abuse in lesbian, gay, bisexual, transgender, and queer (LGBTQ) communities, summed up the problem with this type of rationalization by some abusers: "Frequently we hear batterers say, 'I have a disability so I can't batter,' 'I'm genderqueer so I can't batter,' 'I'm a person of color so I can't batter.' There is no identity that inherently bars people from being batterers."[17] It is of course possible for a person to be a victim of discrimination while simultaneously being a perpetrator of IPV—but reframing transgender abusers as first and foremost victims of transphobia may hinder the ability of survivors and abusers alike to label such relationships as abusive. In sum, though additional research is needed to clarify the extent to which rationalizations are used in T-IPV, qualitative research suggests that T-IPV and C-IPV both are made possible in part by some abusers and survivors recasting abuse as justified or by deflecting attention away from it.

Socialization into IPV-Condoning Attitudes

While the aforementioned rationalizations help some abusers and survivors to either reframe abuse as justified or to deflect attention away from the abuse, some abusers and survivors may more openly embrace IPV in their relationships because they perceive it as a normal conflict resolution strategy. More specifically, in the C-IPV literature, a long-standing explanation of why abuse occurs is the intergenerational transmission of violence. Drawing on social learning theory,[18] the intergenerational transmission of violence theory contends that exposure to interpersonal violence in childhood—such as experiencing child abuse or witnessing interparental IPV—socializes children to justify violence as a normal response to conflict. It is theorized that as a result, many of those same children grow into adults who similarly view abuse as normal, thereby elevating their risk of IPV perpetration and victimization in adulthood.[19] This theory has repeatedly found empirical support in studies with predominantly cisgender samples.[20]

There is reason to suspect that exposure to childhood and family violence also predicts T-IPV perpetration and victimization. Studies indicate that transgender people are two to ten times more likely than cisgender people to experience violent victimization by a family member or someone else close to them,[21] with national US estimates of lifetime family violence victimization prevalence ranging between 10 and 19 percent for transgender individuals.[22] Such experiences may in turn increase risk for T-IPV. Indeed, one study of 412 transgender people in Massachusetts concluded that exposure to family violence predicts IPV victimization for transgender people. Results revealed that experiencing physical or sexual IPV victimization in one's lifetime was associated with having experienced verbal or physical abuse by a family member at any point in life, and it was also associated with having experienced child sexual abuse prior to the age of fifteen.[23] Similarly, a study of 212 transgender women in New York City found that experiencing child sexual abuse victimization was associated with having experienced at least one form of IPV victimization within the past five years.[24] Research is still needed to determine whether the reason for these associations is in fact because, as theorized, exposure to violence in childhood and by family members reshapes attitudes about IPV. Likewise, in addition to testing this theory with regard to predicting T-IPV victimization, research is needed to explore whether these risk factors predict T-IPV perpetration as well. That said, this preliminary evidence suggests that C-IPV and T-IPV may often share a core origin in exposure to childhood and family violence.

Victim Vulnerabilities to Abuse

Whereas the aforementioned rationalizations and IPV-condoning attitudes may reshape how many abusers and survivors perceive IPV, power imbalances between intimate partners often impact the extent to which survivors feel free to challenge, resist, and escape abuse. Consequently, abusers may feel emboldened to initiate and escalate abuse with partners perceived to be vulnerable. Research on C-IPV offers numerous examples of this dynamic. For instance, studies with predominantly cisgender samples find IPV victimization risk to be elevated for people with fewer economic resources, those who belong to more stigmatized populations such as certain minority racial or ethnic groups, and individuals who are undocumented and thus likely to fear contact with law enforcement.[25]

While research has yet to adequately examine power differentials in abusive relationships that involve one or more transgender people—that is, the relative power of abusers and survivors within the same relationship dyad—a growing body of evidence points to a series of risk factors that may increase the vulnerability of transgender people to IPV victimization. For instance, studies indicate that transgender people are more likely to experience IPV victimization if they are undocumented immigrants, have a disability, have formerly been incarcerated, have ever engaged in sex work, or are living with HIV.[26] Although future research is needed to examine the reason for these associations with IPV victimization among transgender people, one plausible explanation is that each factor has the potential to make the individual a more pliable and therefore more appealing target for some abusers. For instance, transgender individuals belonging to one of the aforementioned at-risk categories may be more likely to fear the consequences of seeking help for victimization (e.g., if they fear deportation due to being undocumented, fear arrest for prior sex work, or fear re-incarceration due to being falsely accused by an abuser of violations of parole), to perceive sources of help to be less readily accessible (e.g., if they are immigrants who do not speak the primary language used by IPV victim service agencies, or if they have a disability that inhibits access to transgender-inclusive IPV services), and to view leaving abusers as an untenable loss of emotional and financial support (e.g., if they are impoverished due to employment discrimination against the formerly incarcerated and thus rely financially on the abuser, or if they fear a loss of much-needed emotional and financial support from the abuser to help them cope with a disability or an HIV diagnosis). In each case, an abuser may feel emboldened to initiate and escalate abuse, comforted by the perception that such vulnerable survivors are less likely to resist or to seek help.

In addition to these empirically supported risk factors for IPV victimization among transgender individuals, several other theorized risk factors have been proven to either have only mixed support or to not be significantly predictive at all. For instance, research on transgender youth ages sixteen to twenty-four has found that IPV victimization is not significantly predicted by age, suggesting that transgender adolescents and young adults have similar risk levels.[27] Although research has yet to examine the association between IPV victimization and age with an adult transgender sample, scholars speculate that aging and elderly transgender people may be faced with a series of age-related vulnerabilities to IPV.[28] Evidence is also mixed regarding whether being a member of a racial or ethnic minority group significantly predicts an increased risk of IPV victimization among transgender people.[29] Likewise, evidence is mixed as to whether having ever been homeless predicts an increased risk of IPV victimization for transgender individuals.[30]

Three potential risk factors for T-IPV victimization have not yet been directly tested but do have varying degrees of indirect support: having a smaller social support network, having fewer economic resources, and having children. First, the size of one's social support network has been theorized to covary with IPV victimization risk, in part because abusers may intentionally isolate their partners out of jealousy and to reduce risk of the survivor leaving, because friends and family may help survivors recognize the early warning signs of abuse and thus better avoid and escape it, and because having more friends may represent an eligible dating pool which may increase a survivor's confidence in leaving an unhealthy or abusive relationship.[31] Unfortunately, transgender people in general are at risk of being rejected by transphobic friends and family, thereby often shrinking their social support networks.[32] While not yet directly tested, indirect evidence suggests that the size of social support networks is likely to be associated with IPV victimization among transgender people. For instance, one study found that 30 percent of transgender survivors had an abuser stop them from seeing their friends or family, and 15 percent had an abuser stop them from "engaging with other trans people or attending transgender social groups and support groups."[33]

Second, while also not yet directly tested, indirect evidence hints that having fewer economic resources may increase transgender people's vulnerability to IPV victimization, perhaps in part because this generates greater financial reliance on abusers. For instance, one study found that a nonsignificantly greater percentage of transgender people experience financial abuse (i.e., efforts to limit a survivor's access to and control over financial resources) compared with cisgender people.[34] Qualitative studies also detail instances in which abusers have withdrawn their financial support for medical interventions related to gender expression and gender transition, such as hormone therapies.[35] Although research has not yet clearly demonstrated that having fewer economic resources increases T-IPV victimization risk, the prevalence with which financial abuse occurs in transgender people's relationships suggests that survivors with lower incomes may be particularly vulnerable.

Third and lastly, although not yet directly tested in research, indirect evidence suggests that having children may increase T-IPV victimization risk, perhaps in part because children may provide abusers with a source of control over their partners. For instance, one study found that transgender parents are significantly more likely than cisgender parents to experience abusive tactics that involved their children, including being made to feel guilty about their children, having their children harmed or threatened with harm, or receiving threats of or actually having their children taken away from them.[36] One reason abusers may feel more comfortable leveraging the children of transgender parents is the knowledge that parental rights are substantially weaker for transgender people in many parts of the world. Consider the US, where transgender people may petition to adopt children throughout the nation but are not protected against anti-transgender discrimination during that adoption process in forty-seven of fifty states.[37] Moreover, when transgender people do have or adopt children, many find their transgender status being used against them in custody hearings.[38] Thus, while children are too often used as leverage by abusers of cisgender parents,[39] transgender parents may be particularly vulnerable to IPV given the weakened parental rights for transgender people.

Causal Pathways Unique to T-IPV

While many similarities appear to exist in explaining why T-IPV and C-IPV occur, scholars posit that there are a number of causal pathways unique to T-IPV, each impacted in some way by societal transphobia. These theorized unique pathways can be categorized into (1) transphobia-related perpetration theories and (2) transphobia-related victimization vulnerability theories.

Transphobia-Related Perpetration Theories

By many measures, transphobia is pervasive in large portions of the world. As just one example, a recent report indicated that in the United States, 32 percent of the population agrees or strongly agrees that transgender people have a mental illness, 41 percent is concerned about exposing children to transgender people, and 36 percent believe America has "gone too far" in accommodating transgender people. This same report found that such transphobic attitudes are shared in numerous nations throughout the world.[40] Given this, it is likely that many abusers of transgender intimate partners also have come to accept transphobic views. Building off this assumption, several theories suggest that people who accept transphobic attitudes—or who themselves may have experienced transphobic discrimination—may be more likely to perpetrate IPV. These theories include honour-based violence theory, disempowerment theory, and minority stress theory.

HONOUR-BASED VIOLENCE THEORY
Scholar and social worker Michaela Rogers argues that cisgender people who accept transphobic attitudes may be more likely to abuse transgender people they are close to as a means through which to disassociate themselves from transgender stigma—and ultimately to protect the abuser's "honour" or societal privilege as a cisgender person.[41] Although this honour-based violence theory is described by Rogers in a broad manner to encompass the abuse of transgender people by any of their cisgender family members (e.g., parents, siblings, etc.), it may apply in some instances of T-IPV victimization as well. Research has yet to quantitatively examine whether and the extent to which cisgender people

with a transgender partner are more likely to abuse that partner if they hold transphobic attitudes. However, qualitative research provides several examples of cisgender abusers directly expressing transphobic attitudes toward their transgender partners,[42] such as when one abuser told a transgender survivor, "you're just all f-in freaks."[43]

Indirect support of this theory also can be found in data suggesting that some abusers try to inhibit the ability of transgender survivors to be transgender. For instance, 30 percent of transgender people report that a partner stopped them from telling others about their transgender background or identity, 30 percent have had a partner stop them from expressing their gender through changes in appearance (e.g., via makeup or gendered clothing), and 7 percent have had a partner stop them from receiving gender-affirming medical services (e.g., hormone therapies).[44] This attempt to deny a transgender survivor's ability to be transgender could indicate a cisgender abuser's strong aversion to transgender people in general. Lastly, a study of ninety-seven transgender people who were assigned male at birth found that 10.3 percent reported experiencing IPV "due to their transgender status," potentially indicating that many abusers of transgender intimate partners are motivated in part by anti-transgender animus.[45]

DISEMPOWERMENT AND MINORITY STRESS THEORIES

Whereas honour-based violence theory might help explain why some cisgender abusers perpetrate IPV against transgender individuals, disempowerment theory and minority stress theory both could help explain why some transgender abusers perpetrate IPV against either cisgender or transgender individuals. Specifically, disempowerment theory suggests that some people who feel disempowered by societal discrimination targeted at their own demographic group may choose to perpetrate IPV as a means to regain a sense of power and control in their lives. Disempowerment theory has been speculated to apply to IPV perpetrated by LGBTQ people in general as well as IPV perpetrated by transgender people in particular.[46] In a similar vein, minority stress theory suggests that some people feel extreme stress due to the existence of societal discrimination targeting their own demographic group (e.g., transphobia), and some may attempt to relieve this stress by engaging in aggression (e.g., IPV perpetration).[47] This theory is rooted in the broader criminology literature's strain theory, which can be distilled down to a similar premise that some people cope with the stresses of life by aggressing against others.[48] Minority stress theory has been speculated to help explain IPV perpetration both by cisgender lesbian, gay, bisexual, and queer people and by transgender people of all sexualities.[49] Although feelings of disempowerment and stress are conceptually distinct causal factors, it is likely that feeling disempowered can increase stress and vice versa. Thus, at their cores, disempowerment and minority stress theories both could be understood as predicting that transgender people who encounter greater levels of transphobia in their lives—be it direct experiences with transphobic discrimination or violence, awareness of transphobic discrimination and violence in society at large, or the internalization of transphobic attitudes—are more likely to perpetrate IPV.

Neither disempowerment theory nor minority stress theory has been directly tested in the T-IPV literature. That is, studies have not yet assessed whether the degree to which transgender people feel disempowered by or stress from transphobic discrimination is associated with the likelihood of their perpetrating IPV. Nor has research yet quantitatively examined whether the theorized precipitators of feeling disempowered or stressed (i.e., experienced or perceived transphobic discrimination and internalized transphobic attitudes) themselves predict IPV perpetration by transgender people. That said, indirect evidence hints that these theories may be relevant to understanding T-IPV perpetration. For instance, some transgender abusers purport that their abusive actions are caused in part by the stress associated with transitioning and transphobia, as was the case in the previously detailed story of Serena.[50] It is unclear, however, whether abusers who point to stress as a cause of their abuse are in part reflecting upon actual stress they feel, or whether such stress-related rationalizations are largely exaggerated by abusers in an effort to excuse their behavior.

Further exploration of these two theories in the T-IPV literature is warranted in part because these theories have found preliminary support in the literature on IPV among lesbian, gay, bisexual, and queer (LGBQ) people. As in the T-IPV literature, research has yet to test whether and the extent to which feeling disempowered or stressed by societal homophobia predicts the perpetration of IPV by LGBQ people.

However, research on LGBQ people has begun to examine whether experiencing discrimination and internalizing discriminatory attitudes—factors theorized to cause disempowerment and minority stress—are associated with IPV perpetration. More specifically, research tentatively indicates that LGBQ people are more likely to perpetrate IPV if they have internalized homophobic attitudes,[51] if they experience discrimination,[52] and—likely in part an indicator of perceived societal discrimination against LGBQ people—if they are less out to others about their sexual orientation.[53] Although support for disempowerment theory and minority stress theory in the literature on IPV among LGBQ people does not necessarily mean that similar support will be found in the T-IPV literature, this clearly warrants future examination by scholars.

Transphobia-Related Victimization Vulnerability Theories

In addition to helping explain why some transgender people perpetrate IPV, transphobia may well also explain why certain types of transgender people are more likely to be targeted by abusers. In particular, transgender people who have a heightened awareness of societal transphobia either may feel deserving of abuse or may assume that potential sources of help will be discriminatory, ultimately making it easier for abusers to initiate and escalate abuse without fear that their transgender partners will try to escape.[54] This theory is indirectly supported by research finding that transgender people are more likely to experience IPV victimization if they have experienced anti-transgender hate crimes or bias incidents, bullying as a minor, or general discrimination (but not specifically anti-transgender discrimination).[55] Although the reasons for these associations were not examined in these studies, it is conceivable that experiences with violence and discrimination among transgender people may heighten their awareness of transphobia in society. According to the aforementioned theory, such a heightened awareness of societal transphobia may in turn decrease such individuals' self-esteem and faith in sources of help for IPV survivors, thereby ultimately increasing their appeal to perpetrators as ideal targets who are less likely to challenge or escape abuse.

Relatedly, according to Rogers, stigma power theory suggests that all transgender people are at an elevated risk of victimization because abusers can leverage the stigma associated with being transgender to manipulate and control transgender survivors.[56] Although Rogers put forth stigma power theory to help explain abuse of transgender people perpetrated by anyone close to them, such as family members, it likely can be applied to help explain T-IPV. Research finds that an alarming 27–73 percent of transgender people experience what is often termed "identity abuse," or IPV tactics that employ a person's transgender status as a means by which to exert control.[57] Identity abuse can take many forms, such as threats to out transgender people, transphobic verbal abuse, and intentionally assaulting gendered parts of a transgender person's body, such as breasts.[58] Moreover, transgender survivors are rightly concerned that some traditional sources of help will be transphobic, a fear which abusers may emphasize and rely upon to keep transgender survivors from leaving.[59] It is possible that transgender people are more likely to be targeted by identity abuse and to fear transphobia by potential sources of help if they are out or public to a greater degree about being transgender. Although not yet directly tested, one study of ninety-seven transgender individuals assigned male at birth found IPV victimization to be over three times as prevalent among those who spend more time dressed as women compared to those who spend less time dressed as women.[60] It may be that choosing clothing not associated by society with one's assigned sex at birth often increases the visibility of being transgender, which in turn may—according to this theory—increase one's vulnerability to IPV victimization.

That said, while ample evidence points to abusers utilizing transgender survivors' identities as a locus of control, it is less clear whether this fact can help explain why T-IPV happens in the first place. More specifically, qualitative research is still needed to examine whether some abusers select transgender partners as well as initiate abuse with those partners in part because abusers perceive transgender people to be more readily controlled.

Implications of T-IPV Theories

The movement to address IPV operates at multiple levels, not only in terms of prevention but also in terms of survivor treatment and the reduction of abuser recidivism. At each level, a clear understanding of why abuse occurs can be instrumental in reducing the prevalence and toll of IPV. If this understanding is based solely on C-IPV research, serious concerns emerge as to whether the resulting IPV prevention and intervention models will be inadequate for addressing T-IPV. Thus, a key question posed by this chapter is whether the causes of T-IPV and C-IPV dovetail or diverge.

Although research on the causes of T-IPV remains comparatively scarce, the preliminary answer to this question appears to be "both." On the one hand, T-IPV and C-IPV appear to share a number of causal pathways, including abusers using rationalizations to neutralize potential guilt, survivors being socialized into IPV-condoning attitudes via exposure to childhood and family violence, and a number of factors that increase vulnerability to abuse, such as being an undocumented immigrant or having ever engaged in sex work. On the other hand, T-IPV also appears to occur in part due to abusers and survivors either experiencing transphobic discrimination or internalizing transphobic attitudes, causal pathways that mark T-IPV as often distinct from C-IPV.

Thus, this review suggests that one-size-fits-all efforts to prevent and intervene in IPV may need to be retooled to account for the unique causes of T-IPV. This might involve prevention programs, batterer intervention programs, and survivor mental health treatment plans incorporating elements of basic anti-transphobia education. Anti-transphobia education may in turn help participants and clients identify the ways in which transphobia can be misused to excuse and mask abuse perpetrated either by or against transgender people. Efforts to prevent and intervene in T-IPV would also do well to highlight identity abuse tactics, whereby abusers leverage transphobic stigma as a means to maintaining control over transgender survivors. Helping survivors, abusers, and bystanders to demystify T-IPV's roots and to correctly label abuse as abuse is undoubtedly of vital importance to the efficacy of these efforts to address T-IPV.

Moreover, scholarship on covariates of T-IPV perpetration and victimization may have added utility particularly for victim service providers. In particular, although future verification of research findings is still needed, providers may consider using identification of known T-IPV covariates as possible red flags to trigger IPV screening protocols, and identification of T-IPV among clients in turn should be used to trigger screenings for and treatment of common T-IPV covariates. For example, as reviewed in this chapter, research finds that transgender people are at a significantly greater risk of IPV victimization if they have experienced bullying or sexual abuse during childhood, family violence at any point in life, anti-transgender hate crimes, or general discrimination.[61] Likewise, transgender people have been found to be at an elevated risk of IPV victimization if they have an HIV diagnosis, have a disability, have ever engaged in sex work, have ever been incarcerated, or are undocumented.[62] Service providers should be aware that many transgender individuals face interlocking systems of discrimination and polyvictimization, knowledge that can guide providers in both screening for IPV and addressing its deleterious covariates.

At the same time, much is still unknown about the roots of T-IPV, and so researchers must set their sights on these new avenues of inquiry. Key knowledge gaps highlighted in this chapter include the absence of research on whether T-IPV perpetration (not just victimization) is predicted by childhood and family violence, whether factors increasing victimization vulnerability are better understood as power differentials within a relationship dyad (rather than just as individual-level risk factors), the quantitative extent to which internalizing transphobic attitudes increases risk of perpetration and victimization, and direct exploration of many of the causal mechanisms in prominent theories rather than just the presumed proxies for those mechanisms (e.g., studying whether IPV perpetration is predicted by abusers' feelings of stress and disempowerment generated by transphobia, instead of just utilizing experiences of transphobia as predictors). In addition, several major theories from the C-IPV literature were not reviewed in this chapter due to the absence of corresponding T-IPV research on those theories (e.g., psychological traits and gender norm performance), an oversight in the literature that scholars must work to rectify in the coming years.

Finally, two previously discussed, major methodological adjustments are needed in the T-IPV literature that could substantially expand our collective understanding of the roots of T-IPV: an increased focus on abusers and an influx of longitudinal and retrospective qualitative studies. To the former point, this literature currently offers considerably more insights into theories and risk factors associated with victim vulnerabilities to abuse, in large part because the vast majority of T-IPV research continues to focus solely on victimization. Research on samples that incorporate T-IPV abusers is clearly needed, including both cisgender abusers of transgender intimate partners and transgender abusers of either cisgender or transgender intimate partners. For studies drawing subjects from general transgender populations rather than survivor-specific sampling sites, a simple remedy is to include not only victimization but also perpetration questions within questionnaires and interview protocols.

As for the second methodological recommendation, both longitudinal studies and retrospective qualitative studies are needed to help distinguish causes from outcomes. For instance, it is unclear from current quantitative, cross-sectional studies on transgender people[63] whether anti-transgender hate crime victimization primarily occurs prior to T-IPV victimization (perhaps because hate crime victimization may lower a transgender person's sense of self-worth and thus increase vulnerability to IPV), if instead IPV victimization primarily precedes anti-transgender hate crime victimization (perhaps with hate crime victimization in part precipitated by an abuser outing the victim), if both experiences perhaps are associated primarily because they co-occur with the same underlying factor (e.g., a greater degree of openness about being transgender may independently increase risk of IPV victimization and hate crime victimization), or if methodological limitations of studies have unintentionally double-counted the same experiences (e.g., a study participant may label their same personal experience as both T-IPV identity abuse and as a hate crime). Similarly, it is unclear from existing cross-sectional, quantitative research on transgender people[64] whether becoming HIV positive tends to precede T-IPV victimization (perhaps increasing their emotional and financial dependency and thus their appeal to potential future abusers), whether T-IPV victimization tends to precede becoming HIV positive (perhaps in part due to abusers forcing survivors to engage in unprotected sexual activities), or whether these experiences covary only because both are associated with the same underlying factor (e.g., a greater number of past intimate partners). Longitudinal studies as well as in-depth, retrospective qualitative research could be key in understanding the time order of these associations. These study designs can likewise be invaluable in testing existing theories and in introducing new theories of T-IPV.

Although many questions remain and additional research is needed, the literature indicates that the transphobia-infused roots of T-IPV are unique in numerous ways. As a consequence, serious doubts are cast on the common wisdom that all IPV is the same and should be treated as such. Indeed, this review raises a startling possibility: that many one-size-fits-all programs grounded in the C-IPV literature may be hindering their own efforts to prevent and treat the effects of T-IPV.

NOTES

1. De Grace and Clarke 2012; Whitaker et al. 2006.
2. Austin and Dankwort 1999; Babcock, Green, and Robie 2004.
3. Barner and Carney 2011.
4. Babcock, Green, and Robie 2004; De Grace and Clarke 2012; Stover, Meadows, and Kaufman 2009; Whitaker et al. 2006.
5. Messinger 2017.
6. See Messinger 2017.
7. See Messinger 2017.
8. Sykes and Matza 1957.
9. Hochstetler, Copes, and Williams 2010.
10. E.g., Scott and Straus 2007.
11. Goodmark 2013, 96.
12. Goodmark 2013.
13. Goodmark 2013.
14. munson and Cook-Daniels 2005, 8.
15. Brown 2007, 377.
16. Brown 2007, 375.
17. Perez-Darby 2011, 109.
18. Bandura 1977.
19. Anderson and Kras 2007.
20. For example, see Capaldi et al. 2012; Kitzmann et al. 2003.
21. Browne 2007; Flentje et al. 2016.
22. Grant et al. 2011; James et al. 2016.
23. White Hughto et al. 2017.
24. Parsons et al. 2018.
25. For example, see Capaldi et al. 2012; Erez, Adelman, and Gregory 2009; Wallace and Roberson 2016.
26. Brennan et al. 2012; Goldenberg, Jadwin-Cakmak, and Harper 2018; James et al. 2016. For IPV victimization prevalence estimates in a sample of transgender and gender nonconforming sex workers, see Nemoto, Bödeker, and Iwamoto 2011.
27. Goldenberg, Jadwin-Cakmak, and Harper 2018.
28. Cook-Daniels, 2017; Messinger and Roark, 2019.

29 James et al. 2016 found that transgender people of color reported higher rates of IPV victimization, but this trend did not appear in the research of Goldenberg, Jadwin-Cakmak, and Harper 2018 or Nemoto, Bödeker, and Iwamoto 2011.
30 James et al. 2016 found that transgender people who had experienced homelessness reported higher rates of IPV victimization, but this trend did not appear in the research of Goldenberg, Jadwin-Cakmak, and Harper 2018.
31 See Greenberg 2012; Messinger 2017.
32 James et al. 2016; Klein and Golub 2016.
33 Roch, Morton, and Ritchie 2010.
34 See Turell 2000. Importantly, the association was nonsignificant, although this may have been impacted by the small transgender subsample size ($n = 7$).
35 Goodmark 2013.
36 Turell 2000.
37 Movement Advancement Project 2018.
38 Cooper 2013.
39 Wallace and Roberson 2016.
40 Ipsos Public Affairs 2018.
41 Rogers 2017.
42 E.g., Cook-Daniels 2015.
43 Roch, Morton, and Ritchie 2010, 17.
44 Roch, Morton, and Ritchie 2010.
45 Shipherd et al. 2011, 60–61.
46 McKenry et al. 2006; Messinger 2017; Walker 2015.
47 Brooks 1981.
48 Agnew 1992.
49 Almeida et al. 1994; Balsam and Szymanski 2005; Coleman 1994; Messinger 2011, 2017.
50 E.g., Brown 2007.
51 Balsam and Szymanski 2005; Bartholomew et al. 2008; Edwards and Sylaska 2013; Finneran et al. 2012; Finneran and Stephenson 2014; Kelley et al. 2014; Mendoza 2011. (For exceptions finding perpetration to be unassociated with internalized homophobia, see Carvalho et al. 2011; Chong, Mak, and Kwong 2013; Milletich et al. 2014.)
52 Balsam and Szymanski 2005; Carvalho et al. 2011; Finneran and Stephenson 2014. (For one exception finding perpetration to be associated with experiencing *less* discrimination, see Mendoza 2011.)
53 Edwards and Sylaska 2013; Finneran et al. 2012; Kelley et al. 2014. (For several exceptions finding perpetration to either not be associated with degree of outness or to be associated with a higher degree of outness, see Balsam and Szymanski 2005; Bartholomew et al. 2008; Carvalho et al. 2011.)
54 Messinger 2017.
55 Brennan et al. 2012; Goldenberg, Jadwin-Cakmak, and Harper 2018; Shipherd et al. 2011; White Hughto et al. 2017.

56 Rogers 2017.
57 James et al., 2016; National Coalition of Anti-Violence Programs 2017; Roch, Morton, and Ritchie 2010; Scottish Transgender Alliance 2008; Woulfe and Goodman 2018.
58 Bornstein et al. 2006; Cook-Daniels 2015; FORGE 2013; Goodmark 2013; James et al. 2016; Roch, Morton, and Ritche 2010; Tesch and Bekerian 2015.
59 Amnesty International 2005; Goodmark 2013.
60 Shipherd et al. 2011.
61 Brennan et al. 2012; Goldenberg, Jadwin-Cakmak, and Harper 2018; White Hughto et al. 2017.
62 Brennan et al. 2012; Goldenberg, Jadwin-Cakmak, and Harper 2018; James et al. 2016.
63 Brennan et al. 2012; Goldenberg, Jadwin-Cakmak, and Harper 2018.
64 Brennan et al. 2012.

REFERENCES

Agnew, Robert. 1992. "Foundation for a General Strain Theory of Crime and Delinquency." *Criminology* 30 (1): 47–88.

Almeida, Rhea V., Rosemary Woods, Theresa Messineo, Roberto J. Font, and Chris Heer. 1994. "Violence in the Lives of the Racially and Sexually Different: A Public and Private Dilemma." *Journal of Feminist Family Therapy* 5 (3–4): 99–126.

Amnesty International. 2005. *Stonewalled: Police Abuse and Misconduct against Lesbian, Gay, Bisexual and Transgender People in the US*. London: Amnesty International. www.amnesty.org.

Anderson, James F., and Kimberly Kras. 2007. "Revisiting Albert Bandura's Social Learning Theory to Better Understand and Assist Victims of Intimate Personal Violence." *Women & Criminal Justice* 17 (1): 99–124.

Austin, Juliet B., and Juergen Dankwort. 1999. "Standards for Batterer Programs: A Review and Analysis." *Journal of Interpersonal Violence* 14 (2): 152–168.

Babcock, Julia C., Charles E. Green, and Chet Robie. 2004. "Does Batterers' Treatment work? A Meta-analytic Review of Domestic Violence Treatment." *Clinical Psychology Review* 23 (8): 1023–1053.

Balsam, Kimberly F., and Dawn M. Szymanski. 2005. "Relationship Quality and Domestic Violence in Women's Same-Sex Relationships: The Role of Minority Stress." *Psychology of Women Quarterly* 29 (3): 258–269.

Bandura, Albert. 1977. *Social Learning Theory*. Englewood Cliffs, NJ: Prentice Hall.

Barner, John R., and Michelle Mohr Carney. 2011. "Interventions for Intimate Partner Violence: A Historical Review." *Journal of Family Violence* 26 (3): 235–244.

Bartholomew, Kim, Katherine V. Regan, Doug Oram, and Monica A. White. 2008. "Correlates of Partner Abuse in Male Same-Sex Relationships." *Violence and Victims* 23 (3): 344–360.

Bornstein, Danica R., Jake Fawcett, Marianne Sullivan, Kirsten D. Senturia, and Sharyne Shiu-Thornton. 2006. "Understanding the Experiences of Lesbian,

Bisexual and Trans Survivors of Domestic Violence: A Qualitative Study." *Journal of Homosexuality* 51 (1): 159–181.

Brennan, Julia, Lisa M. Kuhns, Amy K. Johnson, Marvin Belzer, Erin C. Wilson, and Robert Garofalo. 2012. "Syndemic Theory and HIV-Related Risk among Young Transgender Women: The Role of Multiple, Co-occurring Health Problems and Social Marginalization." *American Journal of Public Health* 102 (9): 1751–1757.

Brooks, Virginia R. 1981. *Minority Stress and Lesbian Women*. Lexington, MA: Lexington Books.

Brown, Nicola. 2007. "Stories from Outside the Frame: Intimate Partner Abuse in Sexual-Minority Women's Relationships with Transsexual Men." *Feminism and Psychology* 17 (3): 373–393.

Browne, Kath. 2007. *Count Me in Too: LGBT Lives in Brighton & Hove: Initial Findings: Academic Report*. Brighton, England: Kath Brown and Spectrum. www.realadmin.co.uk.

Capaldi, Deborah M., Naomi B. Knoble, Joann Wu Shortt, and Hyoun K. Kim. 2012. "A Systematic Review of Risk Factors for Intimate Partner Violence." *Partner Abuse* 3 (2): 231–280.

Carvalho, Amana F., Robin J. Lewis, Valerian J. Derlega, Barbara A. Winstead, and Claudia Viggiano. 2011. "Internalized Sexual Minority Stressors and Same-Sex Intimate Partner Violence." *Journal of Family Violence* 26 (7): 501–509.

Chong, Eddie S. K., Winnie W. S. Mak, and Mabel M. F. Kwong. 2013. "Risk and Protective Factors of Same-Sex Intimate Partner Violence in Hong Kong." *Journal of Interpersonal Violence* 28 (7): 1476–1497.

Coleman, Vallerie E. 1994. "Lesbian Battering: The Relationship between Personality and the Perpetration of Violence." *Violence and Victims* 9 (2): 139–152.

Cook-Daniels, Loree. 2015. "Intimate Partner Violence in Transgender Couples: 'Power and Control' in a Specific Cultural Context." *Partner Abuse* 6 (1): 126–139.

Cook-Daniels, Loree. 2017. "Coping with Abuse inside the Family and out: LGBT and/or Male Victims of Elder Abuse." In *Elder Abuse: Research, Practice and Policy*, edited by XinQi Dong, 541–553. Cham, Switzerland: Springer.

Cooper, Leslie. 2013. *Protecting the Rights of Transgender Parents and Their Children: A Guide for Parents and Lawyers*. New York: American Civil Liberties Union, and Washington, DC: National Center for Transgender Equality. https://transequality.org.

De Grace, Alyssa, and Angela Clarke. 2012. "Promising Practices in the Prevention of Intimate Partner Violence among Adolescents." *Violence and Victims* 27 (6): 849–859.

Edwards, Katie M., and Kateryna M. Sylaska. 2013. "The Perpetration of Intimate Partner Violence among LGBTQ College Youth: The Role of Minority Stress." *Journal of Youth and Adolescence* 42 (11): 1721–1731.

Erez, Edna, Madelaine Adelman, and Carol Gregory. 2009. "Intersections of Immigration and Domestic Violence: Voices of Battered Immigrant Women." *Feminist Criminology* 4 (1): 32–56.

Finneran, Catherine, Anna Chard, Craig Sineath, Patrick Sullivan, and Rob Stepheneon. 2012. "Intimate Partner Violence and Social Pressure among Gay Men in Six Countries." *Western Journal of Emergency Medicine* 13 (3): 260–271.

Finneran, Catherine, and Rob Stephenson. 2014. "Intimate Partner Violence, Minority Stress, and Sexual Risk-Taking among US Men Who Have Sex with Men." *Journal of Homosexuality* 61 (2): 288–306.

Flentje, Annesa, Armando Leon, Adam Carrico, Debbie Zheng, and James Dilley. 2016. "Mental and Physical Health among Homeless Sexual and Gender Minorities in a Major Urban US City." *Journal of Urban Health* 93 (6): 997–1009.

FORGE. 2013. *Trans-Specific Power and Control Tactics*. Milwaukee, WI: FORGE. http://forge-forward.org.

Goldenberg, Tamar, Laura Jadwin-Cakmak, and Gary W. Harper. 2018. "Intimate Partner Violence among Transgender Youth: Associations with Intrapersonal and Structural Factors." *Violence and Gender* 5 (1): 19–25.

Goodmark, Leigh. 2013. "Transgender People, Intimate Partner Abuse, and the Legal System." *Harvard Civil Rights–Civil Liberties Law Review* 48 (1): 51–104.

Grant, Jaime M., Lisa A. Mottet, Justin Tanis, Jack Harrison, Jody L. Herman, and Mara Keisling. 2011. *Injustice at Every Turn: A Report of the National Transgender Discrimination Survey*. Washington, DC: National Center for Transgender Equality and National Gay and Lesbian Task Force. www.transequality.org.

Greenberg, Kae. 2012. "Still Hidden in the Closet: Trans Women and Domestic Violence." *Berkeley Journal of Gender, Law & Justice* 27 (2): 198–251.

Hochstetler, Andy, Heith Copes, and J. Patrick Williams. 2010. "'That's Not Who I Am:' How Offenders Commit Violent Acts and Reject Authentically Violent Selves." *Justice Quarterly* 27 (4): 492–516.

Ipsos Public Affairs. 2018. *Global Attitudes toward Transgender People*. New York: Ipsos Public Affairs. www.ipsos.com.

James, Sandy E., Jody. L. Herman, Susan Rankin, Mara Keisling, Lisa Mottet, and Ma'ayan Anafi. 2016. *The Report of the 2015 U.S. Transgender Survey*. Washington, DC: National Center for Transgender Equality. www.ustranssurvey.org.

Kelley, Michelle L., Robert J. Milletich, Robin J. Lewis, Barbara A. Winstead, Cathy L. Barraco, Miguel A. Padilla, and Courtney Lynn. 2014. "Predictors of Perpetration of Men's Same-Sex Partner Violence." *Violence and Victims* 29 (5): 784–796.

Keuroghlian, Alex S., Sari L. Reisner, Jaclyn M. White, and Roger D. Weiss. 2015. "Substance Use and Treatment of Substance Use Disorders in a Community Sample of Transgender Adults." *Drug and Alcohol Dependence* 152:139–146.

Kitzmann, Katherine M., Noni K. Gaylord, Aimee R. Holt, and Erin D. Kenny. 2003. "Child Witnesses to Domestic Violence: A Meta-analytic Review." *Journal of Consulting and Clinical Psychology* 71 (2): 339–352.

Klein, Augustus, and Sarit A. Golub. 2016. "Family Rejection as a Predictor of Suicide Attempts and Substance Misuse among Transgender and Gender Nonconforming Adults." *LGBT Health* 3 (3): 193–199.

McKenry, Patrick C., Julianne M. Serovich, Tina L. Mason, and Katie Mosack. 2006. "Perpetration of Gay and Lesbian Partner Violence: A Disempowerment Perspective." *Journal of Family Violence* 21 (4): 233–243.

Mendoza, Jesmen. 2011. "The Impact of Minority Stress on Gay Male Partner Abuse." In *Intimate Partner Violence in LGBTQ Lives*, edited by Janice L. Ristock, 169–181. New York: Routledge.

Messinger, Adam M. 2011. "Invisible Victims: Same-Sex IPV in the National Violence against Women Survey." *Journal of Interpersonal Violence* 26 (11): 2228–2243.

Messinger, Adam M. 2017. *LGBTQ Intimate Partner Violence: Lessons for Policy, Practice, and Research*. Oakland: University of California Press.

Messinger, Adam M., and Jennifer Roark. 2019. "Transgender Intimate Partner Violence and Aging." In *Transgender Health and Aging: Culturally Competent Care for Transgender Aging Patients*, edited by Magda Houlberg, 79–95. New York: Springer.

Milletich, Robert J., Leslie A. Gumienny, Michelle L. Kelley, and Gabrielle M. D'Lima. 2014. "Predictors of Women's Same-Sex Partner Violence Perpetration." *Journal of Family Violence* 29 (6): 653–664.

Movement Advancement Project. n.d. "Foster and Adoption laws." Accessed July 1, 2018. www.lgbtmap.org.

munson, michael, and Loree Cook-Daniels. 2005. *Transgender Sexual Violence Project: Final Review*. Milwaukee, WI: FORGE. https://web.archive.org/web/20061223190611/http://www.forge-forward.org:80/transviolence/docs/FINAL_narrative_implications.pdf.

National Coalition of Anti-Violence Programs. 2017. *Lesbian, Gay, Bisexual, Transgender, Queer and HIV-Affected Intimate Partner Violence, 2016*. New York: National Coalition of Anti-Violence Programs. http://avp.org.

Nemoto, Tooru, Birte Bödeker, and Mariko Iwamoto. 2011. "Social Support, Exposure to Violence and Transphobia, and Correlates of Depression among Male-to-Female Transgender Women with a History of Sex Work." *American Journal of Public Health* 101 (10): 1980–1988.

Parsons, Jeffrey T., Nadav Antebi-Gruszka, Brett M. Millar, Demetria Cain, and Sitaji Gurung. 2018. "Syndemic Conditions, HIV Transmission Risk Behavior, and Transactional Sex among Transgender Women." *AIDS and Behavior* 22 (7): 1–12.

Perez-Darby, Shannon. 2011. "The Secret Joy of Accountability: Self-Accountability as a Building Block for Change." In *The Revolution Starts at Home: Confronting Intimate Violence within Activist Communities*, edited by Ching-In Chen, Jai Dulani, and Leah Lakshmi Piepzna-Samarasinha, 100–113. Brooklyn, NY: South End Press.

Roch, Amy, James Morton, and Graham Ritchie. 2010. *Out of Sight, out of Mind? Transgender People's Experiences of Domestic Abuse*. Edinburgh: LGBT Youth Scotland and the Scottish Transgender Alliance. www.scottishtrans.org.

Rogers, Michaela. 2017. "Transphobic 'Honour'-Based Abuse: A Conceptual Tool." *Sociology* 51 (2): 225–240.

Scott, Katreena, and Murray Straus. 2007. "Denial, Minimization, Partner Blaming, and Intimate Aggression in Dating Partners." *Journal of Interpersonal Violence* 22 (7): 851–871.

Scottish Transgender Alliance. 2008. *Transgender Experiences in Scotland: Research Summary*. Edinburgh: Equality Network. www.scottishtrans.org.

Shipherd, Jillian C., Shira Maguen, W. Christopher Skidmore, and Sarah M. Abramovitz. 2011. "Potentially Traumatic Events in a Transgender Sample: Frequency and Associated Symptoms." *Traumatology* 17 (2): 56–67.

Stover, Carla Smith, Amy Lynn Meadows, and Joan Kaufman. 2009. "Interventions for Intimate Partner Violence: Review and Implications for Evidence-Based Practice." *Professional Psychology: Research and Practice* 40 (3): 223–233.

Sykes, Gresham M., and David Matza. 1957. "Techniques of Neutralization: A Theory of Delinquency." *American Sociological Review* 22 (6): 664–670.

Tesch, Brian Peter, and Debra A. Bekerian. 2015. "Hidden in the Margins: A Qualitative Examination of What Professionals in the Domestic Violence Field Know about Transgender Domestic Violence." *Journal of Gay and Lesbian Social Services* 27 (4): 391–411.

Turell, Susan C. 2000. "A Descriptive Analysis of Same-Sex Relationship Violence for a Diverse Sample." *Journal of Family Violence* 15 (3): 281–293.

Walker, Julia K. 2015. "Investigating Trans People's Vulnerabilities to Intimate Partner Violence/Abuse." *Partner Abuse* 6 (1): 107–125.

Wallace, Paul Harvey, and Cliff Roberson. 2016. *Family Violence: Legal, Medical, and Social Perspectives*, 8th ed. New York: Routledge.

Wathen, C. Nadine, Jennifer C. D. MacGregor, Masako Tanaka, and Barbara J. MacQuarrie. 2018. "The Impact of Intimate Partner Violence on the Health and Work of Gender and Sexual Minorities in Canada." *International Journal of Public Health* 63 (8): 945–955.

Whitaker, Daniel J., Shannon Morrison, Christine Lindquist, Stephanie R. Hawkins, Joyce A. O'Neil, Angela M. Nesius, Anita Mathew, and Le'Roy Reese. 2006. "A Critical Review of Interventions for the Primary Prevention of Perpetration of Partner Violence." *Aggression and Violent Behavior* 11 (2): 151–166.

White Hughto, Jaclyn M., John E. Pachankis, Tiara C. Willie, and Sari L. Reisner. 2017. "Victimization and Depressive Symptomology in Transgender Adults: The Mediating Role of Avoidant Coping." *Journal of Counseling Psychology* 64 (1): 41–51.

Woulfe, Julie M., and Lisa A. Goodman. 2018. "Identity Abuse as a Tactic of Violence in LGBTQ Communities: Initial Validation of the Identity Abuse Measure." *Journal of Interpersonal Violence*. https://doi.org/10.1177/0886260518760018.

6

The Intersections of Race and Immigration

XAVIER L. GUADALUPE-DIAZ AND CAROLYN M. WEST

In February 2017, Ms. González was living at a local intimate partner violence (IPV) victim shelter in southern Texas after fleeing from an abusive relationship that had been physically violent and threatening to her safety.[1] As a transgender undocumented immigrant, González sought the necessary legal protections that she was lawfully entitled to by filing for court-enforced protection.[2] During the court hearing, González requested and was granted a protective order against her alleged abuser. While still at the courthouse, Immigration Customs Enforcement (ICE) officers detained her after responding to a tip that she would be there seeking protection from IPV. She was transported to a holding facility after her arrest, potentially in violation of the Violence Against Women Act (VAWA), which since 2005 has protected undocumented survivors' information from being used by ICE to detain immigrants. Disturbingly, González's attorney had reason to believe that her abuser was the one who tipped off ICE officers.[3]

As exemplified by González's case, for transgender immigrants and transgender people of color (T-POC), common help-seeking resources for survivors of IPV, such as the police and the courts, can become potential sites for institutional abuse. In turn, fears of being discriminated against by victim service resources can become points of leverage by which abusers can exert control over survivors or—as when abusers tip off immigration law enforcement—exact revenge. Thus, while transgender intimate partner violence (T-IPV) is often presented by scholars and providers as a one-size-fits-all phenomenon—whereby all transgender survivors experience the same IPV tactics and barriers to escape—in reality, transgender survivors who are people of color, immigrants, and/or undocumented face a variety of unique IPV tactics and barriers to escape.

Notably, transgender immigrants and T-POC face a myriad of types of violence that contextualize the lived realities of IPV survivors. While transgender people experience higher rates of interpersonal violence when compared to their cisgender counterparts, T-POC report higher levels of interpersonal, institutional, and structural violence when compared to their white transgender counterparts.[4] Interpersonal violence refers to violence between individuals, and is subdivided into *family and intimate partner violence* and *community violence*. The former category includes child maltreatment, intimate partner violence, and elder abuse, while the latter is broken down into *acquaintance* and *stranger* violence that includes youth violence, assault by strangers, violence related to property crimes, and violence in workplaces and other institutions.[5] Within transgender communities, Black transgender women in particular are disproportionately affected by homicide.[6] Beyond high rates of interpersonal violence, T-POC report high frequencies of both structural and institutional violence when compared to their white transgender counterparts.[7] Institutional violence is committed within social organizations (e.g., violence committed by the police, the military, and the state); these forms of violence occur within or are perpetrated by actors within formal institutions.[8] Structural violence refers to violence that is built into the structure of society, reflecting societal power relationships, and is manifest most obviously in differences in life chances.[9] As this chapter examines, these non-IPV forms of interpersonal, structural, and institutional violence shape the experiences of T-IPV, by exacerbating the negative consequences of IPV and reducing the likelihood that transgender survivors will seek help from institutions in which they fear bias or additional violence.

The current chapter begins with an overview of the social construction of race and how intersectionality complicates how T-IPV is experienced. The proceeding section then highlights the prevalence and dynamics of abuse among transgender immigrants and T-POC, as well as how non-IPV violence (i.e., interpersonal, institutional, and structural violence) shapes these individuals' experiences of T-IPV. Finally, the chapter summarizes key barriers to help seeking that are distinct to transgender immigrant and T-POC survivors of IPV.

Social Construction and Racialization

To better understand T-IPV among racial minority and immigrant communities, it is important to first recognize the ways in which identities are socially constructed and racialized. As in many nations, the social and cultural backdrop in the United States has been characterized by centuries of systemic oppression against racial and ethnic minority groups, including Native Americans, Black and African American communities, Latinx communities, and Asian and Pacific Islander communities.[10] Given this history, this chapter treats the concept of race as a socially constructed category rooted in structured power and inequality. This means that race is understood as a categorization system in which meaning is attached to difference. Within that construction, race is utilized in the organization of society and functions to maintain power differentials between groups.[11]

Furthermore, this chapter examines immigration from a critical perspective that centers *racialization*, the process by which racial characteristics are ascribed to a group, as an aspect of how migration status and identity are constructed.[12] For example, while many immigrants identify as white (e.g., European, Scandinavian, etc.), the concept of "immigrant" is one that is highly racialized in American politics and society.[13] Racialization of immigrants is evident in the ways politicians and policies target particular groups by ascribing unfavorable characteristics to them. Recent examples of this include the maligning of asylum seekers from Latin America as potential "rapists" and "criminals" by political leaders.[14] Similarly, calls from then–presidential candidate Donald Trump to "shut down" Muslim refugees from entering the country by stoking fears of terrorism seek to erroneously ascribe violence as an innate characteristic of Muslims.[15]

Examining transgender identity in isolation fails to capture all of the ways in which race contextualizes transgender lives. Even the term *transgender* reflects a Western orientation toward gender that seeks to create a stable category of those who diverge from the only two culturally and systematically recognized genders. While other cultures recognize a third or multiple genders (both historically and currently), Western scholarship first focused on transgender people to explore the constructs of gender, the social self, the body, and society.[16] Subsequently, as gender and sexuality scholar Johanna Schmidt notes, "writing about trans peoples has shifted to focus less on the concept of transgender itself as a 'unit of analysis,' and more on the issues experienced by trans populations."[17]

Scholars have argued that transgender identity in and of itself should be further examined as a racialized process. In pushing toward a deeper understanding of Black and transgender identity, gender scholar C. Riley Snorton argued that "trans is more about a movement with no clear origin and no point of arrival, and 'blackness' signifies upon an enveloping environment and condition of possibility. Here, trans—in each of its permutations—finds expression and continuous circulation with blackness, and blackness is transected by embodied procedures that fall under the sign of gender."[18] That is to say that throughout history the construction of both race and gender have been falsely presented as immutable and largely independent characteristics—while, in fact, they have intersected through time to create distinct realities that are constantly in flux. Overall, transgender identity must be fully understood within a critical race paradigm to adequately frame issues relevant to violence of all kinds (interpersonal, institutional, and structural). Despite the increasing media representations of celebrity transgender women of color, such as author Janet Mock and actress Laverne Cox, transgender people more broadly face higher rates of violence when compared to their cisgender counterparts, and T-POC are subjected to many more different forms of violence.[19]

Throughout much of the literature on IPV, binary gender—namely, the identities and experiences of cisgender men and women—remains a focal point of analysis, often to the exclusion of equally relevant and intersecting identities. Conversely, *intersectionality theory* has been utilized in some IPV scholarship to illuminate the distinct realities of relationship abuse at the intersections of race, class, gender, sexuality, and other social identities. Intersectionality "provides a means of understanding the experiences of individuals within a context of hierarchal power relations," accounting for how interlocking systems of oppression complicate how identities are understood within social structures.[20] By challenging the choice of IPV scholars to center their focus on binary gender above all other intersecting identities (e.g., race, migration status, etc.), transgender people of color and immigrants have complicated the ways in which violence is experienced by accounting for the contexts of race, ethnicity, immigration, class, sexual orientation, and more. Especially relevant are the intersecting qualities of transphobia, cisnormativity, racism, and xenophobia. Racialized violence and economic vulnerability make T-POC and transgender immigrants distinctly susceptible to multiple forms of interpersonal abuses, including but not limited to IPV. While the demographic identities of abusers relative to survivors may make it possible for abusers to engage in a particular type of identity abuse, this is not always the outcome.

IPV Victimization Prevalence among Transgender Immigrants and T-POC

While obtaining generalizable data on transgender populations remains a challenge, the United States Transgender Survey (USTS) showed that transgender people of color—particularly American Indian, Middle Eastern, and multiracial individuals—and transgender people who were undocumented immigrants reported higher lifetime rates of physical and sexual IPV victimization (such as pushing or shoving, slapping, hitting, or forced sexual activity) as compared to other transgender individuals.[21] They also reported higher lifetime rates of intimate partner coercive control, including experiencing intimidation, emotional harm, and financial harm, having their abuser physically harm others who were important to the respondents, and experiencing controlling tactics related to their transgender status (e.g., being told that they were not a "real" woman or man, being threatened with having their transgender status revealed or outed, and being prevented from taking hormones).[22] (See table 6.1.) Below, IPV victimization prevalence rates are detailed more fully among transgender people of color and transgender immigrants.

African Americans / Black Americans

A study of transgender women with a history of sex work found that, among African Americans ($n = 235$), 43.5 percent had experienced physical IPV in their lifetimes, and 16.4 percent had experienced sexual IPV as an adult.[23] Similarly, data from a cross-sectional survey of transgender

TABLE 6.1. Interpersonal Violence Victimization Rates among
US Transgender Population

Violence Type	Tactic	Victimization Rates, by Race/Ethnicity			
		Black	Latinx	AIAN[1]	ANHPI[2]
Intimate Partner Violence (IPV)	Identity IPV[3] (lifetime)	29%	27%	48%	21%
	Physical or sexual IPV (lifetime)	44%	43%	61%	30%
	Any IPV[4] (lifetime)	56%	54%	73%	43%
Sexual Assault	Sexual assault (lifetime)	53%	48%	65%	41%
	Sexual assault (past year)	13%	13%	17%	11%
	Sexual assault among underground economy workers[5] (past year)	33%	28%	46%	34%
Violence in Family of Origin	Violence by immediate family member (lifetime)	12%	12%	20%	15%
	Experienced family rejection (lifetime)	47%	49%	60%	46%

Notes
[1] AIAN = American Indian and Alaska Native.
[2] ANHPI = Asian, Native Hawaiian, and Pacific Islander.
[3] Identity IPV refers to denigrating, denying, or manipulating aspects of the survivor's identity.
[4] Any IPV encompasses identity, psychological, physical, and/or sexual IPV.
[5] Underground economy refers to sex work, drug sales, and other criminalized activities.
USTS 2015 Survey (n = 27,715)
Sources: James, Brown, and Wilson 2017; James, Jackson, and Jim 2017; James and Magpantay 2017; James and Salcedo 2017.

and gender nonconforming youth from fourteen different cities in the US revealed that, among non-Latinx Black youth (n = 60), 45 percent reported that they had been slapped, punched, kicked, beaten up, or otherwise physically or sexually hurt by an intimate partner.[24] The USTS included the largest available sample of Black transgender individuals to date (n = 796). Overall, 56 percent of African American respondents had experienced some form of IPV, and 44 percent had experienced physical or sexual IPV in particular.[25] Of note, transgender Black men (62 percent) reported slightly higher rates of IPV victimization than transgender Black women (58 percent) and nonbinary Black people (49 percent).[26]

Latinx People

In a sample of transgender women with a history of sex work, among Latinx individuals (n = 110), 36.4 percent had experienced physical

IPV in their lifetimes, and 8 percent had experienced sexual IPV as an adult.[27] The USTS included the largest sample of Latinx transgender individuals to date ($n = 1,473$). Overall, 54 percent of Latinx respondents had experienced some type of IPV during their lifetime, and 43 percent had experienced physical or sexual IPV in particular. As with Black and African American respondents, Latinx transgender men reported the highest rates of IPV, followed by Latinx transgender women and nonbinary Latinx people (58 percent, 54 percent, and 51 percent, respectively).[28] Gender-specific IPV rates from the USTS have not yet been published for other racial and ethnic minority groups, or for immigrants.

American Indians and Alaska Natives

In the USTS, American Indian and Alaska Native respondents ($n = 319$) reported the highest rates of intimate partner abuse. Nearly three-quarters (73 percent) had experienced some form of IPV, and nearly two-thirds (61 percent) had specifically experienced physical or sexual IPV.[29]

Asian Americans, Native Hawaiians, and Pacific Islanders

In a sample of transgender women with a history of sex work, among the Asian/Pacific Islander subsample ($n = 110$), 30.8 percent had experienced physical IPV in their lifetimes, and 16.7 percent had experienced sexual IPV as an adult.[30] The USTS included the largest sample to date of transgender individuals who identified as Asian (including Asian Americans, South Asians, and Southeast Asians) or as Native Hawaiian/Pacific Islander ($n = 783$). Overall, 43 percent of Asians and 50 percent of Native Hawaiians/Pacific Islanders had experienced some form of IPV in their lifetime, and 29 percent of Asians and 44 percent of Native Hawaiians/Pacific Islanders specifically had experienced physical or sexual IPV.[31]

Undocumented Immigrants

An analysis of the USTS found that, among undocumented immigrant transgender respondents ($n = 46$), 68 percent reported experiencing some form of IPV in their lifetimes, with 59 percent specifically reporting physical or sexual IPV.[32]

Polyvictimization and IPV among Transgender People of Color and Immigrants

Evidence shows that T-POC experience higher rates of non-IPV violence when compared to both white transgender and white cisgender populations.[33] For instance, annual reports from the National Coalition of Anti-Violence Programs (NCAVP) regularly report that the majority of transgender homicide victims are people of color, recently referring to this finding as "continuing an alarming multiyear trend."[34] Some estimates report that 91 percent of the murders of transgender and gender nonconforming people between 1995 and 2005 were people of color, primarily transfeminine victims.[35] Recent findings using ICE data also revealed that lesbian, gay, bisexual, and transgender (LGBT) immigrant detainees were ninety-seven times more likely to be sexually assaulted than non-LGBT detainees. More specifically, while LGBT people only accounted for 0.1 percent of the sample, they represented 12 percent of sexual assault victims.[36]

As these examples and this section highlight, engrained legacies of *polyvictimization*—exposure to multiple forms of violence and discrimination, be it interpersonal, structural, or institutional—create distinct realities for T-POC survivors of IPV, individuals who are distinctly vulnerable to discrimination-infused violence, on the basis of not only gender identity but also race, ethnicity, nation of origin, and migrant status. Transgender people's gender identities, like any gender identity, are racialized and contextualized by structures of inequality that exacerbate many of the problems IPV survivors face. In this section, we review the often-overlapping forms of violence and discrimination that T-POC and transgender immigrants are routinely subjected to, and then we proceed to illustrate ways in which this polyvictimization can shape the experiences of transgender survivors.

Transgender Polyvictimization and Race

As illustrated by tables 6.2 and 6.3, T-POC experience alarming rates of institutional violence (i.e., verbal, physical, and sexual assaults committed by actors in law enforcement, educational systems, prisons, places of employment, and public accommodations) and structural violence

TABLE 6.2. Institutional Violence Victimization Rates among US Transgender Population

		Victimization Rates, by Race/Ethnicity			
Violence Type	Tactic	Black	Latinx	AIAN[1]	ANHPI[2]
Police/Law Enforcement	Verbally harassed by police[3,4] (past year)	22%	29%	29%	17%
	Physically attacked by police[3,4] (past year)	12%	5%	9%	4%
	Sexually assaulted by police[3,4] (past year)	6%	5%	5%	7%
Education System	Verbally harassed in school because of gender identity[3] (K–12)	51%	52%	69%	53%
	Physically attacked in school because of gender identity[3] (K–12)	28%	24%	49%	17%
	Sexually assaulted in school because of gender identity[3] (K–12)	19%	16%	22%	13%
Prison	Physically assaulted by prison/jail staff or inmates[4] (past year)	40%	18%	*[5]	*[5]
	Sexually assaulted by prison/jail staff or inmates[4] (past year)	29%	27%	*[5]	*[5]
Employment	Verbally harassed at work because transgender[4] (past year)	14%	14%	27%	12%
	Sexually assaulted at work because transgender[4] (past year)	2%	2%	2%	3%
Public Accommodations	Verbally harassed in public accommodations because transgender[3,4] (past year)	28%	23%	36%	27%
	Physically attacked in public accommodations because transgender[3,4] (past year)	2%	1%	2%	3%

Notes
[1] AIAN = American Indian and Alaska Native.
[2] ANHPI = Asian, Native Hawaiian, and Pacific Islander.
[3] Of those publicly perceived as transgender.
[4] Subsamples limited to those with interactions in the assessed environment (e.g., of those interacting with police, of those who were incarcerated, of those who were employed, of those who visited public accommodations) during the assessed time frame.
[5] No data.
USTS 2015 Survey (*n* = 27,715)
Source: James, Brown, and Wilson 2017; James, Jackson, and Jim 2017; James and Magpantay 2017; James and Salcedo 2017.

TABLE 6.3. Structural Violence Victimization Rates among
US Transgender Population

Violence Type	Tactic	Victimization Rates, by Race/Ethnicity			
		Black	Latinx	AIAN[1]	ANHPI[2]
Economic Marginalization	Living at or near poverty line (currently)	38%	43%	41%	32%
	Unemployed (currently)	20%	21%	23%	10%
	Experienced homelessness (lifetime)	42%	31%	57%	21%
	Experienced homelessness because transgender (past year)	22%	14%	21%	11%
Underground Economy Work	Worked in underground economy[3] (lifetime)	28%	22%	35%	41%
	Engaged in sex work (lifetime)	27%	20%	31%	17%

Notes
[1] AIAN = American Indian and Alaska Native.
[2] ANHPI = Asian, Native Hawaiian, and Pacific Islander.
[3] Underground economy refers to sex work, drug sales, and other criminalized activities.
USTS 2015 Survey (*n* = 27,715)
Source: James, Brown, and Wilson 2017; James, Jackson, and Jim 2017; James and Magpantay 2017; James and Salcedo 2017.

(i.e., harms caused by societal inequities, such as the physical and mental health consequences of economic marginalization and participation in underground economy work). Taken together with the aforementioned high rates of interpersonal violence (see table 6.1), T-POC frequently face intersecting injustices in their lives—which, in turn, foster increasing susceptibilities to IPV.

Systemically, T-POC are more likely to experience economic marginalization and residential segregation than their white counterparts.[37] Partly as a result of racist structural inequality, family rejection, community isolation, and discrimination, T-POC face higher rates of poverty and unemployment than white transgender people.[38] As one example, the National Center for Transgender Equality found that "African American and American Indian transgender people reported some of the worst outcomes regarding discrimination in obtaining a job, violence both in the streets and by law enforcement, accessing health care, and homelessness."[39] T-POC contend with compounding sources of discrimination at the intersections of racism and transphobia that may affect their access to stable employment and earnings potential.[40] For example, in a sample of transgender people living in Washington, DC, researchers found that 57 percent of transgender women of color respondents made below $10,000 a year.[41] This type of severe economic vulnerability heightens other risks such as rates of HIV/AIDS, homelessness, and engagement in high-risk employment such as sex work, which disproportionately affect T-POC and are found to increase IPV victimization risk.[42]

More specifically, researchers have found that transgender women of color are at particular risk for HIV and complications while also reporting serious barriers to health care.[43] Barriers to health care are exacerbated for T-POC, who contend with racist discrimination in health-care provision in addition to fewer resources and insurance coverage.[44] These health risks are especially concerning for T-POC, as research has found a correlation in transgender people between rates of HIV and rates of sexual coercion by intimate partners.[45]

Activists and scholars alike have also focused much attention to the aforementioned high rates of homicide of T-POC—in particular, the high homicide rates of transgender women of color.[46] Drawing on NCAVP transgender homicide data, research has found that transfeminine Black and Latina individuals are at significantly higher risk for homicide than cisfeminine counterparts.[47] In a report published by the Human Rights Campaign and the Trans People of Color Coalition, of the 102 transgender murders between 2013 and 2017, 86 percent of the victims were Black, Hispanic, or Native American.[48]

Transgender Polyvictimization and Immigration

Experiences of transgender immigrant IPV survivors, like that of Ms. González, must be understood in the broader political and social context of xenophobia. While González was likely not the first undocumented survivor of IPV detained by ICE, her story briefly broke on the national stage during a time of heightened xenophobia and a subsequent "crackdown" on immigration. At the time, just one month into a presidency that had been launched using racist vitriol maligning Mexican immigrants as "rapists" and "drug dealers," more attention was focused on the increasing overreach of immigration law enforcement.[49] For instance, recently ICE has been accused of altering evidence to pursue the arrest and detention of undocumented migrants who had not been charged with crimes.[50] In November 2018, the American Civil Liberties Union declared then–Attorney General Jeff Sessions to be the "worst attorney general in U.S. history," citing his extensive record of draconian policies on immigration, some of which they argued were unconstitutional.[51] Indeed, the intense racialization and criminalization of immigrants and of people of color have a long-standing history in the United States.[52] Despite a record-breaking number of deportations that took place under the Obama administration, presidential candidate Trump played to deeply entrenched fears of immigrants, particularly non-white groups, a strategy that has been politically successful throughout US history.[53]

Today, the US is facing a number of human rights violations at its border with Mexico, including escalating cruel immigration treatment such as the unnecessary separation of migrant children from their families, and earning widespread condemnation from the global community on these issues.[54] Beyond the US context, immigrants and refugees face heightened xenophobia globally. In 2016, the Pew Research Center found that Europeans report fears of crime and terrorism as increased numbers of refugees find asylum within European nations.[55] These fears persist despite the fact that comprehensive reviews of the research literature find that higher immigration rates—and higher rates of undocumented immigration—are generally associated with crime rate *decreases*.[56] In Germany, for example, a majority of citizens report fears of immigrant crime waves, yet overall official crime rates are actually at their lowest since 1992.[57] The global rise in nationalist movements can be partially attributed to this growth in migrant xenophobia.

For transgender people seeking to migrate to the US, this hostile climate has placed them at increased risk of institutional violence that can exacerbate existing problems they may be facing (e.g., fleeing from IPV, fear of violence in their native country, etc.). For example, Roxsana Hernandez, a thirty-three-year-old transgender woman, fled her native home of Honduras fearing she would be murdered after several experiences with transphobic violence. Then, when applying for asylum at the US border, she tragically died in ICE custody in what the Transgender Law Center stated was a preventable death.[58] An independent autopsy revealed that Ms. Hernandez had suffered physical abuse while in detention—a finding that echoes claims that transgender migrants in general are at heightened risk for abuse in detention center settings.[59]

For those migrants who are seeking asylum, histories of violence often follow them from their nation of origin to their new destinations. Increasingly restrictive asylum policies—such as those in the US[60]—are particularly worrisome as transgender migrants report frequent aggression, violence, harassment, and death threats from all sectors of society in their nations of origin.[61] Scholars find that transgender immigrants from Latin America are motivated to migrate in part for protection to freely express their gender in a transgender-inclusive society in the US, where they can seek greater economic opportunity.[62] Policy researchers note that, while some public policy is transgender-affirming in Latin American nations like Uruguay, Chile, and Argentina, none of them uniformly provide avenues for gender identity document changes, have laws that prohibit discrimination against transgender people, or provide ready access to gender-affirming surgeries.[63] For many T-POC immigrants already living in the US, daily life is characterized by grappling with residential segregation, higher rates of poverty, lowered economic mobility, violence, and homicide.[64]

Connecting Polyvictimization and T-IPV among People of Color and Immigrants

As reviewed above, T-POC and transgender immigrants face many forms of violence and discrimination—polyvictimization that in turn may exacerbate or foster higher rates of IPV, as well as narrow avenues of escape. Intersectional perspectives in IPV scholarship have helped to capture more of these realities by accounting for multiple identities within structures of inequality.[65] Thus, IPV among T-POC and transgender immigrants must be understood within this broader context of intersecting identities and forms of inequality.

In many instances, discrimination and marginalization drive risk of certain types of violence occurring not only at the hands of strangers and acquaintances but also by intimate partners. For instance, many perpetrators of transgender homicides are current or former intimate partners of their victims,⁶⁶ and research has found links between intimate partner homicide and economic marginalization (i.e., low socioeconomic status), inequality, and residential segregation.⁶⁷ Given that T-POC are disproportionately affected by these aforementioned factors related to intimate partner homicide, this may explain their unique risk to homicide overall. Structural violence like economic marginalization and residential segregation foster higher homicide rates in disadvantaged communities.⁶⁸ Perpetrators of transgender homicides are overwhelmingly cisgender men, many of whom live in the same general area as their victims.⁶⁹ Some cisgender men living alongside T-POC in structurally disadvantaged communities may turn to violent affirmations of masculinity to gain a sense of control in otherwise precarious conditions.⁷⁰

More broadly, because T-POC and transgender immigrants contend with interlocking problems of racism, xenophobia, and heightened economic vulnerability when compared to their white and native-born counterparts,⁷¹ this in turn may increase their dependence on abusers. This is in part because those who experience poverty and unemployment may be more reliant on intimate partners for financial support, health care, and housing, thereby emboldening abusers to initiate and escalate IPV. It is likely also the case that coping with the negative sequelae of IPV victimization (e.g., mental health issues, substance use, suicidality, etc.) is exacerbated by having to simultaneously cope with the fallout of prior polyvictimization.

Moreover, abusers may feel safer in engaging in IPV if they perceive their partners to be less likely to try to escape. Of course, transgender immigrants and T-POC who experience polyvictimization may already have sought help for other forms of non-IPV violence. If their efforts to seek help are met with discrimination and roadblocks, however, it is likely that this will suppress their efforts to reach out again for assistance should they subsequently experience IPV. Unfortunately, barriers to help are extensive for T-POC and transgender immigrants specifically because of the interlocking systems of oppression they too often face. Such challenges that T-POC and transgender immigrants face in seeking help with IPV victimization are explored in greater depth in the next section.

Help Seeking at the Intersections of Transgender Identity, Race, and Immigration

It is evident that experiences of IPV help seeking among both transgender immigrants and native-born transgender people of color are similarly complicated by racism and xenophobia. The formal help-seeking avenues and processes for survivors of IPV who are transgender, POC, and/or immigrants are characterized by several key barriers and challenges from the legal realm through the shelter services response. A recent review of the help-seeking barriers for lesbian, gay, bisexual, transgender, and queer (LGBTQ) survivors of IPV found three major themes: "a limited understanding of the problem of LGBTQ IPV, stigma, and systemic inequities."[72] While these barriers are evident for all LGBTQ survivors, T-POC and transgender immigrants face enhanced stigma and the compounding inequalities of transphobia, xenophobia, and racism. Similarly, transgender immigrants and T-POC may encounter elevated levels of discrimination in IPV victim services and shelters. Despite recent developments with the inclusion of transgender survivors in the 2013 reauthorization of VAWA, researchers, survivors, and advocates continue to find disparities in formal help responses. In the proceeding sections, we review potential problems transgender immigrants and T-POC face in accessing the criminal legal system and police, as well as problems faced in accessing victim services from shelters.

Criminal Legal System

Survivors looking for help from the criminal legal system typically seek immediate safety, forced separation, and/or protective orders, among other options. Help-seeking processes are complicated by both situational and structural factors across all social locations. Situationally, research on cisgender IPV shows that factors such as weapon presence and child witnesses may make survivors more likely to call the police.[73] Other situational factors, such as fear of retaliation and substance use on the part of the survivor, may reduce a survivor's likelihood of involving police.[74]

Fears of transphobia by police may further reduce the likelihood of transgender IPV survivors contacting the police. Consider that, in their sample of over 1,110 LGBTQ respondents, researchers Lisa Langenderfer-Magruder, Darren Whitfield, and Eugene Walls found that transgender people were significantly less likely to report IPV victimization to the police when compared with cisgender lesbian, gay, bisexual, and queer individuals.[75] For the LGBTQ community more broadly, fear of homophobic and cisnormative assumptions by police about victimization may prevent survivors from involving law enforcement voluntarily.[76] For transgender immigrants and T-POC survivors of IPV, histories of transphobic and racist policing permeate perceptions of and experiences with law enforcement. For instance, in one study, Laura, a Black transgender woman survivor of IPV,

> was asked why she felt calling the police was not an option when she was severely beaten. She replied, "I mean I was in mid transition . . . I am still a man on record and my ID and stuff and I'm black. I'm black in [southern state]. It's like first they're going to see I'm this black dude that got beat up by a white man, think that we're gay, then see that I'm trans and that I'm in mid transition and it would be a disaster having to explain all of that and you know the police have a certain way of looking at trans people."[77]

Studies utilizing cisgender samples consistently find that Black and Latinx populations report far more negative perceptions and experiences with law enforcement, which may influence lower crime reporting rates overall.[78]

Studies with cisgender samples find mixed evidence to suggest that perceptions of police are also both gendered and racialized. Importantly, scholars have found that Black cisgender women may be more likely to report IPV victimization to the police than their white counterparts.[79] However, of non-white cisgender women who report IPV to the police, their subsequent evaluations of police responses tend to be more negative, commonly reporting discrimination, racialization, and bias by law enforcement.[80] For those in same-gender relationships, gender-stereotyping and heterosexist biases among law enforcement result in fear of reporting as well as negative experiences.[81]

These studies illustrate that fear of discrimination by police is common among many different minority groups, not just transgender communities. For example, among lesbian, gay, and bisexual survivors of IPV, people of color, cisgender men, and those who have had previous police interventions in IPV cases report higher levels of discomfort in disclosing victimization to the police.[82] For transgender individuals who live at the intersections of multiple stigmatized identities—such as transgender people who are also lesbian, gay, bisexual, queer, and/or POC—fears of contacting the police may be further heightened.

Rigidly gendered perceptions of IPV present another potential problem for transgender immigrant and POC survivors of IPV. Cisnormative ideas of IPV may lead law enforcement to perceive more "masculine" partners as the abuser and more "feminine" partners as the victim.[83] These cisnormative factors intersect with race in a way that may make T-POC more suspicious or less credible to law enforcement. For example, in Laura's earlier quote, she contemplated how police would react to seeing "this black dude that got beat up by a white man," potentially fearing that she may not be treated as a victim.[84] As researcher Kylan Mattias de Vries stated in a study focused on T-POC, "Within the criminal justice system, certain social positions are more stigmatized than others. Individuals within the system rely on these institutional stereotypes to inform their interactions with those who occupy, or are attributed, that social position."[85]

In more policy-based analyses on cisgender IPV, researchers have found that pro-arrest policies influence the rates of arrest when comparing female same-gender couples, male same-gender couples, and male/female different-gender couples. Mandatory arrest policies increased the likelihood of arrest for cisgender female same-gender calls, while these policies had only a minor effect on arrests for cisgender male same-gender calls.[86] The study partially illustrated how mandatory arrest policies affect gendered disparities in arrest by noting a significant change in arresting behavior. Notably, transgender survivors of IPV may be particularly vulnerable to misgendering and revictimization by law enforcement. (See chapter 9 for more on police and T-IPV.) For T-POC, hostile police encounters may be even more common, considering the criminalization of transgender and POC populations.[87] Stereotypes of transgender people as criminal sex workers and drug users permeate police interactions with transgender communities.[88] More specifically, both transgender immigrants and T-POC are characteristically maligned with assumptions of criminality by a criminal legal system that often negates their potential victimizations. Pooja Gehi, an attorney and legal scholar who works with transgender migrant populations, stated that "for low-income transgender people of color . . . the consequences of this system are dire."[89] T-POC are distinctly susceptible to police misconduct, as their transgender status is further compounded by racial and economic inequalities.[90] Black and Latinx transgender women may be more likely than their white counterparts to live and work in heavily policed neighborhoods where they have come to expect both racist and transphobic interactions with law enforcement.[91]

For transgender immigrants, the criminal legal system presents additional challenges as an avenue of help and support. Beyond language and cultural competency issues, transgender immigrant survivors of IPV may feel like they are putting themselves at risk by seeking formal help from the criminal legal system. Disclosing criminal victimization requires formal investigations and participation from a complainant that may draw the attention of officials interested in policing migrant statuses. As previously mentioned, while VAWA offers some protections for immigrants seeking help from IPV from further scrutiny by immigration law enforcement, there have been documented cases in which these protections may have been violated. Transgender immigrants may have a more difficult time obtaining proper identity documentation that is affirming of their gender identity from their home countries and new host nations, which may make them feel that they are not properly able to seek legal recourse against abusers.[92]

Given the broader hostility against immigrants in the US and around the world, abusers of transgender migrants may exploit vulnerabilities and fear of persecution. Researchers Michael Runner, Mieko Yoshihama, and Steve Novick noted that abusers of both undocumented and documented immigrants often use the threat of deportation to silence survivors. As an effective control tactic, abusers can withhold legal information about their residency status and rights to prevent survivors from leaving.[93] Transgender immigrants fleeing severe violence in their countries of origin may be even more fearful of breaking up with abusers who are providing a variety of support in other ways.

Beyond fears of retaliation from the immigration system, transgender immigrant survivors of IPV may also feel heightened social isolation from the broader society. Perceptions of widespread anti-immigrant sentiment can be manipulated by abusers to cut survivors off from avenues of support. Psychologist Janice Ristock noted that, even in cases in which both partners are LGBTQ immigrants, "perpetrators can use this context to further threaten and control their partner while victims may feel that they must not betray their partners, or bring shame to their families, and therefore endure the abuse."[94] Increasing this isolation are the aforementioned restrictive asylum policies emerging in many parts of the world. For instance, in 2018, then–Attorney General Jeff Sessions signaled an end to protections for IPV survivors seeking asylum in the US, stating that "the asylum statute does not provide redress for all misfortune."[95]

Fear of scrutiny from the criminal legal system is further heightened by the well-known hostilities that transgender immigrants face in detention centers and prisons. A study found that one in eight transgender immigrant detainees were placed in solitary confinement, a much higher rate than their cisgender counterparts.[96] Transgender immigrants in detention centers reported higher levels of violence, sexual assault, rape, and harassment.[97] Legal scholar Laurel Anderson noted that, for immigrant transgender women detained in civil custody, "there is an inherent inconsistency between their legal status and their detention conditions. . . . Despite their identification as women, most transgender detainees are housed with men."[98] It would be unrealistic to expect transgender immigrants to voluntarily access the criminal legal system for protection while human rights violations continue to occur within that very structure. In another study, transgender immigrants and T-POC expressed fears of disclosing to police and echoed previous negative encounters, including an immigrant transgender woman who avoided any legal recourse for fear of "getting in trouble."[99]

Shelter Services

For T-POC and transgender immigrant survivors of IPV, IPV victim shelters may have little to offer in adequate services and safety provision. Historically framed toward the needs of white, native-born, cisgender women,[100] shelter programs have broadened their services to create more inclusive environments for people of color, immigrants, and LGBTQ individuals by providing services in multiple languages, creating spaces in their communities, and training staff.[101] However, transgender immigrants and T-POC continue to face a number of challenges when attempting to utilize shelter space and services.

In one study on T-IPV and help seeking, Anna, an immigrant transgender woman, reported on her experience trying to seek help from shelter services. She stated:

> [T]hey wanted to help but they made a big fuss about my trans status. I overheard the staff say "the other residents are going to be scared and the children are going to be scared and it's not going to be the environment that we want here" and then told me they didn't have a room for a single person. So they put me in another room that housed four women in 2 bunk beds and I had one bunk . . . I couldn't wait to get out, I mean the women were not violent to me but they were just not welcoming. . . . [T]hey'd stare at me and when we tried to do the first group counseling like, the women just stared at me or just whispered or something. Even the staff was a little off because I knew from the start they weren't even on the same page about having me there.[102]

On the surface, Anna's experience mirrors that of many transgender survivors who seek help from shelter services, in that she was faced with transphobic shelter staff, residents, and housing policies. However, Anna had to simultaneously contend with a host of additional challenges that, though not exclusive to the lives of people of color and immigrants, were likely exacerbated by xenophobia and racism: for instance, she reported being separated from her immigrant community, being discriminated against for employment, experiencing homelessness and coerced sex work, and being reluctant to seek help from law enforcement for fear of attracting legal scrutiny.[103] Such challenges, which T-POC and transgender immigrants are at a heightened risk of, can unfortunately impede their ability to gain access to and remain in IPV victim shelters. This is because some shelters will perceive the aforementioned challenges as red flags that a person is actually simply homeless and falsely presenting as a victim in order to gain free shelter. According to interviews with IPV shelter staff, some IPV shelters assume all "real" survivors actively seek out and obtain housing and employment, maintain a record free from arrests and criminal convictions, and are willing file a police report so as to seek an order of protection.[104] Failing to conform to these stereotypes of the "legitimate victim"—which may be more difficult for victims who are transgender, people of color, immigrants, or homeless—may result in a survivor being denied admission to or being evicted from an IPV shelter.

Transgender immigrant and T-POC communities are likely to face much higher rates of housing instability than their white and native-born counterparts, which may impact their need for IPV shelter space.[105] The compounding effects of racial residential segregation, transphobic discrimination in housing, and transgender-specific economic vulnerability create a unique need for transgender immigrant and T-POC survivors of IPV.[106] Just as scholars have noted the increased frequency of IPV experienced by Black women, especially those at the economic margins of society,[107] it is important to note the vulnerability of transgender immigrants and T-POC to violence, not only from their intimate partners but also from their families, friends, strangers, and the broader systems that they may interact with.

Studies find that T-POC report especially hostile environments at shelters, stemming from issues ranging from physical space to interpersonal biases from staff and guests.[108] Scholars have noted that racialized assumptions about violence in the lives of people of color influence the response that IPV survivors receive from shelter staff.[109] In the seminal work *Battle Cries: Intimate Partner Violence in the Lives of Black Women*, scholar Hillary Potter concludes that "it is critical that shelter personnel consider how battered Black women are stigmatized in society and how workers in the shelters may themselves accept these stereotypes."[110] Extending this point, shelter services and personnel should be acutely aware of how T-POC are also distinctly stigmatized not only in broader society but also in their own communities.

Shelter services should also consider the significance of transgender physical and mental health issues while acknowledging how these issues are further complicated by race.[111] Isolation may encourage some transgender survivors to stay in abusive relationships but, for T-POC, feelings of isolation may be intensified by widespread rejection in their communities.[112] The high rates of serious violence and homicide experienced by T-POC in their communities may further exacerbate feelings of isolation regardless of IPV victimization status.[113] Hostile living environments and rejection from family or friends may exacerbate the housing insecurities that characterize the lives of transgender immigrants and T-POC.

Conclusions

Overall, T-IPV must be examined within the broader context of race and immigration status. Racism and xenophobia characterize the multitude of risk factors that heighten susceptibility to multiple forms of violence among transgender people who are immigrants and/or people of color. The severe marginalization of both transgender immigrants and T-POC likely fuel higher rates of T-IPV and homicide. Contending with higher rates of housing instability, economic vulnerability, and health issues (e.g., higher rates of HIV/AIDS) worsen IPV situations and the help-seeking process.

Given the complicated history between communities of color and the criminal legal system, alternatives to safety and accountability should be considered. For example, while seeking legal protections such as police intervention or protective orders may be useful for some transgender survivors, transgender immigrants and T-POC may be less likely to pursue or benefit from these options. Some ideas for alternative interventions have been broadly considered under restorative justice frameworks. These include mediations and community conferencing that may or may not involve the criminal legal system. One goal of these alternatives could be to center a survivor's needs while simultaneously encouraging the offender to fully understand and communicate their violation to both the survivor and the entire community. In one example, scholar and activist Mimi Kim has proposed creative solutions to address violence that merge social justice with an anti-violence focus.[114] She cites a call from INCITE! that states: "It is critical that we develop responses to gender violence that do not depend on a sexist, racist, classist, and homophobic criminal justice system."[115] To accomplish this, Kim developed the organization Creative Interventions in Oakland, California, which centers the stories of violence that inform community-based responses to intimate partner and sexual violence. One overarching strategy is that those who are most impacted by violence (e.g., the community at large) have the strongest motivation and solutions for enforcing accountability, healing, and violence prevention. These practices may involve restorative practices that reflect the desires of both survivor and community for what accountability looks like.

IPV victim shelters and services need to be more physically accessible to transgender immigrants and T-POC communities while also extending resources that capture and address the complexities of violence in their lives. Ideally, IPV shelters that work with diverse populations should have accessible materials and resources in the languages of those they seek to serve. Many transgender immigrant survivors of IPV may also need legal assistance with navigating a wide range of citizenship statuses and the potential implications of moving forward with criminal legal recourses.

While shelter services often operate with limited resources and staff, the most comprehensive services would incorporate assistance with permanent housing, employment, and health-care access. Given the compounding inequalities that transgender immigrants and T-POC face, shelter services should be aware of the distinct prevalence of IPV within these populations and extend available space to accommodate their needs. Transgender immigrant and T-POC survivors of IPV may not only be fearing violence from former partners but may also fear greater risk of severe consequences like homelessness, health complications, and homicide.

NOTES

1 CBS News 2017.
2 US Citizenship and Immigration Services n.d.
3 Messinger 2017a; Transgender Law Center 2017.
4 James et al. 2016; Stotzer 2009.
5 Krug et al. 2002.
6 Dinno 2017.
7 Bith-Melander et al. 2010; Singh and McKleroy 2011.
8 Fitzgerald 2017.
9 Fitzgerald 2017.
10 Steinberg 2007.
11 Glenn 2000.
12 Murji and Solomos 2005.
13 Sáenz and Douglas 2015.
14 Jacobs 2018.

15 Johnson 2015.
16 Schmidt 2017.
17 Schmidt 2017, 2.
18 Snorton 2017, 2
19 Testa et al. 2012.
20 Josephson 2005, 86.
21 James et al. 2016.
22 James et al. 2016.
23 Nemoto, Bödeker, and Iwamoto 2011.
24 Goldenberg, Jadwin-Cakmak, and Harper 2018.
25 James et al. 2016.
26 James, Brown, and Wilson 2017.
27 Nemoto, Bödeker, and Iwamoto 2011.
28 James and Salcedo 2017.
29 James, Jackson, and Jim 2017.
30 Nemoto, Bödeker, and Iwamoto 2011.
31 James et al. 2016; James and Magpantay 2017.
32 James et al. 2016.
33 Dinno 2017; Waters 2017.
34 Waters 2017, 9.
35 Wilchins and Taylor 2006.
36 Gruberg 2018.
37 Bith-Melander et al. 2010, 207–220.
38 Bith-Melander et al. 2010, 207–220.
39 National Center for Transgender Equality 2005.
40 Xavier et al. 2005.
41 Edelman et al. 2015.
42 Testa, Jimenez, and Rankin 2014.
43 Kenagy and Bostwick 2005.
44 Xavier et al. 2005.
45 Heintz and Melendez 2006.
46 Waters 2017, 9.
47 Dinno 2017.
48 Lee 2017; Pitofsky 2018.
49 American Civil Liberties Union n.d.
50 Stern 2017.
51 American Civil Liberties Union 2018.
52 Wilson 1973.
53 Leonhardt and Philbrick 2018; Lopez, Gonzalez-Barrera, and Motel 2011.
54 UN News 2016, 2018.
55 Wike, Stokes, and Simmons 2016.
56 Light and Miller 2018; Light, Miller, and Kelly 2017; Ousey and Kubrin, 2018.
57 BBC News Reality Check Team 2018.

58 Sopelsa and Fitzsimon 2018.
59 Anderson 2010.
60 Benner and Dickerson 2018.
61 Chávez 2011.
62 Cerezo et al. 2014.
63 Taylor and Haider-Markel 2014.
64 Morales 2013.
65 Potter 2006; Sokoloff and Dupont 2005; West 2004.
66 Waters 2017.
67 Stöckl et al. 2013.
68 Field and Caetano 2004.
69 Kelley and Gruenewald 2015.
70 Rios 2011.
71 Singh and McKleroy 2011.
72 Calton, Cattaneo, and Gebhard 2016, 2.
73 Perez Trujillo and Ross 2008.
74 Durfee 2012.
75 Langenderfer-Magruder et al. 2016.
76 Wolf et al. 2003.
77 Guadalupe-Diaz and Jasinski 2017, 786.
78 Lai and Zhao 2010.
79 Kaukinen 2004; O'Campo et al. 2002; Pearlman et al. 2003.
80 Liang et al. 2005; Wolf et al. 2003.
81 Seelau and Seelau 2005.
82 Guadalupe-Diaz 2016.
83 Hassouneh and Glass 2008.
84 Guadalupe-Diaz and Jasinski 2017.
85 de Vries 2015, 18.
86 Pattavina et al. 2007.
87 Mogul, Ritchie, and Whitlock 2011.
88 Miles-Johnson 2016.
89 Gehi 2008, 318.
90 de Vries 2015.
91 Roberts 1998.
92 Gehi 2008.
93 Runner, Novick, and Yoshihama 2009.
94 Ristock and Timbang 2005.
95 Benner and Dickerson 2018.
96 Gruberg 2018.
97 Gruberg 2018.
98 Anderson 2010, 2.
99 Guadalupe-Diaz and Jasinski 2017
100 Few 2005.

101   Riggs et al. 2016.
102   Guadalupe-Diaz and Jasinski 2017, 787.
103   Guadalupe-Diaz and Jasinski 2017.
104   Messinger 2017b; VanNatta 2005.
105   Kattari et al. 2016.
106   Whitfield et al. 2014.
107   West 2014.
108   Guadalupe-Diaz and Jasinkski 2017.
109   Kasturirangan, Krishnan, and Riger 2004.
110   Potter 2008, 203
111   Xavier et al. 2005.
112   Guadalupe-Diaz and Jasinski 2017.
113   Teal 2015.
114   Kim 2018.
115   Creative Interventions 2012.

REFERENCES

Akers, Caroline, and Catherine Kaukinen. 2009. "The Police Reporting Behavior of Intimate Partner Violence Victims." *Journal of Family Violence* 24 (3): 159–171.

Allen, Kendra. 2018. "A Hidden Inequity: The Life Expectancy of Transgender Women of Color." *Consumer Health Foundation*, February 5, 2018. www.consumerhealthfdn.org.

American Civil Liberties Union. 2018. "Jeff Sessions Was the Worst Attorney General in Modern American History." *American Civil Liberties Union*. November 9, 2018. www.aclu.org.

American Civil Liberties Union. n.d. "ICE and Border Patrol Abuses." Accessed November 30, 2018. www.aclu.org.

Anderson, Laurel. 2010. "Punishing the Innocent: How the Classification of Male-to-Female Transgender Individuals in Immigration Detention Constitutes Illegal Punishment under the Fifth Amendment." *Berkeley Journal of Gender, Law & Justice* 25 (1): 1–31.

BBC News Reality Check Team. 2018. "Reality Check: Are Migrants Driving Crime in Germany?" *BBC News*, September 13, 2018. www.bbc.com.

Benner, Katie, and Caitlin Dickerson. 2018. "Sessions Says Domestic and Gang Violence Are Not Grounds for Asylum." *New York Times*, June 11, 2018. www.nytimes.com.

Bith-Melander, Pollie, Bhupendra Sheoran, Lina Sheth, Carlos Bermudez, Jennifer Drone, Woo Wood, and Kurt Schroeder. 2010. "Understanding Sociocultural and Psychological Factors Affecting Transgender People of Color in San Francisco." *Journal of the Association of Nurses in AIDS Care* 21 (3): 207–220.

Brown, Taylor N. T., and Jody L. Herman. 2015. *Intimate Partner Violence and Sexual Abuse among LGBT People: A Review of Existing Research*. Los Angeles: The Williams Institute, UCLA School of Law. https://williamsinstitute.law.ucla.edu.

Calton, Jenna M., Lauren Bennett Cattaneo, and Kris T. Gebhard. 2016. "Barriers to Help Seeking for Lesbian, Gay, Bisexual, Transgender, and Queer Survivors of Intimate Partner Violence." *Trauma, Violence, & Abuse* 17 (5): 585–600.

CBS News. 2017. "Undocumented Transgender Woman Filing Domestic Violence Claim Arrested at El Paso Courthouse by ICE, Official Says." *CBS News*, February 16, 2017. www.cbsnews.com.

Cerezo, Alison, Alejandro Morales, Danielle Quintero, and Stephanie Rothman. 2014. "Trans Migrations: Exploring Life at the Intersection of Transgender Identity and Immigration." *Psychology of Sexual Orientation and Gender Diversity* 1 (2): 170–180.

Chávez, Karma R. 2011. "Identifying the Needs of LGBTQ Immigrants and Refugees in Southern Arizona." *Journal of Homosexuality* 58 (2): 189–218.

Creative Interventions. 2012. *Creative Interventions Toolkit: A Practical Guide to Stop Interpersonal Violence*. Oakland, CA: Creative Interventions. www.creative-interventions.org.

de Vries, Kylan Mattias. 2015. "Transgender People of Color at the Center: Conceptualizing a New Intersectional Model." *Ethnicities* 15 (1): 3–27.

Dinno, Alexis. 2017. "Homicide Rates of Transgender Individuals in the United States: 2010–2014." *American Journal of Public Health* 107 (9): 1441–1447.

Durfee, Alesha. 2012. "Situational Ambiguity and Gendered Patterns of Arrest for Intimate Partner Violence." *Violence against Women* 18 (1): 64–84.

Edelman, Elijah A., Ruby Corado, Elena C. Lumby, Roberta H. Gills, Jona Elwell, Jason A. Terry, Jady Emperador Dyer. 2015. *Access Denied: Washington, DC Trans Needs Assessment Report*. Washington: DC Trans Coalition. https://dctranscoalition.wordpress.com.

Few, April L. 2005. "The Voices of Black and White Rural Battered Women in Domestic Violence Shelters." *Family Relations* 54 (4): 488–500.

Field, Craig A., and Raul Caetano. 2004. "Ethnic Differences in Intimate Partner Violence in the US General Population: The Role of Alcohol Use and Socioeconomic Status." *Trauma, Violence, & Abuse* 5 (4): 303–317.

Fitzgerald, Kathleen J. 2017. "Understanding Racialized Homophobic and Transphobic Violence." In *Violence Against Black Bodies*, edited by Sandra E. Weissinger Dwayne A. Mack, and Elwood Watson, pp. 65–82. New York: Routledge.

Gehi, Pooja. 2008. "Struggles from the Margins: Anti-immigrant Legislation and the Impact on Low-Income Transgender People of Color." *Women's Rights Law Reporter* 30:315–346.

Gjorgievska, Aleksandra, & Rothman, Lily. 2014. "Laverne Cox Is the First Transgender Person Nominated for an Emmy—She Explains Why That Matters." *Time*, July 10, 2014. http://time.com.

Glenn, Evelyn Nakano. 2000. "The Social Construction and Institutionalization of Gender and Race." In *Revisioning Gender*, edited by Myra Marx Ferree, Judith Lorber, and Beth B. Hess, 3–43. Walnut Creek, CA: Altamira Press.

Goldenberg, Tamar, Laura Jadwin-Cakmak, and Gary W. Harper. 2018. "Intimate Partner Violence among Transgender Youth: Associations with Intrapersonal and Structural Factors." *Violence and Gender* 5 (1): 19–25.

Goodmark, Leigh. 2013. Transgender People, Intimate Partner Abuse, and the Legal System. *Harvard Civil Rights–Civil Liberties Law Review*, 48 (1): 51–104.

Grindley, Lucas. 2015. State of the Union: These 3 Words Were Used for First Time Ever. *Advocate*, January 20, 2015. www.advocate.com.

Gruberg, Sharita. 2017. *How Police Entanglement with Immigration Enforcement Puts LGBTQ Lives at Risk*. Washington, DC: Center for American Progress. www.americanprogress.org.

Gruberg, Sharita. 2018. "ICE's Rejection of Its Own Rules Is Placing LGBT Immigrants at Severe Risk of Sexual Abuse." *Center for American Progress*, May 30, 2018. www.americanprogress.org.

Guadalupe-Diaz, Xavier. 2016. "Disclosure of Same-Sex Intimate Partner Violence to Police among Lesbians, Gays, and Bisexuals." *Social Currents* 3 (2): 160–171.

Guadalupe-Diaz, Xavier L., and Jana Jasinski. 2017. "'I Wasn't a Priority, I Wasn't a Victim': Challenges in Help Seeking for Transgender Survivors of Intimate Partner Violence." *Violence Against Women* 23 (6): 772–792.

Hassouneh, Dena, and Nancy Glass. 2008. "The Influence of Gender Role Stereotyping on Women's Experiences of Female Same-Sex Intimate Partner Violence." *Violence Against Women* 14 (3): 310–325.

Heintz, Adam Jackson, and Rita M. Melendez. 2006. "Intimate Partner Violence and HIV/STD Risk among Lesbian, Gay, Bisexual, and Transgender Individuals." *Journal of Interpersonal Violence* 21 (2): 193–208.

Henriques, Julian. 2003. "Social Psychology and the Politics of Racism." In *Changing the Subject: Psychology, Social Regulation and Subjectivity*, edited by Julian Henriques, Wendy Hollway, Cathy Urwin, Couze Venn, and Valerie Walkerdine, 76–105. New York: Routledge.

Jacobs, Ben. 2018. "Trump Defends Mexican Rapists Claim during Conspiracy-laden Speech." *Guardian*, April 5, 2018. www.theguardian.com.

James, Sandy E., Carter Brown, and Isaiah Wilson. 2017. *2015 U.S. Transgender Survey: Report on the Experiences of Black Respondents*. Washington, DC and Dallas, TX: National Center for Transgender Equality, Black Trans Advocacy, and National Black Justice Coalition. www.ustranssurvey.org.

James, Sandy E., Jody L. Herman, Sudan Rankin, Mara Keisling, Lisa Mottet, and Ma'ayan Anafi. 2016. *The Report of the 2015 U.S. Transgender Survey*. Washington, DC: National Center for Transgender Equality. www.ustranssurvey.org.

James, Sandy E., Trudie Jackson, and Mattee Jim. 2017. *2015 U.S. Transgender Survey: Report on the Experiences of American Indian and Alaska Native Respondents*. Washington, DC: National Center for Transgender Equality. www.ustranssurvey.org.

James, Sandy E., and Glenn Magpantay. 2017. *2015 U.S. Transgender Survey: Report on the Experiences of Asian, Native Hawaiian, and Pacific Islander Respondents*.

Washington, DC: National Center for Transgender Equality, and New York: National Queer Asian Pacific Islander Alliance. www.ustranssurvey.org.

James, Sandy E., and Bamby Salcedo. 2017 *2015 U.S. Transgender Survey: Report on the Experiences of Latino/a Respondents*. Washington, DC: National Center for Transgender Equality, and Los Angeles: TransLatin@ Coalition. www.ustranssurvey.org.

Johnson, Jenna. 2015. "Trump Calls for 'Total and Complete Shutdown of Muslims Entering the United States.'" *Washington Post*, December 7, 2015. www.washingtonpost.com.

Josephson, Jyl. 2005. "The Intersectionality of Domestic Violence and Welfare in the Lives of Poor Women." In *Domestic Violence at the Margins: Readings on Race, Class, Gender, and Culture*, edited by Natalie J. Sokoloff and Christina Pratt, 83–101. New Brunswick, NJ: Rutgers University Press.

Kasturirangan, Aarati, Sandhya Krishnan, and Stephanie Riger. 2004. "The Impact of Culture and Minority Status on Women's Experience of Domestic Violence." *Trauma, Violence, & Abuse* 5 (4): 318–332.

Kattari, Shanna K., Darren L. Whitfield, N. Eugene Walls, Lisa Langenderfer-Magruder, and Daniel Ramos. 2016. "Policing Gender through Housing and Employment Discrimination: Comparison of Discrimination Experiences of Transgender and Cisgender LGBQ Individuals." *Journal of the Society for Social Work and Research* 7 (3): 427–447.

Kaukinen, Catherine. 2004. "The Help-Seeking Strategies of Female Violent-Crime victims: The Direct and Conditional Effects of Race and the Victim-Offender Relationship." *Journal of Interpersonal Violence* 19 (9): 967–990.

Kelley, Kristin, and Jeff Gruenewald. 2015. "Accomplishing Masculinity through Anti-lesbian, Gay, Bisexual, and Transgender Homicide: A Comparative Case Study Approach." *Men and Masculinities* 18 (1): 3–29.

Kenagy, Gretchen P., and Wendy B. Bostwick. 2005. "Health and Social Service Needs of Transgender People in Chicago." *International Journal of Transgenderism* 8 (2–3): 57–66.

Kim, Mimi. 2006. "Alternative Interventions to Violence: Creative Interventions." *The International Journal of Narrative Therapy and Community Work* 4:45–52.

Kim, Mimi E. 2018. "From Carceral Feminism to Transformative Justice: Women-of-Color Feminism and Alternatives to Incarceration." *Journal of Ethnic & Cultural Diversity in Social Work* 27 (1): 1–15.

Krug, Etienne G., James A. Mercy, Linda L. Dahlberg, and Anthony B. Zwi. "The world report on violence and health." *Lancet* 360, no. 9339 (2002): 1083-1088.

Lai, Yung-Lien, and Jihong Solomon Zhao. 2010. "The Impact of Race/Ethnicity, Neighborhood Context, and Police/Citizen Interaction on Residents' Attitudes toward the Police." *Journal of Criminal Justice* 38 (4): 685–692.

Langenderfer-Magruder, Lisa, Darren L. Whitfield, N. Eugene Walls, Shanna K. Kattari, and Daniel Ramos. 2016. "Experiences of Intimate Partner Violence and Subsequent Police Reporting among Lesbian, Gay, Bisexual, Transgender, and Queer Adults in Colorado: Comparing Rates of Cisgender and Transgender Victimization." *Journal of Interpersonal Violence* 31 (5): 855–871.

Lee, Mark. 2017. *A Time to Act: Fatal Violence against Transgender People in America 2017*. Washington, DC: Human Rights Campaign and Trans People of Color Coalition. www.hrc.org.

Leonhardt, David, and Ian Prasad Philbrick. 2018. "Donald Trump's Racism: The Definitive List." *New York Times*, January 15, 2018. www.nytimes.com.

Lev, Arlene Istar, and Shannon Sennott. 2012. "Understanding Gender Nonconformity and Transgender Identity: A Sex-Positive Approach." In *New Directions in Sex Therapy: Innovations and Alternatives*, 2nd ed., edited by Peggy J. Kleinplatz, 321–336. New York: Taylor & Francis.

Liang, Belle, Lisa Goodman, Pratyusha Tummala-Narra, and Sarah Weintraub. 2005. "A Theoretical Framework for Understanding Help-Seeking Processes among Survivors of Intimate Partner Violence." *American Journal of Community Psychology* 36 (1–2): 71–84.

Light, Michael T., and Ty Miller. 2018. "Does Undocumented Immigration Increase Violence Crime?" *Criminology* 56 (2): 370–401.

Light, Michael T., Ty Miller, and Brian C. Kelly. 2017. "Undocumented Immigration, Drug Problems, and Driving under the Influence in the United States, 1990–2014." *American Journal of Public Health* 107 (9): 1448–1454.

Lopez, Mark Hugo, Ana Gonzalez-Barrera, and Seth Motel. 2011. *As Deportations Rise to Record Levels, Most Latinos Oppose Obama's Policy*. Washington, DC.: Pew Hispanic Center. www.pewhispanic.org.

Messinger, Adam M. 2017a. "The Isolation of Transgender, Undocumented Victims of Domestic Violence." *Huffington Post*, February 21, 2017. www.huffingtonpost.com.

Messinger, Adam M. 2017b. *LGBTQ Intimate Partner Violence: Lessons for Policy, Practice, and Research*. Oakland: University of California Press.

Miles-Johnson, Toby. 2016. "Policing Diversity: Examining Police Resistance to Training Reforms for Transgender People in Australia." *Journal of Homosexuality* 63 (1): 103–136.

Mock, Janet. 2014. *Redefining Realness: My Path to Womanhood, Identity, Love and So Much More*. New York: Atria.

Mock, Janet. 2017. *Surpassing Certainty: What My Twenties Taught Me*. New York: Atria.

Mogul, Joey L., Andrea J. Ritchie, and Kay Whitlock. 2011. *Queer (In)justice: The Criminalization of LGBT People in the United States*. Boston: Beacon Press.

Morales, Eduardo. 2013. "Latino Lesbian, Gay, Bisexual, and Transgender Immigrants in the United States." *Journal of LGBT Issues in Counseling* 7 (2): 172–184.

Murji, Karim, and John Solomos, eds. 2005. *Racialization: Studies in Theory and Practice*. Oxford: Oxford University Press on Demand.

National Center for Transgender Equality. n.d. "Racial & Economic Justice." Accessed November 30, 2018. https://transequality.org.

Nemoto, Tooru, Birte Bödeker, and Mariko Iwamoto. 2011. "Social Support, Exposure to Violence and Transphobia, and Correlates of Depression among Male-to-Female Transgender Women with a History of Sex Work." *American Journal of Public Health* 101 (10): 1980–1988.

O'Campo, Patricia, Karen McDonnell, Andrea Gielen, Jessica Burke, and Yi-hua Chen. 2002. "Surviving Physical and Sexual Abuse: What Helps Low-Income Women?" *Patient Education and Counseling* 46 (3): 205–212.

Ousey, Graham C., and Charis E. Kubrin. 2018. "Immigration and Crime: Assessing a Contentious Issue." *Annual Review of Criminology* 1:63–84.

Pattavina, April, David Hirschel, Eve Buzawa, Don Faggiani, and Helen Bentley. 2007. "A Comparison of the Police Response to Heterosexual versus Same-Sex Intimate Partner Violence." *Violence against Women* 13 (4): 374–394.

Pearlman, Deborah N., Sally Zierler, Annie Gjelsvik, and Wendy Verhoek-Oftedahl. 2003. "Neighborhood Environment, Racial Position, and Risk of Police-Reported Domestic Violence: A Contextual Analysis." *Public Health Reports* 118 (1) 44–58.

Perez Trujillo, Monica, and Stuart Ross. 2008. "Police Response to Domestic Violence: Making Decisions about Risk and Risk Management." *Journal of Interpersonal Violence* 23 (4): 454–473.

Pitofsky, Marina. 2018. "'Epidemic of Violence': 2018 Is Worst for Deadly Assaults against Transgender Americans." *USA Today*, September 28, 2018. www.usatoday.com.

Potter, Hillary. 2006. "An Argument for Black Feminist Criminology: Understanding African American Women's Experiences with Intimate Partner Abuse using an Integrated Approach." *Feminist Criminology* 1 (2): 106–124.

Potter, Hillary. 2008. *Battle Cries: Black Women and Intimate Partner Abuse*. New York: New York University Press.

Riggs, Damien W., Heather Fraser, Nik Taylor, Tania Signal, and Catherine Donovan. 2016. "Domestic Violence Service Providers' Capacity for Supporting Transgender Women: Findings from an Australian Workshop." *British Journal of Social Work* 46 (8): 2374–2392.

Rios, Victor M. 2011. *Punished: Policing the Lives of Black and Latino Boys*. New York: New York University Press.

Ristock, Janice, and Norma Timbang. 2005. "Relationship Violence in Lesbian/Gay/Bisexual/Transgender/Queer [LGBTQ] Communities: Moving beyond a Gender-Based Framework." *Violence against Women Online Resources*. https://vawnet.org.

Roberts, Dorothy E. 1998. "Race, Vagueness, and the Social Meaning of Order-Maintenance Policing." *Journal of Criminal Law & Criminology* 89 (3): 775–836.

Roch, Amy, James Morton, and Graham Ritchie. 2010. *Out of Sight, out of Mind? Transgender People's Experiences of Domestic Abuse*. LGBT Youth Scotland and the Scottish Transgender Alliance. www.scottishtrans.org.

Runner, Michael, Steve Novick, and Mieko Yoshihama. 2009. *Intimate Partner Violence in Immigrant and Refugee Communities: Challenges, Promising Practices and Recommendations*. Princeton, NJ: Robert Wood Johnson Foundation. www.futureswithoutviolence.org.

Sáenz, Rogelio, and Karen Manges Douglas. 2015. "A Call for the Racialization of Immigration Studies: On the Transition of Ethnic Immigrants to Racialized Immigrants." *Sociology of Race and Ethnicity* 1 (1): 166–180.

Schmidt, Johanna M. 2017. "Translating Transgender: Using Western Discourses to Understand Samoan fa'afāfine." *Sociology Compass* 11 (5). https://doi.org/10.1111/soc4.12485.

Seelau, Sheila M., and Eric P. Seelau. 2005. "Gender-Role Stereotypes and Perceptions of Heterosexual, Gay and Lesbian Domestic Violence." *Journal of Family Violence* 20 (6): 363–371.

Singh, Anneliese A., and Vel S. McKleroy. 2011. "'Just Getting Out of Bed Is a Revolutionary Act': The Resilience of Transgender People of Color Who Have Survived Traumatic Life Events." *Traumatology* 17 (2): 34–44.

Snorton, C. Riley. 2017. *Black on Both Sides: A Racial History of Trans Identity*. Minneapolis: University of Minnesota Press.

Sokoloff, Natalie J., and Ida Dupont. 2005. "Domestic Violence at the Intersections of Race, Class, and Gender: Challenges and Contributions to Understanding Violence against Marginalized Women in Diverse Communities." *Violence against Women* 11 (1): 38–64.

Sopelsa, Brooke, and Time Fitzsimon. 2018. "Trans Asylum-Seeker Who Died in ICE Custody Suffered 'Abuse,' Autopsy Finds." *NBC News*, November 28, 2018. www.nbcnews.com.

Steinberg, Stephen. 2007. *Race Relations: A Critique*. Palo Alto, CA: Stanford University Press.

Steinmetz, Katy. 2014, June 9. "America's Transition: Nearly a Year After the Supreme Court Legalized Same-Sex Marriage, Another Social Movement Is Poised to Challenge Deeply Held Cultural Beliefs." *Time*, June 9, 2014, 38–46.

Stern, Mark Joseph. 2017. "Is ICE Altering Evidence and Manipulating Facts in Its Immigration Crackdown?" *Slate*, February 17, 2017. https://slate.com.

Stöckl, Heidi, Karen Devries, Alexandra Rotstein, Naeemah Abrahams, Jacquelyn Campbell, Charlotte Watts, and Claudia Garcia Moreno. 2013. "The Global Prevalence of Intimate Partner Homicide: A Systematic Review." *Lancet* 382 (9895): 859–865.

Stotzer, Rebecca L. 2009. "Violence against Transgender People: A Review of United States Data." *Aggression and Violent Behavior* 14 (3): 170–179.

Taylor, Jami K., and Donald P. Haider-Markel, eds. 2014. *Transgender Rights and Politics: Groups, Issue Framing, and Policy Adoption*. Ann Arbor: University of Michigan Press.

Teal, Janae L. 2015. "'Black Trans Bodies Are under Attack': Gender Non-conforming Homicide Victims in the US 1995–2014." PhD diss., Humboldt State University.

Testa, Rylan J., Crystal L. Jimenez, and Susan Rankin. 2014. "Risk and Resilience during Transgender Identity Development: The Effects of Awareness and Engagement with Other Transgender People on Affect." *Journal of Gay & Lesbian Mental Health* 18 (1): 31–46.

Testa, Rylan J., Laura M. Sciacca, Florence Wang, Michael L. Hendricks, Peter Goldblum, Judith Bradford, and Bruce Bongar. 2012. "Effects of Violence on Transgender People." *Professional Psychology: Research and Practice* 43 (5): 452–459.

Transgender Law Center. 2017. "Undocumented Trans Woman and Survivor of Domestic Violence Arrested while Seeking Safety." *Transgender Law Center*, February 17, 2017. https://transgenderlawcenter.org.

UN News. 2016. "UN Experts Urge US to Address Legacies of the Past, Police Impunity and 'Crisis of Racial Injustice.'" *United Nations*, January 26, 2016. https://news.un.org.

UN News. 2018. "UN Rights Chief Slams 'Unconscionable' US Border Policy of Separating Migrant Children from Parents." *United Nations*. June 18, 2018. https://news.un.org.

US Citizenship and Immigration Services. n.d. "Information on the Legal Rights Available to Immigrant Victims of Domestic Violence in the United States and Facts about Immigrating on a Marriage-Based Visa Fact Sheet." Accessed December 6, 2018. www.uscis.gov.

VanNatta, Michelle. 2005. "Constructing the Battered Woman." *Feminist Studies* 31 (2): 416–443.

Veale, Jaimie, Elizabeth Saewyc, Hélène Frohard-Dourlent, Sarah Dobson, Beth Clark, and the Canadian Trans Youth Health Survey Research Group (2015). *Being Safe, Being Me: Results of the Canadian Trans Youth Health Survey*. Vancouver: Stigma and Resilience Among Vulnerable Youth Centre, School of Nursing, University of British Columbia. www.saravyc.ubc.ca.

Walker, Julia K. 2015. "Investigating Trans People's Vulnerabilities to Intimate Partner Violence/Abuse." *Partner Abuse* 6 (1): 107–125.

Waters, Emily. 2017. *Lesbian, Gay, Bisexual, Transgender, Queer, and HIV Affected Intimate Partner Violence in 2016*. New York: National Coalition of Anti-Violence Programs. http://avp.org.

West, Carolyn M. 2004. "Black Women and Intimate Partner Violence: New Directions for Research." *Journal of Interpersonal Violence* 19 (12): 1487–1493.

West, Carolyn. 2014. *Violence in the Lives of Black Women: Battered, Black, and Blue*. New York: Routledge.

Whitfield, Darren L., N. Eugene Walls, Lisa Langenderfer-Magruder, and Brad Clark. 2014. "Queer is the New Black? Not So Much: Racial Disparities in Anti-LGBTQ Discrimination." *Journal of Gay & Lesbian Social Services* 26 (4): 426–440.

Wike, Richard, Bruce Stokes, and Katie Simmons. 2016. *Europeans Fear Wave of Refugees Will Mean More Terrorism, Fewer Jobs*. Washington, DC: Pew Research Center. www.pewresearch.org.

Wilchins, Riki Anne, and Taneika Taylor. 2006. *50 under 30: Masculinity and the War on America's Youth—A Human Rights Report*. Washington, DC: Gender Public Advocacy Coalition.

Wilson, William J. 1973. *Power, Racism, and Privilege*. New York: Macmillan.

Wirtz, Andrea L., Tonia C. Poteat, Mannat Malik, and Nancy Glass. Forthcoming. "Gender-Based Violence against Transgender People in the United States: A call for Research and Programming." *Trauma, Violence & Abuse*.

Wolf, Marsha E., Uyen Ly, Margaret A. Hobart, and Mary A. Kernic. 2003. "Barriers to Seeking Police Help for Intimate Partner Violence." *Journal of Family Violence* 18 (2): 121–129.

Xavier, Jessica M., Marilyn Bobbin, Ben Singer, and Earline Budd. 2005. "A Needs Assessment of Transgendered People of Color Living in Washington, D.C." *International Journal of Transgenderism* 8 (2–3): 31–4.

PART III

Best Practices in Transgender IPV Service Provision and the Law

7

Providing Appropriate Health-Care Services to Transgender and Gender Nonconforming Survivors of IPV

SHANNA K. KATTARI, HÉCTOR TORRES,
KIM FOUNTAIN, AND ING SWENSON

Providing appropriate mental and medical health services to transgender survivors of intimate partner violence (IPV) is challenged by a lack of treatment models specific to such survivors. Without such models to guide providers, unique aspects of transgender IPV (T-IPV) are often overlooked, and services fail to address transphobic forms of violence. This in turn may potentially exacerbate victimization outcomes, such as through ineffective safety planning, incorrect shelter placement, or dangerous or inappropriate referrals. (See chapter 8 for more on shelters.) In hopes of addressing such gaps, this chapter suggests a model for implementing culturally appropriate services for transgender survivors within medical and mental health-care settings. Drawing on a review of the T-IPV literature and the authors' professional experiences working with this population, the model proposes three core elements: (1) ensuring access to services, (2) promoting broader provider competence, and (3) developing affirmative and culturally responsive services. Taken together, these constitute a model that accounts for the need to address the constellation of interconnected, systemic violence within the lives of transgender survivors of IPV.

Ensuring Access to Medical and Mental Health-Care Services

Transgender populations in general experience high rates of health problems such as depression, anxiety, and substance abuse, reflecting the extreme bias and oppression they face living in a society that too often does not affirm their existence.[1] Moreover, among this population, IPV survivors are at a further elevated risk of depressive symptomology, fear, substance use, HIV, and injury.[2] Thus, transgender survivors require, at the minimum, the same access to victimization-specific medical and mental health services as their cisgender counterparts.

As to whether that needed access to medical and mental health services has materialized, the news is mixed. On the one hand, the last fifteen years have seen improvements in access to health care for transgender survivors.[3] From a slowly growing number of providers and clinics serving transgender individuals to advances in insurance coverage and access,[4] transgender individuals are seeing health-care services beginning to open up to meet their needs. Similarly, a growing number of community-based organizations are training mental health professional students on providing services to transgender people, including but not limited to trainings conducted by the chapter authors and their colleagues in the field.

On the other hand, because advances have been incremental across the broader geographic landscape, access to care and services continues to be a significant challenge for transgender survivors, often leaving them with few options to turn to for assistance in coping with and leaving abusive relationships.[5] Although more research is needed to examine help-seeking patterns, available estimates indicate that 40 percent of transgender survivors seek help from a mental health professional and 21 percent seek help from a medical health professional.[6] While promising, these findings still suggest that the majority of transgender survivors do not disclose victimization to health-care providers.

There are a range of reasons transgender survivors might not seek help for their victimization that have little to do with the inclusivity and accessibility of a given resource, such as a lack of transportation, inability to get the time off from work, concerns related to their immigration status, and worry about leaving children or a pet unattended.[7] That said, two ongoing barriers to accessing health-care services are indeed generated by shortcomings or perceived shortcomings of health-care services themselves: fear of discrimination and concerns regarding identity documents.

Fear of Provider Discrimination

When deciding whether to access services, a transgender IPV survivor will weigh the potential for further risk and may decide that it is not worth the effort if the costs are higher than the benefits. Understanding why many transgender survivors do not disclose victimization to medical and mental health providers can be framed in part by survivors' concerns over the perceived likelihood of experiencing discrimination by providers. Such discrimination concerns may include survivors' lack of confidence in providers' competence or ability to meet their needs, lack of trust and concerns about confidentiality, and concerns about being harassed due to their identity.[8] Research finds that transgender individuals as a population often make the choice to delay or avoid care entirely due to fears about potential discrimination by providers.[9] For instance, an analysis of the US Transgender Survey found that in the past twelve months 23 percent of participants had chosen not to see a doctor when they needed to due to the fear of being mistreated.[10] Research suggests that, relative to mental health providers, medical health providers in particular may suffer from negative perceptions in transgender communities. According to a study of 92 transgender adults (not necessarily IPV survivors), transgender people are more than twice as likely to indicate that they are very or extremely willing to disclose potential future IPV victimization to mental health providers (65 percent) as compared to medical health providers (27 percent), and they are likewise more than twice as likely to presume that mental health providers are very or extremely helpful to IPV survivors (76 percent) as compared to medical health providers (29 percent).[11] Of course, because one of the first points of contact that transgender survivors have at medical and mental health services is with administrative staff, discrimination by staff and the office environment may serve to further exacerbate fears of potential discrimination by providers.[12]

Identity Document Concerns

Another barrier to disclosing IPV victimization to medical and mental health providers revolves around obtaining identification documents. In the US, gender-affirming surgery is required in order to obtain a gender marker change on a birth certificate in nineteen states and on a driver's license in twelve states, a requirement that can be both cost-prohibitive and undesired for many transgender individuals.[13] Perhaps not surprisingly, according to the US Transgender Survey, only 11 percent of transgender people have their correct name and gender listed on all identity documents and records. Moreover, analyses of this study also found that 17 percent of transgender people who requested a name or gender change from their insurance company were denied their request.[14] When a transgender survivor does not have insurance cards and identity documents that match their current name or gender expression, they may forgo accessing mental and physical health-care services when needed. From increasing their fear of being outed as transgender to fear of being accused of insurance fraud or identity theft for having mismatched documents, transgender survivors with outdated identity documents may feel that not accessing services is a better option. For some, this decision may be familiar, having had to make similar choices across their lifespan.[15] Thus, efforts to ensure transgender survivor access to health-care services must entail both decreasing fears of provider discrimination and decreasing barriers to obtaining updated identity documents.

Promoting Provider Competence for Serving Transgender Survivors

Training providers on how to work with transgender survivors of IPV is imperative. This is because, unfortunately, transgender survivors' fears with regards to health-care providers are often based not solely on presumptions about but also direct experiences with provider discrimination. Whether due to personal animus or a lack of basic knowledge about transgender lives and T-IPV, providers who lack cultural responsiveness in their work with transgender individuals may not know to screen for unique T-IPV tactics, may draw on stereotypes that result in excusing perpetrator behavior, or may express transphobic attitudes that deter future help seeking.[16]

Provider Discrimination in Admissions and Services

Transgender community members routinely experience multiple types of discrimination when accessing medical and mental health care, such as verbal harassment and, shockingly, even physical violence from the very people they look to for support.[17] Such discrimination—which may be exacerbated by the experience of IPV—can occur during both the service admissions process as well as during direct service provision.

To begin, discrimination during the admissions process—in the form of denial of service—is unfortunately a common experience among transgender people. Studies on transgender samples (not necessarily IPV survivors) have found that 20–23 percent of transgender people, at some point in their lives, have been denied access to health care due to their gender identity.[18] Moreover, a recent paper by scholars Shanna Kattari and Leslie Hasche reported that 26.7 percent of transgender people experience verbal harassment when trying to access health-care services.[19] Research also finds that 14 percent of transgender people experience multiple types of barriers due to their gender identity when attempting to access emergency medical care.[20]

In addition, many health-care professionals themselves have expressed transphobic attitudes with transgender patients and clients, whether through verbal or physical abuse. For instance, one study reported that 34 percent of lesbian, gay, bisexual, transgender, and queer (LGBTQ) physicians have witnessed transphobic discrimination in the workplace, and a full 65 percent reported having heard derogatory, transphobic comments made by medical providers.[21] Research suggests that 12 percent of transgender people have experienced verbal harassment in a mental health-care setting.[22] Also deeply concerning is that 1–2 percent of transgender people have experienced some type of physical violence in a mental or medical health-care setting.[23] Beyond reporting rates by discrimination type, several studies offer rates of general anti-transgender discrimination experienced in health-care settings. For instance, a recent analysis of the 2008–2009 National Transgender Discrimination Survey found that approximately a fourth (23.4 percent) of respondents had experienced some type of health-care discrimination.[24] Similarly, an analysis of the 2015 US Transgender Survey found that one-third (33 percent) of participants who had seen a health-care provider in the past twelve months had also had at least one negative experience with a health-care provider due to their gender identity.[25] Research also finds that transgender people are frequently provided unequal treatment at emergency departments (13 percent of transgender people), mental health centers (11 percent), rape crisis centers (5 percent), IPV victim shelters (6 percent), and with ambulances or emergency medical technicians (5 percent).[26]

Transgender individuals at the intersection of multiple stigmatized identities are particularly vulnerable to discriminatory practices in accessing medical and mental health services. For instance, transgender individuals with disabilities have been found to be at an elevated risk of experiencing discriminatory treatment in health-care settings, including mental health-care settings, IPV victim shelters, and rape crisis centers.[27] Relative to white transgender people, transgender people of color have also been found to be at an increased risk of discrimination in all three settings.[28] Particularly of note is that multiracial and Latinx transgender individuals are between two and six times more likely to experience discrimination in all three settings than white transgender individuals, and transgender American Indians are more than three times as likely to experience discrimination at IPV victim centers.[29] Thus it appears that the farther a transgender individual is from hegemonic norms, the more potential there is for experiencing higher rates of discrimination and greater obstacles to safety.

Provider Discrimination Under the Guise of Good Intentions

The root of discriminatory practices by some providers does not necessarily always originate in a deeply held animus toward transgender people. To the contrary, discrimination can also emerge when providers are well-intentioned. For example, research finds that some IPV victim service organizations may take an approach of "treating everyone equally," by providing both transgender and cisgender survivors of IPV with access to the same services.[30] While often perceived by providers to be egalitarian and inclusive, a one-size-fits-all approach to services in reality ignores the unique aspects of T-IPV, resulting in cisnormative services that may be less efficacious for transgender survivors. As noted by Derald Wing Sue in his work on microaggressions, this denial of difference is actually a denial of power and the benefits people reap from having such power.[31] In turn, this means that cisgender health-care providers may at times refuse to make their practices more transgender-inclusive out of a subconscious attempt to preserve cisgender privilege, while still claiming to be open and supportive. While there is little research on this specifically regarding providers, Bob Pease speaks to this complex experience of not realizing one's commitment to holding on to privilege and projecting an ideal of inclusiveness while simultaneously upholding systems of power.[32] Such approaches disregard the cultural and physical complexities of transgender medical and mental health needs and risk subjecting transgender survivors to greater harm.

In addition, mental health professionals who critique their transgender clients' identity—such as by perceiving it as a mental illness—may unintentionally imply that transgender people are not equipped to make decisions for themselves in general, which in turn can serve to further disempower transgender survivors. A reason some clinicians might view transgender people as having a mental disorder by default is that this was implied in prior editions of the American Psychiatric Association's *Diagnostic and Statistical Manual of Mental Disorders* (*DSM*)—a classification and diagnostic listing of mental disorders that is ubiquitously used by mental health clinicians in the United States.[33] Despite no longer pathologizing simply being transgender, the current edition of the manual (*DSM-5*) includes gender dysphoria, which refers to the significant distress that some individuals experience from being transgender.[34] The American Psychiatric Association made a position statement where it clarified that this diagnosis is intended in part to support the effectiveness of and need for gender-affirming treatment.[35] However, the *DSM-5*'s subtle shift to pathologizing stress from being transgender (i.e., gender dysphoria)—rather than pathologizing simply being transgender—may not be enough to undo the impact of decades of prior *DSM*s on public perception of transgender people. Indeed, 21 percent of the general population still believe that simply being transgender is a mental illness.[36] Moreover, even a gender dysphoria diagnosis arguably serves to continue pathologizing transgender individuals by misidentifying transgender people as the source of the problem rather than identifying the true source of stress, which is living in a transphobic society that often views and treats transgender people as subhuman. In recognition of some of these challenges, the World Health Organization has stopped categorizing gender identity disorder as a mental disorder.[37] This pinpoints a larger concern, which is that providers are often poorly trained to work with transgender individuals, in part because their educational foundation is based on theories that take the gender binary and heteronormativity as givens. Transphobia is written into science and medicine by maintaining the idea of a gender binary and by valuing scientific opinion over the lived experiences of transgender individuals.[38] The *DSM-5* is an example of a universal authority that has been criticized for presenting gender as a binary concept.[39] Until the *DSM* and foundational theories of behavioral health stop being cisnormative and assuming a gender binary, providers will have additional work to train themselves to be able to work with transgender individuals.

The Effects of Provider Discrimination

Not surprisingly, discrimination by health-care providers can have numerous deleterious effects. It should go without saying that discriminatory denial of services can be quite consequential—for instance, when transgender individuals are turned away from care in urgent and emergency situations, this can lead to an increase of adverse health conditions and, in extreme cases, even death.[40] Providers who understand IPV only through a cisnormative lens may also endanger T-IPV survivors by offering safety planning suggestions that lead to greater vulnerability (e.g., referring survivors to potentially transphobic victim resources, assuming that family members will be supportive, forgetting to remind survivors to pack hormone medications in emergency bags if applicable, etc.).[41] In addition, experiences of transphobic discrimination by medical and mental health-care practitioners are correlated with poor mental health outcomes.[42] For transgender survivors of IPV, an experience of discrimination by health-care providers could seriously add to their trauma. Moreover, when providers lack a basic knowledge of transgender experiences and T-IPV, transgender clients and patients often find themselves in the position of having to be their own advocates. As such, members of this community spend energy and time educating their health-care providers about transgender identities, transgender-specific care, and stigmatizing myths about transgender communities.[43] Thus, as the next section explores, culturally responsive care by providers is critically important when working with this often-marginalized population.[44]

Affirmative and Culturally Responsive Care

Given the costs borne by survivors who work with discriminatory providers, it is perhaps not surprising that empirical evidence points to the benefits of affirmative and culturally responsive care. Research has shown that having a transgender-inclusive primary care provider correlates with transgender individuals feeling comfortable with such providers, along with improved outcomes for transgender people such as lower rates of depression and suicidal ideation.[45] Indeed, the American Psychological Association (APA) has concluded that transgender people "are more likely to experience positive life outcomes when they receive social support or trans-affirmative care."[46] Relatedly, there is evidence that taking graduate courses that directly address how to work with transgender individuals has a positive impact on a clinician's competency and self-efficacy.[47]

Thus, providing culturally responsive care to transgender survivors is not only an ethical responsibility but also more efficacious than cisnormative and discriminatory care. To promote an affirmative and culturally responsive approach to mental and medical health care, this section discusses (1) the need for antidiscrimination and T-IPV knowledge training for providers, as well as approaches to transgender-inclusive (2) victim screening, (3) referrals, (4) core mental health services, and (5) provider organization culture.

Education (and Lack Thereof)

To ensure that medical and mental health-care service provision for transgender survivors is effective, standards of care should be evidence-based, drawing on the best available knowledge from the research literature and evaluation studies.[48] Service provision guidelines represent one potential source of information from which providers can learn best practices. However, much of the mainstream guidance for providers on how to address IPV is cisnormative.[49] Thankfully, a growing number of guidelines are addressing working with transgender clients and patients—if not necessarily specifically IPV-related—such as those published by the APA,[50] the World Professional Association for Transgender Health,[51] the Center of Excellence for Transgender Health,[52] and the Endocrine Society.[53] For T-IPV specifically, core guidelines are found in the APA's "Guidelines for Psychological Practice with Transgender and Gender Nonconforming People."[54] Practitioners can also refer to the US Department of Health and Human Services' "Family Violence Prevention and Services Programs Regulations."[55] Though not for particular disciplines, there are also guidelines for medical and mental health professionals working with transgender survivors, such as those found through the National Training and Technical Assistance Center on LGBTQ Cultural Competency.[56] For practitioners who seek out these guidelines, they will learn current best practices along with the importance of cultural responsiveness. Unfortunately, practitioners are not required to read these transgender-inclusive guidelines, resulting in lower adoption of the recommendations set forth in these publications.

Thus, a more practical, effective approach to provider education would be mandatory trainings—both anti-transphobia training and education on the unique nature of T-IPV.[57] Though there is the imperative for provider trainings, accessing such trainings can be a challenge. The lack of training appears to begin as early on as in graduate school, with many graduate programs in psychology, counseling, and social work not offering educational opportunities to learn about transgender lives. For instance, in 2009, the APA Task Force on Gender Identity and Gender Variance survey found that fewer than 30 percent of psychologists and psychology students are familiar with any transgender-specific clinical topics, potentially indicating that transgender issues are not being integrated into graduate school curriculum.[58] Even when graduate schools offer courses addressing transgender experiences or T-IPV in particular, such courses are generally not required in order to become a licensed behavioral health clinician.[59] This concern is not limited to the mental health field; medical schools face the same criticism.[60] For instance, according to a survey of 166 medical school students in the United Kingdom, only 8.4 percent agreed that they had received education about

LGBTQ health issues, and only 41.5 percent agreed that they would feel confident discussing IPV with an LGBTQ patient.[61]

Moreover, there are countless mental and medical health practitioners who have not previously been trained to develop the necessary skills to work with transgender survivors of IPV.[62] Among providers, accessing trainings that offer more than an introduction to transgender lives and cultural bias is difficult. Even less common are trainings that include a range of topics, from an assessment of cultural competence of a practice to advanced level learning, impact evaluations, continuing education, and ongoing technical assistance. These issues, coupled with the lack of training time for many medical and mental health practitioners as well as the tremendous number of competing training topics, further limits the likelihood of a transgender survivor finding a trained provider.

Clearly there exists a current gap in the knowledge and skills of many health-care providers regarding how to best serve transgender survivors. Training should begin early, starting in graduate school. It is necessary for medical schools, nursing programs, psychology programs, and other provider-oriented graduate programs to increase the amount of mandatory education they offer about this marginalized population, so that health-care providers are better prepared to engage and support transgender patients, including survivors of IPV.[63] In addition, mandatory provider trainings should be implemented in both mental and medical health settings. Building off prior LGBTQ IPV scholarship[64]—as well as the recent call by public health researchers Markie Blumer and colleagues for building providers' awareness, knowledge, and skills when working with transgender populations[65]—provider trainings can achieve multiple goals simultaneously: undermining commonly held myths that erroneously stigmatize transgender lives and transgender survivors, improving provider knowledge about T-IPV (e.g., its unique causes, tactics, and barriers to help seeking), and, ultimately, developing provider skills needed to better serve transgender survivors (e.g., transgender-inclusive screening, referral, and safety-planning techniques).

Screening

In addition to health-care provider trainings, there are many ways to create spaces, processes, and tools that are inclusive and supportive of transgender survivors of IPV. One such area ripe for transgender-inclusivity is IPV victim screenings, during which providers ask patients a series of questions to identify IPV survivors. Those screened positive as survivors can then be directed to appropriate care and referrals. Conducting screenings, intakes, or other forms of initial assessments is a common practice in the service provision world and usually completed at the onset of services. Physicians Kevin Ard and Harvey Makadon have several suggestions for how to engage in this screening process, including starting the process by asking the person if their partner has ever hit, kicked, threatened, or hurt them, or whether they feel safe at home, rather than utilizing stigmatized terminology such as "abuse" or "violence," which survivors may be hesitant to identify with.[66] They also suggest making sure patients are interviewed alone, regardless of the gender of the person who is with them. This is in part to ensure a confidential response and in part to reduce the risk of revictimization, should an abuser masquerade as a friend accompanying the survivor to services. Finally, educating all patients about IPV (regardless of gender, sexual orientation, or whether they screen positively for IPV) offers knowledge to a community that has an increased rate of IPV and also creates space for the patient to bring up issues of IPV later, should they occur.[67] For those who do screen positively as currently or previously experiencing abusive relationships, medical and mental health professionals should have referrals for T-IPV victim assistance providers. For mental health providers who have IPV training, they may also choose to work with the survivor on safety-planning measures.

Of course, when screenings fail to occur, T-IPV victimization among patients will remain invisible to health-care providers, in turn resulting in T-IPV survivors not receiving proper treatment and referrals. Therefore, an important first step toward implementing transgender-inclusive screening is training providers to know when to screen for T-IPV. Although universal screening for all new patients may be warranted in some health-care settings (e.g., mental health services referred by an IPV victim agency), warning flags are often utilized to more selectively trigger screenings. Warning flags can be physical signs or verbalized descriptions of the abuse itself—such as bruises in unusual locations coupled with ill-fitting patient explanations, or patient descriptions of a controlling partner.

In other instances, IPV warning flags may be patient characteristics and experiences that often co-occur with IPV victimization. For instance, mental and medical health-care providers may wish to screen for IPV victimization with transgender patients who have disclosed a disability, have HIV, have engaged in sex work, have been incarcerated, are undocumented immigrants, or have experienced child sexual abuse, family violence, or an anti-transgender hate crime—because each of these have been identified in research as risk factors for IPV victimization among transgender people.[68] Likewise, a position statement approved by the board of the American College of Preventative Medicine proposed that primary care, urgent care, and emergency medical department providers screen patients for IPV victimization if they have experienced any of the many physical health issues associated with IPV (e.g., asthma, chronic pain, gastrological issues, smoking, and substance use).[69] As many transgender people use urgent care or emergency departments as their primary form of health care (due to lack of insurance or fear of discrimination), these interactions may be the only opportunity medical providers have to screen these patients for IPV victimization.[70] Untrained providers may miss these potential indicators of IPV among their transgender patients. Thus, to ensure that screenings are appropriately triggered, health-care provider trainings would do well to incorporate education about common covariates and warning signs of T-IPV.

Once screenings are triggered, it is important that the questions and protocols used by providers to screen for IPV victimization are appropriate for T-IPV. Unfortunately, screening protocols are largely cisnormative and inadequate for use with transgender individuals, as they can render invisible or harm transgender individuals by not including issues specific to this population, such as being misgendered or misnamed or having transition-related clothing or medication withheld.[71] To date, there is not an IPV screening instrument that has been validated for transgender communities, despite the need for one, so extant screening measures that have been validated on largely cisgender samples are used.[72]

To implement T-IPV-specific screenings, three requirements should be incorporated: unique T-IPV tactics, transgender-inclusive language, and respect for transgender lives. First, T-IPV-specific screenings should include questions about unique T-IPV tactics. For example, research has shown that 11 percent of transgender individuals have at some point had a partner threaten to out their identity, 25 percent have had a partner verbally put them down by telling them they are not a "real" woman or man, and 7 percent have had a partner stop them from engaging in gender-affirming medical interventions.[73] Inclusion of such items in screening protocols can ultimately facilitate identifying a greater number of survivors and, for mental health-care providers in particular, can highlight unique traumatic experiences that should be addressed during treatment.

Second, transgender-inclusive language is also important, not only during screening but also throughout the service provision process (e.g., service advertising, treatment, referrals, etc.). Such inclusive language can signal that a provider respects transgender lives, thereby potentially increasing patient trust and willingness to disclose victimization.[74] Scholars note that using patients' self-identified names and pronouns—both by modeling the language used by patients and by directly asking patients about preferred terminology—can lead to more positive interactions.[75] In addition, there can be enormous fluidity in the structure and nature of transgender intimate relationships—ranging between monogamous, polyamorous, platonic, and other relationship types—and so providers must be cognizant of the possibility that survivors do not label their abusers as partners but rather as friends.[76] Therefore, cases that seem like peer victimization may still warrant being treated as potential IPV, with respect to the protocols and services administered. Relatedly, in part due to the pervasiveness of transphobia in households, transgender individuals may adopt a family of choice (consisting of friends and other social support systems). In turn, providers need to be cognizant that some transgender individuals use the term "family" to refer to chosen family and not their family of origin. Gendered terms like *boyfriend* and *girlfriend* also can be problematic for patients with nonbinary partners. Avoiding cisnormative expressions and using transgender-inclusive terminology is essential when working with transgender individuals because it will help in establishing a more trusting relationship with a transgender survivor, which in turn may lead to better medical and mental health outcomes.

Third, and lastly, a key to successfully implementing transgender-inclusive victim screenings—and, for that matter, successful transgender health-care provision more generally—is for providers to be respectful of transgender lives. Transgender individuals are often treated like phenomena rather than human beings—such as when some providers label them solely as "the transgender patient," an oddity rather than simply another patient deserving of equal care and respect.[77] Better care is given when providers focus on transgender patients as individuals to be treated, rather than using those interactions to ask questions about what it means to be transgender, what gender-affirming surgeries someone has had (when not medically relevant), or to show off how "fine" they are with having a transgender patient (e.g., making statements such as, "I have met transgender people before!").[78] Trainers who present on working with transgender survivors sometimes call this process "going sightseeing in someone else's life" and warn against it. Feeling tokenized, being viewed as a spectacle, or being questioned about their level of "trans-ness" can be harmful to patients.

For guidance on developing such transgender-inclusive screenings, health-care providers can consult nonprofit LGBTQ-focused anti-violence organizations such as the NW Network (nwnetwork.org), which hosts annual trainings on LGBTQ IPV screenings, the New York City Anti-Violence Project (avp.org), which produces annual reports on LGBTQ IPV and has been a primary contributor to developing methods and tools for working with LGBTQ IPV survivors, and FORGE (forge-forward.org), which has produced numerous tools for working with transgender survivors. (See chapter 12 for additional information on guidance and resources offered by FORGE.) Once implemented at institutions, transgender-inclusive screening questions and protocols should be reviewed periodically to keep in step with changing and evolving standards. For some settings, an alternative to help facilitate transgender individuals' access to services and provide appropriate IPV screening is to hire peer community health workers and health promoters. Community health workers can be individuals who represent the target population and have competence around working with such individuals. They can be trained to conduct screenings for T-IPV and to provide preventive, outreach, and rehabilitation services. As a result, these individuals can be a bridge that connects transgender individuals and necessary care. While the presence of health workers and health promoters specializing in T-IPV should not be viewed as absolving the rest of a given organization's staff from learning and using T-IPV-specific protocols and tools, they can greatly expand the work of medical and mental health services through greater integration into communities.

Referrals

IPV impacts an individual's life and health in many ways. The complexity of the experience calls for complex solutions. Therefore, providing survivors with relevant and appropriate referrals to other service types (e.g., victim shelters, substance abuse treatment, etc.) is essential to helping patients address needs related to the victimization but beyond the expertise of a given provider. When working with transgender IPV survivors, providers must be able to locate and offer transgender-affirming resources, both locally and online.[79] Furthermore, transgender survivors need help in accessing resources in a safe manner. Providers must be aware that survivors who search for information on or communicate about victim resources from their home or through personal technology can expose themselves to harm from perpetrators, given that perpetrators can track such searches by viewing web browser or phone histories.[80] Rather than a survivor risking retaliation by an abuser for having looked up IPV-related services, it would be better if the first service provider a survivor comes to can offer them a list of referrals, perhaps even facilitating the coordination of appointments. Some providers embed IPV referrals within lists of other types of referrals (e.g., lists of general referrals for food, housing, and transportation), making it easier for clients to safely keep such resources with them if needed. The use of multidisciplinary gender clinics (also known as transgender clinics, in which teams of health-care practitioners provide transgender primary health and medical services) and patient navigators (designated staff that help guide patients through the health-care system) can enhance referral coordination, advocacy for insurance coverage, and successful referrals.[81]

In addition to referring survivors to formal services, health-care providers may wish to consider connecting them with social support. Transgender individuals who receive social support regarding their gender identity and expression are more likely to have much improved quality of life and better outcomes across the board, including significantly ameliorating the negative behavioral health consequences related to experiencing victimization.[82] Providers may consider asking whether survivors feel comfortable seeking support from their families. This can often be difficult for IPV survivors, in part because many abusers isolate their partners from such family connections. Moreover, due to the pervasiveness of transphobia in society, many transgender survivors will not view their families of origin as an accepting and reliable source of help. As such, some transgender individuals develop a supportive family of choice comprised of peers and other nonrelatives. Perhaps this is why one study found that transgender survivors of IPV are over twice as likely to seek help from a friend (77 percent of transgender survivors disclosed to a friend) as compared to family (30 percent).[83] Peers can and do play an important role in helping transgender survivors deal with the aftermath of abuse. To help strengthen the safety net of survivors, providers can encourage transgender survivors to reconnect with and disclose victimization to trustworthy friends who they may have been previously cut off from due to their batterer's isolation tactics. Relatedly, transgender peer support groups offer a shared space in which to work though trauma related to IPV, ultimately helping individuals cope with the effects of abuse and stigma while building resiliency.[84] While individual practices, clinics, or hospitals may not be large enough to support or sustain groups specifically for transgender survivors of IPV, it is worthwhile to connect with other providers who do offer such groups. Similarly, many areas may have resources like this connected to local colleges and universities, or independent anti-violence groups.

Finally, in instances when a given health-care provider has not yet been sufficiently trained to serve transgender survivors, it may be appropriate for providers to consider referring a patient to another health-care provider with greater expertise. Providers should disclose their level of experience working with and knowledge of transgender communities to their transgender clients, consult with other professionals who have experience with transgender individuals, and refer out when they do not feel they have the skill set needed. However, based on the ethical duty of not harming patients, providers should do as much as possible to prepare themselves to be able to work with transgender clients in order to improve continuity of care among the range of accessible resources.

Core Mental Health Services

In addition to tailoring trainings, screening, and referrals, mental health-care providers in particular need to consider tailoring treatment modalities of their core services to better meet the needs of transgender survivors. Beyond meeting the immediate mental health needs commonly associated with IPV victimization, mental health providers can help transgender survivors to address the harms of structural stigma and its negative impact on resilience to trauma. More specifically, based on the literature and the authors' own clinical experience, appropriate mental health care for transgender survivors must intentionally integrate the following core elements: a multisystem framework, a strengths-based and affirmative approach, a trauma-informed approach, and client-centered care.

MULTISYSTEM FRAMEWORK

Appropriately addressing T-IPV through mental health treatment requires that providers employ a multisystem framework, which entails recognizing and addressing the influences of discrimination that transgender patients experience at multiple levels. Social system biases such as stigma, laws and policies, and institutions are part of many transgender individuals' day-to-day reality. Applying a minority stress model to transgender populations, scholars suggest that some transgender individuals experience chronic levels of stress caused by experienced and anticipated anti-transgender discrimination as well as the internalization of transphobic attitudes.[85] In turn, abusers may exploit the minority stress experienced by some transgender survivors in an effort to undermine their self-esteem—such as when some abusers tell survivors they are not "woman" or "man" enough—and to deter victim help seeking, such as by telling survivors that formal support resource systems will not validate a T-IPV survivor's experiences.[86] Because societal discrimination and minority stress can serve to empower abusers of transgender individuals, mental health providers could be valuable assets in helping transgender survivors to navigate not only the effects of abuse itself but also the multisystem discrimination that exacerbates abuse.

STRENGTHS-BASED AND AFFIRMATIVE APPROACH

Transgender survivors often feel a sense of disempowerment due to transphobia as well as IPV victimization.[87] One of the goals of mental health providers is to empower survivors and guide them to develop more effective coping mechanisms. Strengths-based and affirmative approaches can be useful to achieve this.

Simply stated, a strengths-based approach emphasizes clients' strengths. It poses a shift from stressing pathology to focusing on using clients' already existing strengths to reinforce their resiliency and resourcefulness.[88] Added to this, an affirmative approach emphasizes developing a strong therapeutic alliance with clients, whereby the therapist is mindful of societal stigma experienced by transgender clients, embraces transgender identities and relationships, and serves as an advocate for transgender people.[89] Consistent with the minority stress model, pride in one's gender identity is an important resilience factor that can help individuals address external oppressive factors.[90] An integration of both strengths-based and affirmative approaches would highlight how being transgender is a powerful identity, build on a person's specific assets and resiliency factors, and also help the person build supportive communities and connections. This allows for new narratives to form for the transgender person. A client's transgender status can be part of the individual context that informs case conceptualization and delivery of services, as would be the case with any other type of individual difference.[91]

TRAUMA-INFORMED APPROACH

The Substance Abuse and Mental Health Administration (SAMHSA) describes a trauma-informed approach as one in which a provider understands the impact of trauma and avenues for recovery, is able to identify the signs and symptoms of trauma, employs interventions informed by trauma knowledge, and actively avoids retraumatization of clients.[92] A trauma-informed approach is not a prescribed set of practices or a specific intervention but rather an approach that can be implemented by any type of service provider. To facilitate healing, this approach follows six well-known core principles: safety (i.e., assessing for immediate and future danger and establishing a comfortable environment for nonjudgmental exchanges), trustworthiness and transparency (i.e., earning trust through congruence, accuracy and consistency, and honesty), peer support (i.e., offering survivor groups for other transgender individuals with firsthand experience of trauma in order to help reduce feelings of isolation and increase connectivity), collaboration and mutuality (i.e., providing the opportunity for a collaborative relationship to be established so that clients can be more actively engaged in decision-making about their well-being), empowerment, voice, and choice (i.e., viewing clients as and encouraging clients to be resilient, as well as recognizing that client experiences are unique, which requires an individualized approach to care informed by the client), and cultural, historical, and gender issues (i.e., recognition of social and historical oppression and being culturally informed and responsive). Discussing these principles in detail would be beyond the scope of this chapter, but it is recommended that every practitioner who works with clients exposed to trauma should explore these six principles more in depth.[93]

A trauma-informed approach is essential in working with T-IPV survivors.[94] A central tenet of IPV is power and control, which may present on the interpersonal level as well as at the institutional and societal levels. Feeling out of control, survivors of trauma often begin to fear that they are damaged to the core and beyond redemption.[95] When providers acknowledge and attend to societal transphobia, this helps to establish a trusting relationship with clients who have experienced T-IPV, giving these survivors an opportunity to use their voice, to regain their sense of safety, and to be central in their own empowerment. In working with transgender people to maintain their sense of self-worth in a society that often devalues them and systematically denies them access to health care and mental health services, mental health providers can help transgender survivors to develop or strengthen the skills needed to maintain their own safety nets. This can help ensure that the tools perpetrators rely upon to establish and maintain power and control are less effective.

Trauma-informed care also necessitates that providers understand the impact of gatekeeping in furthering trauma. For transgender individuals interested in gender-affirming medical interventions, many may require letters of support from mental health-care providers to access hormone therapies and medical procedures covered by health insurers. Gatekeeping is the practice of mental health-care providers having the power to choose whether these transgender individuals are deserving of such a letter of support.[96] Instead of relying solely on the preferences of transgender clients, some providers practice gatekeeping by screening transgender individuals for "readiness for transition," which for some transgender clients means not receiving a letter of support.[97] Providers use the standards of care to deny support letters to those they deem not "transgender enough" and cite cases of those who have detransitioned as a result of moving too quickly. The authors have learned through their clinical experience that, because of the unique power that mental health providers hold over determining whether transgender people are able to receive gender-affirming medical interventions, transgender clients may feel pressured during therapy sessions to present their lives as stable and uncomplicated. A transgender person may decide to hide experiences of trauma, violence, or other challenging issues from their providers in order to get their needs met.[98] Consequently, transgender survivors of IPV may be less likely to receive needed services to address their experiences with abuse.[99]

CLIENT-CENTERED CARE

Client-centered care is grounded in the understanding that clients are human beings and, as such, have intrinsic potential for self-actualization. In an exploration of the potential of using client-centered interventions with lesbian, gay, bisexual, and transgender adolescents, Jim Lemoire and Charles Chen suggested that client-centered interventions can provide these individuals with a safe space and a therapeutic alliance, which facilitates self-exploration and self-understanding.[100] Such a safe space and therapeutic alliance are achievable through the use of the three core principles of client-centered interventions: (1) congruence (i.e., encouraging harmony and agreement between the concept of who the client wants to be and their behavior), (2) empathy (i.e., understanding and sharing a client's experience and related emotions), and (3) unconditional positive regard (i.e., accepting and supporting clients without conditions and regardless of what they do or say). Placing a transgender person in charge of their life and their treatment is necessary for supporting their empowerment and further self-determination.[101] In doing so, providers acknowledge that the client can make informed decisions about their life; this also strengthens the therapeutic alliance. This client-centered lens is crucial given that the medical model has historically stated that transgender people need permission from mental health providers to access certain types of medical treatment. Listening to individual clients, asking them probing questions to understand their needs and where they hope to be, and supporting them on their pathway—rather than relying on a predetermined idea of what all transgender people must want—allows a provider to offer the most effective support for their clients.

Transgender individuals face a tremendous constellation of systemic obstacles to living full, authentic, and safe lives. Such obstacles are put into place through interpersonal interactions, and the negative effects and messaging can be deeply internalized. These processes become part of the internal messaging that act as individual barriers to transgender people accessing services. Such barriers must be addressed if transgender people are going to begin trusting providers enough to seek the services and support they need.

Improving Organizational Culture

If transgender survivors are to receive assistance that attends to their full, authentic selves, barriers must be addressed throughout an organization or agency, from management to frontline staff. In doing so, medical and mental health providers will increase their ability to offer more transgender-friendly environments within their organizations.[102] Research suggests that it is important to consider starting further up the care pipeline by working to recruit, train, and retain transgender community members in roles such as peer educators, support staff, case managers, and, ultimately, mental and medical health providers.[103] When there are members of a community in positions of power (such as medical providers working with patients), they are able to not only advocate for inclusive practices but also model them for their peers.

Conclusion

Medical and mental health-care providers should work toward creating more equitable practices, interventions, and policies for transgender survivors of IPV. The range of relatively low-cost, simple strategies to improve the experiences of transgender survivors seeking care will ultimately also improve experiences for all survivors seeking care, given the emphasis on nuanced, culturally responsive care. Clinicians and physicians can demonstrate their willingness to strive for cultural competence by using gender-inclusive language, accessing information about and conducting research on best practices in supporting members of this population, and pursuing continual education regarding this topic. Moreover, organizations offering IPV survivor services should mandate education for their providers about T-IPV and working with this population. Relatedly, national organizations such as the APA, the American Medical Association, and other mental and medical health-care groups should ensure that their accredited graduate programs are adequately preparing future professionals to work with transgender individuals in all settings. In doing so, mental and medical health-care providers will demonstrate their competence in providing knowledgeable services, which in turn will help to establish trust. Through this trusting relationship, the transgender survivor will be more likely to share important information and to accept the guidance of the provider.

While it can be a delicate balance to make sure one is amplifying the voice of transgender IPV survivors rather than speaking over them or speaking for them, the more medical providers and mental health professionals work together to enact meaningful and effective change toward transgender inclusivity, the better health outcomes will be for their patients and clients across the board.

NOTES
1 Grant et al. 2011; James et al. 2016.
2 Brennan et al. 2012; Goldenberg, Jadwin-Cakmak, and Harper 2018; Keuroghlian et al. 2015; Parsons et al. 2018; Pitts et al. 2006; Roch, Morton, and Ritchie 2010.
3 Thompson, Karnik, and Garofalo 2016.
4 Thompson, Karnik, and Garofalo 2016.
5 Brown et al., 2016.
6 Kurdyla, Messinger, and Ramirez, 2019; Roch, Morton, and Ritchie 2010.
7 Collins et al. 2018.
8 Brown et al. 2016; Greenberg 2012.
9 Hughto, Reisner, and Pachankis 2015; One Colorado Education Fund 2015; Seelman et al. 2017.
10 James et al. 2016.

11 Kurdyla, Messinger, and Ramirez, 2019.
12 Redfern and Sinclair 2014.
13 Movement Advancement Project 2018.
14 James et al. 2016.
15 Shires and Jaffee 2015.
16 Harcourt 2013.
17 Grant et al. 2011; Institute of Medicine 2011; Jillison 2002; One Colorado Education Fund 2011.
18 Institute of Medicine 2011; Kenagy and Bostwick 2005.
19 Kattari and Hasche 2016.
20 Kenagy and Bostwick 2005.
21 Eliason, Dibble, and Robertson 2011.
22 Grant et al. 2011.
23 Grant et al. 2011; Kattari and Hasche 2016.
24 Kattari and Hasche 2016.
25 James et al. 2016.
26 Grant et al. 2011.
27 James et al. 2016; Kattari et al. 2017; Seelman et al. 2017.
28 James et al. 2016; Kattari et al. 2015; Kattari et al. 2017.
29 Kattari et al. 2017.
30 Hines and Douglas 2011; Renzetti 1996; Shelton 2018.
31 Sue 2010.
32 Pease 2013.
33 Kamens 2011.
34 American Psychological Association 2013.
35 Drescher, Haller, and the APA Caucus of Lesbian, Gay and Bisexual Psychiatrists 2012.
36 Bame 2017.
37 Haynes 2019.
38 Takahashi 2016.
39 Daley and Mulé 2014.
40 Jillison 2002.
41 Blumer, Ansara, and Watson 2013; FORGE 2013.
42 Riggs, Coleman, and Due 2014.
43 Keiswetter and Brotemarkle 2010; Poteat, German, and Kerrigan 2013; Xavier et al. 2005.
44 Allen-Meares 2007; Chettih 2012.
45 Kattari et al. 2016; Riggs, Coleman, and Due 2014.
46 APA 2015.
47 Bidell 2013.
48 Richmond, Burnes, and Carroll 2012; Thompson, Karnik, and Garofalo 2016.
49 Liang et al. 2005.
50 APA 2015.

51 Coleman et al. 2012.
52 Deutsch 2016.
53 Hembree et al. 2009.
54 APA 2015.
55 45 C.F.R. 1370 (2016).
56 Anti-Violence Project n.d.
57 Barrett and Sheridan 2017; Furman et al. 2017; Messinger 2017.
58 APA 2015; APA Task Force on Gender Identity and Gender Variance 2009.
59 Liang et al. 2005.
60 Obedin-Maliver et al. 2011.
61 Parameshwaran et al. 2017.
62 Barrett and Sheridan 2017; Ford et al. 2013; Makadon, Potter, and Goldhammer 2008.
63 Fallin-Bennett 2015.
64 E.g., Fountain et al. 2009; Haymes et al. 1999.
65 Blumer, Ansara, and Watson 2013.
66 Ard and Makadon 2011.
67 Ard and Makadon 2011.
68 Brennan et al. 2012; Goldenberg, Jadwin-Cakmak, and Harper 2018; James et al. 2016; White Hughto et al. 2017.
69 Phares et al. n.d.
70 Phares et al. n.d.
71 New York Anti-Violence Project 2017.
72 Goldenberg, Jadwin-Cakmak, and Harper 2018.
73 James et al. 2016; Roch, Morton, and Ritchie 2010. See Messinger 2017 for a review of unique T-IPV tactics.
74 Richmond, Burnes, and Carroll 2012.
75 Pitts et al. 2009.
76 Barrett and Sheridan 2017.
77 Ard and Makadon 2011.
78 Wagner et al. 2016.
79 Richmond, Burnes, and Carroll 2012.
80 Dragiewicz et al. 2018; Woodlock 2017.
81 Thompson, Karnik, and Garofalo 2016.
82 Barrett and Sherida 2017; Brill and Pepper 2008; Pinto, Melendez, and Spector 2008.
83 Kurdyla, Messinger, and Ramirez 2019.
84 White Hughto et al. 2015.
85 Messinger 2017; Meyer 2003.
86 See Messinger 2017.
87 Calton, Cattaneo, and Gebhard 2016.
88 Jones-Smith 2014; Singh and McKleroy 2011.
89 Yerke and DeFeo 2016.

90 Hendricks and Testa 2012.
91 Mattocks et al. 2014.
92 SAMHSA 2014.
93 For a review of these principles of a trauma-informed approach, see SAMHSA n.d.
94 Richmond, Burnes, and Carroll 2012.
95 van der Kolk 2015.
96 Budge 2015.
97 Benson 2013.
98 Ard and Makadon 2011.
99 Hendricks and Testa 2012.
100 Lemoire and Chen 2005.
101 Knutson and Koch 2018.
102 Leyva, Breshears, and Ringstad 2014.
103 Furman et al. 2017; Mansh, Garcia, and Lunn 2015.

REFERENCES

Allen-Meares, Paula. 2007. "Cultural Competence: An Ethical Requirement." *Journal of Ethnic & Cultural Diversity in Social Work* 16 (3–4): 83–92.

American Psychiatric Association. 2013. *Diagnostic and Statistical Manual of Mental Disorders, Fifth Edition (DSM-5)*. Arlington, VA: American Psychiatric Association.

American Psychological Association. 2015. "Guidelines for Psychological Practice with Transgender and Gender Nonconforming People." *American Psychologist* 70 (9): 832–864.

American Psychological Association's Task Force on Gender Identity and Gender Variance. 2009. *Report of the Task Force on Gender Identity and Gender Variance*. Washington, DC: American Psychological Association. www.apa.org.

Anti-Violence Project. n.d. "Training and Technical Assistance Center." Accessed November 30, 2018. https://avp.org.

Ard, Kevin L., and Harvey J. Makadon. 2011. "Addressing Intimate Partner Violence in Lesbian, Gay, Bisexual, and Transgender Patients." *Journal of General Internal Medicine* 26 (8): 930–933.

Bame, Yael. 2017. "21% of Americans Believe That Being Transgender Is a Mental Illness." *YouGov.com*, May 17, 2017. https://today.yougov.com.

Barrett, Betty Jo, and Daphne Vanessa Sheridan. 2017. "Partner Violence in Transgender Communities: What Helping Professionals Need to Know." *Journal of GLBT Family Studies* 13 (2): 137–162.

Benson, Kristen E. 2013. "Seeking Support: Transgender Client Experiences with Mental Health Services." *Journal of Feminist Family Therapy* 25 (1): 17–40.

Bidell, Markus P. 2013. "Addressing Disparities: The Impact of a Lesbian, Gay, Bisexual, and Transgender Graduate Counselling Course." *Counselling and Psychotherapy Research* 13 (4): 300–307.

Blumer, Markie L. C., Y. Gavriel Ansara, and Courtney M. Watson. 2013. "Cisgenderism in Family Therapy: How Everyday Clinical Practices Can Delegitimize People's Gender Self-Designations." *Journal of Family Psychotherapy* 24 (4): 267–285.

Brennan, Julia, Lisa M. Kuhns, Amy K. Johnson, Marvin Belzer, Erin C. Wilson, and Robert Garofalo. 2012. "Syndemic Theory and HIV-Related Risk among Young Transgender Women: The Role of Multiple, Co-occurring Health Problems and Social Marginalization." *American Journal of Public Health* 102 (9): 1751–1757.

Brill, Stephanie, and Rachel Pepper. 2008. *The Transgender Child: A Handbook for Families and Professionals*. New York: Simon and Schuster.

Brown, Adrienne, Simon M. Rice, Debra J. Rickwood, and Alexandra G. Parker. 2016. "Systematic Review of Barriers and Facilitators to Accessing and Engaging with Mental Health Care among At-Risk Young People." *Asia-Pacific Psychiatry* 8 (1): 3–22.

Budge, Stephanie. 2015. "Psychotherapists as Gatekeepers: An Evidence Based Case Study Highlighting the Role and Process of Letter Writing for Transgender Clients." *Psychotherapy* 52 (3): 287–297.

Calton, Jenna M., Lauren Bennett Cattaneo, and Kris T. Gebhard. 2016. "Barriers to Help Seeking for Lesbian, Gay, Bisexual, Transgender, and Queer Survivors of Intimate Partner Violence." *Trauma, Violence, & Abuse* 17 (5): 585–600.

Chettih, Mindy. 2012. "Turning the Lens Inward: Cultural Competence and Providers' Values in Health Care Decision Making." *Gerontologist* 52 (6): 739–747.

Coleman, Eli, Walter Bockting, Marsha Botzer, Peggy Cohen-Kettenis, Griet DeCuypere, Jamie Feldman, Lin Fraser et al. 2012. "Standards of Care for the Health of Transsexual, Transgender, and Gender-Nonconforming People, Version 7." *International Journal of Transgenderism* 13 (4): 165–232.

Collins, Elizabeth A., Anna M. Cody, Shelby Elaine McDonald, Nicole Nicotera, Frank R. Ascione, and James Herbert Williams. 2018. "A Template Analysis of Intimate Partner Violence Survivors' Experiences of Animal Maltreatment: Implications for Safety Planning and Intervention." *Violence against Women* 24 (4): 452–476.

Daley, Andrea, and Nick J. Mulé. 2014. "LGBTQs and the *DSM-5*: A Critical Queer Response." *Journal of Homosexuality* 61 (9): 1288–1312.

Deutsch, Madeline B., ed. 2016. *Guidelines for the Primary and Gender-Affirming Care of Transgender and Gender Nonbinary People*. San Francisco: Center of Excellence for Transgender Health, University of California, San Francisco.

Dragiewicz, Molly, Jean Burgess, Ariadna Matamoros-Fernández, Michael Salter, Nicolas P. Suzor, Delanie Woodlock, and Bridget Harris. 2018. "Technology Facilitated Coercive Control: Domestic Violence and the Competing Roles of Digital Media Platforms." *Feminist Media Studies* 18 (4): 609–625.

Drescher, Jack, Ellen Haller, and the American Psychiatric Association Caucus of Lesbian, Gay and Bisexual Psychiatrists. 2012. *Position Statement on Access to Care for Transgender and Gender Variant Individuals*. Washington, DC: American Psychiatric Association.

Eliason, Michele J., Suzanne L. Dibble, and Patricia A. Robertson. 2011. "Lesbian, Gay, Bisexual, and Transgender (LGBT) Physicians' Experiences in the Workplace." *Journal of Homosexuality* 58 (10): 1355–1371.

Fallin-Bennett, Keisa. 2015. "Implicit Bias against Sexual Minorities in Medicine: Cycles of Professional Influence and the Role of the Hidden Curriculum." *Academic Medicine* 90 (5): 549–552.

Ford, Chandra L., Terra Slavin, Karin L. Hilton, and Susan L. Holt. 2013. "Intimate Partner Violence Prevention Services and Resources in Los Angeles: Issues, Needs, and Challenges for Assisting Lesbian, Gay, Bisexual, and Transgender Clients." *Health Promotion Practice* 14 (6): 841–849.

FORGE. 2013. "Safety Planning with Transgender Clients FAQ." *FORGE*, January 2013. http://forge-forward.org/.

Fountain, Kim, Maryse Mitchell-Brody, Stephanie A. Jones, and Kaitlin Nichols. 2009. *Lesbian, Gay, Bisexual, Transgender and Queer Domestic Violence in the United States in 2008*. New York: National Coalition of Anti-Violence Programs. http://avp.org.

Furman, Ellis, Paula Barata, Ciann Wilson, and Tiyondah Fante-Coleman. 2017. "'It's a Gap in Awareness': Exploring Service Provision for LGBTQ2S Survivors of Intimate Partner Violence in Ontario, Canada." *Journal of Gay & Lesbian Social Services* 29 (4): 362–377.

Goldenberg, Tamar, Laura Jadwin-Cakmak, and Gary W. Harper. 2018. "Intimate Partner Violence among Transgender Youth: Associations with Intrapersonal and Structural Factors." *Violence and Gender* 5 (1): 19–25.

Grant, Jaime M., Lisa A. Mottet, Justin Tanis, Jack Harrison, Jody L. Herman, and Mara Keisling. 2011. *Injustice at Every Turn: A Report of the National Transgender Discrimination Survey*. Washington, DC: National Center for Transgender Equality and National Gay and Lesbian Task Force. www.transequality.org.

Greenberg, Kae. 2012. "Still Hidden in the Closet: Trans Women and Domestic Violence." *Berkeley Journal of Gender, Law & Justice* 27 (2): 198–251.

Harcourt, Jay. 2013. "Understanding the Experiences of Lesbian, Bisexual and Trans Survivors of Domestic Violence: A Qualitative Study." In *Current Issues in Lesbian, Gay, Bisexual, and Transgender Health*, edited by Jay Harcout, 175–198. New York: Routledge.

Haymes, Richard S., Carl Locke, Clarence Patton, and Diane Dolan-Soto. 1999. *Lesbian, Gay, Transgender and Bisexual (LGTB) Domestic Violence in 1998: New York City Edition*. New York: The Anti-Violence Project and the National Coalition of Anti-Violence Programs. http://avp.org.

Haynes, Susan. 2019. "The World Health Organization Will Stop Classifying Transgender People as Having a 'Mental Disorder.'" *Time*, May 28, 2019. www.time.com.

Hembree, Wylie C., Peggy Cohen-Kettenis, Henrietta A. Delemarre-van de Waal, Louis J. Gooren, Walter J. Meyer III, Norman P. Spack, Vin Tangpricha, and Victor M. Montori. 2009. "Endocrine Treatment of Transsexual Persons: An Endocrine Society Clinical Practice Guideline." *Journal of Clinical Endocrinology & Metabolism* 94 (9): 3132–3154.

Hendricks, Michael L., and Rylan J. Testa. 2012. "A Conceptual Framework for Clinical Work with Transgender and Gender Nonconforming Clients: An Adaptation of the Minority Stress Model." *Professional Psychology: Research and Practice* 43 (5): 460–467.

Hines, Denise A., and Emily M. Douglas. 2011. "The Reported Availability of US Domestic Violence Services to Victims Who Vary by Age, Sexual Orientation, and Gender." *Partner Abuse* 2 (1): 3–30.

Hughto, Jaclyn M. White, Sari L. Reisner, and John E. Pachankis. 2015. "Transgender Stigma and Health: A Critical Review of Stigma Determinants, Mechanisms, and Interventions." *Social Science & Medicine* 147:222–231.

Institute of Medicine. 2011. *The Health of Lesbian, Gay, Bisexual, and Transgender People: Building a Foundation for Better Understanding.* Washington, DC: The National Academies Press.

James, Sandy E., Jody L. Herman, Susan Rankin, Mara Keisling, Lisa Mottet, and Ma'ayan Anafi. 2016. *The Report of the 2015 US Transgender Survey: Executive Summary.* Washington, DC: National Center for Transgender Equality. www.ustrans survey.org.

Jillison, Irene Anne. 2002. "Opening Closed Doors: Improving Access to Quality Health Services for LGBT Populations." *Clinical Research and Regulatory Affairs* 19 (2–3): 153–190.

Jones-Smith, Elsie. 2014. *Strengths-Based therapy: Connecting Theory, Practice and Skills.* Thousand Oaks, CA: Sage.

Kamens, Sarah R. 2011. "On the Proposed Sexual and Gender Identity Diagnoses for *DSM-5*: History and Controversies." *Humanistic Psychologist* 39 (1): 37–59.

Kattari, Shanna K., and Leslie Hasche. 2016. "Differences across Age Groups in Transgender and Gender Non-conforming People's Experiences of Health Care Discrimination, Harassment, and Victimization." *Journal of Aging and Health* 28 (2): 285–306.

Kattari, Shanna K., N. Eugene Walls, and Stephanie Rachel Speer. 2017. "Differences in Experiences of Discrimination in Accessing Social Services among Transgender/Gender Nonconforming Individuals by (Dis)ability." *Journal of Social Work in Disability & Rehabilitation* 16 (2): 116–140.

Kattari, Shanna K., N. Eugene Walls, Stephanie Rachel Speer, and Leonardo Kattari. 2016. "Exploring the Relationship between Transgender-Inclusive Providers and Mental Health Outcomes among Transgender/Gender Variant People." *Social Work in Health Care* 55 (8): 635–650.

Kattari, Shanna K., N. Eugene Walls, Darren L. Whitfield, and Lisa Langenderfer-Magruder. 2015. "Racial and Ethnic Differences in Experiences of Discrimination in Accessing Health Services among Transgender People in the United States." *International Journal of Transgenderism* 16 (2): 68–79.

Kattari, Shanna K., N. Eugene Walls, Darren L. Whitfield, and Lisa Langenderfer Magruder. 2017. "Racial and Ethnic Differences in Experiences of Discrimination in Accessing Social Services among Transgender/Gender-Nonconforming People." *Journal of Ethnic & Cultural Diversity in Social Work* 26 (3): 217–235.

Keiswetter, Sesa, and Becky Brotemarkle. 2010. "Culturally Competent Care for HIV-Infected Transgender Persons in the Inpatient Hospital Setting: The Role of the Clinical Nurse Leader." *Journal of the Association of Nurses in AIDS Care* 21 (3): 272–277.

Kenagy, Gretchen P., and Wendy B. Bostwick. 2005. "Health and Social Service Needs of Transgender People in Chicago." *International Journal of Transgenderism* 8 (2–3): 57–66.

Knutson, Douglas, and Julie M. Koch. 2018. "Person-Centered Therapy as Applied to Work with Transgender and Gender Diverse Clients." *Journal of Humanistic Psychology*. https://doi.org/10.1177/0022167818791082.

Keuroghlian, Alex S., Sari L. Reisner, Jaclyn M. White, and Roger D. Weiss. 2015. "Substance Use and Treatment of Substance Use Disorders in a Community Sample of Transgender Adults." *Drug and Alcohol Dependence* 152:139–146.

Kurdyla, Victoria, Adam M. Messinger, and Milka Ramirez. 2019. "Transgender Intimate Partner Violence and Help-Seeking Patterns." *Journal of Interpersonal Violence*. https://doi.org/10.1177/0886260519880171.

Langenderfer-Magruder, Lisa, N. Eugene Walls, Darren L. Whitfield, Samantha M. Brown, and Cory M. Barrett. 2016. "Partner Violence Victimization among Lesbian, Gay, Bisexual, Transgender, and Queer Youth: Associations among Risk Ractors." *Child and Adolescent Social Work Journal* 33 (1): 55–68.

Lemoire, S. Jim, and Charles P. Chen. 2005. "Applying Person-Centered Counseling to Sexual Minority Adolescents." *Journal of Counseling & Development* 83 (2): 146–154.

Lennon, Erica, and Brian J. Mistler. 2014. "Cisgenderism." *Transgender Studies Quarterly* 1 (1–2): 63–64.

Leyva, Valerie L., Elizabeth M. Breshears, and Robin Ringstad. 2014. "Assessing the Efficacy of LGBT Cultural Competency Training for Aging Services Providers in California's Central Valley." *Journal of Gerontological Social Work* 57 (2–4): 335–348.

Liang, Belle, Lisa Goodman, Pratyusha Tummala-Narra, and Sarah Weintraub. 2005. "A Theoretical Framework for Understanding Help-Seeking Processes among Survivors of Intimate Partner Violence." *American Journal of Community Psychology* 36 (1–2): 71–84.

Makadon, Harvey J., Jennifer Potter, and Hilary Goldhammer. 2008. *The Fenway Guide to Lesbian, Gay, Bisexual, and Transgender Health*. Philadelphia: ACP Press.

Mansh, Matthew, Gabriel Garcia, and Mitchell R. Lunn. 2015. "From Patients to Providers: Changing the Culture in Medicine toward Sexual and Gender Minorities." *Academic Medicine* 90 (5): 574–580.

Mattocks, Kristin M., Michael R. Kauth, Theo Sandfort, Alexis R. Matza, J. Cherry Sullivan, and Jillian C. Shipherd. 2014. "Understanding Health-Care Needs of Sexual and Gender Minority Veterans: How Targeted Research and Policy Can Improve Health." *LGBT Health* 1 (1): 50–57.

Messinger, Adam M. 2017. *LGBTQ Intimate Partner Violence: Lessons for Policy, Practice, and Research*. Oakland: University of California Press.

Meyer, Ilan H. 2003. "Prejudice, Social Stress, and Mental Health in Lesbian, Gay, and Bisexual Populations: Conceptual Issues and Research Evidence." *Psychological Bulletin* 129 (5): 674–697.
Meyer, Ilan H., and David M. Frost. 2013. "Minority Stress and the Health of Sexual Minorities." *Handbook of Psychology and Sexual Orientation*, edited by Charlotte J. Patterson and Anthony R. D'Augelli, 252–266. New York: Oxford University Press.
Movement Advancement Project. 2018. "Equality Maps." www.lgbtmap.org.
New York Anti-Violence Project. 2017. *Transgender IPV Toolkit*. New York: New York Anti-Violence Project. https://avp.org.
Obedin-Maliver, Juno, Elizabeth S. Goldsmith, Leslie Stewart, William White, Eric Tran, Stephanie Brenman, Maggie Wells, David M. Fetterman, Gabriel Garcia, and Mitchell R. Lunn. 2011. "Lesbian, Gay, Bisexual, and Transgender-Related Content in Undergraduate Medical Education." *JAMA: The Journal of the American Medical Association* 306 (9): 971–977.
One Colorado Education Fund. 2011. *Invisible: The State of LGBT Health in Colorado*. Denver, CO: One Colorado Education Fund. https://one-colorado.org.
One Colorado Education Fund. 2015. *Transparent: The State of Transgender Health in Colorado*. Denver, CO: One Colorado Education Fund. https://one-colorado.org/
Parameshwaran, Vishnu, Beatrice C. Cockbain, Miriam Hillyard, and Jonathan R. Price. 2017. "Is the Lack of Specific Lesbian, Gay, Bisexual, Transgender and Queer/Questioning (LGBTQ) Health Care Education in Medical School a Cause for Concern? Evidence from a Survey of Knowledge and Practice among UK Medical Students." *Journal of Homosexuality* 64 (3): 367–381.
Parsons, Jeffrey T., Nadav Antebi-Gruszka, Brett M. Millar, Demetria Cain, and Sitaji Gurung. 2018. "Syndemic Conditions, HIV Transmission Risk Behavior, and Transactional Sex among Transgender Women." *AIDS and Behavior* 22 (7): 1–12.
Pease, Bob. 2013. *Undoing Privilege: Unearned Advantage in a Divided World*. London: Zed Books.
Phares, Tanya M., Suzanne Harrison, Connie Mitchell, Kevin Sherin, M. D. Randall Freeman, Kate Lichtenberg, and Amer Shakil. n.d. "Intimate Partner Violence (IPV) Screening and Intervention." The American College of Preventative Medicine Position Statement.
Pinto, Rogério M., Rita M. Melendez, and Anya Y. Spector. 2008. "Male-to-Female Transgender Individuals Building Social Support and Capital from within a Gender-Focused Network." *Journal of Gay & Lesbian Social Services* 20 (3): 203–220.
Pitts, Marian K., Murray Couch, Hunter Mulcare, Samantha Croy, and Anne Mitchell. 2009. "Transgender People in Australia and New Zealand: Health, Well-Being and Access to Health Services." *Feminism & Psychology* 19 (4): 475–495.
Pitts, Marian, Anthony Smith, Anne Mitchell, and Sunil Patel. 2006. *Private Lives: A Report on the Health and Wellbeing of GLBTI Australians*. Melbourne: Australian Research Centre in Sex, Health and Society, La Trobe University. www.glhv.org.au.

Poteat, Tonia, Danielle German, and Deanna Kerrigan. 2013. "Managing Uncertainty: A Grounded Theory of Stigma in Transgender Health Care Encounters." *Social Science & Medicine* 84:22–29.

Redfern, Jan S., and Bill Sinclair. 2014. "Improving Health Care Encounters and Communication with Transgender Patients." *Journal of Communication in Healthcare* 7 (1): 25–40.

Renzetti, Claire. 1996. "The Poverty of Services for Battered Lesbians." *Journal of Gay & Lesbian Social Services* 4 (1): 61–68.

Richmond, Kate A., Theodore Burnes, and Kate Carroll. 2012. "Lost in Trans-Lation: Interpreting Systems of Trauma for Transgender Clients." *Traumatology* 18 (1): 45–57.

Riggs, Damien W., and Clare Bartholomaeus. 2016. "Australian Mental Health Nurses and Transgender Clients: Attitudes and Knowledge." *Journal of Research in Nursing* 21 (3): 212–222.

Riggs, Damien W., Katrina Coleman, and Clemence Due. 2014. "Healthcare Experiences of Gender Diverse Australians: A Mixed-Methods, Self-Report Survey." *BMC Public Health* 14 (1): 230.

Roch, Amy, James Morton, and Graham Ritchie. 2010. *Out of Sight, out of Mind? Transgender People's Experiences of Domestic Abuse*. Edinburgh: LGBT Youth Scotland and the Scottish Transgender Alliance. www.scottishtrans.org.

Seelman, Kristie L. 2015. "Unequal Treatment of Transgender Individuals in Domestic Violence and Rape Crisis Programs." *Journal of Social Service Research* 41 (3): 307–325.

Seelman, Kristie L., Matthew J. P. Colón-Diaz, Rebecca H. LeCroix, Marik Xavier-Brier, and Leonardo Kattari. 2017. "Transgender Noninclusive Healthcare and Delaying Care because of Fear: Connections to General Health and Mental Health among Transgender Adults." *Transgender Health* 2 (1): 17–28.

Shelton, Samuel Z. 2018. "A Queer Theorist's Critique of Online Domestic Violence Advocacy: Critically Responding to the National Coalition against Domestic Violence Web Site." *Journal of Homosexuality* 65 (10): 1275–1298.

Shipherd, Jillian C., Kelly E. Green, and Sarah Abramovitz. 2010. "Transgender Clients: Identifying and Minimizing Barriers to Mental Health Treatment." *Journal of Gay & Lesbian Mental Health* 14 (2): 94–108.

Shires, Deirdre A., and Kim Jaffee. 2015. "Factors Associated with Health Care Discrimination Experiences among a National Sample of Female-to-Male Transgender Individuals." *Health & Social Work* 40 (2): 134–141.

Singh, Anneliese A., and Vel S. McKleroy. 2011. "'Just Getting Out of Bed Is a Revolutionary Act': The Resilience of Transgender People of Color Who Have Survived Traumatic Life Events." *Traumatology* 17 (2): 34–44.

Substance Abuse and Mental Health Services Administration. 2014. *Trauma-Informed Care in Behavioral Health Services*. Washington, DC: US Department of Health and Human Services.

Substance Abuse and Mental Health Services Administration. n.d. "Programs." www.samhsa.gov.

Sue, Derald Wing. 2010. *Microaggressions in Everyday Life: Race, Gender, and Sexual Orientation*. Hoboken, NJ: John Wiley & Sons.

Takahashi, Alexis. 2016. "How Transphobia Gets Written into Science and Medicine." *Free Radicals*, January 9, 2016. https://freerads.org.

Thompson, Hale M., Niranjan S. Karnik, and Robert Garofalo. 2016. "Centering Transgender Voices in Research as a Fundamental Strategy toward Expansion of Access to Care and Social Support." *Journal of Adolescent Health* 59 (3): 241–242.

van der Kolk, Bessel A. 2015. *The Body Keeps the Score: Brain, Mind, and Body in the Healing of Trauma*. New York: Penguin Books.

Wagner, Phillip E., Adrianne D. Kunkel, Mary Beth Asbury, and Frances Soto. 2016. "Health (Trans)gressions: Identity and Stigma Management in Trans* Healthcare Support Seeking." *Women & Language* 39 (1): 49–74.

White Hughto, Jaclyn M., John E. Pachankis, Tiara C. Willie, and Sari L. Reisner. 2017. "Victimization and Depressive Symptomology in Transgender Adults: The Mediating Role of Avoidant Coping." *Journal of Counseling Psychology* 64 (1): 41–51.

White Hughto, Jaclyn M. White, Sari L. Reisner, and John E. Pachankis. 2015. "Transgender Stigma and Health: A Critical Review of Stigma Determinants, Mechanisms, and Interventions." *Social Science & Medicine* 147:222–231.

Woodlock, Delanie. 2017. "The Abuse of Technology in Domestic Violence and Stalking." *Violence against Women* 23 (5): 584–602.

Xavier, Jessica M., Marilyn Bobbin, Ben Singer, and Earline Budd. 2005. "A Needs Assessment of Transgendered People of Color Living in Washington, DC." *International Journal of Transgenderism* 8 (2–3): 31–47.

Yerke, Adam, and Jennifer DeFeo. 2016. "Redefining Intimate Partner Violence beyond the Binary to Include Transgender People." *Journal of Family Violence* 31: 975–979.

8

Best Practices in Shelter Provision

BRIAN TESCH

Across all sociodemographic group identities, intimate partner violence (IPV) continues to be a major public health problem throughout the world.[1] Research notes that transgender individuals in particular experience high rates of IPV victimization, often experiencing both abusive tactics and help-seeking barriers shaped by the overall marginalization of transgender communities that exists within cisnormative societies.[2] Unfortunately, despite transgender individuals experiencing IPV at rates similar to or higher than cisgender individuals, transgender IPV (T-IPV) is too often overlooked in the construction of social service shelters and operating policies at victim service organizations—including, notably, IPV victim shelters.[3]

Transgender survivors often experience discrimination within IPV victim shelters, not only from staff but also from cisgender survivors in residence at the same shelter. These negative shelter experiences are not just relegated to the more "mainstream" emergency shelters; transgender survivors also have reported negative experiences with IPV shelters designed specifically to work with LGBTQ communities.[4] Similarly, studies have found that many shelter staff members feel uncertain about how best to assist transgender survivors, even when staff members have professed wanting to make their shelters more transgender-inclusive.[5] For instance, when interviewed about how they could make IPV victim services more suitable to the unique needs of transgender survivors, one service provider indicated not knowing how, offering only that they "couldn't say; [we] just need more."[6] Clearly, then, evidence-based approaches are needed to guide shelters in developing services and policies that better address T-IPV.

Given the unique challenges facing IPV victim shelters in providing culturally sensitive and effective services for transgender survivors, this chapter reviews some of the shelter policies and procedures that currently exist and examines how they impact transgender survivors. Additionally, the chapter discusses why and how IPV shelters might be better able to tailor their services to best assist transgender survivors. First, the chapter provides a brief overview of how feminist IPV theory became the ideological foundation for many IPV victim shelters and how it contributes to the discrimination and cisnormative behavior that is seen in some shelters. In addition, the chapter proposes how shelters can best alter their services in order to help transgender survivors of IPV.

"We Have a Problem": The Emergence of Cisnormative Shelters

During the late 1960s and early 1970s, the battered women's movement arose in large part to address the pervasive problem of IPV perpetrated by heterosexual, cisgender men against their heterosexual, cisgender, female romantic partners.[7] To provide survivors with a safe place to escape abuse, the first IPV victim shelters were created in response to this problem.[8] Since that time, the overall number of shelters has grown exponentially. For instance, in the United States, only a handful of shelters were operating in 1976, and just eight years later there were well over five hundred shelters assisting IPV survivors.[9] While many of these early IPV shelters operated with very limited funding and could provide only a small number of social, legal, and medical services for their clients (in many cases, the shelters could provide only temporary emergency housing and nothing more), present-day IPV shelters have evolved into large multiservice IPV agencies that provide not only emergency housing but also varying combinations of on-site and off-site counseling services, safety planning resources, support groups, and referrals for such external resources as legal aid and child-related services.[10]

While the increase of societal awareness of IPV resulted in the creation of new and effective social services to address this problem, these resources were developed based on heterosexual cisgender women's experiences with IPV. IPV was originally often understood as being rooted in a patriarchal power structure within society, and it was believed that it could be situationally addressed through the application of feminist IPV theory.[11] Overall, this explanation for IPV can be described as a neo-Marxist feminist framework that has provided the theoretical justification for the construction of present-day shelter services.[12] Although comprised of numerous smaller and often competing theories, the body of work termed *feminist IPV theory* at its core contends the following: that patriarchal gender inequality and hegemonic masculine gender norms within society encourage and enable heterosexual, cisgender men to abuse their heterosexual, cisgender, female romantic and/or intimate partners.[13]

Unfortunately, this has resulted in many mainstream IPV shelters being cisnormative in nature—focused primarily on serving cisgender IPV survivors. Consequently, some—though not all—shelters (1) refuse to admit transgender survivors, (2) subject transgender survivors to transphobic discrimination, and/or (3) require transgender survivors to utilize services designed for cisgender IPV survivors. Each of these issues is discussed in greater detail below.

Exclusionary Admission Practices at IPV Shelters

Many transgender survivors of IPV encounter a great deal of difficulty when attempting to access services provided by cisnormative IPV shelters.[14] For many transgender survivors, the simple act of reaching out to IPV shelters for help in escaping incidents of abuse is fraught with fear, confusion, and worry because of concerns that some shelters may respond negatively to survivors who are not cisgender.[15] Many transgender survivors perceive that shelters partnered with larger social service agencies will either not be inclusive of them due to shelter staff discriminating against them, or that individuals in the shelter will be openly hostile and transphobic toward them.[16] Often these fears about the possibility of experiencing prejudice and transphobia result in many transgender survivors choosing not to even attempt to access services from these shelters.[17]

Transgender survivors who do attempt to access emergency services from mainstream IPV shelters are often confronted with inconsistent admissions policies and procedures that differ from shelter to shelter. While there are mainstream IPV shelters with policies that explicitly deny services to transgender individuals, some IPV shelters have created policies that solely focus on the comfort of the cisgender women who access their services.[18] These policies often require transgender women to either prove that they have had gender-affirming surgical interventions or provide documentation from a medical doctor or a mental health professional that explicitly states that they are currently in the process of transitioning.[19] In another example of transgender-exclusionary policy, some IPV agencies will admit transgender individuals into their program only if the other residents in the facility are unaware that the person is transgender.[20] Still other agencies admit transgender survivors into their facilities only on a case-by-case basis, with no guarantee that they will be admitted.[21]

In those instances where an IPV emergency shelter denies access to their services to transgender survivors, shelter staff often argue that their refusal to admit transgender individuals is based on their agency's desire to protect the overall health and safety of their cisgender female clients by designating the shelter a heterosexual, cisgender "woman-only" space.[22] Such single-gender admission policies may be perceived by some shelter staff as reducing the risk of heterosexual, cisgender female survivors being exposed to and potentially retraumatized by the mannerisms and physical features of cisgender men.[23]

An extension of this logic may in turn be used by shelter staff to justify denying admission to transgender survivors of IPV who either identify as men or who were assigned male at birth.[24] Although emerging from a well-intentioned desire to protect cisgender women, admissions policies that exclude transgender people from emergency shelter services place the comfort of cisgender IPV survivors over the safety and welfare of their transgender counterparts. Such policies are no different than the idea of an emergency shelter turning away an individual who is tall because many shelter residents were abused by someone who was tall, or a shelter banning the admittance of blue-eyed individuals because a client was victimized by someone with blue eyes. Transgender survivors should not be denied access to emergency shelters just because their gender identity or birth-assigned sex is similar to that of another client's abuser. Moreover, the argument presumes that survivors were abused by men and should be shielded from all reminders of abusers, even the masculine features of fellow survivors, when exposure to such triggers in a safe environment may actually better facilitate reintegration into everyday life when it is time to leave the shelter.[25]

Other agencies have cited concerns that transgender survivors pose a safety risk within shelters because these individuals could physically or sexually assault their cisgender female clients.[26] The myth of transgender people as dangerous may emerge from an erroneous belief—popularized by a number of prominent US politicians—that cisgender men intentionally masquerade as transgender women as a means to gain access to women-only spaces (such as restrooms or victim shelters) and assault cisgender women.[27] Although some IPV shelters may use this argument to purportedly protect residents from victimization, there is no evidence that transgender survivors physically or sexually assault people in shelters (or in public restrooms, for that matter). In fact, research studies have consistently demonstrated that transgender individuals are at a much higher risk of being victims of violent crime than perpetrators of it.[28] This myth is particularly damaging not only because it portrays transgender people as dangerous but also because it denies the very existence of transgender people, by implying they are really just nefarious cisgender people in disguise. For transgender survivors, this myth may unfortunately hinder their ability to be trusted and admitted by some IPV shelters.

At present, most shelters in the US are now legally required to admit individuals based on their gender identity rather than their assigned sex at birth.[29] In 2013, the primary piece of federal legislation designed to address IPV, the Violence Against Women Act, was reauthorized to include provisions that prevent shelters that receive grant funding from the US Department of Justice from discriminating on the basis of gender identity.[30] Furthermore, many shelters that operate in larger metropolitan areas are now required by state statutes to admit individuals based on their gender identity rather than their assigned sex, and an admissions policy based on birth-assigned sex would essentially be breaking the law.[31] Unfortunately, this law is not readily enforceable, and many IPV shelters still engage in discriminatory admissions practices toward transgender individuals.

Transphobic Discrimination in IPV Shelters

Although there are some IPV social service agencies that have transgender exclusionary policies in place that deny transgender survivors access to their emergency shelter programs, there are many other IPV service agencies that are willing to accept individuals into their programs regardless of their gender identity. However, while an emergency shelter may be willing to assist transgender survivors, the reality is that some agencies may actually do more harm than good by subjecting transgender individuals to practices, policies, and shelter staff members who behave in a transphobic manner toward them.[32] This transphobic behavior is reported as being widespread in IPV shelters and is often cited by transgender survivors as the primary reason they might not turn to local shelters for help, even in instances where help is desperately needed.[33]

One primary concern that many transgender survivors have is the seeming lack of knowledge and awareness of shelter staff about transgender individuals.[34] Multiple surveys of cisnormative IPV social service agency staff members have found that only a small percent of agencies have specifically offered trainings to their staff on how to effectively work with LGBTQ communities, and an even smaller percentage of these emergency shelters have conducted trainings with their staff in how to appropriately work specifically with transgender individuals.[35] In many instances, shelter staff members are not given any specialized training in how to best work with transgender survivors or even transgender individuals in general.[36] Perhaps as a consequence of inadequate training protocol, it is not uncommon for transgender survivors to be asked invasive, disrespectful, and unnecessary questions by shelter staff during admission (e.g., "Have you had surgery on your genitals?") or for staff members to use incorrect pronouns when interacting with transgender survivors.[37]

Some transgender survivors have even reported instances where shelter staff have been physically or verbally abusive toward them (e.g., calling them derogatory names because of being transgender) or disclosed their transgender identity or history to others without their consent.[38] Unfortunately, these incidents of transphobia from IPV shelter staff are not isolated, and many transgender survivors report that they will choose to forego seeking shelter services in the future because they do not wish to risk experiencing transphobia while coping with IPV-induced trauma.[39] Although bigotry may never be completely eradicated, mandatory, transgender-inclusive trainings for shelter staff may be a key step in the right direction.

Transgender Individuals Accessing Cisgender IPV–Oriented Services

Ideally, transgender survivors would be able to access either LGBTQ-specific or mainstream emergency shelter services where staff members are trained on reducing bias. Unfortunately, many transgender survivors do not live near any LGBTQ-specific IPV victim service providers, and the local IPV victim service providers that are available to them may not have invested in LGBTQ sensitivity and T-IPV knowledge trainings for their staff members.[40] It is important to note that while there are IPV service agencies that are able to provide a wide range of services to all individuals (both cisgender and transgender), many of these agencies are located only in large urban centers with sizeable LGBTQ communities.[41] Transgender survivors who live in remote or rural areas often must cope with what is available to them, even if it is not helpful in addressing their needs.

One major problem that transgender survivors often encounter when seeking help from local mainstream IPV agencies is that many agencies utilize a one-size-fits-all universal approach to working with IPV survivors. This means that agencies operate by using the same gender-neutral interactions with all individuals, regardless of any experiences of abuse, prejudice, or other problems that these survivors may have because of being transgender.[42] For those agencies that have adopted this "universal" approach, all of the interactions and treatment modalities that are put into practice are the same for all individuals; even all of the components of the initial paperwork and intake process are the same for everyone.[43] While this universal, gender-neutral approach may be beneficial from an administrative standpoint in terms of streamlining both treatment administration and bureaucratic record keeping, it can obfuscate a transgender survivor's personal experiences of abuse that were focused on their gender identity.[44] The use of gender neutrality by some shelters could also alienate nonbinary and gender nonconforming individuals by not even allowing intake staff to inquire about an individual's correct pronouns.[45]

Another problem that many transgender survivors may encounter should they access mainstream IPV shelter services is that many of these services still frame their understanding of IPV in cisnormative, heterosexist, and transphobic terms. Many IPV shelters still use a heterosexual and cisgender neo-Marxist feminist conceptualization of IPV. This conceptualization of IPV is readily apparent both in how these organizations discuss IPV with their clients and in how these agencies portray the problem of IPV to the overall community at large.[46] A transgender survivor may feel unwelcome at cisgender IPV–oriented agencies, such as when these agencies only display cisgender, heterosexual women in all of their promotional and informational material. This may occur even when an agency has policies in place to work with individuals from all backgrounds.[47]

Transgender survivors in need of emergency shelter services may encounter another problem when attempting to find bed space at their local IPV shelter. Many mainstream IPV shelters that operate in smaller communities are often the only IPV shelter in that particular geographic area (and may be the only shelter within dozens to hundreds of miles), which means that transgender survivors are often competing with other individuals for placement in shelters that have a finite number of beds available for the entire community.[48] In such cases, mainstream shelters may give priority to IPV survivors with children, or they may be more likely to deny entry to those who might be considered disruptive to their other clients.[49] Unfortunately, many transgender individuals often face a great deal of hostility and prejudice from the broader society because of the erroneous belief that a child will be emotionally harmed by being raised by a transgender individual.[50] This unsubstantiated belief about a transgender person inherently being a danger to their children (biological or otherwise) has resulted in instances where child custody is taken away from them.[51] Given that transgender individuals may thus not have children, or may have had their children taken away by the courts, they could face reduced prioritization for entry into emergency shelter services.[52]

One increasingly popular option that IPV shelters may use when they do not have any available beds is to place individuals in a hotel or motel.[53] For many mainstream IPV social service agencies, paying for a hotel or motel room for an IPV survivor can seem like an ideal solution to provide emergency housing for those individuals that shelter staff may be leery about allowing into their shelter space.[54] However, this solution might actually be harmful for transgender survivors—both from a therapeutic and a humane standpoint. Transgender survivors who have been given housing in hotels or motels report feeling isolated by their placement in such housing, because these individuals do not have access to the round-the-clock therapeutic and emotional support provided by shelter staff to those who have beds in the emergency shelter space.[55] Many transgender survivors have reported that this isolation can lead to feeling even more alone and rejected by mainstream shelter services (and by society overall), and this has resulted in transgender survivors ultimately leaving the shelter (even in some cases returning to their abuser).[56]

Finally, it is important to note that this inability of transgender survivors to access services from mainstream cisnormative IPV shelters can have a major impact on their recovery from abuse in terms of their overall self-esteem. Some transgender survivors have reported that denial of services from IPV shelters was especially painful because it reinforced all of the negative core beliefs that mainstream society has about transgender individuals (beliefs that transgender individuals often internalize about themselves).[57] These transgender survivors often report that their negative experience with IPV emergency shelter services has resulted in an increased use in alcohol and other drugs, and it also has resulted in many transgender survivors returning to their abusers.[58]

Alternate Forms of Housing and Support for T-IPV Survivors

Whether it is because they were denied access to an IPV victim emergency housing shelter, or because they refused to seek help from social service organizations in the first place, many transgender survivors come to rely upon alternative social networks for support when trying to escape an abusive situation. Unfortunately, many transgender survivors cannot ask for help from family members or friends because in many instances these individuals are unwilling to accept them because of their gender identity, and thus are unwilling to provide assistance.[59] This lack of access to family and friends has created a need for transgender survivors to create new, alternative networks of support, and also to use other non-IPV social service agencies to find the help they need.

One source of support that many transgender survivors have been known to use is informal social networks. Research into T-IPV has found that prior to reaching out to IPV shelter services, many transgender individuals will often turn to other LGBTQ community members for emergency housing, safety, and protection from abusive partners.[60] Despite not benefitting from therapeutic services offered at some shelters, transgender survivors have reported that they found support through informal LGBTQ networks, and that this support was invaluable and lifesaving for them as they tried to leave their abusive relationship.[61] Furthermore, these informal LGBTQ social networks of support for transgender survivors also serve as a way to disseminate information throughout the community; individuals who have had prior negative experiences with IPV staff or organizations may warn others in the community to stay away from them, thus giving a social service organization a bad reputation within its local LGBTQ community.[62]

Another option that transgender survivors have turned to for alternate emergency housing is their local homeless shelter network. The use of local homeless shelters to shield individuals from serious incidents of abuse is not a recent phenomenon; many cisgender men have needed to stay in homeless shelters in order to escape IPV because of the difficult time that cisgender men have had in accessing IPV emergency shelter services.[63] Unfortunately, the use of homeless shelters may be detrimental for transgender survivors because these agencies may be ill-equipped to serve both transgender survivors and transgender people more generally. For instance, many homeless shelters have similar admissions policies as those of IPV emergency shelters; due to the gender-segregated nature of many homeless shelters, transgender individuals often are placed in separate areas of the homeless shelter or are located based on their assigned sex at birth.[64] There have been incidents where transgender survivors were required to wear clothing associated with their assigned sex at birth rather than their gender identity in order to spend the night in the homeless shelter.[65] Other homeless shelters have elected to not concern themselves with sensitivity concerning gender identity, and have gone so far as to advertise that transgender individuals are not allowed in the shelter.[66]

A final avenue of support that is utilized by some transgender survivors is LGBTQ-focused social service organizations that operate within their community. Unfortunately, many of these LGBTQ-specific organizations do not specialize in IPV victim services, and many of these services are not even able to assist transgender individuals because no agency staff members are knowledgeable about transgender identities.[67] This potential for a lack of staff knowledgeable about IPV and/or transgender identity can mean that LGBTQ service agencies might not make the best referrals for transgender survivors, because they are unclear about what the treatment needs are for individuals in this situation.[68]

Unfortunately for transgender survivors, the current cisnormative and heteronormative emergency shelter system that is in place may at times be unable to handle just how complex, multifaceted, and multidimensional the problem of IPV can be for someone who is transgender. Given the difficulty that many transgender survivors have in accessing mainstream IPV services, there should be a concerted effort to make existing emergency shelter services more accepting of transgender individuals, while also creating targeted IPV services that serve the needs of the transgender community.

Transforming IPV Shelters to Be More Inclusive of Transgender Survivors

So how do heteronormative and cisnormative IPV emergency shelters start to become more inclusive of transgender survivors? One of the easiest ways would be to address the lack of training and education in many IPV shelters regarding transgender issues. Many emergency IPV shelters may want to assist transgender survivors in escaping abusive relationships, but these services could be unaware that their current policies and procedures, as well as the lack of awareness and understanding that shelter staff may display toward transgender individuals, could make transgender survivors uncomfortable and could ultimately result in them leaving the shelter.[69]

In order for an IPV emergency shelter to become more transgender-inclusive, it must start addressing the needs of transgender survivors by examining and altering its policies and procedures, addressing the behaviors and attitudes of all shelter staff by providing trainings around transgender issues, and changing the ways in which it does outreach within its community. The following section outlines some ways in which all of these issues can be addressed by IPV agencies so that transgender survivors' needs can be effectively met and they can begin to heal from the abuse they have experienced.

The first and arguably most crucial step that an IPV social service program must take is to train its staff members to be aware of transgender individuals' needs.[70] As was previously stated, many research studies have already demonstrated the exceptional regularity with which transgender survivors have negative experiences with IPV shelter staff.[71] These negative experiences are so widespread that it is not uncommon for transgender individuals to warn other transgender survivors to stay away from certain agencies altogether because of the negative experiences that they (and many others) have had with them.[72] Fortunately for many IPV agencies, a T-IPV-specific educational component in staff trainings can be easy to implement, and it has been shown to be extremely effective in improving how shelter staff members interact with transgender survivors.[73] Studies have shown that, when IPV shelter staff are trained to be sensitive to how gender identity and transphobia shape the experience of T-IPV victimization, these staff members become more keenly aware of their own biases and misconceptions, and they become more welcoming, accepting, and respectful toward transgender survivors.[74]

Another proactive step that IPV shelters can take concerns how these shelters integrate the needs of transgender communities into their programs by educating cisgender shelter residents about transgender lives.[75] This introductory education for cisgender survivors about transgender individuals can have two key immediate benefits: it can decrease the risk that cisgender survivors will feel uncomfortable with or even triggered by the presence of transgender survivors at the same shelter, and it can decrease the risk of transgender survivors being treated in a discriminatory manner by cisgender survivors at the shelter. As was mentioned previously, some IPV shelters exclude transgender survivors because of the possibility that any hint of maleness—including from transgender survivors assigned male at birth or transgender survivors who identify as men—could potentially remind heterosexual, cisgender female survivors at the shelter of cisgender male abusers, thereby triggering traumatic memories.[76] Teaching cisgender shelter members about transgender communities would permit shelter staff the opportunity to undercut the myth that transgender women and nonbinary individuals assigned male at birth are "really" men, as well as the myth that all men (cisgender and transgender alike) are inherently dangerous. This in turn may decrease the potential for heterosexual, cisgender female survivors to associate their male cisgender abusers with transgender survivors.[77] Furthermore, teaching cisgender IPV survivors about transgender communities can decrease transphobia within the shelter, ultimately serving to create a more supportive and accepting shelter environment for transgender survivors.

Many IPV social service agencies must examine what their policies are, as well as how these policies have impacted transgender survivors in the past, so as to determine whether their agency has effectively assisted this community.[78] An example of this is the treatment recommendations that many IPV shelters make for their clients, specifically that survivors should sever all contact with their abusive partner and terminate the romantic relationship.[79] While this may be an ideal goal for any survivor of IPV, many transgender individuals rely on their romantic partners for financial and emotional support,[80] reliance that can be exacerbated by employment discrimination and social isolation in transgender communities. Terminating the relationship may thus be more feasible if such forms of support can be replaced, such as by shelters that assist transgender survivors in locating employment and support groups that are welcoming of transgender individuals. IPV shelters should develop services beyond one-size-fits-all treatment approaches by focusing on recommended strategies that may better serve transgender survivors.[81]

It also is important for IPV shelters to examine their intake paperwork and admissions procedures to see if these processes are inclusive of transgender individuals and not transphobic in terms of their content or their questions. For many transgender survivors, their first interactions with IPV agencies can make them very anxious because of their overall fear that the agency will not be accepting of transgender individuals.[82] By having intake paperwork include questions about pronouns, gender identity, and T-IPV-specific abusive tactics the survivor may have experienced, transgender survivors may come to recognize that the agency is actually working toward transgender inclusivity and is going to be sensitive to the needs of transgender communities.[83]

In terms of community engagement, it is crucial for IPV emergency treatment programs to reach out and build relationships with other area transgender and LGBTQ social service agencies, and with the local transgender community in general, in order to conduct more effective outreach to transgender survivors. Because of transphobic discrimination that transgender individuals may experience when seeking assistance from IPV victim service providers, many transgender survivors will forego accessing these services and will instead look for help within the LGBTQ community.[84] By conducting outreach with LGBTQ social service agencies and the LGBTQ community at large, IPV shelters can not only make the community aware of their existence as a potential referral source for transgender survivors, but also show a willingness to be more accessible and available to the transgender community.

It is also important that any educational and treatment programs offered by IPV shelters include discussions and materials that specifically address T-IPV victimization. Although research into T-IPV is a relatively new field of research inquiry, a number of studies have demonstrated that T-IPV operates in wholly unique ways that make it fundamentally different than other forms of IPV.[85] Many T-IPV perpetrators engage in transphobic abusive tactics, such as destroying personal items utilized for transitioning (e.g., cosmetics, wigs, chest binders, etc.), hiding or destroying hormone medications, and refusing to refer to the survivor by their correct pronouns.[86] (See chapter 2 for a review of T-IPV-specific tactics.) Social service agencies need to make transgender survivors aware of the fact that these behaviors are forms of IPV, and that abusers may be targeting their gender identity as means of control.[87]

Finally, it is important that IPV emergency shelters include T-IPV issues in their outreach to the community and make certain that their community at large is aware of the fact that anyone can experience IPV. The reality is that most people have a cisnormative understanding of IPV, even though research has consistently demonstrated that IPV can take unique forms in transgender communities.[88] While many IPV shelter programs may be aware of the fact that IPV crosses all demographic categories, and may even offer shelter space and IPV treatment to all individuals (regardless of sex, gender identity, and gender expression), some shelter staff may still hold the erroneous belief that the only real, legitimate victims are cisgender, heterosexual women abused by male partners.[89] Such views may encourage transgender survivors to not identify their own experiences as legitimate abuse and, therefore, not seek out needed help.⁹⁰ IPV social service agencies should make certain that their community outreach includes depictions of T-IPV so that all potential IPV survivors are aware of the fact that they are experiencing instances of abuse, and that there are services available to them.

It is important to note that many major cities with large LGBTQ communities do have IPV services that work exclusively with LGBTQ survivors of abuse. This may seem like an ideal solution to address the need for IPV services that are understanding of the unique factors inherent in LGBTQ IPV. Furthermore, many transgender survivors who have sought treatment from LGBTQ service providers have spoken about being very happy with the experience, and how these agencies and the staff who worked in them were able to provide an excellent level of support that ultimately helped them to leave their abusive relationships.⁹¹

However, although LGBTQ-specific IPV shelters are often an excellent option for the transgender survivors who can access them, these shelters are by no means a perfect solution. One primary problem is that LGBTQ IPV emergency shelters are more often located in large cities with sizeable LGBTQ communities.⁹² While potentially lifesaving for transgender survivors living in or near these large cities, many transgender survivors live in remote or rural areas that do not have any LGBTQ-specific services. For these survivors, the quality of services provided by LGBTQ IPV shelters located far away is something of a moot point if they cannot physically get to these particular shelters.

Another problem that exists for some LGBTQ IPV emergency shelter services has to do with the agencies themselves and how well they address T-IPV. Many LGBTQ IPV social service agencies focus primarily on assisting cisgender lesbian, gay, and bisexual (LGB) IPV survivors.⁹³ These LGBTQ IPV services may not have experience assisting in cases of T-IPV, either because they do not encounter incidents of T-IPV regularly or because they assume that T-IPV and cisgender LGB IPV are so similar that the same victim services can be used for the entire LGBTQ population.⁹⁴ Unfortunately, cisgender LGB IPV and T-IPV are not identical and therefore their services should not be either. Thus, in LGBTQ IPV emergency shelters oriented more toward addressing cisgender LGB IPV, transgender survivors may not get tailored services, and they may even find themselves ostracized within the shelter by some clients and staff.[95]

Final Thoughts

Over the past forty years, our overall understanding of IPV has shifted dramatically. We have moved away from a purely heteronormative and cisnormative understanding of what IPV is as a social problem to a much more expansive viewpoint, one that acknowledges that anyone can experience IPV victimization.[96] The impact of IPV often can be compounded for groups that are already experiencing marginalization within mainstream society, including transgender individuals.[97] Because IPV victim shelters do not always recognize that their services are cisnormative, they often may struggle in fully addressing the needs of transgender survivors. Many shelters have policies and procedures in place that can ban transgender individuals from staying in their shelters, and shelters that do admit transgender survivors often created an unwelcoming atmosphere, including staffing individuals who may overtly or covertly engage in transphobic behavior against clients.

Perceptions of—and too often the reality of—shelters as exclusionary and discriminatory institutions have resulted in some transgender individuals avoiding the IPV social service system all together. To address the concerns of these survivors, several steps can be taken. These include implementing transgender-inclusive policies and procedures (such as including various options for gender identity in all admissions materials), training staff to be sensitive to the needs of transgender individuals, and creating a shelter space that is not cisnormative in its assumptions related to IPV victimization. Of course, changes beyond shelters are also needed to enhance the safety of transgender survivors; for instance, legislation needs to be created that better protects transgender individuals from IPV, the full range of victim services (e.g., police, victim hotlines, etc.) needs to continue to increase their sensitivity to the needs of transgender IPV survivors, and, more generally, societies must work toward embracing a conceptualization of gender beyond the binary—and toward embracing a world in which respect is extended to all people regardless of gender expression or identity.[98] However, until we are able to move away from societal transphobia and tolerance of violence toward LGBTQ individuals, we need to make certain that IPV shelters serve their intended purpose of protecting anyone and everyone from violence—regardless of their gender identity.

NOTES

1 Goodman and Epstein 2008; Island and Letellier 1991; Tesch et al. 2010; Tjaden, Thoennes, and Allison 1999.
2 Goodmark 2013; Kidd and Witten 2007; Stotzer 2009; Tesch and Bekerian 2015; Witten and Eyler 1999
3 Messinger 2017.
4 Tesch and Bekerian 2015.
5 Tesch and Bekerian 2015.
6 Tesch and Bekerian 2015.
7 Abrar, Lovenduski, and Margetts 2000; Goodman and Epstein 2008; Merrill 1996; Walker 1999.
8 Gelles and Cornell 1985; Hutchings 1988.
9 Gelles and Cornell 1985.
10 Gelles and Cornell 1985; Stover and Lent 2014; Wallace and Roberson 2016; Waugh and Bonner 2002.
11 Cannon, Lauve-Moon, and Buttell 2015; Cattaneo and Goodman 2015; Gelles and Cornell 1985; Goodman and Epstein 2008; Hutchings 1988; Stover and Lent 2014; Tesch et al. 2010.
12 Abrar, Lovenduski, and Margetts 2000; Cannon, Lauve-Moon, and Buttell 2015; Goodman and Epstein 2008.
13 Cannon, Lauve-Moon, and Buttell 2015; Cattaneo and Goodman 2015; Dutton and Nicholls 2005; Stith, Williams, and Rosen 1990; Wade and Ferree 2015.
14 Tesch et al. 2010; Tesch and Bekerian 2015.
15 Bornstein et al. 2006; Greenberg 2012.
16 Bornstein et al. 2006.
17 Ford et al. 2013; Greenberg 2012.
18 Ford et al. 2013; Greenberg 2012.
19 Greenberg 2012; Seelman 2015.
20 Goodmark 2013.
21 Greenberg 2012.
22 Riggs et al. 2016.
23 Quinn 2010.
24 Greenberg 2012; Riggs et al. 2016; Yerke and DeFeo 2016.
25 Quinn 2010.
26 Smith 2015.
27 Gabriel 2016; Juzwiak 2016.
28 Stotzer 2009; Witten 2009.

29 Goodmark 2013.
30 US Department of Justice 2014.
31 Goodmark 2013.
32 Stotzer, Silverschanz, and Wilson 2013.
33 Bornstein et al. 2006; Greenberg 2012; Stotzer, Silverschanz, and Wilson 2013.
34 Ford et al. 2013; Stotzer, Silverschanz, and Wilson 2013.
35 Seelman 2015; Yerke and DeFeo 2016.
36 Stotzer, Silverschanz, and Wilson 2013; Yerke and DeFeo 2016.
37 Seelman 2015; Stotzer, Silverschanz, and Wilson 2013.
38 Stotzer, Silverschanz, and Wilson 2013; Yerke and DeFeo 2016.
39 Ford et al. 2013; Stotzer, Silverschanz, and Wilson 2013; Yerke and DeFeo 2016.
40 Seelau, Seelau, and Poorman 2003; Stotzer, Silverschanz, and Wilson 2013.
41 Goodmark 2013; Seelau, Seelau, and Poorman 2003; Stotzer, Silverschanz, and Wilson 2013.
42 Seelman 2015.
43 Seelman 2015; Stotzer, Silverschanz, and Wilson 2013; Yerke and DeFeo 2016.
44 Ford et al. 2013; Seelman 2015; Stotzer, Silverschanz, and Wilson 2013.
45 Ford et al. 2013; Seelman 2015; Stotzer, Silverschanz, and Wilson 2013.
46 Ford et al. 2013; Riggs et al. 2016; Shelton 2018.
47 Ford et al. 2013; Riggs et al. 2016; Shelton 2018.
48 Baker, Cook, and Norris 2003.
49 Smith 2015.
50 Ethics Committee of the American Society for Reproductive Medicine 2015.
51 Carter 2006; Ethics Committee of the American Society for Reproductive Medicine 2015.
52 Stotzer, Silverschanz, and Wilson 2013.
53 Greenberg 2012; Sullivan and Rumptz 1994.
54 Sullivan and Rumptz 1994.
55 Greenberg 2012; Tesch and Bekerian 2015.
56 Greenberg 2012.
57 Ford et al. 2013; Greenberg 2012.
58 Bornstein et al. 2006.
59 Ford et al. 2013; Greenberg 2012; Yerke and DeFeo 2016.
60 Bornstein et al. 2006; Goodmark 2013.
61 Bornstein et al. 2006.
62 Riggs et al. 2016; Stotzer, Silverschanz, and Wilson 2013.
63 Letellier 1996.
64 Greenberg 2012; Stotzer, Silverschanz, and Wilson 2013.
65 Greenberg 2012.
66 Stotzer, Silverschanz, and Wilson 2013.
67 Stotzer, Silverschanz, and Wilson 2013; Tesch and Bekerian 2015.
68 Greenberg 2012; Stotzer, Silverschanz, and Wilson 2013; Tesch and Bekerian 2015.
69 Riggs et al. 2016; Stotzer, Silverschanz, and Wilson 2013; Yerke and DeFeo 2016.

70 Ford et al. 2013; Riggs et al. 2016; Stotzer, Silverschanz, and Wilson 2013; Tesch and Bekerian 2015.
71 See Yerke and DeFeo 2016.
72 Bornstein et al. 2006; Riggs et al. 2016.
73 Ford et al. 2013; Riggs et al. 2016; Stotzer, Silverschanz, and Wilson 2013.
74 Goldberg and White 2011; Riggs et al. 2016.
75 Quinn 2010; Staiger et al. 2009.
76 Quinn 2010.
77 Quinn 2010.
78 Greenberg 2012; Stotzer, Silverschanz, and Wilson 2013; Tesch and Bekerian 2015.
79 Goodmark 2013.
80 Goodmark 2013.
81 Seelman 2015.
82 Riggs et al. 2016; Stotzer, Silverschanz, and Wilson 2013; Tesch and Bekerian 2015.
83 Riggs et al. 2016; Wade and Ferree 2015; Yerke and DeFeo 2016.
84 Bornstein et al. 2006; Greenberg 2012.
85 Brown 2011; Goodmark 2013; Tesch and Bekerian 2015.
86 Brown 2011; Tesch and Bekerian 2015.
87 Goldberg and White 2011; Goodmark 2013.
88 Island and Letellier 1991; Renzetti 1992.
89 Shelton 2018.
90 Bornstein et al. 2006; Shelton 2018.
91 Bornstein et al. 2006.
92 Goodmark 2013; Tesch and Bekerian 2015.
93 Tesch and Bekerian 2015.
94 Goldberg and White 2011; Tesch 2011; Tesch and Bekerian 2015.
95 Tesch and Bekerian 2015.
96 Goodman and Epstein 2008; Tjaden, Thoennes, and Allison 1999.
97 Witten 2009.
98 Wade and Ferree 2015.

REFERENCES

Abrar, Stefania, Joni Lovenduski, and Helen Margetts. 2000. "Feminist Ideas and Domestic Violence Policy Change." *Political Studies* 48: 239–262.

Baker, Charlene K., Sarah L. Cook, and Fran H. Norris. 2003. "Domestic Violence and Housing Problems: A Contextual Analysis of Women's Help-Seeking, Received Informal Support, and Formal System Response." *Violence Against Women* 9 (7): 754–783.

Bornstein, Danica R., Jake Fawcett, Marianne Sullivan, Kirsten D. Senturia, and Sharyne Shiu-Thornton. 2006. "Understanding the Experiences of Lesbian,

Bisexual and Trans Survivors of Domestic Violence: A Qualitative Study." *Journal of Homosexuality* 51 (1): 159–181.

Brown, Nicola. 2011. "Holding Tensions of Victimization and Perpetration: Partner Abuse in Trans Communities." In *Intimate Partner Violence in LGBTQ Lives*, edited by Janice L. Ristock, 153–168. New York: Routledge.

Cannon, Clare, Katie Lauve-Moon, and Fred Buttell. 2015. "Re-theorizing Intimate Partner Violence through Post-Structural Feminism, Queer Theory, and the Sociology of Gender." *Social Sciences* 4:668–687.

Carter, Kari J. 2006. "The Best Interest Test and Child Custody: Why Transgender Should Not Be a Factor in Custody Determinations." *Health Matrix: The Journal of Law-Medicine* 16 (1): 209–236.

Cattaneo, Lauren B., and Lisa A. Goodman. 2015. "What Is Empowerment Anyway? A Model for Domestic Violence Practice, Research, and Evaluation." *Psychology of Violence* 5 (1): 84–94.

Dutton, Donald G., and Tonia L. Nicholls. 2005. "The Gender Paradigm in Domestic Violence: Research and Theory." *Aggression and Violent Behavior* 10:680–714.

Ethics Committee of the American Society for Reproductive Medicine. 2015. "Access to Fertility Services by Transgender Persons: An Ethics Committee Opinion." *Fertility and Sterility* 104 (5): 1111–1115.

Ford, Chandra L., Terra Slavin, Karin L. Hilton, and Susan L. Holt. 2013. "Intimate Partner Violence Prevention Services in Los Angeles: Issues, Needs, and Challenges for Assisting Lesbian, Gay, Bisexual, and Transgender Clients." *Health Promotion Practice* 14 (6): 841–849.

Gabriel, Trip. 2016. "Ted Cruz, Attacking Donald Trump, Uses Transgender Bathroom Access as a Cudgel." *New York Times*, April 30, 2016. www.nytimes.com.

Gelles, Richard J., and Claire P. Cornell. 1985. *Intimate Violence in Families*. New York: Sage.

Goldberg, Joshua M., and Caroline White. 2011. "Reflections on Approaches to Trans Anti-Violence Education." In *Intimate Partner Violence in LGBTQ Lives*, edited by Janice L. Ristock, 56–77. New York: Routledge.

Goodman, Lisa A., and Deborah Epstein. 2008. *Listening to Battered Women: A Survivor-Centered Approach to Advocacy, Mental Health, and Justice*. Washington, DC: American Psychological Association.

Goodmark, Leigh. 2013. "Transgender People, Intimate Partner Abuse, and the Legal System." *Harvard Civil Rights–Civil Liberties Law Review* 48 (1): 51–104.

Greenberg, Kae. 2012. "Still Hidden in the Closet: Trans Women and Domestic Violence." *Berkeley Journal of Gender, Law & Justice* 27 (2): 198–251.

Han, Erin L. 2003. "Mandatory Arrest and No-Drop Policies: Victim Empowerment in Domestic Violence Cases." *Boston College Third World Law Journal* 23 (1): 159–191.

Hutchings, Nancy. 1988. *The Violent Family: Victimization of Women, Children, and Elders*. New York: Human Sciences Press.

Island, David, and Patrick Letellier. 1991. *Men Who Beat the Men Who Love Them*. New York: Harrington Park Press.

Juzwiak, Rich. 2016. "North Carolina Governor Is Back at It Again With the Trans-Predators Narrative in Campaign Video." *Jezebel*, September 7, 2016. https://theslot.jezebel.com.

Kidd, Jeremy D., and Tarynn Witten. 2007. "Transgender and Transsexual Identities: The Next Strange Fruit—Hate Crimes, Violence, and Genocide against the Global Trans-Communities." *Journal of Hate Studies* 6 (1): 31–63.

Letellier, Patrick. 1996. "Twin Epidemics: Domestic Violence and HIV Infection among Gay and Bisexual Men." *Journal of Gay & Lesbian Social Services* 4 (1): 69–81.

Merrill, Gregory S. 1996. "Ruling the Exceptions: Same Sex Battering and Domestic Violence Theory." In *Violence in Gay and Lesbian Domestic Partnerships*, edited by Claire M. Renzetti and Charles H. Miley, 9–22. New York: Harrington Park Press.

Messinger, Adam M. 2017. *LGBTQ Intimate Partner Violence: Lessons for Policy, Practice, and Research*. Oakland: University of California Press.

Mirchandani, Rekha. 2006. "'Hitting Is Not Manly': Domestic Violence Court and the Re-imagination of the Patriarchal State." *Gender & Society* 20 (6): 781–804.

Quinn, M.-E. 2010. *Open Minds Open Doors: Transforming Domestic Violence Programs to Include LGBTQ Survivors*. Boston: The Network/La Red. www.ncdsv.org.

Renzetti, Claire. 1992. *Violent Betrayal: Partner Abuse in Lesbian Relationships*. Newbury Park, CA: Sage.

Riggs, Damien W., Heather Fraser, Nik Tayler, Tania Signal, and Catherine Donovan. 2016. "Domestic Violence Service Providers' Capacity for Supporting Transgender Women: Findings from an Australian Workshop." *British Journal of Social Work* 46 (8): 2374–2392.

Seelau, Eric P., Shelia M. Seelau, and Paula B. Poorman. 2003. "Gender and Role-Based Perceptions of Domestic Abuse: Does Sexual Orientation Matter?" *Behavior Sciences and the Law* 21 (2): 199–214.

Seelman, Kristie L. 2015. "Unequal Treatment of Transgender Individuals in Domestic Violence and Rape Crisis Programs." *Journal of Social Service Research* 41:307–325.

Shelton, Samuel Z. 2018. "A Queer Theorist's Critique of Online Domestic Violence Advocacy: Critically Responding to the National Coalition against Domestic Violence Web Site." *Journal of Homosexuality* 65 (10): 1275–1298.

Smith, Carla M. 2015. "Examining Access Barriers to Emergency Domestic Violence Shelter Services for Transgender Identified Survivors of Intimate Partner Violence in New York State." PhD diss., St. John Fisher College.

Staiger, Petra K., Fritha Melville, Leanne Hides, Nicolas Kambouropoulos, and Dan I. Lubman. 2009. "Can Emotion-Focused Coping Explain the Link between Posttraumatic Stress Disorder Severity and Triggers for Substance Use in Young Adults?" *Journal of Substance Abuse Treatment* 36 (2): 220–226.

Stith, Sandra M., Mary Beth Williams, and Karen H. Rosen. 1990. *Violence Hits Home: Comprehensive Treatment Approaches to Domestic Violence*. New York: Spring.

Stotzer, Rebecca L. 2009. "Violence against Transgender People: A Review of United States Data." *Aggression and Violent Behavior* 14 (3): 170–179.
Stotzer, Rebecca L., Perry Silverschanz, and Andre Wilson. 2013. "Gender Identity and Social Services: Barriers to Care." *Journal of Social Service Research* 39:63–77.
Stover, Carla S., and Kimberly Lent. 2014. "Training and Certification for Domestic Violence Service Providers: The Need for a National Standard Curriculum and Training Approach." *Psychology of Violence* 4 (2): 117–127.
Sullivan, Cris M., and Maureen H. Rumptz. 1994. "Adjustment and Needs of African-American Women Who Utilized a Domestic Violence Shelter." *Violence and Victims* 9 (3): 275–286.
Tesch, Brian. 2011. "Violence in the Transgender Home." *Psychologist* 24 (11): 796–797.
Tesch, Brian P., and Debra Bekerian. 2015. "Hidden in the Margins: A Qualitative Examination of What Professionals in the Domestic Violence Field Know about Transgender Domestic Violence." *Journal of Gay and Lesbian Social Services* 27:391–411.
Tesch, Brian, Debra Bekerian, Peter English, and Evan Harrington. 2010. "Same-Sex Domestic Violence: Why Victims Are More at Risk." *International Journal of Police Science and Management* 12 (4): 526–535.
Tjaden, Patricia, Nancy Thoennes, and Christine J. Allison. 1999. "Comparing Violence over the Life Span in Samples of Same-Sex and Opposite Sex Cohabitants." *Violence and Victims* 14 (4): 413–425.
US Department of Justice. 2014. *Frequently Asked Questions: Nondiscrimination Grant Condition in the Violence against Women Reauthorization Act of 2013*. Washington, DC: US Department of Justice. www.justice.gov.
Wade, Lisa, and Myra Marx Ferree. 2015. *Gender: Ideas, Interactions, Institutions*. New York: W.W. Norton.
Walker, Lenore E. 1999. "Psychology and Domestic Violence around the World." *American Psychologist* 54 (1): 21–29.
Wallace, Paul Harvey, and Cliff Roberson. 2016. *Family Violence: Legal, Medical, and Social Perspectives*. New York: Routledge.
Warshaw, Carole. 1996. "Domestic Violence: Changing Theory, Changing Practice." *Journal of the American Medical Women's Association* 51(3): 87–91.
Waugh, Fran, and Michelle Bonner. 2002. "Domestic Violence and Child Protection: Issues in Safety Planning." *Child Abuse Review* 11 (5): 282–295.
Witten, Tarynn M. 2009. "Graceful Exits: Intersections of Aging, Transgender Identities, and the Family/Community." *Journal of GLBT Family Studies* 5 (1/2): 35–61.
Witten, Tarynn M., and A. Evan Eyler. 1999. "Hate Crimes and Violence against the Transgendered." *Peace Review* 11 (3): 461–468.
Yerke, Adam F., and Jennifer DeFeo. 2016. "Redefining Intimate Partner Violence beyond the Binary to Include Transgender People." *Journal of Family Violence* 31 (8): 975–979.

9

Best Practices in Policing

KAE GREENBERG

Authors, historians, and activists have repeatedly pointed out that the birth of what became known as the "gay rights movement" was in fact a response to the persistent harassment of lesbian, gay, bisexual, transgender, and queer (LGBTQ)[1] people by the police at such locations as the Stonewall Inn in New York City and Compton's Cafeteria in San Francisco. Less well known is the fact that the individuals at the epicenter of such tipping points were often transgender, particularly transgender women of color (see chapter 6 for more on race).[2] Even less acknowledged, in an age when it is common for police to march in LGBTQ pride parades,[3] is that the discrimination transgender people face at the hands of the police continues today.[4]

The history of interactions between transgender people and the police is fraught with mistrust and violence, causing many transgender people to hesitate to bring the police into their lives when they are at their most vulnerable. For example, the term "walking while trans" arose to reflect the repeated harassment of transgender women of color by the police, who often profile transgender women as sex workers.[5] But to conclude in this time of #BlackLivesMatter that transgender people hesitate to call the police solely because of their gender identity is to ignore the intersectional identities that many transgender people have. A white transgender person may be far likelier to call the police than a Black transgender person, who may fear how police arriving to deal with a violent situation might react.[6] As the police represent a primary resource for many people experiencing intimate partner violence (IPV), this reluctance to contact police could increase the risk of survivors of transgender IPV (T-IPV) remaining with their abusers.

The challenges and unique concerns that transgender people face in relation to the police are myriad. Some are similar to those faced by cisgender people, and some are unique. A transgender IPV survivor may wonder if by calling the police they are exposing themselves to the possibility of being revictimized. A survivor whose abuser is transgender may wonder if calling the police will put the transgender abuser in a dangerous situation, at risk of being harmed or discriminated against by police, when the survivor only wants the violence to stop. After undergoing trauma, transgender survivors may wonder if they still have the strength to endure being potentially disbelieved or incorrectly gendered by the police.

Across the United States and in many other parts of the world, owing to the persistent agitation of LGBTQ activists in their jurisdictions, police departments have begun to implement guidelines that dictate how officers should interact with transgender people.[7] Although these guidelines relate primarily to interactions when police are making an arrest,[8] one can glean from these guidelines what these departments have identified as important when dealing with transgender people generally. Similarly, through common omissions in guidelines, one can identify what steps police departments still must take to improve their treatment of and interactions with transgender people.

This chapter presents a set of best practice principles for police when interacting with transgender IPV survivors and perpetrators. To do so, this chapter reviews applicable organization reports and scholarly research, and also includes my own experience working with transgender people in the criminal legal system as a public defender. As with any best practices, there is no one-size-fits-all solution to policing IPV, and effective policing will continue to require officers to act upon experience and judgment as unique situations arise. Nonetheless, recommendations in this chapter can serve as an impetus for gradual, paradigmatic shifts in police policy regarding T-IPV.

That said, so-called best practices for law enforcement alone are not enough, and potentially bolster a racist and discriminatory system.[9] Transgender law professor and legal advocate Dean Spade cautions us to be wary of fighting for reforms that only make the criminal justice system stronger.[10] It is important to note that the police represent just one of numerous resources for survivors of T-IPV, and that supporters should grant survivors the autonomy to consider non-police options should survivors not wish to engage with the criminal justice system.

Why Transgender People Are Afraid of the Police

To implement best practices in T-IPV policing reforms, we first need to understand the current landscape that we are attempting to change with respect to the broader relationship between law enforcement and transgender communities. The history of transgender people's interactions with law enforcement is rife with examples of oppression and abuse. As the activist collective INCITE! explains, "From enforcement of historical laws prohibiting people from wearing apparel associated with a different gender, to present day enforcement of social expectations regarding use of gender-segregated facilities such as restrooms, law enforcement agents have explicitly policed the borders of the binary gender system."[11] In part, based solely on transgender people's clothing choices to express their gender identity, the police historically viewed them as lawbreakers rather than as citizens in need of their services.[12] The very moment enshrined as the inception of the modern transgender movement—the Stonewall riots, June 28, 1969—marks when transgender women of color, butch women, "Stonewall girls," and other gender nonconforming individuals said "enough" to being mistreated by the police because of their identity and fought back.[13]

One common police practice today that drives a wedge between the police and transgender communities is "quality of life" (QOL) policing.[14] QOL policing grew out of the "broken windows" theory that "allowing broken windows and other signs of 'disorder' to exist in a neighborhood quickly leads, if left unchecked, to an explosion of serious crime by 'signaling that the community is not in control.'"[15] In QOL policing, police target typically noncriminal activities or summary offenses, such as sleeping in public or urinating in public.[16] Activists and scholars have contended that since its inception, QOL policing has commonly been used to target minority groups, including transgender people.[17] It was first rolled out during the administration of Mayor Rudy Giuliani in New York City Police Department's Sixth Precinct, in which the West Village—a traditional haven for transgender people—is located.[18] The Center for American Progress and Movement Advancement Project have highlighted what makes this policy problematic for transgender people, pointing out the way that "quality-of-life policing grants extensive discretion to individual law enforcement officers. Because of this, underlying biases can easily come to bear in interactions between people and police."[19] The police are given the discretion to choose whom to arrest and whom to ignore, and their private biases come—either intentionally or unintentionally—into play.[20]

Some police also use their discretion in arresting people for QOL crimes to particularly harass transgender women of color, whom they may incorrectly assume are engaging in sex work. This phenomenon is common enough that, as referenced earlier, the phrase "walking while trans" was coined.[21] In their work, the collective INCITE! has found that "frequently, officers use vaguely worded 'quality of life' regulations prohibiting, among many other things, 'loitering' and 'loitering with intent to solicit,' as well as 'obstructing vehicular traffic,' 'public lewdness,' 'public nuisance,' and 'disorderly conduct,' to harass, detain, and arrest individuals they believe to be involved in sex work, and particularly street based sex work."[22] Charging a transgender woman with "loitering with intent to solicit" allows the police officer to bypass the fact that the transgender woman was not observed interacting with either a "prospective John" or an undercover vice cop. In other instances, some police will accuse the transgender woman directly of sex work, regardless of what they observed. One transgender Latina woman from Jackson Heights, Queens, recounts, "Another night I was on 82nd and Roosevelt Avenue. I went to get tacos and Pepsi at a taco stand. At that time I saw the police van patrolling like always. They looked at me but I thought to myself, 'don't worry you are not doing anything wrong.' But then I saw the police get out of the van and they approached me. They threw my food to the floor, handcuffed me and arrested me. They accused me of sex work."[23] Going through one's daily routine can be enough to get arrested.

Such discrimination is particularly present for transgender people of color, who have to deal with the bias of some police officers against not only transgender people but also people of color generally. As Mitchyll Mora, a staff member of Streetwise and Safe, puts it, "The policing of Brown and Black people begins with the color of our skin, our race, our ethnicity, and our youth, but it does not end there."[24] For example, Kloe Jones, a twenty-three-year-old transgender woman in Chicago, explains, "There's a lot of people from the South and West Side. [Boystown] is a predominantly white neighborhood, but this is all we have. There have been muggings and robbings up here, and [white residents] look at the

African Americans who come to the Center [on Halsted, an LGBTQ community organization], as if somehow it's their fault."[25] Because transgender people of color may not conform to whom police expect to see in certain neighborhoods, they are commonly targeted for extra surveillance when they are in those areas.[26]

Some transgender people also come into contact with law enforcement because of their reliance on survival crimes, such as theft or sex work, to deal with the repercussions of transphobia in their lives. For example, transgender children and youth, having been kicked out of home because of their gender, are disproportionately homeless, with 20–40 percent of homeless youth identifying as LGBTQ.[27] This situation often leads these young people to engage in survival crimes.[28] In fact, family rejection and homelessness have been found to be the top predictors that LGBTQ youth will end up in the criminal justice system, because of the heavy police surveillance of the disproportionately LGBTQ homeless population.[29] One transsexual youth remembered:

> [I didn't really think about], you know, trading sex for anything whenever I first moved here. And then whenever I got here, I realized that it was just so popular because there were so many people in my situation that were unemployed and they needed money and that it was just so widely, you know, it was so easy to get into. So I was a very conservative person. I didn't really think about doing that but times got really, really hard and I didn't eat for about a week and I didn't have anywhere to stay. I was sneaking on the train and so I decided that I was going to clean myself up a little bit. Decided to go out there and do what I have to do.[30]

A well-documented pattern of abusive behavior by the police toward transgender people exists.[31] This abuse is too often the result not of "just a few bad apples" but rather of the systemic targeting of transgender people discussed earlier.[32] One type of abuse is the apathy exhibited by many police officers to using proper pronouns and names when interacting with transgender people.[33] Scholar Vivian Namaste writes, "The interactions between police officers and transgendered [sic] prostitutes [sic] offer additional evidence of police harassment, both subtle and overt. Officers would ask MTF transsexuals for their male names, even when these individuals had their documentation legally changed."[34] This disrespect can escalate into the use of directly threatening language. As one transgender woman recalled to Namaste, "One of the arresting officers commented that 'People like you should all be killed at birth.'"[35] Police have also been documented targeting areas where transgender people hang out and then arresting them on a more serious charge than solicitation, such as "crimes against nature." Such a charge puts an arrested transgender person at risk of ending up on the sex offender registry.[36] The abuse by some police is heightened for transgender people of color.[37] Take for example the 2015 well-publicized shooting of Mya Hall, a Black transgender woman who, having become lost as she was driving in Baltimore, accidentally drove into a National Security Agency parking lot.[38] Rather than asking questions, the police automatically opened fire, killing Hall.

With such a history, the distrust that many transgender people have for the police today is hardly surprising. For instance, as part of the 2015 US Transgender Survey, the authors asked participants about their contact with and feelings about the police. Forty percent said that they had interacted with the police in the previous year, and, of those respondents who also reported that police thought or knew they were trans, an alarming 57 percent said that they had never been or were only sometimes treated with respect.[39] Relatedly, 57 percent of all 27,715 respondents to the survey stated that they were generally uncomfortable asking the police for help.[40]

Of course, this sense of unease about the police impacts not only transgender people in general but survivors of T-IPV in particular. This point is poignantly illustrated by the experiences of a sex worker beaten by her boyfriend when he discovered that she was transgender. The survivor recounted, "I couldn't phone the police. What am I going to say? 'Oh, I had my boyfriend here and he just found out I had a penis and almost killed me'?! They would have just humiliated me, you know. It would have been a big joke."[41] These concerns of many T-IPV survivors regarding the police are reviewed in the next section.

T-IPV Survivors' Hesitancy to Call the Police

Besides pervasive mistrust of police interactions beyond the context of IPV, there are also circumstances unique to T-IPV that cause many transgender people to pause before calling for police help. If a transgender person is in a relationship with another transgender person, they may hesitate to call the police because of the potential negative consequences of doing so, such as the partner (or themselves, if mistakenly arrested) being housed with people of a different gender identity while incarcerated. As Amnesty International has found, "Some LGBT individuals who are survivors of domestic violence reportedly hesitate to contact law enforcement officials for fear of being arrested, or because they worry about how their partner would be treated in police custody."[42] For example, 59 percent of transgender women in male prisons are assaulted, versus 4 percent of cisgender men.[43] Although they may not be able to cite the precise statistics, it is likely that most transgender people are aware of the risks transgender people face while incarcerated.

T-IPV survivors are also at increased risk of arrest owing to mandatory arrest policies.[44] A mandatory arrest policy specifies that if officers find probable cause in an IPV case, they must make an arrest.[45] The policy's ostensible purpose is to force police to take IPV seriously and not just give the perpetrator a stern "talking to."[46] However, as legal scholar Adele Morrison contends, "Essentially, the policies have given police another reason to enter already over-policed communities and to arrest and prosecute those who are already most arrested and prosecuted."[47] Many studies have shown that mandatory arrest laws have increased the number of dual arrests, increasing the number of survivors who end up arrested.[48] The arrest of the survivor instead of the abuser is so common in some localities that in Los Angeles, for example, STOP Domestic Violence Project, an IPV program of the Los Angeles LGBT Center, actually runs a support group for IPV survivors who have been incorrectly arrested as the offender and referred for treatment.[49]

One reason that transgender people may be arrested when they call the police is that some police view them as less trustworthy because they are transgender.[50] LGBTQ authors and attorneys Joey Mogul, Andrea Ritchie, and Kay Whitlock write, "Archetypes of transgender people as deceptive, mentally unstable, and sexually degraded permeate responses to domestic violence committed against them as much as they do other law enforcement activities."[51] Consequently, when police officers arrive at a crime scene, they may be less likely to believe a transgender person who is revealing violence committed against them. Law enforcement's common disbelief of transgender people can be exacerbated if, upon answering a call, the police officers do not initially realize that the person who has called them is transgender. The activists of INCITE! find that "transgender survivors of domestic violence are particularly poorly treated by responding police, and are frequently arrested or detained for mental health evaluations. Advocates and survivors alike report that once a transgender woman's gender identity is discovered by law enforcement officers or disclosed to them by an abuser, she is treated as if she has deceived the police, and often subjected to verbal abuse, arrest, and violence by law enforcement officers."[52] A study by the National Coalition of Anti-Violence Programs found that 40 percent of transgender survivors disclosed that they had experienced police violence when reporting their IPV victimization.[53]

Because many transgender women do not fit the cisgender, hyperfeminine stereotype of "victim," they can be at risk of arrest by the very police they may have called to assist them. The image of the "battered woman" that police are supposed to aid is that of a middle-class, white, cisgender woman.[54] The police frequently apply such a stereotype when deciding whom to arrest at a call for IPV. As Andrea Ritchie points out, "police base their decisions regarding who is the abuser . . . on raced and gendered presumptions and stereotypes—the abuser must be the 'bigger' partner, the more 'butch' partner, the woman of color, or the person who is less fluent in English."[55] Although the author here is referring specifically to female same-gender relationships, the reliance of police on these gendered stereotypes likely holds true in some T-IPV police calls as well. An officer who does not believe the survivor's gender identity may make an incorrect determination that the survivor is actually an abuser by erroneously applying stereotypes. Simply put, Ritchie adds, "Where domestic violence against transgender women is concerned, officers often laugh, or say, 'You're a man, too. You can handle yourself.'"[56] In writings by sociologists Xavier Guadalupe-Diaz and Jana Jasinski, a transgender survivor is quoted as recalling, "I mean I was in mid transition . . . I am still a man on record and my ID and stuff and I'm black. I'm black in [southern state]. It's like first they're going to see I'm this black dude that got beat up by a white man, think that we're gay, then see that I'm trans and that I'm in mid transition and it would be a disaster having to explain all of that and you know the police have a certain way of looking at trans people."[57]

A final particular barrier to T-IPV survivors' willingness to call the police is their fear that reactions by the police may increase their body dysphoria. Transgender people commonly have a complicated relationship with their own bodies, and certain parts of their anatomy may be the site of trauma or dysphoria.[58] T-IPV survivors may have the additional concern that they might have to undergo a police "gender check," a search done for the sole purpose of examining a person's anatomy. The DC Trans Coalition has documented a case where "a trans woman reported domestic abuse to Metro Police Department (MPD). When officers arrived, both she and her significant other were arrested and detained. She was housed in a cell with men and forced to strip naked repeatedly in front of other inmates."[59] In cases where transgender survivors have experienced sexual IPV, they may be loath to subject themselves to the gathering of evidence via a rape kit. Organizer Ana Clarissa Rojas Durazo explains, "Almost all interviews in a recent study of survivors of sexual abuse said that they were re-traumatized by the medical examination procedures. First, because there is an underlying assumption that they are not to be believed, material evidence must be collected from their bodies as they are objectified and invaded, penetrated a second time by medical intervention. And like mandatory arrest policies, the now common medical mandatory reporting policies also deem the survivors inaudible and irrelevant by insisting that criminal charges be imposed without their consent."[60]

Analysis of Police Directives for Interactions with Transgender People

Many police districts around the country have recognized that they need to codify procedures to address the specific issues facing transgender people. This realization is a result of work done and recommendations made on the federal level, as well as the activism of and advocacy by LGBTQ organizations and transgender people more generally.[61] Although they typically address similar issues, the rules vary by locality. And, as will be seen in the next section, these policies alone have not been enough to curtail the occurrence and adverse effects of discriminatory, transphobic practices by some police officers. These policies are drafted with an eye toward dealing with transgender arrestees. However, it is not a far stretch to assume that the ways in which the police are trained to deal with transgender people generally will have a significant impact on how they deal with those transgender individuals who are also IPV survivors.

Although they likely do not constitute all of the policies across the United States, I have been able to review sixteen policies of police departments in localities ranging from major metropolitan areas to small towns. They are Los Angeles, California; Hartford, Connecticut; Washington, DC; Atlanta, Georgia; Chicago, Illinois; Boston and Worcester, Massachusetts; Chevy Chase, Frederick, Anne Arundel, and Baltimore, Maryland; Minneapolis, Minnesota; Philadelphia, Pennsylvania; Salt Lake City, Utah; Seattle, Washington; and the Bay Area Rapid Transit (BART) system of San Francisco, California. When examining the policies, I not only looked at each separately but also endeavored to compare what issues they collectively covered and how they did so.

Many of these departmental policies begin with an introduction clarifying the reasons for the policy, usually stating that its inclusion is an acknowledgment that discrimination and bias have often plagued transgender people's interactions with the police. The introductions also typically refer to an overarching goal of treating people with dignity and respect, regardless of their gender identity. For example, the Salt Lake City Police Department's policy reads:

> Consistent with the Mission Statement and Core Values of the Salt Lake Police Department all members will safeguard the rights of all people, without consideration of a person's actual or perceived race, color, sex, gender, gender identity/expression, religious creed, sexual orientation, age, national origin, ancestry, handicap or disability. These goals cannot be met unless all persons are treated with the courtesy and dignity inherently due every person as a human being. Therefore, all members will act, speak, and conduct themselves in a professional manner towards an individual, or group of individuals, who identify as transgender or an associated subgroup. Members will not make discourteous, or disrespectful remarks regarding another person's actual or perceived gender, gender identity/expression, or sexual orientation.[62]

This policy makes two important points. It establishes that being respectful to transgender people is only giving them the respect that is due every human being. This should be self-evident, but it is important to have it in black and white, especially in the opening of a policy that will address using proper pronouns and names. Respecting a transgender person's name and pronouns is a necessary (though not sufficient) component of treating them with the dignity they deserve. It also ties the proper treatment of transgender people to the mission statement of the police department itself.

Of the sixteen law enforcement directives that I have examined, all but one has a section dedicated to defining common terms related to transgender people. Some, such as the guidelines developed for the Worcester Police Department, make it clear that the transgender people who use what the guidelines term an "adopted name" should not be perceived as trying to lie or obfuscate.[63] The Hartford Police Department's policy has the important inclusion of language stating that, although the document's definitions are meant to instruct officers and are accepted by much of the transgender community, they may not be the definitions or terms that every community member uses, and it therefore advises officers to use the same terms used by the community member with whom they are dealing.[64] Typically, all of the policies identify "transgender" as an umbrella term under which other identities fall. This has the benefit of making the policies all-inclusive, covering anyone whose birth-assigned sex does not align with their gender identity or expression. From a practical policy standpoint, such directives remove some of the ability of responding officers to screen people out as not meeting the criteria used in the statement of the policy; the policy is inclusive rather than exclusionary. Under it, individual officers cannot decide, for example, that someone is "not trans enough," or has not had enough medical intervention, to be covered by the protective umbrella of the policy.

Every policy reviewed orders police officers to use a transgender person's chosen name and pronouns when speaking with them. The policies also consistently require that, if they do not yet know, officers ask transgender individuals what pronoun they use. On the plus side, having this plainly laid out in the guidelines reduces the risk that officers will try to guess—potentially incorrectly—a person's gender identity and pronouns. The Chevy Chase Police Department's directive encourages officers to determine what pronouns to use based on clues from a person's gender expression, such as clothing.[65] However, instructing officers to ask only in cases where they are unsure precludes the officers from asking when they are fairly sure yet incorrect. For example, some transgender people may not be out as transgender at work, and thus dress for work in a way consistent with their birth-assigned sex, but actually prefer different pronouns than those indicated by their work clothes. Two people wearing the same suit and tie may prefer different pronouns. A better rule would be to have officers make no assumptions and require them to ask everyone what name and pronouns they use. As I tell people when I conduct training sessions on transgender criminal justice issues, "You may offend people by asking them, but I can guarantee that you are offending people when you are not asking."

Although these policies direct officers to use a transgender person's chosen name in their interpersonal interactions with them, the officers are required to put the name that appears on a person's government-issued identification documents on all forms, listing the chosen name as an "also known as" (a.k.a.). On its face, this might seem to make sense to avoid confusion, or to make sure that, even if someone has been arrested before under a different name, they are consistently booked under their "legal" name.[66] But this policy can cause extensive problems down the line for a transgender person who is booked as a defendant (given that, as already noted, many transgender survivors of IPV are mistakenly arrested as the aggressors). In Philadelphia, for example, the police paperwork becomes the basis for the charging documents, which are the basis for the case title. A person arrested as "John Doe," for example, and listed as such on the paperwork, will then be the defendant in the case *Commonwealth v. John Doe*, even if the person's chosen name is "Jane." Every time that person appears in court, they will be inevitably outed as transgender, thereby potentially putting them at risk of mistreatment and discrimination in the courtroom. (See chapter 10 for more on legal issues.) As the reviewed police directives require that both names be listed—and given that both names follow a person through the court system—it would make more sense to enter the person's legal name as their a.k.a. and put their chosen name as their name on all paperwork.

As already discussed, all of the police department policies reviewed explicitly order officers to refer to transgender people by the pronouns that they ask for, and the policies generally tell officers to classify the person's gender based on the gender marker on their government-issued ID. In the absence of government-issued ID, however, officers are commonly required to classify the person based on the "existence (or lack thereof) of male genitalia."[67] This language is problematic and essentialist (basing a person's gender entirely upon their physical characteristics, as well as improperly assigning a gendered term to physical characteristics, such as referring to a penis as "male genitalia."). If, for the purpose of classification, a police officer asks a transgender woman whether she has male genitalia, that is a way of discounting her gender identity. The policies should allow for a person's self-disclosed gender identity to be their gender designation on all forms, regardless of what their government-issued ID may currently say.

When it comes to how frisks and searches should be conducted, the guidelines begin to differ widely. Every policy I reviewed states that searches shall not be done for the purpose of identifying the gender of the person being addressed—that is, no "genital checks." Repeated searches of transgender people and groping of their genital area by police are a well-documented and pervasive problem.[68] Some of the policies differentiate between the rules for pat downs or frisks of transgender people and the rules for searches of them. A pat down or frisk occurs when an officer runs the flat of the hand over the outside of a subject's clothing to determine whether the person is armed or in possession of contraband. Policies that specifically mention a pat down state that it can be done by an officer of any gender, regardless of the preferences of the subject.

In the case of a search, however, some policies, such as that of the Boston Police Department, state that a transgender person should be searched by an officer of the gender of their choice.[69] Other policies, such as the Chevy Chase Police Department's, require that two officers be present during a search.[70] The inference to be drawn from having a second officer present is that it will prevent the abuse of the transgender person. The Frederick Police Department's policy requires that one of the officers who is present be a supervisor.[71] Some policies, such as that of the Philadelphia Police Department, fall short, requiring only that searches be done based on government-issued ID (meaning that the gender marker on the person's ID controls the gender of the officer who does the search), although an officer of a specific gender can be present if the transgender person requests it. These policies make strides toward recognizing the vulnerability of transgender people in police custody, as well as their autonomy in regard to their gender, but not all go far enough. The policy of the Metropolitan Police Department (Washington, DC) includes a provision that no officer can refuse to search a transgender person because of the person's transgender status.[72] This addition militates against officers making transgender people feel uncomfortable by refusing to search them. Affording transgender people the ability to specify the gender of the person conducting their search more fully represents the transgender person's self-determination, allowing them to make their own decisions as to what will prove best for their safety.

All of the policies I reviewed that address transportation require that transgender people in police custody be transported and housed separately. The Metropolitan Police Department's policy also includes a provision that the mileage at the beginning and end of the transport be recorded, for the additional protection of the transgender transportee.[73] This is due to an unfortunate history of police requesting sexual favors from arrestees;[74] recording the mileage limits officers' ability to take side trips in which such abuses can occur.

There are several other provisions in the police directives reviewed that should be included in overall best practices. For example, many of the policies contain a provision that a transgender person should not be forced to remove any items related to their gender expression (such as a wig or any prosthetics) unless their removal is required for safety or the items are ones that a cisgender person would also be required to remove. As another example, the Atlanta Police Department's policy specifically states that the chief of police is responsible for making sure that all of the procedures outlined in its directive are followed by lower officers.[75] This stipulation is important because without proper supervision, these policies may not be adhered to. The Philadelphia Police Department's policy requires that officers use the chosen name and pronouns of a person when communicating with the media.[76] The policies of both the Baltimore and Atlanta police departments also refer to the position (often held by an LGBTQ officer) of liaison to the LGBTQ community, with the Baltimore Police Department's policy tasking this liaison with keeping track of all calls for police assistance by the LGBTQ community.[77] It is through this kind of review that agencies are able to determine how closely their officers are adhering to policies. Several policies state that being transgender cannot be used as prima facie evidence of criminal activity. This is significant as it relates to issues connected to transgender people being stopped for "walking while trans" (e.g., a police officer cannot use the fact that someone is transgender as evidence that they are a sex worker). Many policies also caution officers that they should reveal someone's transgender status only for legitimate law enforcement purposes (such as letting the next officers who will interact with the transgender individual know so that they will not use the wrong name or pronouns). Minneapolis's policy acknowledges the existence of nonbinary and gender nonconforming people, and references the use of the gender neutral pronoun they, but falls short of making any comprehensive guidelines as to interactions with nonbinary and gender nonconforming people.[78] Only one policy, that of the Hartford Police Department, explicitly refers to making sure that a transgender person can use the appropriate bathroom.[79] No single policy, however, encompasses all of these necessary additions to their general requirements.

Best Practices for Police Serving Transgender Communities

Although police agencies are starting to adopt policies governing their interaction with transgender communities, national distrust of the police by transgender people remains high. As previously mentioned, according to the 2015 US Transgender Survey, 57 percent of transgender people are either somewhat or very uncomfortable with calling the police for help.[80] There are two steps that police departments must take to further bridge the divide between themselves and transgender communities: (1) strengthen existing departmental policies and create new policies so as to better regulate relations with the local transgender community, and (2) go beyond just writing policies to increasing the transgender community's trust in the police.

The Racial Justice Action Center (RJAC) has compiled an example ideal policy—"Model Protocols for Interactions with Trans, Intersex, and Gender Nonconforming Individuals"—that covers some of the areas where the enacted policies fall short. In addition, RJAC's model protocols require that police officers receive training, including refresher courses, facilitated by representatives of the community, so that no officer has an excuse for not following the guidelines when out on the street. Finally, and most importantly, RJAC's model protocols explicitly include "teeth," meaning that police officers are held accountable for violations.[81] The authors of the RJAC model protocols write, "The department shall have zero tolerance for any member's sexual misconduct or harassment directed toward a trans, intersex, or gender nonconforming individual. Any substantiated claim of sexual contact or harassment may result in termination of the member's employment, civil penalties, or other punitive actions as deemed appropriate."[82] Language similar to this has been incorporated into the policies adopted by police departments in Harris County, Texas, and Santa Rosa, California.[83] It is the enforcement of such punitive measures that will enable these policies to have actual impact. As researchers James Copple and Patricia Dunn point out, "Though data on this subject is quite limited, the studies that do exist reinforce the point that policy change does not necessarily lead to change on the ground."[84] Without sanctions, there is no real incentive for a policy to be followed, and it may be consistently ignored.[85]

It is also necessary for police departments to ensure that there is proper oversight of officers by their superiors. Copple and Dunn write, "Bias and discrimination against LGBTQ+ people happen in the day-to-day life of a community. Addressing these issues should be embedded into everything police chiefs are doing—e.g., senior officers should go out on the streets to see what junior officers are doing."[86] As mentioned earlier, the Atlanta Police Department's policy puts the onus on the chief of police to make sure that officers are following the proper protocols.[87] Furthermore, the implementation of these policies must be regularly audited.[88]

Beyond incorporating guidelines specific to transgender people, there are other steps that police departments must take to establish the trust of transgender communities. Police departments need to incorporate the tenets of community policing into their work. Community policing is a style of policing that prioritizes community–police relationships as a way to improve the efficacy of the police force (a far more collaborative, trust-building approach than the top-down, often-stigmatizing strategy of "broken windows" policing).[89] Community policing focuses on equipping police to work with diverse communities through targeted intensive training that both utilizes community members and integrates anti-bias training.[90] Police districts should also institute specific LGBTQ competency training. Specific cultural competency training is in line with suggestions by Lambda Legal in their report "Protected and Served?" This report argues that police should "implement mandatory cultural competency training for employees at all levels of the department, with content specific to the duties of the personnel being trained. The training should address issues relevant to the LGBTQ community. These trainings should be led by non-police personnel and with participation and input of community members."[91] These training sessions must be provided regularly, including refreshers for those who have attended previous sessions; a single session at the police academy does not suffice.[92] Importantly for dealing with IPV, new police recruits are supposed to learn de-escalation skills. Writing about trust building, researchers Caitlin Gokey and Susan Shah state, "Teaching de-escalation skills is essential to keeping situations under control while maintaining a positive or constructive interaction."[93] It is through community policing, through a focus on officers being trained in serving a diverse community, including transgender people, that the necessary bridges can be formed.

To help build community trust, the police department in Virginia Beach, Virginia, supports the acknowledgment and dissemination of examples showing where law enforcement caused past injustices.[94] As previously discussed, friction between transgender people and the police has a long history due to the practice of police targeting transgender individuals for harassment and abuse. Acknowledging past as well as recent wrongs could go a long way toward helping to close the rift between transgender people and the police, as it is often a lack of such transparency that can sow distrust. Such public transparency by police should include updates regarding the status of police investigations into the homicides of transgender people, a continuing epidemic in our society, so that people will know that such deaths are being rigorously investigated.[95] The Virginia Beach Police Department takes its recruits to the Holocaust Museum in Washington, DC, and in Richmond, VA, reporting that it uses this trip "as an opportunity to illustrate the power of abusive government and the use of police to support oppressive governmental actions."[96] Many of the past abuses of transgender people by the police arose out of the police enforcing (in a discriminatory fashion) laws that were already on the books, such as sumptuary laws (e.g., laws that criminalized people for wearing clothing associated with the "opposite" gender) and sodomy laws.[97] Having police understand and acknowledge their institution's role in oppression should help them also to monitor themselves when dealing with members of the transgender community.

Police departments should also allow for community oversight. For example, Philadelphia has a Police Advisory Commission that meets and reviews police procedures and outcomes. Its mission, according to the mandate of the City of Philadelphia, is "to improve the relationship between the police department and the community. The Commission, in its diversity of composition and in its functioning, is intended to represent the point of view of the Philadelphia citizenry."[98] The Police Advisory Commission includes transgender members.[99] Having an advisory board that meets regularly is one of the recommendations put forward by former president Barack Obama's Task Force on 21st Century Policing.[100] Other cities, such as Baltimore and Atlanta, have LGBTQ liaisons in the police department who are responsible for tracking incidents that involve LGBTQ people and acting as a conduit for community concerns and oversight. The Atlanta liaison, per the Atlanta police directive, "shall provide an internal source of support to employees on LGBT matters. The LGBT Liaison shall promote cooperation between the Atlanta Police Department and the community, while taking a leading role in building a vital link between the police and the LGBT community. To that aim, the unit shall collaborate with community leaders, residents and businesses within the City of Atlanta to design and implement public safety projects and programs."[101] These liaisons serve as specific people to whom LGBTQ constituents can communicate their concerns, thereby creating for the LGBTQ community an entry point into what might otherwise feel like an opaque policing system.

Finally, transgender people have intersecting identities, meaning that they can be not only transgender but also, for example, a person of color. Historically, policies such as "stop and frisk" drive a wedge between police and communities of color because of the overpolicing of those communities. Police policies regarding stop and frisk have been the subject of extensive litigation in Philadelphia and New York City, where the courts have found that the police are targeting people of color, stopping them, and performing pat down searches without meeting the constitutional threshold for such searches.[102] A police department that is truly interested in improving community relations needs to take these intersecting identities into account and take steps to end policies such as stop and frisk. As recommended by Copple and Dunn, "Law enforcement agencies and municipalities should refrain from practices requiring officers to issue a predetermined number of tickets, citations, arrests, or summonses, or to initiate investigative contacts with citizens for reason not directly related to improving public safety, such as generating revenue."[103] This recommendation recognizes that officers are more likely to engage in discriminatory profiling practices if there is a financial incentive or a required quota for them to meet. Catherine Hanssens and her co-authors propose that "all federal law enforcement agencies . . . adopt anti-discrimination and anti-profiling provisions . . . prohibiting the use of race, color, ethnicity, national origin, immigration status, religion, gender, disability, sexual orientation, or gender identity as a factor, to any extent or degree, in establishing reasonable suspicion or probable cause . . . except as part of an actual and apparently credible description of a specific suspect or suspects in a criminal investigation."[104] Similarly, the National Center for Transgender Equality has urged Congress to pass the End Racial Profiling Act, a bill that forbids the police from using actual or perceived race, ethnicity, national origin, religion, gender, gender identity, or sexual orientation when making determinations on whom to stop.[105]

Best Practices for Police Serving T-IPV Survivors

Whereas the best practices reviewed in the previous section focused on how police departments can better serve transgender people in general—including but not limited to IPV survivors—this section delves into additional recommended best practices for law enforcement interactions specifically with T-IPV survivors. To begin, there are many IPV tactics that are unique to T-IPV (see chapter 2). For example, one type of abuse that police should be specifically conscious of and sensitive about is the targeting of gendered body parts by perpetrators in such a way as to denigrate transgender survivors.[106] Consider that, if a transgender man typically binds to modify his chest's appearance, an abuser may either verbally or physically single out his chest in an effort to emasculate him and make him feel like a failed man. Police should be aware that a transgender person might not use traditional or scientific language to describe their body parts, especially those that typically carry gendered meaning (e.g., a transgender man may describe his upper torso as his "chest," his "chesticles," or his "pecs," rather than "breasts"). Police should be sure to echo in a respectful manner the language that a transgender person uses to describe their body.[107] Furthermore, since abusers may have targeted these sensitive areas for abuse, police should be aware that certain investigative procedures, such as a rape kit or even taking photographs, can be significantly retraumatizing for a transgender person, and therefore they should ensure that their investigative demeanor and practices are sensitive to this.[108] While police should always treat all survivors with patience and compassion, they should recognize that discussing issues relating to their bodies may be unusually difficult for transgender survivors.

Police should also make sure that all of their printed materials are inclusive of transgender identities. It is important that survivors not feel ignored by the very materials that the police are handing out to help them. This could include making all references to survivors and perpetrators gender-neutral, so as not to assume the pronouns of either. Police departments should seek out providers of transgender-specific services and have those relationships in place so that they can provide appropriate referrals for transgender survivors. FORGE, a national transgender anti-violence organization, maintains a list of three hundred transgender-focused social support groups across the country that can be used as a resource.[109]

Police districts should also place stricter limits on the use of dual and mandatory arrest policies. Dual arrest policies are especially problematic for survivors of T-IPV, as they are frequently employed to arrest both survivor and perpetrator.[110] This echoes the guidance released by the US Department of Justice found in "Identifying and Preventing Gender Bias in Law Enforcement Response to Sexual Assault and Domestic Violence": "Law Enforcement agencies also should discourage dual arrests in domestic violence cases, wherever feasible. . . . Arresting the wrong party or both parties increases the likelihood that the offender will act again, and discourages the victim from reporting future incidents."[111] As discussed earlier, many transgender people call the police for help only to find themselves arrested along with their abuser because the police officer cannot sort out what happened.

As discussed in the previous section, police officers should be trained in LGBTQ competence. However, this should not be a "one-and-done" kind of training. Trainings need to be comprehensive and to identify the specific issues that may arise when dealing with transgender survivors of IPV; they must go beyond the "transgender 101" style of training that covers only basic transgender competency. Police training must specifically address avoiding the use of stereotypes when making arrests in T-IPV situations. There exists an intersection between stereotypes and victim blaming: the perception that transgender survivors are bringing the abuse on themselves through their dress and "lifestyle."[112] Recognizing the use of stereotypes when making arrests should also hopefully address the issue of victim blaming by removing the inclination to make determinations about someone's role in an altercation based on their gender identity and expression.

Police training should also acknowledge and respond to the checkered history between the police and transgender people.[113] Police should be trained not to treat a transgender person's reticence or evasiveness as a sign that they are lying, as this attitude may come from the antagonistic history between the police and transgender communities.[114] If police are educated as to the potential roots of a transgender survivor's discomfort, they will be less likely to use the results of that discomfort as a way of discrediting the stories of survivors.

The fact that training should focus on bias and cultural awareness was stressed by participants in the 2015 Roundtable Discussion for Identifying and Preventing Gender Bias in Law Enforcement Response to Sexual Assault and Domestic Violence.[115] A survey of transgender people conducted by the Solutions Not Punishment Collective found that 26 percent of all transgender women surveyed (and 38 percent of all transgender women of color) who called the police for help were instead arrested.[116] Although not limited to IPV-specific incidents, these numbers indicate the way that police can use stereotypes when determining whom to arrest. The Baltimore Police Department has specifically addressed this issue by requiring that "when responding to calls for service relating to domestic violence, assault, or other concerns, members shall not make assumptions about which individuals may be victims and/or suspects based on the individual's gender identity, gender expression, and/or sexual orientation."[117] Police training must address specific issues surrounding T-IPV to eliminate the pervasive practice of transgender survivors being arrested instead of or alongside the perpetrator.

Alternatives to Calling the Police

Although the focus of this piece is on best practices for police departments for their interactions with survivors and perpetrators of T-IPV, transgender people may not wish to contact the police at all, a decision that should be respected. Law professor Leigh Goodmark points out how involving the criminal legal system deprives people of the ability to determine "how the violence in their lives should be addressed."[118] In the United States and in many other parts of the world, when criminal charges are brought by the government against an abuser, it is the agents of the government (district attorneys, primarily) who determine the course of the case, not the survivors themselves. Options such as transformative justice prioritize the needs of the survivor and help them recover from their trauma, whereas the goal of the carceral state is to punish and lock up offenders.[119]

Conclusion

The conflictual history of transgender people and law enforcement has led to extensive distrust of the police, which makes transgender people reluctant to call the police, particularly when they have been victimized and are at their most vulnerable. Mistrust cannot be eradicated through the mere creation of policies—best practices go beyond policy, beyond words. Police departments must confront the causes of this mistrust head on, taking responsibility for past failings. They must be responsive to community concerns and requests, and prove through both actions and policy that they are committed to a respectful relationship with transgender people. They must seek to ameliorate mistrust in a way that takes into account transgender people's intersecting identities and thus their potential exposure to multiple forms of discrimination (e.g., eliminating

Figure 9.1. Best Practices in Policing Related to Transgender Intimate Partner Violence

1. Develop police department policies ensuring respectful interactions with transgender individuals
2. Form a community-based police oversight board that monitors police protocols pertaining to transgender communities
3. Appoint an LGBTQ-community liaison within the police force
4. End the use of stop and frisk
5. Publicly acknowledge and vow to address transphobic discrimination of the past and present by police
6. Mandate recurring police officer trainings, covering "transgender 101," stereotypes, and T-IPV
7. Create transgender-inclusive IPV survivor brochures and other informational materials (including transgender-specific victim service referrals)
8. Curtail the use of mandatory and dual arrest policies
9. Respect and support the decision of some T-IPV survivors to seek help from nonpolice resources

transphobia alone in a police force will not protect transgender people of color from racial discrimination by police). Finally, rather than focusing solely on "improving" the police, we should simultaneously be turning our attention to the creation and support of noncriminal legal measures. Regardless of what the goal may be, there are concrete best practices that police can use to foster trust between themselves and transgender communities. Police departments must do the following. (See figure 9.1.)

First, police departments should promulgate or update directives to specifically address police interactions with the transgender community. At a minimum, these directives must mandate that police be respectful of transgender people's identities through the use of proper pronouns and names, and act in such a way as to guarantee the safety of both transgender victim and arrestee. These policies should also specifically reference as well as provide guidelines for interactions with nonbinary people. These policies must also include mechanisms for assuring accountability (including punishment and sanctions) of officers who deviate from them.

Second, police departments should assemble oversight boards that include members of the communities impacted by police tactics, specifically including transgender people. These oversight boards must be given the ability to review police protocols and make suggestions as to modifications reflective of the ever-changing landscape. Ideally, these oversight boards should have the ability to review information and data regarding arrests in order to identify any potentially unintended but harmful patterns of targeting and arrest.

Third, police departments should appoint, in tandem with oversight boards, an LGBTQ liaison to whom transgender community members can bring their concerns and be guaranteed trans-competent services.

Fourth, police departments should end the use of stop and frisk. This is necessary to increase trust in the police, specifically by communities of color, including transgender people of color.

Fifth, police departments should engage in activities that increase trust between themselves and transgender communities. This includes, in particular, acknowledging the antagonistic past between the transgender and law enforcement communities.

Sixth, police departments should require officer trainings covering both transgender competency and the unique nature of T-IPV. These must not be "one-and-done" style trainings, and they must go beyond basic transgender competency around terms and pronouns. They must address the use of stereotypes and their impact on police activities head-on. Police must understand the distinct ways that T-IPV manifests in order to recognize and handle T-IPV scenarios properly.

Seventh, police departments should create materials (e.g., brochures, website information, etc.) for IPV survivors that are transgender inclusive. Both within and in addition to these materials, police must identify appropriate referrals for transgender survivors.

Eighth, police departments should curtail the use of mandatory and dual arrest policies. These policies have an extensive history of resulting in the arrest of transgender IPV survivors and therefore are antithetical to increasing trust between transgender communities and the police.

Ninth and lastly, police departments should allow their services to be victim directed. Police should respect that a T-IPV survivor (especially if someone other than the survivor called the police) may not want to have the police involved and may wish, instead, to pursue alternatives to arrest and punishment of the perpetrator.

NOTES

1 In this chapter, when discussing people whose gender identity does not align with the sex assigned to them at birth, I generally use the umbrella term *transgender*. However, there are some people who use other terms to identify themselves. Where other terms, such as *transsexual*, are used in this chapter, it

is because of the self-identification of interviewed individuals in the research literature.
2   National Center for Transgender Equality 2016.
3   Russell 2018.
4   K. Stryker 2019. See also Mogul, Ritchie, and Whitlock 2011.
5   Greenberg 2012, 214.
6   In discussing the way that police treatment and perception of him have changed post-transition, Trystan Cotten, a Black transgender man, states, "I'll never call the police again." Although his story does not deal with IPV, the statement makes stark reference to the fact that a Black person, especially a Black man, may hesitate to see the police as the source of his salvation. Bahrampour 2018.
7   Police districts as far apart as Queensland, Australia, and Baltimore, Maryland, to name just two. Queensland Police Service 2016; Baltimore Police Department 2016.
8   See, e.g., Philadelphia Police Department 2013.
9   It has been argued that the system itself, by the criminalization of Black and Brown bodies, is only accomplishing what it was designed to do. See Alexander 2010.
10 See, generally, Spade 2015. I find it important to note here that, even as a person who advocates for necessary reforms to police procedure (and prisons), because these systems cause harm to many transgender IPV survivors and perpetrators alike who come into contact with them I do so with the hopes of a prison abolitionist.
11 INCITE! Women of Color Against Violence 2018, 42.
12 This is due, in part, to laws that were designed specifically to criminalize "cross-dressing." Sears 2015.
13 The purpose of this chapter is not to dwell on the past but to look to a future informed by that past. For more about the background of the modern transgender rights movement, see S. Stryker 2008.
14 Center for American Progress and Movement Advancement Project 2016, 45.
15 INCITE! Women of Color Against Violence 2018, 17.
16 INCITE! Women of Color Against Violence 2018, 17.
17 For example, in Philadelphia, as I can attest, having worked shifts in arraignment court, even though possession of a small amount of marijuana was made only a citation offense by the city council, many people of color were still being arrested and charged for it. Despite the council's having made it known that they did not want such possession to be criminalized, Philadelphia police continued to use marijuana possession as a reason to stop and arrest people. At every encounter, therefore, it is up to the individual officer to choose whether they will issue a citation rather than execute an arrest.
18 Sylvia Rivera Law Project 2007, 16.
19 Center for American Progress and Movement Advancement Project 2016, 45.
20 Center for American Progress and Movement Advancement Project 2016, 45.

21 Lawyer and activist Pooja Gehi writes, "'Walking while trans,' a play on the well-known phrase 'driving while black,' is a term used by clients of Sylvia Rivera Law Project ('SRLP') to describe the intense police scrutiny trans people of color experience while walking on the streets of New York City. Many of my clients are stopped for no reason other than their perceived gender-nonconformity, and as a result, are charged with a range of survival crimes such as loitering for the purposes of prostitution, obstruction of government conduct, disorderly conduct, or lewd conduct." Gehi 2012, 369.
22 INCITE! Women of Color Against Violence 2018, 26.
23 Make the Road New York 2012, 22.
24 Hanssens et al. 2014, 10.
25 Center for American Progress and Movement Advancement Project 2016, 45.
26 The collective FIERCE (fiercenyc.org) has done incredible work organizing around this issue in New York, focusing on access to the Chelsea Piers in the gentrified neighborhood of the West Village.
27 Majd, Marksamer, and Reyes 2009, 71. Finding transgender-specific data can be difficult, as the *T* is normally lumped in with the *LGB*.
28 Majd, Marksamer, and Reyes 2009, 72.
29 Hanssens et al. 2014, 4.
30 Dank et al. 2015, 21.
31 Dwyer 2015.
32 Dwyer et al. 2017.
33 I gained personal knowledge of this level of abuse from reviewing police arrest reports for transgender people arrested in Philadelphia. Commonly, transgender people are referred to as "men with purses," and all of the documents use the person's given name and incorrect pronouns. This holds true whether the transgender person is the arrestee or the putative victim.
34 Namaste 2000, 170.
35 Namaste 2000, 169.
36 US Department of Justice, Civil Rights Division 2011, 36.
37 Farr 2016, 25.
38 Ritchie 2017, 1.
39 James et al. 2016, 185.
40 James et al. 2016, 185.
41 Namaste 2000, 172.
42 Amnesty International 2005, 41.
43 Arkles 2009, 517.
44 Ritchie 2006, 140.
45 Goodmark 2017, 61–64.
46 Goodmark 2017, 61–64.
47 Morrison 2003, 106.
48 Hirschel and Buzawa 2002.
49 Amnesty International 2005, 50.

50 Bettcher 2007.
51 Mogul, Ritchie, and Whitlock 2011, 137.
52 INCITE! Women of Color Against Violence 2018, 39.
53 Waters 2017, 32.
54 Morrison 2006, 1078.
55 Ritchie 2006, 140.
56 Ritchie 2017, 191.
57 Guadalupe-Diaz and Jasinski, 2017, 786.
58 Kirkup 2013, 52.
59 DC Trans Coalition, n.d., 23.
60 Durazo 2006, 187.
61 The New York Police Department does not have a specific policy for transgender people. The department has, however, updated its patrol documents overall to address issues brought to it by the city's transgender community. I have been unable to find another jurisdiction that has similarly modified its overall guidelines.
62 Salt Lake City Police Department 2018.
63 Worcester Police Department 2014.
64 Hartford Police Department n.d.
65 Chevy Chase Police Department 2015.
66 "Legal" is in quotation marks because of a misnomer relating to what can constitute a legal name, which may vary across jurisdictions. A person may need to get a court-ordered name change in order to change their identity documents, but at least in Pennsylvania that does not stop their chosen name from being their legal name. 54 Pa.C.S.A. § 701(b) provides, in part, that "a person may at any time adopt and use any name if such name is used consistently, nonfraudulently and exclusively." Therefore, the name one uses every day could arguably be considered a legal name even if the person has not submitted government forms completing a name change procedure.
67 E.g., Chicago Police Department 2015; Frederick Police Department 2014; Philadelphia Police Department 2013. The version of the Pennsylvania Police Directive utilized in this writing has since been amended and updated in substantial ways in 2019. It was too late, however, to incorporate an analysis of that policy into the chapter due to the printing schedule.
68 Mogul, Ritchie, and Whitlock 2011.
69 Boston Police Department 2013.
70 Chevy Chase Police Department 2015.
71 Frederick Police Department 2014.
72 Metropolitan Police Department, District of Columbia 2015.
73 Metropolitan Police Department, District of Columbia 2015.
74 The recent US Transgender Survey found that 6–27 percent of all transgender people interviewed were subject to physical or sexual assault by officers with whom they interacted. James et al. 2016, 187.
75 Atlanta Police Department 2015.

76 Philadelphia Police Department 2013. This requirement is a result of press reports about transgender people who were victims of crime in Philadelphia. Researchers Burke and colleagues explain: "Not isolated to law enforcement, the use of improper terminology can cause strain between transgender communities and the community at large. On July 14, 2013, Diamond Williams was brutally murdered and dismembered after the suspect discovered that Diamond was a transgender woman. Her body was located in an isolated field. 'Initial news articles about Williams' death described her as a "male prostitute dressed as a woman,"' language offensive to many transgender persons and allies. Some of the other orders within directive 152 include keeping transgender arrestees isolated from the general inmate population and referring to transgender victims, witnesses, or arrestees by their preferred names, particularly when addressing the media." Burke, Owen, and Few-Demo 2015.
77 Atlanta Police Department 2015; Baltimore Police Department 2016.
78 Minneapolis Police Department 2016.
79 Hartford Police Department, n.d.
80 James et al. 2016, 185.
81 Racial Justice Action Center, n.d.
82 Racial Justice Action Center, n.d., 5.
83 Harris County Police Department 2017; Santa Rosa Police Department 2015.
84 Copple and Dunn 2017, 11.
85 Copple and Dunn 2017, 11. Note that the Virginia Beach Police Department's guidelines generally include not only sanctions for misconduct but also strategies for positive reinforcement. Hungerford and Pastrana 2016, 9.
86 Copple and Dunn 2017, 20.
87 Atlanta Police Department 2015.
88 Copple and Dunn 2017, 27.
89 Gokey and Shah 2016, 5.
90 Gokey and Shah 2016, 41.
91 Lambda Legal 2015.
92 Copple and Dunn 2017, 32.
93 Gokey and Shah 2016, 43.
94 Hungerford and Pastrana 2016, 6.
95 Copple and Dunn 2017, 60.
96 Hungerford and Pastrana 2016, 6.
97 See Sears 2015.
98 City of Philadelphia, n.d.
99 City of Philadelphia, n.d.
100 Copple and Dunn 2017, 19.
101 Atlanta Police Department 2015.
102 Bailey v. City of Philadelphia, No. 10-5952 (E.D. Pa. Feb. 24, 2015).
103 Copple and Dunn 2017, 14.
104 Hanssens et al. 2014, 14.

105 Tobin, Freedman-Gurspan, and Mottet 2015, 29.
106 Greenberg 2012, 217–218.
107 FORGE 2014.
108 Brown 2011, 155.
109 FORGE 2014.
110 Goodmark 2013, 76.
111 US Department of Justice 2015, 20.
112 Parsons 2014, 4. See also Center for American Progress and Movement Advancement Project 2016, 12.
113 Carpenter and Marshall 2017.
114 FORGE 2014.
115 Police Executive Research Forum 2016, 15.
116 Solutions Not Punishment Coalition 2016, 11.
117 Baltimore Police Department 2016.
118 Goodmark 2017, 104.
119 Chrysalis Collective 2016, 189.

REFERENCES

Alexander, Michelle. 2010. *The New Jim Crow: Mass Incarceration in the Age of Colorblindness.* New York: New Press.

Amnesty International. 2005. *Stonewalled: Police Abuse and Misconduct against Lesbian, Gay, Bisexual, and Transgender People in the US.* London: Amnesty International. www.amnesty.org.

Anne Arundel County Police Department. 2017. "Interactions with Transgender Individuals," policy no. 2007. www.powerdms.com/public/aac/documents/1278177.

Arkles, Gabriel. 2009. "Safety and Solidarity across Gender Lines: Rethinking Segregation of Transgender People in Detention." *Temple Political & Civil Rights Law Review* 18:515–560.

Atlanta Police Department. 2015. "Transgender Interactions," policy no. APD.SOP.6180. www.atlantapd.org.

Bahrampour, Tara. 2018. "Crossing the Divide." *Washington Post*, July 22, 2018. www.washingtonpost.com.

Baltimore Police Department. 2016. "Lesbian, Gay, Bisexual, and Transgender Involved Incidents," policy no. 720. www.powerdms.com/public/BALTIMOREMD/documents/55009.

Barrett, Betty Jo, and Vanessa Sheridan. 2017. "Partner Violence in Transgender Communities: What Helping Professionals Need to Know." *Journal of GLBT Family Studies* 13 (2): 137–162.

Bay Area Rapid Transit Police Department. 2015. "Interactions with Individuals Identifying as Transgender," policy no. 403. www.bart.gov.

Bettcher, Talia Mae. 2007. "Evil Deceivers and Make-Believers: On Transphobic Violence and the Politics of Illusion." *Hypatia* 22 (3): 43–65.

Boston Police Department. 2013. "Transgender Policy," policy no. SO 13–025. http://bpdnews.com.
Brown, Nicola. 2011. "Holding Tensions of Victimization and Perpetration: Partner Abuse in Trans Communities." In *Intimate Partner Violence in LGBTQ Lives*, edited by Janice L. Ristock, 153–168. New York: Routledge.
Burke, Tod W., Stephen S. Owen, and April Few-Demo. 2015. "Law Enforcement and Transgender Communities." *FBI Law Enforcement Bulletin*, June 11, 2015. https://leb.fbi.gov.
Carpenter, L., and Barrett Marshall. 2017. "Walking While Trans: Profiling of Transgender Women by Law Enforcement, and the Problem of Proof." *William & Mary Journal of Women & the Law* 24:5–38.
Center for American Progress and Movement Advancement Project. 2016. *Unjust: How the Broken Criminal Justice System Fails LGBT People*. Washington, DC: Center for American Progress, and Denver: Movement Advancement Project. www.lgbtmap.org.
Chevy Chase Police Department. 2015. "Interactions with Transgender Individuals," policy no. 5-16.1. www.chevychasevillagemd.gov.
Chicago Police Department. 2015. "Interactions with Transgender, Intersex, and Gender Nonconforming (TIGN) Individuals," policy no. G02-01-03. http://directives.chicagopolice.org.
Chrysalis Collective. 2016. "Beautiful, Difficult, Powerful: Ending Sexual Assault through Transformative Justice." In *The Revolution Starts at Home: Confronting Intimate Violence within Activist Communities*, 2nd ed., edited by Ching-In Chen, Jai Dulani, and Leah Lakshi Piepzna-Samarasinha, 189–206. Oakland, CA: AK Press.
City of Philadelphia. n.d. "Police Advisory Commission: Mission." Accessed July 1, 2018. www.phila.gov.
Copple, James E., and Patricia M. Dunn. 2017. *Gender, Sexuality, and 21st Century Policing: Protecting the Rights of the LGBTQ+ Community*. Washington, DC: Office of Community Oriented Policing Services. https://cops.usdoj.gov.
Dank, Meredith, Jennifer Yahner, Kuniko Madden, Isela Banuelos, Lilly Yu, Andrea Ritchie, Mitchyll Mora, and Brendan Conner. 2015. *Surviving the Streets of New York: Experiences of LGBTQ Youth, YMSM, and YWSW Engaged in Survival Sex*. Washington, DC: Urban Institute. www.urban.org.
DC Trans Coalition. n.d. *Police and the Trans Community: Metropolitan Police Academy SLU Training*. Washington, DC: DC Trans Coalition. https://dctranscoalition.wordpress.com.
Durazo, Ana Clarissa Rojas. 2006. "Medical Violence against People of Color and the Medicalization of Domestic Violence." In *Color of Violence: The INCITE! Anthology*, edited by INCITE! Women of Color against Violence, 179–190, Durham, NC: Duke University Press.
Dwyer, Angela. 2015. "Teaching Young Queers a Lesson: How Police Teach Lessons about Non-heteronormativity in Public Spaces." *Sexuality & Culture* 19 (3): 493–512.

Dwyer, Angela, Matthew Ball, Christine Bond, Murray Lee, and Thomas Crofts. 2017. *Exploring LGBTI Police Liaison Services: Factors Influencing Their Use and Effectiveness According to LGBTI People and LGBTI Police Liaison Officers.* Canberra, Australia: Criminology Research Grants. http://crg.aic.gov.au.

Farr, Patrick. 2016. "Queer Victims: Reports of Violence by LGBTQI Survivors Result in Violent Assaults by Police." Master's thesis, Arizona State University.

Ford, Chandra L., Terra Slavin, Karin I. Hilton, and Susan L. Holt. 2013. "Intimate Partner Violence Prevention Services and Resources in Los Angeles: Issues, Needs, and Challenges for Assisting Lesbian, Gay, Bisexual, and Transgender Clients." *Health Promotion Practice*, 14 (November): 841–849.

FORGE. 2014. "Responding to Transgender Victims of Sexual Assault: Victim Issues." www.ovc.gov.

Frederick Police Department. 2014. "Interactions with Transgender Persons," policy no. 580. www.cityoffrederick.com.

Gehi, Pooja. 2012. "Gendered (In)security: Migration and Criminalization in the Security State." *Harvard Journal of Law & Gender* 35:357–398.

Gokey, Caitlin, and Susan Shah, eds. 2016. *How to Support Trust Building in Your Agency: Police Perspectives: Building Trust in a Diverse Nation, no. 3.* Washington, DC: Office of Community Oriented Policing Services.

Goodmark, Leigh. 2013. "Transgender People, Intimate Partner Abuse, and the Legal System." *Harvard Civil Rights–Civil Liberties Law Review* 48 (1): 51–104.

Goodmark, Leigh. 2017. "Should Domestic Violence Be Decriminalized?" *Harvard Journal of Law & Gender* 40:53–113.

Greenberg, Kae. 2012. "Still Hidden in the Closet: Trans Women and Domestic Violence." *Berkeley Journal of Gender, Law & Justice* 27 (2): 198–251.

Guadalupe-Diaz, Xavier L. 2013. "Victims outside the Binary: Transgender Survivors of Intimate Partner Violence." PhD diss., University of Central Florida.

Guadalupe-Diaz, Xavier L., and Jana Jasinski. 2017. "'I Wasn't a Priority, I Wasn't a Victim': Challenges in Help Seeking for Transgender Survivors of Intimate Partner Violence." *Violence against Women* 23 (6): 772–792.

Hanssens, Catherine, Aisha C. Moodie-Mills, Andrea J. Ritchie, Dean Spade, and Urvashi Vaid. 2014. *A Roadmap for Change: Federal Policy Recommendations for Addressing the Criminalization of LGBT People and People Living with HIV.* New York: Center for Gender & Sexuality Law at Columbia Law School. www.law.columbia.edu.

Harris County Police Department. 2017. "Lesbian, Gay, Bisexual, Transgender and Intersex (LGBTI)," policy no. 413. www.harriscountyso.org.

Hartford Police Department. n.d. "Appropriate Treatment of Detained Transgender Individuals," policy no. DD 17-01. www.hartford.gov.

Hirschel, David, and Eve Buzawa. 2002. "Understanding the Context of Dual Arrest with Directions for Future Research." *Violence against Women* 8 (12): 1449–1473.

Hungerford, Kelly E., and Nathalie M. F. Pastrana. 2016. *Virginia Beach Police Department in the 21st Century: A Response to the President's Task Force Report.* Virginia Beach, VA: Virginia Beach Police Department. www.vbgov.com.

INCITE! Women of Color Against Violence, eds. 2006. *Color of Violence: The INCITE! Anthology*. Durham, NC: Duke University Press.

INCITE! Women of Color Against Violence. 2018. *Law Enforcement Violence against Women of Color and Transgender People of Color: A Critical Intersection of Gender Violence and State Violence*. INCITE! Women of Color Against Violence. www.incite-national.org.

James, Sandy E., Jody L. Herman, Susan Rankin, Mara Keisling, Lisa Mottet, and Ma'ayan Anafi. 2016. *The Report of the 2015 U.S. Transgender Survey*. Washington, DC: National Center for Transgender Equality. www.ustranssurvey.org.

Kirkup, Kyle. 2013. *Best Practices in Policing and LGBTQ Communities in Ontario*. Toronto: Ontario Association of Chiefs of Police. www.oacp.on.ca.

Lambda Legal. 2015. *Protected and Served?* New York: Lambda Legal. www.lambdalegal.org.

Langenderfer-Magruder, Lisa, Darren L. Whitfield, N. Eugene Walls, Shanna K. Kattari, and Daniel Ramors. 2016. "Experiences of Intimate Partner Violence and Subsequent Police Reporting among Lesbian, Gay, Bisexual, Transgender, and Queer Adults in Colorado: Comparing Rates of Cisgender and Transgender Victimization." *Journal of Interpersonal Violence* 3 (5): 855–871.

Los Angeles Police Department. 2012. "Police Interactions with Transgender Individuals," policy no. 1.12. www.lapdonline.org.

Lydon, Jason. 2015. *Coming Out of Concrete Closets: A Report on Black & Pink's National LGBTQ Prison Survey*. With Kamaria Carrington, Hana Low, Reed Miller, and Mahsa Yazdy. Omaha, NE: Black & Pink. www.blackandpink.org.

Majd, Katayoon, Jody Marksamer, and Carolyn Reyes. 2009. *Hidden Injustice: Lesbian, Gay, Bisexual, and Transgender Youth in Juvenile Courts*. San Francisco and Washington, DC: Legal Services for Children, National Juvenile Defender Center, and National Center for Lesbian Rights. www.nclrights.org.

Make the Road New York. 2012. *Transgressive Policing: Police Abuse of LGBTQ Communities of Color in Jackson Heights*. Brooklyn, NY: Make the Road New York. https://maketheroadny.org.

Messinger, Adam M. 2017. *LGBTQ Intimate Partner Violence: Lessons for Policy, Practice, and Research*. Oakland: University of California Press.

Metropolitan Police Department, District of Columbia. 2015. "Handling Interactions with Transgender Individuals," policy no. PCA 501-02. https://go.mpdconline.com.

Minneapolis Police Department. 2016. "Interactions with Transgender and Gender Non-conforming Individuals," policy no. 7-3001. www.minneapolismn.gov.

Mogul, Joey, Andrea J. Ritchie, and Kay Whitlock. 2011. *Queer (In)justice: The Criminalization of LGBT People in the United States*. Boston: Beacon Press.

Morrison, Adele. 2003. "Queering Domestic Violence to 'Straighten Out' Criminal Law: What Might Happen When Queer Theory and Practice Meet Criminal Law's Conventional Responses to Domestic Violence." *Southern California Review of Law & Women's Studies* 13:81–160.

Morrison, Adele. 2006. "Changing the Domestic Violence (Dis)course: Moving from White Victim to Multicultural Survivor." *UC Davis Law Review* 39:1063–1118.
Namaste, Vivian. 2000. *Invisible Lives: The Erasure of Transsexual and Transgendered People.* Chicago: University of Chicago Press.
National Center for Transgender Equality. 2016. "Stonewall: 47 Years Later." *National Center for Transgender Equality,* June 28, 2016. https://transequality.org.
New Smyrna Beach Police Department. 2008. "Interactions with Transgender Individuals," policy no. FS 901. www.cityofnsb.com.
Orloff, Leslye E., Mary Ann Dutton, Giselle Aguilar, and Nawal Ammar. 2003. "Battered Immigrant Women's Willingness to Call for Help and Police Response." *UCLA Women's Law Journal* 13 (1): 43–100.
Parsons, Brett. 2014. "Audio Transcript: United States Department of Justice Community Relations Service: Law Enforcement and the Transgender Community." September 9, 2014. www.justice.gov.
Pasulka, Nicole. 2014. "The Women Who Helped Change How Police Treat Transgender People." *BuzzFeed,* July 10, 2014. www.buzzfeed.com.
Philadelphia Police Department. 2013. "Department Interactions with Transgender Individuals," policy no. 152. www.phillypolice.com.
Pitts, Marion, Anthony Smith, Anne Mitchell, and Sunil Patel. 2006. *Private Lives: A Report on the Health and Wellbeing of GLBTI Australians.* Melbourne: Australian Research Centre in Sex, Health and Society, La Trobe University. www.glhv.org.au.
Police Executive Research Forum. 2016. *Identifying and Preventing Gender Bias in Law Enforcement Response to Sexual Assault and Domestic Violence: A Roundtable Discussion.* Washington, DC: Office of Community Oriented Policing Services. www.nccpsafety.org.
Queensland Police Service. 2016. *Good Practice Guide for Interaction with Transgender Clients.* Queensland, Australia: Queensland Police Service. www.police.qld.gov.au.
Racial Justice Action Center. n.d. "Model Protocols for Interactions with Trans, Intersex, and Gender Nonconforming Individuals." April 13, 2018. www.rjactioncenter.org.
Ritchie, Andrea J. 2006. "Law Enforcement Violence against Women of Color." In *Color of Violence: The INCITE! Anthology,* edited by INCITE! Women of Color against Violence, 138–156, Durham, NC: Duke University Press.
Ritchie, Andrea J. 2017. *Invisible No More: Police Violence against Black Women and Women of Color.* Boston: Beacon Press.
Ritchie, Andrea J., and Delores Jones-Brown. 2017. "Policing Race, Gender, and Sex: A Review of Law Enforcement Policies." *Women and Criminal Justice* 27 (1): 21–50.
Roch, Amy, James Morton, and Graham Ritchie. 2010. *Out of Sight, Out of Mind? Transgender People's Experiences of Domestic Abuse.* Edinburgh: LGBT Youth Scotland and the Scottish Transgender Alliance. www.scottishtrans.org.
Russell, Emma K. 2018. "Carceral Pride: The Fusion of Police Imagery with LGBTI Rights." *Feminist Legal Studies* 26 (3): 331–350.
Salt Lake City Police Department. 2018. "Transgender Individuals," policy no. 344.1. www.slcdocs.com.

Santa Rosa Police Department. 2015. "PREA (Prison Rape Elimination Act) LGBTI (Lesbian, Gay, Transgender, Bisexual, Intersex) Inmates," policy no. O-008. http://santarosasheriff.org.

Sears, Clare. 2015. *Arresting Dress: Cross-Dressing, Law, and Fascination in Nineteenth-Century San Francisco*. Durham, NC: Duke University Press.

Seattle Police Department. 2016. "Interaction with Transgender Individuals," policy no. 16.2000. www.seattle.gov.

Solutions Not Punishment Coalition (SNaP Co). 2016. *"The Most Dangerous Thing Out Here Is the Police": Trans Voices on Police Abuse and Profiling in Atlanta*. East Point, GA: Solutions Not Punishment Coalition. http://snap4freedom.org.

Spade, Dean. 2015. *Normal Life: Administrative Violence, Critical Trans Politics, and the Limits of Law*. Durham, NC: Duke University Press.

Spalek, Basia. 2008. *Communities, Identities, and Crime: Lesbian, Gay, Bisexual and Transgender Communities: Crime, Victimization, and Criminal Justice*. Bristol, England: Policy Press.

Stryker, Kitty. 2019. "Targeting the Opposition: The Long, Troubling History of Cops at Pride Parades," *Bitch Media*, June 24, 2019. www.bitchmedia.org.

Stryker, Susan. 2008. *Transgender History*. Berkeley, CA: Seal Press.

Stubbs, Julie, and Julia Tolmie. 2005."Defending Battered Women on Charges of Homicide: The Structural and Systemic versus the Personal and Particular." In *Women, Mental Disorder and the Law*, edited by Wendy Chan, Dorothy E. Chunn, and Robert Menzies, 191–210. London: Glasshouse Press.

Sylvia Rivera Law Project. 2007. *"It's War in Here": A Report on the Treatment of Transgender and Intersex People in New York Men's Prisons*. New York: Sylvia Rivera Law Project. https://srlp.org.

Tobin, Harper Jean, Raffi Freedman-Gurspan, and Lisa Mottet. 2015. *A Blueprint for Equality: A Transgender Federal Agenda*. Washington, DC: National Center for Transgender Equality. www.transequality.org.

US Department of Justice. 2015. *Identifying and Preventing Gender Bias in Law Enforcement Response to Sexual Assault and Domestic Violence*. Washington, DC: US Department of Justice. www.justice.gov.

US Department of Justice, Civil Rights Division. 2011. *Investigation of the New Orleans Police Department*. Washington, DC: US Department of Justice. www.justice.gov.

Vitale, Alex. 2017. *The End of Policing*. New York: Verso.

Waters, Emily. 2017. *Lesbian, Gay, Bisexual, Transgender, Queer, and HIV-Affected Intimate Partner Violence in 2016*. New York: National Coalition of Anti-Violence Programs. http://avp.org.

Worcester Police Department. 2014. "Transgender Policy," policy no. 495. www.worcesterma.gov.

Yarbrough, Marilyn, and Crystal Bennett. 2000. "Cassandra and the 'Sistahs': The Peculiar Treatment of African American Women in the Myth of Women as Liars." *Journal of Gender, Race & Justice* 3:625–657.

10

Legal System Reform

LEIGH GOODMARK

When a person is abused, often the first advice given is to engage the legal system in some way: call the police or seek a protective order. While that advice is well-meaning, it is also problematic. The legal system often fails to respond protectively or productively for people subjected to abuse. For no one is this truer than for transgender individuals.

Transgender intimate partner violence (T-IPV) survivors often avoid interacting with the legal system, believing that the system has little to offer at best and can be traumatizing and harmful at worst. Reporting rates make it clear that transgender survivors rarely access the legal system. A survey by the National Coalition of Anti-Violence Programs (NCAVP) found that only 39 percent of lesbian, gay, bisexual, transgender, and queer (LGBTQ) survivors of IPV interacted with law enforcement in some way, whether voluntarily or involuntarily, and only 33 percent sought a protective order.[1] Transgender survivors report IPV to police less frequently than cisgender survivors[2] or cisgender lesbian, gay, and bisexual survivors.[3] This hesitation about using the legal system may reflect a belief that transgender survivors will not be protected by the law, as well as concerns about interactions with legal system personnel.

This chapter examines the barriers preventing some T-IPV survivors from seeking protection under the law. The chapter will also explore the complicated relationships between T-IPV survivors and actors within the legal system: police, lawyers, judges, and court staff. (See chapter 9 for more on police.) It will make apparent the intentional and unintentional barriers these actors create for transgender individuals seeking legal relief from intimate partner violence. Finally, this chapter will suggest ways that legal system actors can create a more hospitable climate within that system for transgender individuals subjected to abuse.

Barriers to Legal Remedies for Transgender IPV

In the US legal system, individuals subjected to abuse usually seek protection in one of two ways: by pursuing a case through the criminal system or by seeking restraining orders (often known as civil protection orders) in the civil system. In each case, T-IPV survivors face unique barriers in accessing legal remedies, barriers which are reviewed below.

Criminal Charges

In most states in the US, pursuing criminal charges requires that the police investigate and determine that there is sufficient evidence to believe that a crime has occurred; making an arrest requires probable cause to believe that a criminal offense has been committed. Once the police have determined whether they believe a crime has occurred, prosecutors decide whether to pursue charges. Those who harm their intimate partners can be convicted for behavior that falls within the general criminal law (e.g., assault and battery) or for specific crimes of IPV. If convicted, those who do harm can be incarcerated, fined, mandated to complete a batterer intervention program, and/or ordered to comply with other conditions designed to safeguard the person subjected to abuse.[4] In many places, courts can also enter criminal protective orders with or without the assent of the person subjected to abuse at any point in the life of a case. Those orders bar people who are accused and/or convicted of IPV from contacting, threatening, harassing, or otherwise engaging their partners.[5]

This route is, in theory, accessible to transgender individuals. The general laws of assault and battery—which are the crimes most frequently charged in the context of IPV—do not make reference to the relationship between or the gender of the parties. Those laws vary by state, but most simply require that one party has injured, attempted to cause injury to, or induced fear of injury in another. Even in states with specialized IPV misdemeanor laws, the laws make reference to the relationships between the parties (for example, family or household members, people with a child in common, current or former cohabitants, people who are or were engaged in romantic or dating relationships, etc.) without specifying the gender of the parties.

But the criminal law may not address the unique kinds of harms experienced by T-IPV survivors. The legal system tends to focus on addressing abusive acts that cause or threaten physical harm.[6] Emotional and psychological abuse are not crimes in most jurisdictions. The law generally does not criminalize a form of IPV specific to the transgender community: identity abuse. Identity abuse includes outing a survivor's transgender identity or history without consent, undermining and belittling a survivor's gender identity (for example, by preventing a transgender survivor from expressing their gender identity or refusing to use their proper pronouns or name), using transphobic language, and isolation from the transgender community.[7] (See chapter 3 for more on identity abuse.) Although identity abuse is extremely debilitating for transgender survivors, it is unlikely to be actionable under the criminal law—or, for that matter, the civil law—of most states in the United States and many other nations.

Protective Orders

In the civil system, IPV survivors can petition courts on their own behalf for relief from abuse by asking for civil protection orders. Civil protection orders can require that abusers refrain from continuing to assault, threaten, or harass their victims; bar abusers from approaching or making contact with their victims; and provide economic and other forms of relief to survivors. Civil protection orders are enforceable both through civil and criminal contempt, and, in many states, violation of a protective order is a separate crime.[8]

In the last several years, the final overt legal barriers preventing transgender individuals from accessing protective orders in the United States have fallen. In the past, some state protective order laws restricted access to those orders to individuals in different-gender female/male relationships; transgender people in same-gender relationships could have been prevented from obtaining protective orders under such laws.[9] But the language creating that potential obstacle was removed by state legislatures from Montana's protective order statute in 2013 and from Louisiana's statute in 2017. Similar language in South Carolina's protective order statute was found to be unconstitutional in 2017 by the South Carolina Supreme Court in *Doe v. State*.[10] European nations' protective order laws do not prevent transgender individuals subjected to violence from seeking protection.[11] South Africa's law is similarly inclusive.[12]

But the laws governing protective orders may discourage T-IPV survivors from obtaining them. Forms of abuse specific to transgender survivors (like identity abuse) do not provide a basis for entering a civil protection order in most states.[13] Moreover, protective orders often lack remedies to address the unique needs of those affected by T-IPV (for example, a prohibition on outing survivors as transgender). The inability to secure protection for or relief from these forms of abuse may prevent T-IPV survivors from using the legal system.

Discrimination by Law Enforcement

Transgender people's survivors must also contend with the possibility of discrimination by those administering the legal system. Transgender communities have historically had, and continue to experience, a fraught relationship with many of the professionals who staff the legal system, including law enforcement, lawyers, judges, court staff, and correctional officers.

Discomfort Reporting Victimization to Law Enforcement

Many transgender survivors are uncomfortable contacting the police. Research suggests that only 12–18 percent of transgender survivors report their victimization to the police.[14] Transgender survivors are more likely to access almost any other type of resource than the police.[15] Eighty-three percent of transgender people assume that police will be either only somewhat or not at all helpful to victims of IPV,[16] and 57 percent of transgender people are somewhat or very uncomfortable asking police for assistance regarding any type of crime.[17]

Transgender people's mistrust of police is so pervasive that some organizations no longer recommend that T-IPV survivors contact police in emergency situations. (See chapter 9 for more on police.) The recorded messages of most IPV service providers include some variation on this phrase: "If you are in immediate danger, hang up and dial 911." That advice is designed to ensure that police are notified of the situation and can quickly respond. But the NW Network—a Seattle-based anti-violence organization providing services to the LGBTQ community—removed that language from its outgoing message some time ago. It did so, according to executive director Connie Burk, because the organization recognized that some police have the potential to pose a significant danger to its client community.[18]

Police Discrimination and the Transgender Community

Wariness about calling the police may stem from concerns that some police officers are transphobic, and that calling the police might expose transgender people to harassment and violence. Such concerns have historic roots. For example, as late as the 1980s in the US, police were responsible for enforcing laws requiring individuals to wear at least three pieces of clothing corresponding with their birth-assigned sex, laws which police used to arrest transgender individuals for disorderly conduct.[19] Police regularly raided the bars and bathhouses where transgender women congregated.[20] Transgender women were at the forefront of the clash with police during the raid that started the Stonewall riots.[21]

Many transgender people report discrimination by police.[22] According to the 2008–2009 National Transgender Discrimination Survey, 22 percent of transgender people have been harassed by police.[23] Fifty-seven percent of respondents to the 2015 US Transgender Survey who, in the past year, interacted with police who thought or knew they were transgender, stated that police never or only sometimes treated them respectfully, and 58 percent reported some form of mistreatment by police, including verbal harassment (20 percent), physical attack (4 percent), sexual assault (3 percent), or engaging in unwanted sex to avoid arrest (1 percent).[24] As in research on predominantly cisgender samples, among transgender samples, people of color are more likely than whites to report mistreatment by police.[25]

Police regularly misgender transgender individuals, using the wrong gender pronouns or honorifics for them. Scholar Vivian Namaste recalls police calling transgender women "sir," "boy," or "guy" and asking, "What are you? Are you a guy or a girl? We don't like these fucking half-breeds."[26] Police also refer to transgender individuals as "it."[27] Forty-nine percent of transgender individuals who interacted with police who thought or knew they were transgender reported to the 2015

US Transgender Survey that police misgendered them.²⁸ This persistent misgendering makes transgender survivors less likely to call police. As Rebecca, a transgender woman and IPV survivor, explained, "I had two cops before just refuse to call me by my girl name before I had everything changed and they still called me he. They'd kind of exchanged glances at each other and stuff. I mean I don't know, maybe I'm just paranoid and expected that but then again it's something I think about. How will they see me, will that play a role in how they treat me or believe me or something? Like if I have to explain myself before I can even explain my being a victim?"²⁹

Police Discrimination and Transgender Survivors

Transgender survivors report discrimination by officers responding to their requests for assistance. The 2016 NCAVP survey found that 7 percent of LGBTQ IPV survivors who interacted with law enforcement regarding their victimization described officers they encountered as hostile and 12 percent reported that officers were indifferent.³⁰ Some police ignore the IPV victimization experienced by transgender individuals altogether, failing to respond or refusing to take reports. As Joey Mogul and colleagues note, "Many transgender survivors of domestic violence report that when the police do respond to interpersonal violence committed against them, once officers determine they are transgender, they either simply leave, saying something along the lines of, 'Oh guys, it's a man, forget it …'"³¹

Police interactions with transgender survivors may be colored by cisgender IPV stereotypes of what "real" abusers and victims look like. For example, when one transgender man called the police, he noted that they seemed skeptical of his story:

> I mean maybe they saw her and saw me and then expected that I was the one starting things. She had just gotten off work so she was all in a business skirt and pretty and all but they don't know what she had just done. I bet they thought it was just like a common heterosexuals couple fight and so they were just ready to blame me because I was more masculine or just looked stronger or something I don't know. Instead of just like evaluating the situation they were quick to jump to conclusions about things.³²

Moreover, some transgender survivors are arrested as abusers—even when they ask law enforcement for help. As lawyer Pooja Gehi explained, "When my clients who are survivors of domestic violence call the police for assistance, they often end up getting arrested either instead of, or along with, their abuser. . . . Rather than investigate the situation, police officers tend to arrest based on assumptions and often explain that since they were 'confused,' they just arrested everyone."[33] When a transgender woman called police in the District of Columbia to report that she had been strangled by her male partner, for example, police referred to her as "mister," arrested her, and detained her for hours at the police station. She was charged with assaulting her partner; those charges were later dropped.[34] Transgender survivors are especially likely to be arrested when they fight back against their partners.[35] For transgender women, fighting back creates a catch-22. If they fight back, they are more likely to be arrested. If they fail to fight back,[36] police might be more skeptical of their stories, asking, "Well, she's a man; why can't [she] fight back?"[37] The problem of wrongful arrest of transgender survivors is exacerbated by the operation of preferred and mandatory arrest laws, which incentivize or require police to make arrests in cases of IPV whenever they have probable cause to do so.[38] Calling the police also creates the possibility that a transgender survivor will be arrested on old or unrelated charges. For instance, after repeated calls about IPV, police in Los Angeles refused to arrest the abuser of a transgender woman, instead arresting the survivor for solicitation.[39]

Discrimination in the Court System

Transphobic Harassment and the Courts

Transgender survivors confront harassment and incivility when they engage the court system. Judges and court staff sometimes misgender transgender individuals and seem uncomfortable in their presence. Judges, like police officers, have been heard referring to transgender individuals as "it."[40] Advocates report that some court staff are particularly flustered when transgender individuals' gender identity and gender expression do not seamlessly mesh, and they may respond to that discomfort by avoiding interactions with transgender litigants and instead talking to transgender litigants' lawyers.[41] Some court clerks ridicule transgender litigants, talking and laughing about the "trans case."[42]

Court clerks may also require transgender individuals to use the names that appear on their government-issued identification documents in court pleadings, even when that documentation is inconsistent with a litigant's gender expression. The refusal to use names that are consistent with a transgender individual's gender expression creates particular problems for the enforcement of protective orders; for example, officers may be unwilling to enforce an order issued to Jeff when they encounter Jennifer. And legal system actors may ignore a transgender individual's request to use their chosen name and pronouns as punishment for failing to comply with the system's demands. One probation officer, for instance, used a transgender person's chosen name and pronouns until they missed a meeting, at which point the probation officer reverted to the transgender person's given name.[43]

Transphobic Legal Strategies and the Courts

Lawyers sometimes utilize transphobic myths to win cases against transgender individuals. One such myth is that transgender people are inherently deceitful because they lie about their gender. As lawyer and LGBTQ rights activist Andrea Ritchie notes, courts often view transgender individuals as "fraudulent, deceitful, violent, or mentally unstable because of their perceived gender disjuncture."[44] Lawyers use this myth to cast doubt about the stories told by transgender individuals in court. For example, in the case of a transgender woman on trial for the murder of an off-duty police officer, the prosecutor asked the jury, "How can you trust this person? He tells you he is a woman; he is clearly a man."[45] Lawyers also can weaponize names and pronouns, consistently using the wrong pronouns not only to rattle transgender witnesses but also to subtly cast aspersions on their credibility.[46]

A final transphobic legal strategy in criminal proceedings has been called the "trans panic defense," which attempts to justify IPV as a natural reaction to discovering one's partner is transgender.[47] The trans panic defense was used, for example, on behalf of the young men who murdered transgender teenager Gwen Araujo, with whom they had been sexually and romantically involved.[48] Although not explicitly permitted by the law of any state, the trans panic defense has been used to bolster insanity and provocation defenses and claims of self-defense.[49] In the context of an insanity defense, the trans panic defense is used to argue that the sudden revelation of a victim's anatomy or birth-assigned sex causes the perpetrator to become temporarily insane or diminishes the perpetrator's capacity to appreciate the wrongfulness of their violence.[50] To establish provocation (and thus justify a finding of voluntary manslaughter rather than murder), a male perpetrator may argue that "the average heterosexual man would have been provoked into a heat of passion if he had discovered that the person with whom he had been sexually intimate was not a 'real' female, but a person with male genitalia pretending to be a woman."[51] Provocation is used in court to partially justify the crime; the defendant is viewed as "less guilty than an unprovoked killer."[52] The trans panic defense also has been used to bolster self-defense claims, enabling defendants to argue that "they reasonably believed the victim was about to cause them serious bodily harm because of the victim's . . . gender identity."[53]

Allowing defendants to use a trans panic defense sends a message to transgender survivors: not only are you not able to get assistance here, but, in fact, your gender identity is so alien and upsetting to others that you can be abused with impunity, and your abuser will not be held fully responsible for using deadly force against you. According to the American Bar Association, allowing trans panic defenses "subjects victims to secondary victimization by asking the jury to find the victim's . . . gender identity blameworthy for the defendant's actions."[54] Such defenses are "designed to stir up and reinforce the . . . anti-transgender emotions and stereotypes that led to the assault in the first place."[55] As a result, in 2013 the American Bar Association passed a resolution urging state, federal, and tribal governments to bar the use of the trans panic defense.[56] California passed such a law in 2014, precluding defendants from claiming that they were provoked to engage in criminal behavior by the "discovery of, knowledge about, or potential disclosure of the victim's actual or perceived gender, gender identity, gender expression, or sexual orientation."[57] Illinois passed a similar law in 2017, and several other states have considered such laws.[58] In those states where the trans panic defense still operates, however, it serves to remind transgender survivors that their claims are unwelcome in the courts.

Discrimination in the Correctional System

After they have been arrested, people accused of perpetrating IPV may be temporarily housed in jails while awaiting trial, and those convicted in court can be sentenced to incarceration in jails or prisons. Whether in jails or prisons, correctional staff often refuse to recognize the gender identity of transgender individuals. Transgender people are regularly denied requests to be searched by or housed with individuals of the same gender identity.[59] In May 2018, the US Federal Bureau of Prisons deleted language from its "Transgender Offender Manual" that stated that housing would be decided "by gender identity when appropriate," replacing that standard with determinations on a "case-by-case basis" and assigning inmates based on gender identity "in rare cases."[60] Transgender individuals may also have to verify and reverify their gender for jail or prison staff. As one transgender man explained, "When I was in solitary, a cop asked me about my gender. I told him I was male, and he told me I sounded female. Next thing I knew, I was being taken to the jail doctor to spread my legs and have him confirm my gender. It was humiliating."[61]

Incarceration also exposes transgender individuals to significant dangers. The 2015 US Transgender Survey found that among respondents who had been incarcerated in the last year, 20 percent were sexually assaulted by staff or other inmates and 23 percent were physically assaulted.[62] According to Mogul and colleagues, transgender women are particularly vulnerable when housed in men's jails and prisons, where they are routinely subjected to "excessive, abusive, and invasive searches, groping their breasts, buttocks, or genitalia," and staff "repeatedly leering at them while they shower, disrobe, or use the bathroom."[63] While incarcerated, transgender individuals are rarely referred to by the names and pronouns they request, are often denied medical care related to their gender, and are often segregated from the general population, ostensibly for their own safety.[64]

Multiply Marginalized Transgender Communities

The barriers and prejudices of the legal system prevent many transgender individuals from seeking relief from IPV through the legal system.

For transgender individuals with additional marginalized identities and experiences, those barriers and prejudices loom exponentially larger. This is particularly true for transgender people who are racial or ethnic minorities, undocumented immigrants, or sex workers. (See chapter 6 for more on T-IPV, race, and immigration.)

Transgender People of Color

Although the US Transgender Survey revealed that transgender individuals of color suffer IPV at higher rates than white individuals,[65] they may be even less likely than white transgender individuals to seek the assistance of the legal system. People of color, for example, report higher rates of being treated disrespectfully by police: 72 percent of American Indian, 70 percent of Black, 66 percent of multiracial, 62 percent of Latinx, and 57 percent of Asian transgender people say that they are never or only sometimes treated with respect by police, as opposed to 52 percent of white transgender individuals.[66] A 2012 study of Latina transgender women in Los Angeles County found that law enforcement officers had verbally abused 66 percent, physically assaulted 21 percent, and sexually assaulted 24 percent of the respondents.[67] Racism and fear of racial bias informs transgender individuals' experiences with police when they report IPV. Rebecca, for example, having lived her early life as "a black teenage boy," believed that police would be suspicious of her and judge her if she sought assistance after being abused.[68]

Transgender Undocumented Immigrants

Undocumented transgender individuals also are likely to be abused by intimate partners; 68 percent of undocumented transgender individuals report having experienced IPV in their lifetimes.[69] But like other marginalized groups, undocumented transgender individuals are leery of asking the legal system for help. As Anna, an undocumented transwoman, explained, "Oh gosh definitely no I would have never called the police. I mean like what are they going to do? I am a transsexual woman and I'm an immigrant and also I mean, I was doing illegal things like hormone sharing and I don't think they would've believed that my ex was forcing me to have sex for money. I mean they would've been seen me like a stereotype like what he used to say you know—I think that's true they would've just gotten me into trouble too."[70]

Interactions with police and courts at this particular moment in US history are especially fraught for undocumented individuals. At the beginning of the Trump administration's crackdown on undocumented individuals, one of the first stories on immigration enforcement to grab the public's attention was that of a transgender woman who was detained by Immigration and Customs Enforcement officers after seeking protection from IPV at the El Paso County courthouse.[71] (For more on this case, see chapter 6.) In Houston, where Latinx people make up 44 percent of the population, reports of IPV dropped 16 percent in 2017; other cities with large immigrant populations, including Los Angeles, San Diego, and Denver, all have reported similar declines.[72] Undoubtedly, the reluctance of transgender immigrants to seek assistance accounts for some part of that decline. Transgender individuals fare particularly badly in immigration detention. Fifty-two percent of those who have ever been detained were isolated in some way: 17 percent were held in separate areas for transgender or lesbian, gay, or bisexual people, and 42 percent were placed in solitary confinement, some for as long as six months.[73] While in immigration detention, 23 percent were physically assaulted, 15 percent were sexually assaulted, 19 percent were threatened with sexual assault, 29 percent were denied access to hormones, and 22 percent were denied gender-appropriate clothing.[74] The Trump administration's stance on both transgender individuals (as seen, for example, in the ban on transgender individuals serving in the military and in the administration's rescission of guidance on the treatment of transgender students)[75] and undocumented people[76] sends a clear message that seeking legal assistance in this climate is not only fruitless, but likely unwise.

Moreover, undocumented transgender individuals who are detained now have fewer grounds on which to challenge their detention. In *Matter of A-B-*, then–Attorney General Jeff Sessions overruled a Board of Immigration Appeals decision granting asylum to an undocumented woman based on El Salvador's failure to protect her from her ex-husband's abuse both during and after their marriage. In his decision, Sessions significantly narrowed the grounds for seeking asylum on the basis of IPV and other abuse carried out by private individuals. Sessions wrote, "The mere fact that a country may have problems effectively policing certain crimes—such as domestic violence or gang violence—or that certain populations are more likely to be victims of crime, cannot itself establish an asylum claim."[77] This passage has been widely read to threaten access to asylum not only for individuals experiencing IPV, but also for transgender individuals more broadly.[78] Without the ability to raise previously available defenses in immigration court if detained, undocumented transgender individuals have little to gain and much to lose when considering turning to the legal system for assistance. (For more on T-IPV and immigration, see chapter 6).

Transgender Sex Workers

Transgender individuals subjected to abuse sometimes avoid the legal system because that system fails to code what they have experienced as IPV. The abuse that transgender women experience in intimate relationships, for instance, is often dismissed as an unfortunate byproduct of engaging in sex work. Profiling of transgender women as sex workers is disturbingly common. Eleven percent of respondents to the US Transgender Survey that had interacted with police officers who thought or knew they were trans reported that police officers assumed they were sex workers, numbers that were even higher for transgender women of color, including Black (33 percent), multiracial (30 percent), Latina (25 percent), American Indian (23 percent), and Asian (20 percent) transgender women.[79] Arrests for "walking while trans" or carrying "sexual paraphernalia" (condoms) are so common that the Legal Aid Society sued the New York City Police Department over the practice.[80]

Sex workers who allege intimate partner violence may be seen as less credible because they are engaged in criminal activity. These credibility concerns are more acute for more marginalized transgender individuals, such as low-income people and people of color.[81] Because some personnel in the legal system assume that transgender women engage in intimate relationships only in the context of sex work, protection is sometimes denied to transgender women who are abused in intimate relationships, whether or not they are engaged in sex work at the time.[82]

Conclusions

The legal system is the primary response to IPV in many nations in the world, including the United States. But for many T-IPV survivors, the legal system is not a viable option in seeking to address IPV. At best, the system creates needless obstacles for transgender individuals; at worst, it humiliates and revictimizes them. Fundamental change to the system is necessary if it is to become a source of support for T-IPV survivors.

First, police and court staff must stop harassing, dehumanizing, and violating transgender individuals. The abusive treatment of transgender individuals by some legal system professionals is directly responsible for the entirely reasonable belief among transgender survivors that the legal system will not provide them with justice. Transgender victims of abuse will not develop faith in the legal system's ability to provide them with protection without a radical change in the way that the system interacts with them.

Next, law enforcement officers, lawyers, and court personnel should have clear written protocols for addressing T-IPV victimization. Those protocols should start with the most basic principles—treating transgender survivors and perpetrators of violence with civility and dignity—and require that all legal system professionals use the names and pronouns consistent with each individual's gender identity. The protocols should also identify and debunk commonly held misconceptions about transgender individuals (around credibility and sex work, for example) and about abuse of transgender individuals (e.g., that abuse of a transgender woman by a cisgender male partner is a "fair fight"). Courts should issue orders that reflect the individual's gender identity (for example, issuing protective orders first in the name a transgender individual is actually using and then, if necessary, in the person's legal name). Training should be provided on these protocols at regular intervals, given the frequent turnover in the legal system.

Legal system professionals should also receive training on implicit biases (around race, immigration status, and gender identity, to start) and have the opportunity to reflect on those biases in the specific context of T-IPV. Recognizing one's implicit biases can be a first step toward overcoming the impulse to act on those biases and toward checking biased behavior. Employing and increasing the visibility of transgender personnel within the legal system could also help to mitigate bias, as well as create a sense of safety and security for those who seek to use the legal system. Moreover, the legal system should exclude evidence supporting so-called trans panic defenses and similar transphobic arguments. Jurors should be instructed (as per the American Bar Association's resolution) not to allow bias or prejudice based on gender identity to affect their decisions. US states and other nations should follow California's and Illinois's example and preclude defendants from offering evidence that they were provoked by the discovery or disclosure of a person's birth-assigned sex.

Change in any system is slow and moves in fits and starts. But T-IPV survivors have needs that must be met now. Waiting for the legal system to evolve to a place where transgender individuals feel safe seeking help from that system will mean that many, many transgender individuals are left without recourse after violence. (See chapter 4 for more on barriers to help). Developing options beyond the legal system for responding to IPV is therefore essential; such options would provide transgender survivors ways to access justice without having to interact with the legal system. These options could include restorative practices, economic resources, and community-based programs like the NW Network's Friends Are Reaching Out (FAR Out) program, which works with LGBTQ survivors and their friends and families to develop supportive networks to respond to IPV.[83] While all IPV survivors should have access to the legal system if they want it, recognizing and meeting the needs of those individuals who are less likely to voluntarily use the system is a key component of any societal response to IPV.

NOTES

1 Waters 2017, 25.
2 Langenderfer-Magruder et al. 2016, 864.
3 NCAVP 2010, 32.
4 Goodmark 2012, 9–10.
5 Suk 2006, 16–17.
6 Goodmark 2012, 40–41.
7 Woulfe and Goodman 2018, 4–5.
8 Goodmark 2012, 17.
9 Goodmark 2013, 84–85.
10 Doe v. State, 421 S.C. 490 (2017).

11 European Institute for Gender Equality 2016, 7.
12 Domestic Violence Act 116 of 1998 (South Africa).
13 Stapel 2007, 255.
14 Kurdyla, Messinger, and Ramirez, 2019; Langenderfer-Magruder et al. 2016, 863; Roch, Morton, and Ritchie 2010.
15 Kurdyla, Messinger, and Ramirez, 2019; Roch, Morton, and Ritchie 2010.
16 Kurdyla, Messinger, and Ramirez, 2019.
17 James et al. 2016, 185.
18 Burk 2014.
19 Hovey 2009, 104.
20 Ogles 2018.
21 Schlaffer 2016.
22 Guadalupe-Diaz and Jasinski 2017, 784.
23 Grant et al. 2011, 158.
24 James et al. 2016, 185–86.
25 Fedina et al. 2017, 154; James et al. 2016, 186.
26 Namaste 2000, 170–71.
27 Namaste 2000, 170–71.
28 James et al. 2016, 186.
29 Guadalupe-Diaz and Jasinski 2017, 785.
30 Waters 2017, 12.
31 Mogul, Ritchie, and Whitlock 2011, 138.
32 Guadalupe-Diaz and Jasinski 2017, 785.
33 Gehi 2008, 325–26.
34 INCITE! Women of Color Against Violence, n.d., 39.
35 Arkles 2009, 520.
36 Arkles 2009, 520.
37 B. et al. 2001, 147.
38 Goodmark 2012, 107–10.
39 INCITE! Women of Color Against Violence, n.d., 39.
40 Goodmark 2013, 79.
41 Goodmark 2013, 81.
42 Goodmark 2013, 81.
43 Goodmark 2013, 81.
44 Ritchie 2006, 108.
45 Mogul, Ritchie, and Whitlock 2011, 76.
46 Goodmark 2013, 81.
47 Lee and Kwan 2014, 79.
48 Barrett and Sheridan 2017, 151; Lee and Kwan 2014, 106–107.
49 Lee and Kwan 2014, 79–80.
50 American Bar Association 2013, 6–7.
51 Lee and Kwan 2014, 105–106.
52 Lee and Kwan 2014, 100.

53 American Bar Association 2013, 1.
54 American Bar Association 2013, 4.
55 American Bar Association 2013, 4.
56 American Bar Association 2013, 1.
57 Lee and Kwan 2014, 108; 2014 Cal. Legis. Serv. ch. 684 (A.B. 2501) (West).
58 National LGBT Bar Association 2018.
59 Guadalupe-Diaz and Jasinski 2017, 785.
60 Gathright 2018.
61 James et al. 2016, 188.
62 James et al. 2016, 191.
63 Mogul, Ritchie, and Whitlock 2011, 107.
64 Mogul, Ritchie, and Whitlock 2011, 110–12.
65 James et al. 2016, 207.
66 James et al. 2016, 186.
67 Galvan and Bazargan 2012, 6.
68 Guadalupe-Diaz and Jasinski 2017, 786.
69 James et al. 2016, 206.
70 Guadalupe-Diaz and Jasinski 2017, 786.
71 Villasana 2017.
72 Engelbrecht 2018.
73 James et al. 2016, 194.
74 James et al. 2016, 195.
75 Cooper and Gibbons-Neff 2018; Peters, Becker, and Davis 2017.
76 Rucker and Weigel 2018.
77 Matter of A-B-, 27 I & N Dec 316 (A.G. 2018), 316.
78 Haynes 2018.
79 James et al. 2016, 187.
80 Whitford 2018.
81 MacKenzie & Marcel 2009, 84.
82 Goodmark 2013, 80.
83 Goodmark 2018, 85.

REFERENCES

American Bar Association. 2013. "Resolution 113A." www.americanbar.org.

Arkles, Gabriel. 2009. "Safety and Solidarity across Gender Lines: Rethinking Segregation of Transgender People in Detention." *Temple Political and Civil Rights Law Review* 18(2): 515–560.

B., Valerie, Victoria Cruz, Theresa Jefferson, Lisi Lord, David Pumo, and Grace A. Telesco. 2001. "Lesbian, Gay, Bisexual, and Transgender Communities and Intimate Partner Violence." *Fordham Urban Law Journal* 29 (1): 121–58.

Barrett, Betty Jo, and Daphne Vanessa Sheridan. 2017. "Partner Violence in Transgender Communities: What Helping Professionals Need to Know." *Journal of GLBT Family Studies* 13(2): 137–162.

Burk, Connie. 2014. "The Possibilities and Limits of Criminal Justice Reform." Remarks at CONVERGE! Reimagining the Movement to End Gender Violence. University of Miami School of Law, Miami, FL, February 7–8, 2014.

Cooper, Helene, and Thomas Gibbons-Neff. 2018. "Trump Approves New Limits on Transgender Troops in the Military." *New York Times*, March 24, 2018. www.nytimes.com.

Engelbrecht, Cora. 2018. "Fewer Immigrants Are Reporting Domestic Abuse. Police Blame Fear of Deportation." *New York Times*, June 3, 2018. www.nytimes.com.

European Institute for Gender Equality. 2016. *Analysis of National Definitions of Intimate Partner Violence*. Vilnius, Lithuania: European Institute for Gender Equality. http://eige.europa.eu.

Fedina, Lisa, Bethany L. Backes, Hyun-Jin Jun, Roma Shah, Boyoung Nam, Bruce G. Link, and Jordan E. DeVylder. 2018. "Police Violence among Women in Four U.S. Cities." *Preventive Medicine* 106:150–156.

Galvan, Frank H., and Mohsen Bazargan. 2012. *Interactions of Latina Transgender Women with Law Enforcement*. Los Angeles: Beinestar Human Services.

Gathright, Jenny. 2018. "The Guidelines for Protection of Transgender Prisoners Just Got Rewritten." *National Public Radio*, May 12, 2018. www.npr.org.

Gehi, Pooja. 2008. "Struggles from the Margins: Anti-immigrant Legislation and the Impact on Low-Income Transgender People of Color." *Women's Rights Law Reporter* 30:315–346.

Goodmark, Leigh. 2012. *A Troubled Marriage: Domestic Violence and the Legal System*. New York: New York University Press.

Goodmark, Leigh. 2013. "Transgender People, Intimate Partner Abuse, and the Legal System." *Harvard Civil Rights–Civil Liberties Law Review* 48 (1): 51–104.

Goodmark, Leigh. 2018. *Decriminalizing Domestic Violence: A Balanced Policy Approach to Intimate Partner Violence*. Berkeley: University of California Press.

Grant, Jamie M., Lisa A. Mottet, Justin Tanis, Jack Harrison, Jody L. Herman, and Mara Keisling. 2011. *Injustice at Every Turn: A Report of the National Transgender Discrimination Survey*. Washington, DC: National Center for Transgender Equality and National Gay and Lesbian Task Force. www.transequality.org.

Guadalupe-Diaz, Xavier L., and Jana Jasinski. 2017. "'I Wasn't a Priority, I Wasn't a Victim': Challenges in Help Seeking for Transgender Survivors of Intimate Partner Violence." *Violence against Women* 23 (6): 772–792.

Haynes, Dina. 2018. "Misogyny and Racism in Sessions' Unraveling of Asylum Law." *Gender Policy Report*, June 18, 2018. http://genderpolicyreport.umn.edu.

Hovey, Jaime E. 2009. "Nursing Wounds: Why LGBT Elders Need Protection from Discrimination and Abuse Based on Sexual Orientation and Gender Identity." *Elder Law Journal* 17 (1): 95–123.

INCITE! Women of Color Against Violence. n.d. *Law Enforcement Violence against Women of Color and Trans People of Color: A Critical Intersection of Gender Violence and State Violence*. Redmond, WA: INCITE! Women of Color Against Violence. www.incite-national.org.

James, Sandy E., Jody L. Herman, Suan Rankin, Mara Keisling, Lisa Mottet, and Ma'ayan Anafi. 2016. *The Report of the 2015 U.S. Transgender Survey*. Washington, DC: National Center for Transgender Equality. www.ustranssurvey.org.

Kurdyla, Victoria, Adam M. Messinger, and Milka Ramirez. 2019. "Transgender Intimate Partner Violence and Help-Seeking Patterns." *Journal of Interpersonal Violence*. https://doi.org/10.1177/0886260519880171.

Langenderfer-Magruder, Lisa, Darren L. Whitfield, N. Eugene Walls, Shanna K. Kattari, and Daniel Ramors. 2016. "Experiences of Intimate Partner Violence and Subsequent Police Reporting among Lesbian, Gay, Bisexual, Transgender, and Queer Adults in Colorado: Comparing Rates of Cisgender and Transgender Victimization." *Journal of Interpersonal Violence* 31 (5): 855–871.

Lee, Cynthia, and Peter Kwan. 2014. "The Trans Panic Defense: Masculinity, Heteronormativity, and the Murder of Transgender Women." *Hastings Law Journal* 66: 77–132.

MacKenzie, Gordene, and Mary Marcel. 2009. "Media Coverage of the Murder of U.S. Transwomen of Color." In *Local Violence, Global Media: Feminist Analyses of Gendered Representations*, edited by Lisa M. Cuklanz and Sujata Moorti, 79–106. New York: Peter Lang.

Mogul, Joey L., Andrea J. Ritchie, and Kay Whitlock. 2011. *Queer (In)justice: The Criminalization of LGBT People in the United States*. Boston: Beacon Press.

Namaste, Vivian. 2000. *Invisible Lives: The Erasure of Transsexual and Transgendered People*. Chicago: University of Chicago Press.

National Coalition of Anti-Violence Programs. 2010. *Survival, Support and Resilience: Stories of LGBTQ Survivors and Victims of Domestic/Intimate Partner Violence*. New York: National Coalition of Anti-Violence Programs.

National LGBT Bar Association. n.d. "Gay and Trans Panic Defense." Accessed January 17, 2020. https://lgbtbar.org.

Ogles, Jacob. 2018. "30 Infamous Police Raids of Gay Bars and Bathhouses." *Advocate*, February 2, 2018. www.advocate.com.

Peters, Jeremy W., Jo Becker, and Julie Hirschfield Davis. 2017. "Trump Rescinds Rules on Bathrooms for Transgender Students." *New York Times*. February 22, 2017. www.nytimes.com.

Ritchie, Andrea J. 2006. "Law Enforcement Violence against Women of Color." In *Color of Violence: The INCITE! Anthology*, edited by INCITE! Women of Color against Violence, 138–156. Durham, NC: Duke University Press.

Roch, Amy, James Morton, and Graham Ritchie. 2010. *Out of Sight, out of Mind? Transgender People's Experiences of Domestic Abuse*. Edinburgh: LGBT Youth Scotland and the Scottish Transgender Alliance. www.scottishtrans.org.

Rucker, Philip, and David Weigel. 2018. "Trump Advocates Depriving Undocumented Immigrants of Due-Process Rights." *Washington Post*, June 24, 2018. www.washingtonpost.com.

Schladen, Marty. 2017. "ICE Detains Alleged Domestic Violence Victim." *El Paso Times*, February 15, 2017. www.elpasotimes.com.

Schlaffer, Natasha. 2016. "The Unsung Heroines of Stonewall: Marsha P. Johnson and Sylvia Rivera." *Femmes Fatales*, October 23, 2016. https://sites.psu.edu.

Stapel, Sharon. 2007. "Falling to Pieces: New York State Civil Legal Remedies Available to Lesbian, Gay, Bisexual, and Transgender Survivors of Domestic Violence." *New York Law School Law Review* 52 (2): 247–77.

Suk, Jeannie. 2006. "Criminal Law Comes Home." *Yale Law Journal* 116 (1): 5–70.

Villasana, Jose. 2017. "ICE Agents Arrest Transgender Woman Who Filed Protective Order against Ex-boyfriend." *KVIA ABC 7*, February 15, 2017. www.kvia.com.

Waters, Emily. 2017. *Lesbian, Gay, Bisexual, Transgender, Queer, and HIV-Affected Intimate Partner Violence in 2016*. New York: National Coalition of Anti-Violence Programs. http://avp.org.

Whitford, Emma. 2018. "When Walking While Trans Is a Crime." *The Cut*, January 31, 2018. www.thecut.com.

Woulfe, Julie M., and Lisa A. Goodman. 2018. "Identity Abuse as a Tactic of Violence in LGBTQ Communities: Initial Validation of the Identity Abuse Measure." *Journal of Interpersonal Violence*. https://doi.org/10.1177/0886260518760018.

PART IV

Future Directions and Conclusions

11

Beyond the Gender Binary

Trans/forming IPV Prevention Using a Public Health Framework

REBECCA HOWARD, SHARYN J. POTTER,
TAYLOR FLAGG, MARY M. MOYNIHAN,
AND ZACHARY AHMAD-KAHLOON

Transgender individuals experience alarming rates of discrimination, harassment, and violence across the lifespan.[1] Research has shown that this population is at the highest risk of intimate partner violence (IPV) and sexual violence (SV)[2] compared to cisgender women or men.[3] Even so, few IPV and SV prevention programs acknowledge transgender individuals. That is, prevention programs often focus on violence between cisgender, heterosexual individuals where the assumed perpetrator is a cisgender man and the assumed survivor is a cisgender woman.[4] This approach neglects an entire population of lesbian, gay, bisexual, transgender, and queer (LGBTQ) survivors and abusers, including cisgender men in relationships with cisgender men, cisgender women in relationships with cisgender women, and relationships involving at least one partner who is a transgender woman, transgender man, or nonbinary individual. Additionally, gendered language related to IPV and SV such as "violence against women" and "battered women's shelters" also overlooks cisgender men and transgender individuals as survivors of these forms of violence.[5] The exclusion of transgender individuals in IPV research and public health interventions is problematic because it contributes to a cisnormative and heteronormative model of IPV and ignores the specific needs of transgender people.[6] (See chapter 13 for more on transgender IPV research.) To better protect this vulnerable population, violence prevention programs must begin to treat the victimization of transgender individuals as a serious public health problem that should be addressed and prevented.

Intimate partner violence involves an intentional pattern of power and control perpetrated by a current or former intimate partner. Perpetrators use various violent and controlling behaviors to subjugate their partner, including physical, emotional, and economic abuse. Sexual assault and other forms of SV are often part of this pattern.[7] Even when SV does not occur within a long-term, committed relationship, the majority of SV is perpetrated by someone the survivor knows, such as a friend, acquaintance, family member, or neighbor. Additionally, abuse in sexual relationships (even sexual relationships that are shorter and nonromantic) is often considered to be within the spectrum of IPV. Research finds that 25–47 percent of transgender individuals experience sexual violence in an intimate partner relationship during their lifetime.[8] Because of this overlap, a number of prevention programs aim to simultaneously address SV and IPV, in part because the two are so often interconnected. For these reasons, a discussion of IPV prevention programming should simultaneously consider SV prevention programming.

Research shows that transgender people experience high rates of harassment and discrimination that affect their mental health and well-being.[9] Transgender individuals are also more vulnerable to violence in intimate partner relationships,[10] yet less likely to seek community resources, medical care, or law enforcement assistance.[11] As detailed in a United Nations Special Report on sexual violence among vulnerable populations, cisgender women —as with other types of minority groups—may encounter discrimination that can "exacerbate the institutional failures with regard to the State response to rape and sexual violence."[12] Transgender individuals may feel mistrustful of medical providers or law enforcement due to past experiences of transphobic discrimination by these systems, which can cause them to avoid seeking help and therefore lead to further victimization and compounded health problems.[13]

Violent victimization can have serious negative effects on an individual's long-term and short-term mental and physical health,[14] yet few IPV and SV prevention programs focus on violence against, or within, the transgender community.[15] (See chapter 7 for more on health services.) Given the adverse health and economic outcomes of IPV and SV, preventing and responding to these types of violence is critical for the health and safety of transgender individuals. In this chapter, we use a public health framework to outline the importance of addressing many societal factors that lead to perpetration of violence committed against transgender people. Moreover, the lack of resources afforded to transgender individuals puts them at greater risk for IPV and SV.[16] A public health approach demonstrates the steps that can be taken to minimize this risk and reduce violence in our communities.

Prevention Using a Public Health Framework

Effective strategies for prevention of IPV and SV are often rooted in theories of public health, which focus on reducing the collective cost of violence and improving collective well-being, to provide the maximum benefit for the largest number of people.[17] Research finds that IPV and SV victimization can greatly impact a survivor's mental health, physical health, economic potential, and overall well-being.[18] Health outcomes are even poorer for transgender survivors, as many transgender individuals already experience negative mental health symptoms from minority stress and discrimination.[19] Additionally, research shows that many transgender individuals are not accepted by their family of origin and often rely on an intimate partner for safety and support, which can make the consequences of IPV even more distressing.[20] A public health approach to violence prevention theorizes that violence against anyone has a negative impact on the community and society in which they live. Therefore, it is critically important to find solutions to end violence among transgender people, not only for the individuals who are personally victimized but also for the benefit of the community as a whole.

A public health violence prevention model is based on the idea that interpersonal violence can be prevented by taking action to address the factors that influence the acceptance and use of violence by others.[21] Therefore, to address IPV and SV among transgender individuals, we must first identify the factors that put this population at risk, such as persistent societal transphobia and discrimination.[22] For instance, transgender individuals are at greater risk of experiencing IPV if they have been victims of discrimination, bullying, or anti-transgender hate crimes or bias incidents.[23] Unfortunately, such IPV risk factors are pervasive in part because transphobia is so widespread. The Trans PULSE Project, a survey of 433 transgender people aged sixteen or older, found that 98 percent of respondents had experienced at least one form of transphobia.[24] Results of the 2008–2009 National Transgender Discrimination Survey revealed that 63 percent of participants had experienced at least one serious act of discrimination that had a major impact on their quality of life and ability to sustain themselves emotionally or financially. These negative outcomes include loss of employment, eviction, bullying, harassment, physical assault, sexual assault, homelessness, or denial of medical services—all due to bias on the basis of gender identity or expression.[25] Additionally, transphobic policies such as North Carolina's so-called bathroom bill, which attempted to ban transgender people from using restrooms corresponding with their gender identity,[26] and the Trump administration's policy to ban and later only allow certain transgender individuals to serve in the military,[27] affirm assumptions at the societal level that transgender people are "less than" and do not deserve equal rights under the law.

A public health framework is grounded in a belief that these discriminatory attitudes toward transgender people can be changed through prevention and education. As explained in the National Sexual Violence Resource Center's (NSVRC) guide to prevention programming for LGBTQ individuals, "people are not born homophobic, biphobic, racist, sexist, transphobic or classist"—rather, these are learned behaviors that are perpetuated by community and societal norms.[28] Therefore, we can reduce violence in our communities by changing the norms, beliefs, and behaviors in our culture to become accepting of transgender individuals.

The public health approach to violence prevention includes four important steps rooted in the scientific method.[29] These steps include (1) defining the problem, (2) identifying risk and protective factors, (3) developing and testing prevention strategies, and (4) assuring widespread adoption of the prevention strategy. Based on the "Public Health Approach to Violence Prevention" framework from the Centers for Disease Control and Prevention (CDC), we outline these four steps with a focus on the victimization of transgender individuals who experience IPV and SV.[30] For this example, we choose to focus on transgender youth and young adults, as most IPV and SV prevention programs are targeted at high school- and college-age students. This age group (sixteen to twenty-four years old) not only is at the highest risk for violence,[31] but also is the most likely to be positively affected by prevention programming due to continuing cognitive and social development.[32]

Step 1: Defining the Problem

The first step in the public health framework for preventing violence is to understand the *who, what, where, when, why*, and *how* of the problem. These questions are usually answered by reviewing data and scientific research about violence in a given community. Unfortunately, the dearth of available data related to transgender individuals causes challenges when defining the problem of transgender IPV and SV. According to public health experts Esther Meerwijk and Jae Sevelius, "the population size of transgender individuals in the United States is not well-known, in part because official records, including the US Census, do not include data on gender identity."[33] It is nearly impossible to frame the problem when the majority of data on rates of violence exclude transgender people and/or identities.[34] For that reason, at this time, public health practitioners must use findings from a variety of sources to create a more complete picture of the issue. See table 11.1 for example questions and answers regarding how to begin formulating prevention programming responses to transgender IPV and SV.

TABLE 11.1. Defining the Problem: Example Questions and Answers

Questions	Answers
1. Who is the target audience?	Transgender youth
2. What are you trying to prevent?	IPV and SV victimization among transgender individuals
3. When is the problem occurring?	Victimization often begins early (before age 18) and continues on throughout lifespan[i]
4. Where is the problem occurring?	Transgender IPV and SV can occur anywhere[ii]
5. Why is the problem occurring?	Societal transphobia; lack of transgender resources; transgender youth have many risk factors for IPV and SV and few protective factors (see table 11.2)
6. How many people are affected by the problem?	Approximately 1 in 2 transgender individuals experience IPV and SV in their lifetime[iii]

[i] James et al. 2016.
[ii] Reisner et al. 2014.
[iii] James et al. 2016.

Step 2: Identifying Risk and Protective Factors

Identifying factors that make someone more or less likely to experience violence can be helpful in determining where prevention efforts need to be focused. Risk factors refer to the circumstances or characteristics that make people more likely to be a survivor or perpetrator of violence. Protective factors work as a buffer against risk factors, and refer to the circumstances that decrease the likelihood of violence and the impact of negative health outcomes if violence does occur.[35] Risk factors do not cause violence, and, as the CDC notes, the "presence of risk factors does not mean that a person will always experience violence."[36] For example, although identifying as transgender is a risk factor for IPV and SV, this does not mean that all transgender individuals will experience violence.[37] In fact, effective prevention can act as a protective factor against violence for those in transgender communities.[38] For a list of risk and protective factors for transgender individuals, see table 11.2 (as well as chapter 5).

Step 3: Developing and Testing Prevention Strategies

According to the CDC, prevention strategies should be rigorously tested through the scientific method to see if they prevent violence. This testing phase includes gathering data from community assessments of the program, interviewing stakeholders, and conducting focus groups with community members to "increase program acceptability among the intended audience."[39] A program is considered effective if scientific testing supports that it reduces violence in a community.[40] Strategies that are shown to be effective in this step are then disseminated and implemented broadly.

In 2014, the Obama administration's White House Task Force to Protect Students from Sexual Assault commissioned a review and report that noted bystander intervention as one of the most promising prevention strategies, as it engages everyone in the community rather than just victims or perpetrators and "provides [individuals] with skills to help when they see behavior that puts others at risk."[41] The report, authored by CDC health scientist Sarah DeGue and colleagues, highlighted Bringing in the Bystander and Green Dot as two of the best bystander

TABLE 11.2. Risk and Protective Factors for Transgender IPV and SV

Risk Factors for Transgender IPV and SV	Protective Factors for Transgender IPV and SV
• Past victimization experiences[i] • Racial minority status[ii] • Substance abuse[iii] • HIV exposure or diagnosis[iv] • Family neglect[v] • Housing instability/homelessness[vi] • Past history of sex work or incarceration[vii] • Depression/suicidal ideation[viii] • Bullying/harassment[ix] • Hostile school climate[x]	• Transgender role models[xi] • Family and peer support[xii] • Peer norms about safe sex[xiii] • Opportunities and recognition for pro-social school involvement[xiv] • Positive/transgender-friendly school climate, including Gay-Straight Alliances[xv] • Availability and access to transgender sexual and health education resources[xvi] • Antidiscrimination policies and laws[xvii]

[i]Goldenberg, Jadwin-Cakmak, and Harper 2018.
[ii]Coulter and Rankin 2017.
[iii]Brennan et al. 2012.
[iv]Brennan et al. 2012.
[v]Ryan et al. 2010.
[vi]Guadalupe-Diaz and Jasinksi 2017.
[vii]Goldenberg, Jadwin-Cakmak, and Harper 2018.
[viii]Grant et al. 2011.
[ix]Goldenberg, Jadwin-Cakmak, and Harper 2018.
[x]Johns et al. 2018.
[xi]Johns et al. 2018.
[xii]Johns et al. 2018; Ryan et al. 2010; Simons et al. 2013.
[xiii]Mustanski et al. 2015.
[xiv]Marx and Kettrey 2016.
[xv]Marx and Kettrey 2016.
[xvi]Mustanski et al. 2015.
[xvii]Johns et al. 2018.

intervention prevention programs.[42] However, these programs were categorized as promising rather than effective because of "strict evidential criteria for primary prevention, requiring outcome measures to demonstrate a significant reduction in incidence of sexual violence perpetration."[43] This high standard for effective prevention programming demonstrates the importance of the rigorous scientific evaluation that must be completed before a prevention program is disseminated widely or considered effective.

Step 4: Ensuring Widespread Adoption

Once a prevention program has been identified as promising or effective, schools, colleges, health centers, and other organizations are encouraged to adapt the program for their community. Public health approaches often incorporate evidence-based programs, such as bystander intervention, that meet the community's needs. According to the CDC, training and technical assistance for prevention programs should be offered to community practitioners to ensure that the prevention strategies are implemented as they were intended.

There are several online registries for finding evaluated prevention models. However, few programs have been demonstrated to prevent violence among transgender communities.[44] According to the NSVRC, IPV and SV prevention programming for transgender individuals should be culturally informed and tailored to the specific needs of transgender communities.[45] In a survey of LGBTQ individuals, most respondents believed that sexual violence is a problem in LGBTQ communities, and that sexual violence prevention tailored to LGBTQ communities is needed.[46] However, the same respondents also believed that open dialogue about sexual violence in LGBTQ communities is not occurring, and an even higher percentage of respondents disagreed that their local community is well-equipped to handle incidents of sexual violence in LGBTQ communities.[47] To effectively address and prevent transgender IPV and SV, transgender individuals must feel that prevention programs are appropriate for them and represent their identities. This is consistent with research showing that when target audience members see people who look like them or their peers in the prevention strategy, the prevention message is more likely to resonate.[48]

Currently, few scientifically based prevention programs are culturally specific for this marginalized group.[49] The NSVRC suggests that IPV and SV prevention efforts must focus on creating positive change by working to advance transgender equality, sexual health, and healthy relationships.[50] When transgender prevention programs are introduced, it is important for these programs to target change at multiple levels of the social ecological model, a public health archetype that is explained below.

Social Ecological Model

Public health practitioners often point to a social ecological model that incorporates individual, relationship, community, and societal-level factors influencing the likelihood of violence.[51] The social ecological model indicates that prevention is necessary for every level of social interaction.[52] In IPV and SV prevention work, the social ecological model is often used to demonstrate the complex interplay among different factors in our social environment that influence the likelihood that violence will exist in a given community.[53]

While high school– and college-age individuals (i.e., sixteen to twenty-four years old) are recognized to be at the highest risk for IPV and SV,[54] not all individuals are at equal risk for victimization, and certain populations are more likely to experience violence.[55] The social ecological model can be used to examine the effects of potential prevention strategies by addressing the risk and protective factors that influence whether a person will experience IPV or SV.[56] Understanding risk and protective factors in the context of different levels of the social ecological model is an essential aspect of creating scientifically based programs that will effectively address and prevent SV and IPV among transgender communities.[57]

Comprehensive prevention programs should leverage all of the levels of the social ecological model, rather than only focusing on one level. Furthermore, prevention messages must be consistent across all levels, as well: individual, relationship, community, and societal.[58]

Individual-Level Influences

The first level of the social ecological model identifies biological and personal history factors that can increase a person's risk for victimization or perpetration.[59] Research shows that young people ages sixteen to twenty-four years old are at the highest risk for IPV and SV victimization and perpetration, so primary prevention should ideally begin before this age.[60] Individual-level risk factors that contribute to youth dating violence victimization include depression and suicidal ideation, family maltreatment and abuse, lack of peer and social acceptance, poor school performance, and substance abuse.[61] These same factors are present at heightened levels in transgender youth, as these individuals often face discrimination and bullying by classmates, friends, and family.[62] For transgender individuals, their identity in itself puts them at higher risk for violence victimization, as they are often the target of transphobic hate crimes.[63] Additionally, transgender youth are more likely to be rejected by their family of origin, which can leave them vulnerable to homelessness, addiction, sex work, SV victimization, and IPV victimization.[64] The CDC notes that protective factors for transgender youth against IPV, SV, and other forms of violence include family and peer support and access to Gay-Straight Alliances (GSAs; also known as Genders and Sexualities Alliances) and other transgender-positive community organizations.[65]

Prevention strategies at the individual level are often designed to promote attitudes, beliefs, and behaviors that prevent violence, with the goal of impacting the individual factors that affect the likelihood of being a victim or perpetrator of violence. These approaches can include education and life skills training to increase awareness of IPV and SV and situations in which it might occur.[66] Other examples include empowering students through bystander intervention strategies so an individual is better prepared to confront a dangerous situation.[67] It is important to note that many of the individual-level risk factors, such as bullying, hate crimes related to gender identity, child abuse, and suicidality, are caused and impacted by institutionalized and societal transphobia. Designing prevention strategies at each specific level should be done with an understanding of the broader context of discrimination that impacts the individual's experience. However, transgender individuals may experience challenges in implementing these individual-level strategies that cisgender individuals do not face. They may be resistant to bystander intervention for fear of mistreatment by formal supports (e.g., police) or discrimination from the bystanders around them.[68] (See chapter 9 for more on police.) Instead, prevention practitioners should discuss violence within a social justice framework that gives examples of transgender relationships and that notes the complexities of sex and gender identity, in order to gain credibility from transgender individuals.[69]

Relationship-Level Influences

The second level of the social ecological model examines close relationships that may increase the risk of experiencing violence. Prevention strategies at this level should address relationships with peers, intimate partners, and family members.[70] Since IPV and SV often occur in close interpersonal relationships, educating high school– and college-age students about the importance of healthy relationships and sexual lives can prevent violence from occurring in the future.[71] Healthy relationship education should not only focus on cisgender-only romantic relationships but also those involving one or more transgender individuals, as well as power and control that exists in workplaces, with advisors, and in platonic friendships. While power and control dynamics are often seen in intimate partnerships, such dynamics can also emerge within platonic friendships, at workplaces, and between advisors and students. Giving students the ability to identify potentially abusive dynamics and what to do when they are confronted with them can empower students to change their culture. (See chapter 5 for more on theoretical explanations of transgender IPV.)

Like members of other marginalized communities, transgender individuals face unique challenges in the way they experience IPV and SV. For example, an abusive partner may target a transgender person's unique vulnerabilities and use them to dominate and control them.[72] This can include threatening to reveal the survivor's transgender identity or history, withholding finances necessary for gender-affirming medical services, withholding items the survivor uses to express their gender identity, or insulting the survivor's body or clothing choices.[73] In addition, transgender individuals may face family rejection that in turn makes them more vulnerable to structural and interpersonal victimization.[74]

Therefore, prevention at the relationship level should focus on educating parents and families on the importance of supporting their child's psychosocial development, regardless of their gender identity, as family acceptance of transgender adolescents has been shown to increase positive health outcomes (e.g., self-esteem, social support, and general health) and protect against negative health outcomes (e.g., depression, substance abuse, and suicide).[75] Prevention strategies designed at this level should then include discussing the abusive behaviors of IPV in a way that includes unique transgender IPV tactics rather than only cisgender IPV tactics. These strategies can also include discussing unique myths about transgender IPV to help undermine attitudes condoning transgender IPV. This allows for participants to engage in a broader conversation regarding IPV that reflects transgender people's lives and experiences. Relationship-level prevention also includes mentoring and peer programs that are designed to reduce conflict and foster healthy interpersonal relationships, using examples and language that is transgender-inclusive.[76]

Community-Level Influences

The community level of the social ecological model includes the settings (e.g., schools, workplaces, and neighborhoods) in which social relationships occur, and seeks to identify the characteristics of these settings that are associated with risk factors for violence. Community-level prevention involves empowering all individuals to stop violence and emphasizes a group commitment to maintaining a safe community.[77] Prevention at this level must confront and reform the social expectations and norms of the community that lead to violence.

To reduce violence among transgender individuals, community members must come together to engage in strategies that prevent violence and discrimination against these individuals. For example, a review of protective factors for transgender youth by CDC health scientist Michelle Johns and colleagues found that the presence of transgender-inclusive organizational resources, including GSAs and other visible LGBTQ groups and allies in schools, improved self-advocacy skills and resilience among transgender youth.[78] Schools can also improve the climate for transgender youth by implementing policies that show these students that they are accepted and protected in the community, including strict antidiscrimination policies, school-wide education on the topic of gender identity–based discrimination for students, faculty, and staff, and the implementation of gender-neutral bathrooms.[79]

Educational psychologists Robert Brown and Valerie Gortmaker also recommend that colleges implement a campus climate study focused on the experiences and needs of LGBTQ students.[80] These studies can serve to "empower LGBTQ students by demonstrating that the institution cares enough to be concerned about them and their needs."[81] The results of campus climate studies can help transgender students, as well as cisgender lesbian, gay, bisexual, and queer (LGBQ) students, see that they are not alone in their experiences, and also can help college administrators improve the quality of life for these students through policy changes.

Societal-Level Influences

The fourth level of the social ecological model looks at the broad societal factors that help create a climate in which violence is encouraged or inhibited. These factors include social and cultural norms such as tolerance of transphobia, as well as genderism and rigid definitions of "masculinity" and "femininity." Other factors include the health, economic, education, and social policies that help to maintain economic or social inequalities between groups in society.[82]

Today we see a wider normative intolerance for IPV and SV than in generations past, as cultural sexism has decreased and behaviors to prevent violence have become the norm.[83] However, violence remains a prevalent problem in transgender communities that will not be thwarted without wider social change. Prevention at the societal level of the social ecological model involves shifting common beliefs and attitudes to address social issues in new ways. For example, in the US, laws in twenty states prohibit discrimination against transgender people. Their protections vary, but many laws ban discrimination in employment, housing, and public accommodations like restaurants, hospitals, and retail stores. While these laws are a step in the right direction, there is still far to go, and the majority of states currently have no explicit prohibitions against discrimination based on gender identity in their state law.[84] Additionally, recent federal policies show a lack of regard for transgender individuals, such as the Trump administration's guidance that the words *transgender* and *diversity* should be avoided by the CDC and other agencies of the US Department of Health and Human Services in all budget reports.[85] For numerous additional examples of anti-transgender policy and guidance in the US under the Trump administration, see the web page "Trump's Record of Action against Transgender People" produced by the National Center for Transgender Equality.[86]

In a qualitative study of transgender individuals, psychologist Susan Turell and colleagues found that many participants had other issues in their lives that were more "urgent" than IPV, including gender-based discrimination and violence in broader social contexts. Participants also noted that mental health problems caused by marginalization, including depression and drug abuse, were more immediate health needs than IPV prevention.[87] Thus, to solve the problems of IPV and SV in transgender communities, alongside the introduction of transgender-specific violence prevention programs, we must also simultaneously work to eradicate societal transphobia and marginalization, which not only can increase the isolation of transgender IPV survivors but also in and of themselves have many negative health impacts.

Primary Prevention

Additionally, a comprehensive approach must include primary, secondary, and tertiary prevention strategies to stop violence from happening, as well as respond to violence after it occurs.[88] Primary prevention refers to attitudes, behaviors, and social conditions aimed at preventing IPV and SV before they happen. This can include universal interventions "directed at the general population, as well as selected interventions aimed at those who may be at increased risk for sexual violence," whether in terms of perpetration or victimization.[89] Secondary prevention aims to stop violence while it is being perpetrated and also addresses a survivor's immediate needs in the aftermath of a crime. Tertiary prevention refers to long-term follow-up and support for survivors, to deal with the lasting consequences of violence for both the survivor and the larger community.[90] (See table 11.3 for an example of a comprehensive framework for reducing IPV and SV against transgender individuals that leverages the four levels of the social ecological model.)

Although beyond the scope of the present chapter, numerous resources exist in the literature to aid in the development of secondary and tertiary prevention efforts.[91] In this section, primary prevention issues are discussed in the context of addressing transgender IPV and SV. Primary prevention is considered the cornerstone of good public health, as these strategies are aimed to prevent health problems before they occur.[92] Primary violence prevention can be challenging, as community leaders must determine when to begin prevention, whom to target, and how to do it. Additionally, primary prevention programming must be culturally and linguistically appropriate for the identified community.[93] For that reason, prevention activities may vary across communities and population types. For transgender students, prevention programming focused on age group may not resonate with their identity. This can make transgender students feel less likely to participate or less connected.

When deciding on primary violence prevention programs for transgender—as well as LGBQ—communities, the NSVRC notes three broad areas of focus to consider.[94] First, prevention should focus on healthy relationships among transgender individuals, as well as the development of positive intracommunity relationships and structural supports. Second, organizations that provide resources to IPV and SV survivors should be culturally competent in issues faced by transgender communities, including risks such as revictimization, lack of access to support services, and health disparities. Third and lastly, a focus should be made on the development of community norms and supports that contribute to the ability of transgender individuals to thrive, while addressing risks associated with hate crimes and violence originating outside transgender communities. It is important for prevention programs to understand and acknowledge transgender communities, including the causes and consequences of violence within and against them. Next, we outline new techniques and research in primary prevention education that are transgender-inclusive and promising in their ability to reduce violence and raise awareness about IPV and SV. These include GSAs, online interventions, and bystander interventions.

GSAs

The NSVRC notes that effective IPV and SV prevention can involve programs that address discrimination (e.g., transphobia and homophobia), such as GSAs.[95] Originally founded as Gay-Straight Alliances and now often called Genders and Sexualities Alliances, these groups create safe environments in schools for students to support each other and learn about and educate their school on different forms of oppression based on gender identity and sexual orientation. As another example, the Stand and Serve Club is part of a program in Arizona that addresses dating violence, sexual violence, homophobia, sexism, and other forms of violence, and could be adapted for LGBTQ communities. This club

TABLE 11.3. Strategies for Reducing Transgender IPV and SV Using a Social Ecological Framework

	Level of the Social Ecological Model			
	Individual	Relationship	Community	Societal
Intervention Targets	Biological/personal history factors • Demographics (e.g., age, gender, race, sexuality) • Prior victimization • Alcohol and drug use	Close relationships • Peers • Romantic and sexual partners • Teachers, counselors, professors • Parents	Social Environments • Middle and high schools • Colleges • Community centers • Health centers	Inequalities • Transphobia • Genderism • Intersecting prejudice, such as racism, classism, and heterosexism
Reduction Strategies	• Helping students strengthen skills and knowledge to prevent violence among all individuals, with special focus on acceptance of differences (e.g., GSAs)	• Engaging peer groups and adults in strengthening group skills and knowledge to prevent transphobia and violence	• Engaging community members in strategies to prevent violence and change norms to support transgender-inclusive and violence-free environments	• Implementing policies that address transgender inequalities and promote equity among all groups
Prevention Actions	• Supporting youth when they come out as transgender. • Teaching individuals bystander intervention skills to intervene against oppressive remarks/actions against transgender individuals.	• Interrupting transphobic comments. • Creating institutions and workplaces with transgender-friendly spaces.	• Ensuring comprehensive sexuality education programs are widely available in all schools and communities. • Incorporating examples of transgender intimate partner violence and sexual violence in all violence prevention program exercises.	• Positively representing transgender identities and relationships in the media. • Providing transgender individuals equal rights and protections under the law in every nation, state, and community.

- Using gender-inclusive language to describe violence (e.g., sexual violence and intimate partner instead of "violence against women").
- Assuring that prevention educators are knowledgeable about and comfortable with discussing the complexities of transgender identities and experiences, as well as implications for violence prevention.

- Strengthening parental, family, and school support of transgender youth and their relationships.
- Providing support systems and resources for transgender youth that are widely available.

- Designating gender-neutral bathrooms on high school and college campuses.
- Allowing transgender students to attend prom in their preferred clothing and gender expressions.
- Designing education programs specifically for transgender communities and their allies.
- Training crisis center advocates and shelter staff about the needs of transgender intimate partner violence survivors.

- Enacting school anti-bullying and anti-harassment policies to protect transgender students.
- Guaranteeing access to marriage equality under the law.
- Ensuring equality in adoption processes.
- Providing access to affirming health care for transgender people.

Prevention efforts should span across all levels

was formed on the belief that preventing one form of violence in a community can prevent them all, as the underlying conditions that lead to their existence are rooted in oppression.[96]

In a meta-analysis by doctoral candidate Robert Marx and sociologist Heather Kettrey, schools with GSAs were associated with significantly lower levels of school-based victimization and fear for safety among LGBTQ students.[97] The meta-analysis drew upon fifteen quantitative studies that measured victimization outcomes for students at schools with GSAs or other school-based gender and sexuality diversity clubs, compared to students at schools without such programs. The results of the study support GSAs as a means of protecting transgender as well as cisgender LGBQ youth from school-based victimization, as results showed strong evidence of an association between the presence of GSAs in schools and lower reports of victimization among adolescents.[98] Moving forward, GSAs should be considered as an important resource for preventing IPV and SV among transgender students, as these organizations could be an effective avenue for dispersing prevention programming to vulnerable students.

Online Interventions

Most school-based sexual health programs do not meet the needs of transgender youth. Transgender individuals also have few accessible role models for healthy relationships and, as medical researchers Brian Mustanski and colleagues note, they "may have less parental support for and monitoring of their romantic and sexual activities."[99] Therefore, the internet is an important, and underutilized, resource in the development of sexual health among transgender youth. A study by Mustanski and colleagues showed positive outcomes from an online-based sexual health promotion program for LGBTQ youth.[100] The program consisted of five intervention modules, with a quiz after each module about the materials presented. The findings showed significant positive effects on several aspects of sexual health, including knowledge of sexual functioning, HIV/AIDS, sexually transmitted infections, and contraceptives. Additionally, significant positive effects were found for several aspects of healthy relationships, including increased communication skills and sexual assertiveness, and decreased justification of violence.[101] These results show promise for the continued development and expansion of online programs for transgender youth, which could possibly be implemented in GSAs or via other transgender-friendly community resources, as a way to target this vulnerable group and potentially prevent IPV and SV.

Bystander Interventions

Many high schools and colleges have moved to bystander intervention strategies that encourage individuals to engage with their friends, peers, and others to confront and change social norms that contribute to violence.[102] These bystander approaches are designed to engage everyone in the community as allies against violence, and can also involve role models in the campus community, including coaches, athletes, professors, and parents.[103]

Bystander intervention is an important tool for creating a safe and inclusive environment for all students and may be critical to supporting cisgender LGBQ students.[104] However, transgender individuals may not feel as comfortable as cisgender individuals to use the bystander method to confront a dangerous situation, as many transgender people are aware of the risk of transphobic hate in communities and from formal supports (e.g., police, medical providers, and crisis centers). Still, bystander intervention can help to protect transgender people in violent relationships, as the goal of the strategy is to motivate individuals in the community to intervene in a potentially dangerous situation, regardless of who the victim or perpetrator is.

Research suggests that peers can serve as powerful role models in encouraging nondiscriminatory behavior with respect to transgender individuals.[105] Social worker and political scientist Laura Wernick and colleagues found that seeing other students intervene in instances of harassment or victimization of LGBTQ individuals was significantly and positively related to the likelihood that the student respondents would intervene.[106] Since cisgender, heterosexual students are usually the majority population on campus, it is important to foster bystander intervention skills among this group.[107] Cisgender, heterosexual individuals are uniquely positioned to intervene in situations of violence and discrimination against transgender individuals because they often have access to social capital with their peers, intimate knowledge of interpersonal and social dynamics, and access to locations that supervisory adults do not.[108] More research must be done to involve transgender individuals in bystander intervention by creating safer spaces where these individuals feel less vulnerable against hate crimes and discrimination and therefore more likely to stand up for themselves and others.

Conclusions

Despite the strict scientific standard for evaluating primary violence prevention programs,[109] there is no requirement to include examples of transgender individuals in prevention programming for it to be deemed evidence-based. This is problematic, as it leaves out an entire population that may not relate to the cisgender relationship structure exemplified in many prevention programs. Small changes could make transgender individuals feel more included in these programs, as well as improve the efficacy of these programs in reducing IPV and SV specifically among transgender program participants. Specifically, transgender individuals are marginalized in society, and their identities should be represented in prevention programs to reduce levels of victimization and perpetration among this vulnerable group. To better guide these needed programmatic changes, further research must focus on refining and evaluating prevention programs addressing IPV, SV, and other forms of violence among transgender communities, as this group has been proven to experience heightened levels of violence throughout their lifetime.

For now, communities must find creative ways to implement effective prevention to protect transgender individuals. While primary prevention is the cornerstone of public health, secondary and tertiary prevention are also critical in supporting survivors who experience SV and IPV. Transgender individuals face many barriers to help seeking, including fear of discrimination by formal supports. Many structural factors deter a transgender survivor from receiving the services they need after an assault, and a lack of inclusive resources may make this population especially vulnerable to IPV.[110] For example, experiencing homelessness or housing instability may lead a transgender individual to rely on their intimate partner for housing, and thus they may not report IPV for fear that they would no longer have a place to stay. Many services, such as emergency or temporary housing or shelter services, are gender-segregated and sometimes dangerous to transgender individuals.[111] In this regard, Susan Turell and colleagues concluded that it was unlikely that transgender survivors would access mainstream community services and would more likely seek out support within the transgender and broader LGBTQ communities.[112] Therefore, it is important to educate transgender communities on how to help others access resources that are transgender-sensitive.

As the NSVRC notes, preventing IPV and SV for transgender individuals is ultimately about creating "safe, affirming, and respectful environments" for all people.[113] Transgender individuals face discrimination and oppression in their day-to-day lives that make them more susceptible to violence. Using a public health model, we can begin to change the cultural and community norms that allow violence to continue to disproportionately affect this population, in hopes of creating healthier personal lives and relationships for transgender individuals.

NOTES

1. James et al. 2016.
2. According to the Centers for Disease Control and Prevention, "sexual violence" involves a range of acts including attempted or completed forced or alcohol/drug-facilitated penetration (i.e., rape), being made to penetrate someone else, verbal (nonphysical) pressure that results in unwanted penetration (i.e., sexual coercion), unwanted sexual contact (e.g., fondling), and noncontact unwanted sexual experiences (e.g., verbal harassment or voyeurism). While SV can be perpetrated within an intimate partner relationship, it can also involve assault by family, friends, acquaintances, or strangers. Basile et al. 2016.
3. T. Brown and Herman 2015; Cantor et al. 2015; Dank et al. 2014.
4. Ford et al. 2013.
5. N. Brown 2007.
6. N. Brown 2007; Goldenberg, Jadwin-Cakmak, and Harper 2018.
7. Murray et al. 2007.
8. Risser, et al. 2005; Roch, Morton, and Ritchie 2010; Turell, 2000.
9. Cantor et al. 2015; Johns et al. 2018; Kosciw et al. 2015.
10. T. Brown and Herman 2015; Goldenberg, Jadwin-Cakmak, and Harper 2018.
11. Turell et al. 2012; Yerke and DeFeo 2016.
12. Coomaraswamy 1997, 10.
13. James et al. 2016; Yerke and DeFeo 2016.
14. Basile et al. 2007; Potter et al. 2018.
15. Marine and Nicollazzo 2017; Potter, Fountain, and Stapleton 2012.

16 Goldenberg, Jadwin-Cakmak, and Harper 2018.
17 Basile et al. 2016.
18 Banyard et al. 2017; Coker et al. 2002; Potter et al. 2018; Smith et al. 2017.
19 Goldenberg, Jadwin-Cakmak, and Harper 2018; James et al. 2016; Messman and Leigh 2019.
20 Barrett and Sheridan 2017; Factor and Rothblum 2007; Klein and Golub 2016.
21 Basile et al. 2016.
22 Goldenberg, Jadwin-Cakmak, and Harper 2018; Grossman, Park, and Russell 2016.
23 Brennan et al. 2012; Goldenberg, Jadwin-Cakmak, and Harper 2018; Shipherd et al. 2011; White Hughto et al. 2017.
24 Barrett and Sheridan 2017; Marcellin et al. 2013.
25 Grant et al. 2011.
26 Robertson 2018.
27 Hirschfield Davis and Cooper 2017.
28 NSVRC 2012, 1.
29 Brome et al. 2004.
30 CDC 2015.
31 Catalano 2012; Sinozich and Langton 2014.
32 Lee, Guy, and Perry 2007.
33 Meerwijk and Sevelius 2017, 1.
34 Messman and Leslie 2019.
35 Mercy et al. 2002.
36 CDC 2015, 1.
37 Dank et al. 2014.
38 CDC 2018.
39 Brome et al. 2004, 3.
40 Langhinrichsen-Rohling and Capaldi 2012.
41 DeGue et al. 2014, 359.
42 DeGue et al. 2014.
43 Fenton et al. 2016, 36.
44 Marx and Kettrey 2016; Mustanski et al. 2015; Potter, Fountain, and Stapleton 2012.
45 NSVRC 2012.
46 Todahl et al. 2009.
47 Todahl et al. 2009.
48 Potter 2012; Potter, Moynihan, and Stapleton 2011.
49 Marine and Nicolazzo 2017; Potter, Fountain, and Stapleton 2012; Turell et al. 2012.
50 NSVRC 2012.
51 Bronfenbrenner 1977.
52 Basile et al. 2016.
53 NSVRC 2012; Potter 2016.

54 Catalano 2012; Sinozich and Langton 2014.
55 Eaton, Davis, and Noonan 2007; Kaukinen 2014.
56 Dahlberg and Krug 2002.
57 Basile et al. 2016.
58 Basile et al. 2016.
59 Basile et al. 2016.
60 Catalano 2012; Sinozich and Langton 2014.
61 Vezina and Hebert 2007.
62 Carmel, Hopwood, and Dickey 2014; Henry et al. 2018.
63 James et al. 2016.
64 Goldenberg, Jadwin-Cakmak, and Harper 2018.
65 CDC 2018; Marx and Kettrey 2016; Ryan et al. 2010; Simons et al. 2013.
66 Mustanski et al. 2015; Senn et al. 2015.
67 Potter 2016.
68 Potter, Fountain, and Stapleton 2012; Yerke and DeFeo 2016.
69 Marine and Nicollazzo 2017.
70 Carr 2005.
71 Mustanski et al. 2015.
72 Brown 2011; Yerke and DeFeo 2016.
73 FORGE 2011; White and Goldberg 2006.
74 Klein and Golub 2016
75 Ryan et al. 2010; Simons et al. 2013.
76 Marx and Kettrey 2016.
77 Basile et al. 2016.
78 Johns et al. 2018.
79 Johns et al. 2018.
80 Brown and Gortmaker 2009.
81 Brown and Gortmaker 2009, 430.
82 Basile et al. 2016.
83 Potter 2016.
84 Transgender Law Center, n.d.
85 Byne 2018.
86 National Center for Transgender Equality 2018.
87 Turell et al. 2012.
88 Dills, Fowler, and Payne 2016.
89 DeGue et al. 2014, 347.
90 Brome et al. 2004.
91 Basile et al. 2016; Brome et al. 2004.
92 Basile et al. 2016.
93 Potter 2012; Potter, Moynihan, and Stapleton 2011.
94 NSVRC 2012.
95 NSVRC 2012.
96 NSVRC 2012; Peer Solutions 2018.

97 Marx and Kettrey 2016.
98 Marx and Kettrey 2016.
99 Mustanski, Greene, and Ryan 2015, 221.
100 Mustanski et al. 2015.
101 Mustanski et al. 2015.
102 Banyard and Moynihan 2011; Coker et al. 2015; Potter et al. 2015.
103 Bannon and Foubert 2017.
104 Dessel, Goodman, and Woodford 2017.
105 Wernick, Kulick, and Inglehart 2013.
106 Wernick, Kulick, and Inglehart 2013.
107 Dessel, Goodman, and Woodford 2017.
108 Flaspohler et al. 2009; Lipson 2001; O'Connell, Pepler, and Craig 1999; Wernick, Kulick, and Inglehart 2013.
109 DeGue 2014.
110 Goldenberg, Jadwin-Cakmak, and Harper 2018.
111 Cook-Daniels 2015.
112 Turell et al. 2012.
113 NSVRC 2012, 18.

REFERENCES

Bannon, R. Sean, and John D. Foubert. 2017. "The Bystander Approach to Sexual Assault Risk Reduction: Effects on Risk Recognition, Perceived Self-efficacy, and Protective Behavior." *Violence and Victims* 32 (1): 46–59.

Banyard, Victoria L., Jennifer M. Demers, Ellen S. Cohn, Katie M. Edwards, Mary M. Moynihan, Wendy A. Walsh, and Sally K. Ward. 2017. "Academic Correlates of Unwanted Sexual Contact, Intercourse, Stalking, and Intimate Partner Violence: An Understudied but Important Consequence for College Students." *Journal of Interpersonal Violence.* https://doi.org/10.1177/0886260517715022.

Banyard, Victoria L., and Mary M. Moynihan. 2011. "Variation in Bystander Behavior Related to Sexual and Intimate Partner Violence Prevention: Correlates in a Sample of College Students." *Pyschology of Violence* 1 (4): 287–301.

Barrett, Betty J, and Daphne V. Sheridan. 2017. "Partner Violence in Transgender Communities: What Helping Professionals Need to Know." *Journal of GLBT Family Studies* 13 (2): 137–162.

Basile, Kathleen C., Jieru Chen, Michele C. Black, and Linda E. Saltzman. 2007. "Prevalence and Characteristics of Sexual Violence Victimization among U.S. Adults, 2001–2003." *Violence and Victims* 22 (4): 437–448.

Basile, Kathleen C., Sarah DeGue, Kathryn Jones, Kimberley Freire, Jenny Dills, Sharon G. Smith, and Jerris L. Raiford. 2016. *STOP SV: A Technical Package to Prevent Sexual Violence*. Atlanta: Centers for Disease Control and Prevention.

Brennan, Julia, Lisa M. Kuhns, Amy K. Johnson, Marvin Belzer, Erin C. Wilson, Robert Garofalo, and Adolescent Medicine Trials Network for HIV/AIDS Interventions. 2012. "Syndemic Theory and HIV-related Risk among Young Transgender

Women: The Role of Multiple, Co-occurring Health Problems and Social Marginalization." *American Journal of Public Health* 102 (9): 1751–1757.

Brome, Margaret, Janet Saul, Karen Lang, Rebeca Lee-Pethel, Neil Rainford, and Jocelyn Wheaton. 2004. *Sexual Violence Prevention: Beginning the Dialogue*. Atlanta: Centers for Disease Control and Prevention.

Bronfenbrenner, Urie. 1977. "Toward an Experimental Ecology of Human Development." *American Psychologist* 32 (7): 513–531.

Brown, Nicola. 2007. "Stories from Outside the Frame: Intimate Partner Abuse in Sexual-Minority Women's Relationships with Transsexual Men." *Feminism and Psychology* 17 (3): 373–393.

Brown, Nicola. 2011. "Holding Tensions of Victimization and Perpetration: Partner Abuse in Trans Communities." In *Intimate Partner Violence in LGBTQ Lives*, edited by Janice L. Ristock, 153–168. New York: Routledge.

Brown, Robert D., and Valerie J. Gortmaker. 2009. "Assessing Campus Climates for Lesbian, Gay, Bisexual, and Transgender (LGBT) Students: Methodological and Political Issues." *Journal of LGBT Youth* 6:416–435.

Brown, Taylor N. T., and Jody L. Herman. 2015. *Intimate Partner Violence and Sexual Abuse among LGBT People: A Review of Existing Research*. Los Angeles, CA: The Williams Institute, UCLA School of Law. http://williamsinstitute.law.ucla.edu.

Byne, William. 2018. "Resilience and Action in a Challenging Time for LGBT Rights." *LGBT Health* 5 (1): 1–5.

Cantor, David, Bonnie Fisher, Susan Chibnall, Carol Bruce, Reanne Townsend, Gail Thomas, and Hyunshik Lee. 2015. *Report on the AAU Campus Climate Survey on Sexual Assault and Sexual Misconduct*. Rockville, MD: Westat.

Carmel, Tamar, Ruben Hopwood, and Lore M. Dickey. 2014. "Mental Health Concerns." In *Trans Bodies, Trans Selves: A Resource for the Transgender Community*, edited by Laura Erickson-Schroth, 305–332. New York, NY: Oxford University Press.

Carr, Joetta L. 2005. "American College Health Association Campus Violence White Paper." Baltimore, MD.

Catalano, Shannan. 2012. *Intimate Partner Violence in the United States, 1993–2010*. Washington DC: US Department of Justice, Office of Justice Programs, Bureau of Justice Statistics.

Centers for Disease Control and Prevention. 2015. "The Public Health Approach to Violence Prevention." www.cdc.gov.

Centers for Disease Control and Prevention. 2018. "Protective Factors for LGBT Youth: Information for Health and Education Professionals." www.cdc.gov.

Coker, Ann, Keith Davis, Ileana Arias, Sujata Desai, Maureen Sanderson, Heather Brandt, and Paige Smith. 2002. "Physical and Mental Health Effects of Intimate Partner Violence for Men and Women." *American Journal of Preventive Medicine* 23 (4): 260–268.

Coker, Ann, Bonnie Fisher, Heather Bush, Suzanne Swan, Corrine Williams, Emily Clear, and Sarah DeGue. 2015. "Evaluation of the Green Dot Bystander Intervention to Reduce Interpersonal Violence among College Students across Three Campuses." *Violence against Women* 21 (12): 1507–1527.

Cook-Daniels, Loree. 2015. "Intimate Partner Violence in Transgender Couples: 'Power and Control' in a Specific Cultural Context." *Partner Abuse* 6 (1): 126–139.

Coomaraswamy, Radhika. 1997. *Report of the Special Rapporteur on Violence against Women, Its Causes and Consequences*. Geneva: United Nations Economic and Social Council Commission on Human Rights.

Coulter, Robert W. S., and Susan R. Rankin. 2017. "College Sexual Assault and Campus Climate for Sexual- and Gender-Minority Undergraduate Students." *Journal of Interpersonal Violence* (2017). https://doi.org/10.1177/0886260517696870.

Dahlberg, Linda, and Etienne Krug. 2002. "Violence—A Global Public Health Problem." In *World Report on Violence and Health*, edited by Etienne G. Krug, Linda L. Dahlberg, James A. Mercy, Anthony B. Zwi, and Rafael Lozano, 3–21. Geneva: World Health Organization.

Dank, Meredith, Pamela Lachman, Janine Zweig, and Jennifer Yahner. 2014. "Dating Violence Experiences of Lesbian, Gay, Bisexual and Transgender Youth." *Journal of Youth and Adolescence* 43: 846–857.

DeGue, Sarah, Linda Anne Valle, Melissa K. Holt, Greta M. Massetti, Jennifer L. Matjasko, and Andra Teten Tharp. 2014. "A Systematic Review of Primary Prevention Strategies for Sexual Violence Perpetration." *Aggression and Violent Behavior* 19 (4): 346–362.

Dessel, Adrienne B, Kevin D. Goodman, and Michael R. Woodford. 2017. "LGBT Discrimination on Campus and Heterosexual Bystanders: Understanding Intentions to Intervene." *Journal of Diversity in Higher Education* 10 (2): 101–116.

Dills, Jenny, Dawn Fowler, and Gayle Payne. 2016. *Sexual Violence on Campus: Strategies for Prevention*. Atlanta, GA: National Center for Injury Prevention and Control, Centers for Disease Control and Prevention. www.cdc.gov.

Eaton, Danice K, Kristen S. Davis, and Rita K. Noonan. 2007. "Associations of Dating Violence Victimization with Lifetime Participation, Initiation of Risk Behaviors." *Journal of Interpersonal Violence* 22 (5): 585–602.

Factor, Rhonda J., and Esther D. Rothblum. 2007. "A Study of Transgender Adults and Their Non-transgender Siblings on Demographic Characteristics, Social Support, and Experiences of Violence." *Journal of LGBT Health Research* 3 (3): 11–30.

Fenton, Rachel Anne, Helen L. Mott, Kieran McCartan, and Philip Rumney. 2016. *A Review of Evidence for Bystander Intervention to Prevent Sexual and Domestic Violence in Universities*. London: Public Health England.

Flaspohler, Paul D., Jennifer L. Elfstrom, Karin L. Vanderzee, Holli E. Sink, and Zachary Birchmeier. 2009. "Stand By Me: The Effects of Peer and Teacher Support in Mitigating the Impact of Bullying on Quality of Life." *Psychology in the Schools* 46 (7): 636–649.

Ford, Chandra L., Terra Slavin, Karin L. Hilton, and Susan L. Holt. 2013. "Intimate Partner Violence Prevention Services and Resources in Los Angeles: Issues, Needs, and Challenges for Assisting Lesbian, Gay, Bisexual, and Transgender Clients." *Health Promotion Practice* 14 (6): 841–849.

FORGE. 2011. *Transgender Domestic Violence and Sexual Assault Resource Sheet*. Milwaukee, WI: FORGE. https://avp.org.

Goldenberg, Tamar, Laura Jadwin-Cakmak, and Gary W. Harper. 2018. "Intimate Partner Violence among Transgender Youth: Associations with Intrapersonal and Structural Factors." *Violence and Gender* 5 (1): 19–25.

Grant, Jaime M., Lisa A. Mottet, Justin Tanis, Jack Harrison, Jody L. Herman, and Mara Keisling. 2011. *Injustice at Every Turn: A Report of the National Transgender Discrimination Survey*. Washington DC: National Center for Transgender Equality and National Gay and Lesbian Task Force. www.transequality.org.

Grossman, Arnold H., Jung Yeon Park, and Stephen T. Russell. 2016. "Transgender Youth and Suicidal Behaviors: Applying the Interpersonal Psychological Theory of Suicide." *Journal of Gay and Lesbian Mental Health* 20:329–349.

Guadalupe-Diaz, Xavier L., and Jana Jasinski. 2017. "'I Wasn't a Priority, I Wasn't a Victim': Challenges in Help Seeking for Transgender Survivors of Intimate Partner Violence." *Violence Against Women* 23 (6): 772–792.

Henry, Richard S., Paul B. Perrin, Bethany M. Coston, and Jenna M. Calton. 2018. "Intimate Partner Violence and Mental Health among Transgender/Gender Nonconforming Adults." *Journal of Interpersonal Violence*. https://doi.org/10.1177/0886260518775148.

Hirschfield Davis, Julie, and Helene Cooper. 2017. "Trump Says Transgender People Will Not Be Allowed in the Military." *New York Times*, July 26, 2017. www.nytimes.com.

James, Sandy E., Jody L. Herman, Susan Rankin, Mara Keisling, Lisa Mottet, and Ma'ayan Anafi. 2016. *The Report of the 2015 U.S. Transgender Survey*. Washington DC: National Center for Transgender Equality. www.ustranssurvey.org.

Johns, Michelle Marie, Oscar Beltran, Heather L. Armstrong, Paula E. Jayne, and Lisa C. Barrios. 2018. "Protective Factors among Transgender and Gender Variant Youth: A Systematic Review by Socioecological Level." *Journal of Primary Prevention* 39 (3): 263–301.

Kaukinen, Catherine. 2014. "Dating Violence among College Students: The Risk and Protective Factors." *Trauma Violence & Abuse* 15 (4): 283–296.

Klein, Augustus, and Sarit A. Golub. 2016. "Family Rejection as a Predictor of Suicide Attempts and Substance Misuse among Transgender and Gender Nonconforming Adults." *LGBT Health* 3 (3): 193–199.

Kosciw, Joseph G., Emily A. Greytak, Noreen M. Giga, Christian Villenas, and David J. Danischewski. 2015. *The 2015 National School Climate Survey: The Experiences of Lesbian, Gay, Bisexual and Transgender Youth in Our Nation's Schools*. New York: GLSEN. www.glsen.org.

Langhinrichsen-Rohling, Jennifer, and Deborah M. Capaldi. 2012. "Clearly We've Only Just Begun: Developing Effective Prevention Programs for Intimate Partner Violence." *Prevention Science* 13 (4): 410–414.

Lee, David S., Lydia Guy, and Brad Perry. 2007. *Sexual Violence Prevention*. Linthicum, MD: American College Health Association.

Lipson, Jodi. 2001. *Hostile Hallways: Bullying, Teasing, and Sexual Harassment in School*. Washington, DC: American Association of University Women Educational Foundation. www.aauw.org.

Marcellin, Roxanne Longman, Ayden Scheim, Greta Bauer, and Nik Redman. 2013. "Experiences of Transphobia among Trans Ontarians." *Trans PULSE E-Bulletin* 3 (2): 1–2.

Marine, Susan B., and Z. Nicollazzo. 2017. "Campus Sexual Violence Prevention Educators' Use of Gender in Their Work: A Critical Exploration." *Journal of Interpersonal Violence*. https://doi.org/10.1177/0886260517718543.

Marx, Robert A., and Heather H. Kettrey. 2016. "Gay-Straight Alliances Are Associated with Lower Levels of School-Based Victimization of LGBTQ+ Youth: A Systematic Review and Meta-Analysis." *Journal of Youth and Adolescence* 45:1269–1282.

Meerwijk, Esther L., and Jae M. Sevelius. 2017. "Transgender Population Size in the United States: A Meta-regression of Population-Based Probability Samples." *American Journal of Public Health* 107 (2): e1–e8.

Mercy, James A., Alexander Butchart, David Farrington, and Magdalena Cerda. 2002. "Youth Violence." In *World Report on Violence and Health*, edited by Etienne G. Krug, Linda L. Dahlberg, James A. Mercy, Anthony B. Zwi, and Rafael Lozano, 25–62. Geneva: World Health Organization.

Messman, Jenna B., and Leigh A. Leslie. 2019. "Transgender College Students: Academic Resilience and Striving to Cope in the Face of Marginalized Health." *Journal of American College Health* 67 (2): 161–173.

Murray, Christine E., Keith Mobley, Anne P. Buford, and Megan M. Seaman-DeJohn. 2007. "Same-Sex Intimate Partner Violence." *Journal of LGBT Issues in Counseling*, 1 (4): 7–30.

Mustanski, Brian, George J. Greene, Daniel Ryan, and Sarah W Whitton. 2015. "Feasability, Acceptability, and Initital Efficacy of an Online Sexual Health Promotion Program for LGBT Youth: The Queer Sex Ed Intervention." *Journal of Sex Research* 52 (2): 220–230.

National Center for Transgender Equality. n.d. "Trump's Record of Action against Transgender People." Accessed November 30, 2018. https://transequality.org.

National Sexual Violence Resource Center. 2012. *Guide for Transformative Prevention Programming: Sexual Violence and Individuals Who Identify as LGBTQ*. Enola, PA: National Sexual Violence Resource Center and Pennsylvania Coalition against Rape.

O'Connell, P. A. U. L., Debra Pepler, and Wendy Craig. 1999. "Peer Involvement in Bullying: Insights and Challenges for Intervention." *Journal of Adolescence* 22 (4): 437–452.

Peer Solutions. n.d. "Stand and Serve Club." Accessed July 2, 2018. www.peersolutions.org.

Potter, Sharyn J. 2012. "Using a Multi-media Social Marketing Campaign to Increase Active Bystanders on the College Campus." *Journal of American College Health* 60 (4): 282–295.

Potter, Sharyn J. 2016. "Reducing Sexual Assault on Campus: Lessons from the Movement to Prevent Drunk Driving." *American Journal of Public Health* 106 (5): 822–829.

Potter, Sharyn J., Kim Fountain, and Jane G. Stapleton. 2012. "Addressing Sexual and Relationship Violence in the LGBT Community Using a Bystander Framework." *Harvard Review of Psychiatry* 20 (4): 201–208.

Potter, Sharyn J., Rebecca M. Howard, Sharon Murphy, and Mary M. Moynihan. 2018. "Long-Term Impacts of College Sexual Assaults on Women Survivors' Educational and Career Attainments." *Journal of American College Health*, 66 (6): 496–507.

Potter, Sharyn J., Mary M. Moynihan, and Jane G. Stapleton. 2011. "Using Social Self-Identification in Social Marketing Aimed at Reducing Violence against Women on Campus." *Journal of Interpersonal Violence* 26 (5): 971–990.

Potter, Sharyn J., Jane G. Stapleton, Kari Mansager, and Charles Nies. 2015. "Adapting and Piloting the Know Your Power Bystander Social Marketing Campaign for a Diverse Campus Population." *Cases in Public Health Communication and Marketing* 8:71–93.

Risser, Jan M. H., Andrea Shelton, Sheryl McCurdy, John Atkinson, Paige Padgett, and Bernardo Useche. 2005. "Sex, Drugs, Violence, and HIV Status among Male-to-Female Transgender Persons in Houston, Texas." *International Journal of Transgenderism*. 8 (2–3): 67–74.

Robertson, Gary D. 2018. "Tension over North Carolina's 'Bathroom Bill' Lingers." *Boston Globe*, March 31, 2018. www.bostonglobe.com.

Roch, Amy, James Morton, and Graham Ritchie. 2010. *Out of Sight, out of Mind? Transgender People's Experiences of Domestic Abuse*. Edinburgh: LGBT Youth Scotland and the Scottish Transgender Alliance. www.scottishtrans.org.

Ryan, Caitlin, Stephen T. Russell, David Huebner, Rafael Diaz, and Jorge Sanchez. 2010. "Family Acceptance in Adolescence and the Health of LGBT Young Adults." *Journal of Child and Adolescent Psychiatric Nursing* 23 (4): 205–213.

Senn, Charlene Y., Misha Eliasziw, Paula C. Barata, Wilfreda E. Thurston, Ian R. Newby-Clark, H. Lorraine Radtke, and Karen L. Hobden. 2015. "Efficacy of a Sexual Assault Resistance Program for University Women." *New England Journal of Medicine* 372:2326–35.

Shipherd, Jillian C., Lauren Mizock, Shira Maguen, and Kelly E. Green. 2012. "Male-to-Female Transgender Veterans and VA Health Care Utilization." *International Journal of Sexual Health* 24 (1): 78–87.

Simons, Lisa, Sheree M. Schrager, Leslie F. Clark, Marvin Belzer, and Johanna Olson. 2013. "Parental Support and Mental Health among Transgender Adolescents." *Journal of Adolescent Health* 53 (6): 791–793.

Sinozich, Sofi, and Lynn Langton. 2014. *Rape and Sexual Assault among College-Age Females, 1995–2013*. Washington, DC: US Department of Justice, Office of Justice Programs, Bureau of Justice Statistics.

Smith, Sharon G., Jieru Chen, Kathleen C. Basile, Leah K. Gilbert, Melissa T. Merrick, Nimesh Patel, Margie Walling, and Anurag Jain. 2017. *The National Intimate Partner and Sexual Violence Survey (NISVS): 2010–2012 State Report.* Atlanta: National Center for Injury Prevention and Control, Centers for Disease Control and Prevention.

Todahl, Jeffrey L., Deanna Linville, Amy Bustin, Jenna Wheeler, and Jeff Gau. 2009. "Sexual Assault Support Services and Community Systems: Understanding Critical Issues and Needs in the LGBTQ Community." *Violence against Women* 15:952–976.

Transgender Law Center. n.d. "Equality Maps." Accessed July 2, 2018. https://transgenderlawcenter.org.

Turell, Susan. 2000. "A Descriptive Analysis of Same-Sex Relationship Violence for a Diverse Sample." *Journal of Family Violence* 15 (3): 281–293.

Turell, Susan, Molly Herrmann, Gary Hollander, and Carol Galletly. 2012. "Lesbian, Gay, Bisexual, and Transgender Communities' Readiness for Intimate Partner Violence Prevention." *Journal of Gay & Lesbian Social Services* 24 (3): 289–310.

Vezina, Johanne, and Martine Hebert. 2007. "Risk Factors for Victimization in Romantic Relationships of Young Women: A Review of Empirical Studies and Implications for Prevention." *Trauma, Violence, & Abuse* 8 (1): 33–66.

Wernick, Laura J., Alex Kulick, and Marita H. Inglehart. 2013. "Factors Predicting Student Intervention when Witnessing Anti-LGBTQ Harassment: The Influence of Peers, Teachers, and Climate." *Children and Youth Services Review* 35 (2): 296–301.

White, Caroline, and Joshua Goldberg. 2006. "Expanding on Our Understanding of Gendered Violence: Violence against Trans People and Their Loved Ones." *Canadian Women's Studies* 25 (1–2): 124–127.

White Hughto, Jaclyn M., and Sari L. Reisner. 2016. "A Systematic Review of the Effects of Hormone Therapy on Psychological Functioning and Quality of Life in Transgender Individuals." *Transgender Health* 1 (1): 21–31.

Yerke, Adam F., and Jennifer DeFeo. 2016. "Redefining Intimate Partner Violence beyond the Binary to Include Transgender People." *Journal of Family Violence* 31: 975–79.

12

Training Service Providers to Identify and Overcome Service Barriers in Working with Transgender IPV Survivors

MICHAEL MUNSON AND LOREE COOK-DANIELS

The intimate partner violence (IPV) and sexual assault intervention fields developed out of the women's movement, as women in consciousness-raising groups realized how pervasive these forms of violence are. Unfortunately, because the groups were generally for women only, their participants did not hear men's stories of abuse. They therefore understandably concluded that IPV and sexual assault are *women's* problems rather than *human* problems, and set about educating the public accordingly. That education effort was profoundly successful. Not only did the general public's picture of IPV and sexual assault become that of a man assaulting a woman, but even Congress was influenced by the effective grassroots organizing. When it came time in 1994 to develop a federal system to address these newly recognized types of violence, Congress gave it a name that effectively shut down all alternative ways of thinking about this violence: the Violence Against Women Act.

At the inception of the Violence Against Women Act, transgender individuals were not part of the public discourse and were not at all addressed in the act or in the accompanying policy development and discussions. Now, however, transgender women, transgender men, and nonbinary individuals are starting to more frequently recognize that they also have experienced intimate partner violence and would ideally like to seek services. Similarly, service providers have started to identify that transgender people are impacted by IPV and want to begin better serving this population. However, there is still a wide gap between the needs of transgender survivors and the services of mainstream service providers. A bridge must be built between the two, and movement is necessary from both starting positions. In this chapter, we will identify the major barriers confronting both survivors and service providers and discuss our approaches to overcoming those barriers and building the much-needed bridge between the two groups. In doing so, we draw upon our respective roles as Policy and Program Director and Executive Director of FORGE, a United States–based organization that, for more than a decade, has been training victim service providers on how to better meet the needs of transgender, nonbinary, and gender nonconforming victims of intimate and sexual violence.

More on Ideology

Over the years, efforts have been made around the margins to expand the picture that "violence against women" creates. Lesbian, gay, bisexual, transgender, and queer (LGBTQ) anti-violence groups typically use the term *intimate partner violence* in part to make room for abusive dynamics that might happen in same-gender partnerships or relationships with one or more transgender persons. *Gender-based violence*, a term first defined by a United Nations body in 1993, has recently been increasingly popular, often in another effort to widen the lens on who is affected by intimate partner violence and sexual assault.[1] Unfortunately, this term is perhaps even less inclusive of transgender survivors than previous terms, for two reasons. One is that the definition typically specifies violence that "results from power inequalities that are based on gender roles," a definition that does not fit how many transgender people view their relationship dynamics.[2] Moreover, "gender" is a core term within transgender communities, used more often in more ways than is the case in more general society. Given transgender communities' far more pervasive and nuanced discussions of gender, use of that term by mainstream agencies may feel not just wrong to transgender individuals, but even somehow off-putting. It is as if the agencies have adopted another culture's word even though they do not speak that culture's language or understand what that culture means by the term.

Terms can create barriers in other ways. One of the most popular theories about what "causes" IPV is "oppression": people with less social "power" and "privilege" are abused by partners with more "power" and "privilege."[3] This view obscures the obvious fact that it is not always the socially less-valued member of a relationship who is victimized; transgender individuals and other members of oppressed communities can and do abuse their seemingly more privileged partners. More importantly, the use of the oppression model in training situations insidiously divides audiences into "us" and "them," with transgender (or other minority populations) on one side and cisgender service providers on the other. Although cisgender service providers are often urged to see themselves as "allies" to the oppressed minorities they serve, many may get the message that they and their clients are not only not the same, but also that the cisgender service providers somehow belong in the "oppressor" group. That is hard to hear. So hard, in fact, that many people simply shut down in self-defense.

During provider trainings, FORGE has found that it is entirely possible to talk about violence and health disparities without framing it within an oppression model. We cultivate a sense that "we're all in this together," in part by starting all of our in-person and online trainings by talking about FORGE's twin guiding philosophies: we are trauma-informed, and we are empowerment-based. We explain these approaches by noting that whether we are working with survivors or service providers, we are always aware that there are likely a large number of trauma survivors in the room, and we want to honor their survivorship. We say the same about our goal of empowerment: just as survivors often need empowerment, so do service providers. We usually affirm that most service providers have excellent skills and "know what to do" if they do not get distracted by the fact that a survivor is transgender, and that the purpose of the training is to help them gain that confidence. With this opening, we establish a sense that survivors and service providers are not so different from each other, and often need the same things. We also assure participants that we respect their professional skills and are meeting them as helpful peers rather than setting up a hierarchy even within the training itself.

In recent years, we have often situated our violence and health disparities statistics within a context of the Adverse Childhood Experiences (ACE) study.[4] The ACE study is an incredibly important body of work that proves that, in the general population, there are lifelong negative physical as well as mental health consequences of experiencing trauma. The ACE study focuses on how childhood traumas affect many aspects of a person's development, which limits its applicability to what happens after someone experiences trauma as an adult. However, we view that as a minor drawback given the importance of the study's many other findings.

During provider trainings, we explain the ACE study's findings: a count of how many of ten specific adverse childhood experiences (such as neglect, abuse, and family disruptions like divorce, parental mental illness, or parental incarceration) someone has experienced will directly correlate with their risks of a wide variety of physical and mental health conditions. The more ACEs a person has, the more likely they are to use alcohol or drugs, experience cancer, and so forth. This is true of everyone. From there, we speculate that there may be transgender-specific ACEs (denial of identity, bullying, being thrown out of the house, being unable to use a bathroom that aligns with their gender, etc.) that may help explain why many transgender individuals' health disparity rates are even higher than those of high-ACE general populations. In this way we acknowledge that transgender individuals often experience very high rates of violence and discrimination that negatively impact health, but we do so in the context of a ubiquitous human problem: when people experience traumatic events, there can be long-term negative consequences.

Barriers from the Transgender Survivor Side of the Service Gap

In 2011, FORGE conducted an institutional review board–approved survey that included 1,005 transgender respondents. This was an online survey in which participants were recruited via email lists and social media. Respondents were asked about their knowledge and experience with fourteen types of victim service agencies (mostly IPV shelters and sexual assault agencies, but also services such as victim compensation programs), whether they would use or refer a transgender friend to those agencies, and if not, why not. Nearly half (48 percent) of respondents said they could find their local IPV shelter, but the only type of service they were *less* likely to use was a rape crisis line. A little over a third (39 percent) "would use" an IPV shelter if needed; the low was 37 percent for rape crisis lines, and the high was 72 percent for LGBTQ community centers. FORGE analyzed the write-in responses for why the respondents would not or might not use an agency. The following data reflect all survey answers for all fourteen service types, ordered by the most frequently stated responses. The quotes, however, are specific to IPV shelters or programs.

Fear

Transgender people talked about their fears of abuse, hostility, rejection, derision, judgment, discrimination, being outed, being mistreated by other clients, being denied services, and being the only transgender person in the group. For example, participants noted "fear of mistreatment," "fear of being turned away or discriminated [against]," and "although there are a few places that may be safe, Transfolk may still be ridiculed when they stay there. Sometimes by the staff."

Worry about Welcome

FORGE describes an agency as "transgender-welcoming" when a new transgender client senses that an agency's environment and attitude are friendly and respectful. Will people be "comfortable" with me? Will I be "accepted"? Will people be hostile? Survey participants named feelings of not being welcome at IPV shelters and programs. For example, participants noted that "local shelters DO NOT WELCOME US!" and that providers "don't want me there."

Worry about Cultural Competency

Once a transgender person feels "welcomed" by an agency, the next question may well be about its cultural competency, which FORGE defines as having staff who are informed on how to respectfully treat transgender people. When we train, we describe this as transgender people wondering: Will I be asked invasive questions? Will they use my name and pronouns correctly? Will I have to educate my provider? Can they deal with my body? For example, one participant shared the following: "They don't advertise as being trans-friendly or conscious, and list that services are available without regard to 'sexual preference' which is offensive. There's nothing on their website which would lead anyone to believe they're open and supportive." Another participant summed up this point, noting concerns over "spotty competency" among providers.

Do Not Know What Agency Is or How to Find It

Most people have reason to use victim service agencies infrequently, and so may not know what services exist, what they offer, or how to find them. When FORGE asked transgender people about fourteen types of services, many responded with variations of "What is this? I never heard of it." In addition, services may not be available everywhere; rural survivors may find it particularly difficult to access services. Participants expressed concerns over "not knowing how to access where these are, or their availability" and "if it existed, sure [I would use it] . . . it doesn't [exist] here."

Reputation

Many transgender people will only approach a new service agency if they have heard from others that it treats transgender people well. Transgender communities are very interconnected and tightly knit. When one person has a negative experience at an agency or with a particular provider, the word spreads very quickly. One person's negative experience—shared with someone else—can dramatically influence the entire community and paint the service agency as "unwelcoming," "culturally incompetent," or as having any number of other negative qualities (even if the agency is actually highly welcoming and skilled in working with transgender survivors). The end result is that the agency's reputation is severely damaged and, more importantly, survivors who need services do not get them. For instance, several participants expressed such concerns over agency reputations: "I've heard domestic violence shelters are unsafe and/or unfriendly to trans folks," and, "Shelters in particular have a very spotty record about being respectful towards trans people. I've heard of, and known, MANY people who were turned away or mistreated on account of being transgender."

Woman-Focused Agencies

As noted above, most IPV programs are organized around a "violence against women" or "gender-based violence" philosophy. Consequently, transgender people of any gender identity are often unsure if they will be welcomed at these services (and they often have not been). When talking about their reluctance to access some services, transgender respondents to FORGE's survey cited the name of the agency as suggesting they only serve women (such as "the Women's Crisis Center"), unclear policies about who the agency serves, and website and brochure language that talk only about women and children. Transgender people reported that these signals that they may not be welcome at the agency led to feelings of erasure and hopelessness about where to seek services. For instance, participants noted the following: "I know a trans woman who, just a few years ago, was turned away from a shelter like this in a blizzard, state of emergency conditions and was told that the shelter was for women, not men who dress like women," "This is a program for only women, I don't know how they would deal with trans people," and "They service ONLY women and children."

Shame, Stigma, and Embarrassment

Shame, embarrassment, and stigma are common for nearly all survivors. Transgender survivors, too, may experience these strong emotions. Transgender people also may have some additional concerns. For example, transgender people may desire more privacy and time to complete bathing and grooming activities than cisgender shelter residents might. Transgender survivors also may have embodied the shame placed upon them by society about being transgender or having a body that does not align with other peoples' expectations. Several participants expressed these feelings of shame (e.g., "public shame" and "general fear & embarrassment") as reasons for not seeking help.

Seeking Help Might Make Things Worse

Many transgender survivors fear that seeking services will make things worse. Fears around being retraumatized are common. For some transgender people, past abuse happened in institutional settings such as medical offices or during interactions with police. Just the fact that they might have been previously assaulted may be enough to retraumatize them. If they attempted to find services and help in the past and were not successful, they may be less likely to try again now. Because so many transgender people have been denied services or treated poorly in the past, they have a realistic fear that seeking services now will make things worse (again). A number of participants shared this reason for not seeking help, reporting sentiments such as "heard too many horror stories from survivors," "get real, not worth the risk," and "any program that is not for trans [people] would be a potential source for disrespect on top of already being traumatized."

Lack of Trust

Transgender people may lack trust in specific providers, in types of services, and in systems as a whole—based on previous negative experiences, rumors or reputations spread throughout the community, or projection. There are often deep concerns about police and potential police misconduct. Many transgender people have experienced inappropriate behavior at the hands of police and are very hesitant to have any kind of interaction with them. The same is true for medical providers or others in positions of authority. Several participants expressed such feelings that hindered their help seeking. One respondent shared, "Don't think it would help. Nobody cares about old transwomen." Another offered, "Years ago I volunteered for this service, and later tried to access services for myself. They weren't able to help me and I would have severe reservations about recommending them to a trans friend." A third stated, "Some Trans people are very used to being treated adversely, in many different agencies. I for one have not reported things because I don't trust the police."

Desire to Seek Help Elsewhere

We all have our individual preferences. Some of us would never feel comfortable in a support group, for instance, or in a group shelter—we would rather sleep on a friend's couch. Many transgender people are far more comfortable seeking help from the general practitioner they have known for years than seeing a new specialist, particularly if that might mean having to disclose their transgender status or history to a new provider. Some transgender people would choose to be around other transgender people (such as in a transgender support group) even if the setting had nothing to do with directly helping with IPV or trauma symptoms. This sentiment was expressed through such write-in responses as "would go to friends/family first" and "prefer to rely on own community."

Service Is Unwanted or Unneeded

In a similar vein, some transgender people told us they would not access some types of services because they do not think they would ever need or want them. Sometimes transgender people do not want to access services because they simply do not know what the benefit would be or they think there will be more red tape or hassle involved than there actually would be. For instance, participants noted: "I would hope I wouldn't need to, that friends would be supportive and I would not need to go to strangers," "I take care of my self, and can not answer to/for others," and "I believe that I can take care of myself no matter what."

Systemic Problems

It is widely known that privacy may be sacrificed in group shelters. Survivors of all genders (transgender and cisgender) may not be believed. Survivors often need to jump through hoops in order to access services, and there sometimes is a wait list for services. All of these problems may be even more troubling for transgender survivors, who may believe they have fewer overall resources to begin with or may have concerns about the double and triple layers of potential discrimination and revictimization they may experience within these systems. Participants expressed this concern in a variety of ways, sharing: "Safety and confidentiality concerns"; "I'm not in a violent situation right now, but if I was, shelters are often cissexist and don't follow harm reduction philosophies (set excessive rules for survivors)"; "Fear of lack of privacy with housing"; and "Communal living (with strangers) is a nightmare and residents may be transphobic."

Barriers from the Provider Side of the Service Gap

FORGE's experience in working with both service providers and transgender survivors themselves is that oftentimes the barriers to serving transgender survivors have less to do with their being transgender and more to do with providers' explicit or implicit belief that intimate partner violence is something that only cisgender women experience. When a transgender person—of any gender vector—seeks their services, they may simply not fit the service provider's long-held picture of a victim. This is a problem not just for transmasculine and gender nonconforming individuals who may not "look female" to providers, but also for transgender women if their gender history is known or suspected. With this in mind, in 2015 FORGE interviewed staff from twenty IPV shelters that worked with transgender people and/or cisgender men in addition to cisgender female survivors.[5] Although all of these shelters felt their integration efforts were ultimately successful, many reported having to overcome barriers from staff, other residents, community members, and/or their own boards of directors. Interestingly, there appeared to be more pushback regarding admitting cisgender men than serving transgender people (of any gender vector).

Three of the most frequent concerns staff had about accepting cisgender men into shelter were that they would sexually assault women or children in the shelter, start abusive relationships with the women in shelter, or pretend to be survivors in order to gain access to their female partner who was already sheltering there. Regarding the latter concern, one study participant queried, "Can we be sure that man is a victim?" These concerns, of course, reflect the violence against women paradigm in which women are the only (or at least "the vast majority of") victims and men are the only (or "vast majority of") perpetrators. This is a myth that is, unfortunately, still widespread. In fact, research is clear that men frequently experience intimate partner violence. A recent national study found that heterosexual men experienced IPV at rates close to those of heterosexual women (29 percent to 35 percent), and that bisexual men (along with bisexual women and lesbians) experienced more IPV (37 percent, 61 percent, and 44 percent, respectively) than did heterosexual women (35 percent).[6] (See table 12.1.) Transgender-specific rates may be even more surprising. FORGE's data (from the aforementioned 2011 survey of 1,005

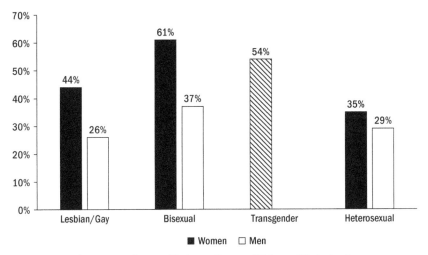

Figure 12.1. Lifetime Prevalence of Intimate Partner Violence Victimization
Sources: James et al. 2016; Walters, Chen, and Breiding 2013.

transgender respondents) indicates that transmasculine folks experience primary types of violence as adults at even higher rates than do transfeminine folks, with the sole exception of hate violence. (See figure 12.2.)

When we asked staff at gender-integrated shelters about the objections they encountered, objections to sheltering transgender people were often described as problems with "LGBT" clients. The most commonly reported "transgender-specific" objections were as follows: staff feared that gay men and transgender women would molest children in the shelter; staff feared offending LGBT survivors by not saying the right thing, and also they felt that they needed more education so as to not offend survivors; staff feared being made fun of; there were worries about bathrooms; and both cisgender male staff and residents sometimes objected to the idea of serving transgender women or gay men, with a particular problem seeming to be cisgender male residents who did not want to room with gay men.

Staff members also said they feared the reaction of cisgender women survivors and supporters. One described this reaction as, "Can't they just get a hotel or get a job and move on; they don't have kids to worry about so do they really need shelter?" Another said that since clients are women who were abused by men, they should not have to be around

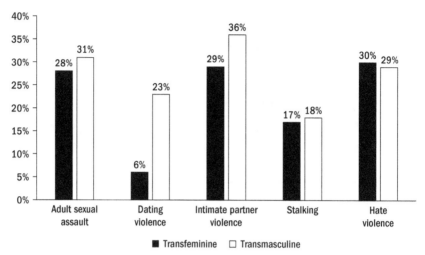

Figure 12.2. Lifetime Rates of Violence by Gender Vector
Note: N = 1,005 transgender respondents.
Sources: FORGE 2011.

men at all. A third staffer shared that one woman reported to a staff member that she did not want to share a house with a lesbian because the lesbian looked like a man and frightened her. Still another respondent reported that a female funder was a conservative Christian who objected to the shelter being at an LGBTQ pride event.

Interestingly, many shelter staff members reported that they received the most community pushback from other shelters and IPV programs. One person shared that, "There were a couple times there were service providers [elsewhere in the county] that didn't think [sheltering transgender people and non-transgender men] was safe and were shocked." Another reported, "There were some 'old school' providers who run a men's winter shelter through a church and have this 'pull men up by their bootstraps' kind of setup that truly balked at our agency serving men." A similar sentiment was: "[Other shelters] have more of a problem serving non-trans men than LGBTQ people. They worry about men being in with women survivors." One staff member shared: "We had pushback about serving men in general back in the '90s and early 2000s. The [domestic violence] movement was very hostile about serving men. We had to be somewhat militant at times, including very nasty fights both locally and in the state coalition level. There was a lot of pushback. We had to stand up and sometimes to the point of appearing militant and not willing to step down." Another offered, "We're kind of the black sheep among our peers. We've been serving men since the beginning and other shelters always judged us. So we're used to pushing the buck in our area."

Training and Publications to Build Bridges

FORGE's trainings and publications are custom-designed with the specific audience in mind and seek to meet the needs of people with a variety of learning styles. Consequently, we use many different techniques in different settings. The following outlines many of our most-used strategies and topics, along with explanations for why we use them.

It's the Law (in Many Cases)

In March 2013, Congress reauthorized the Violence Against Women Act (VAWA) and created a new condition that service-providing grantees must meet, prohibiting discrimination based on gender identity and sexual orientation—categories that were added to the existing nondiscrimination provisions based on actual or perceived sex, race, color, religion, national origin, or disability.[7] The addition, aimed at protecting the LGBTQ portion of the population, might have resulted in relatively small changes in the way that agencies funded by the Office on Violence Against Women (OVW) work.

However, when the US Department of Justice (DOJ) issued its frequently asked questions (FAQ) guidance document in April 2014, explaining how it expected the new provisions to be implemented, it became clear that agencies could be required to make more substantive changes. Among other things, the FAQ addressed two service provision models used widely by many agencies that service IPV survivors: designing sex-segregated or sex-specific services, and providing "comparable" services to those not eligible for the program's primary services.

The FAQ explains that programming is "sex-segregated" when males and females receive services in separate settings and "sex-specific" when it is designed differently for males and females. Both "sex-segregated" and "sex-specific" programming places individuals in a position to "choose" to identify with a particular sex. These types of programming are permissible if the agency "[can] articulate clearly why sex-segregation or sex-specific programming was necessary to the essential operation of the program," although the FAQ also cautions that "the justification cannot rely on unsupported assumptions or overly broad sex-based generalizations." Furthermore, agencies offering sex-segregated or sex-specific services must consider "the impact the division of services will have on transgender individuals seeking services and whether similarly situated recipients providing the same services have been successful in providing services effectively in a manner that is not sex-segregated or sex-specific."[8]

If agencies do provide sex-segregated services, they must offer "comparable" services to those who cannot be accommodated by those services:

> A comparable service is one that is designed to confer a substantially equal benefit. Factors that DOJ will consider, either individually or in the aggregate as appropriate, in determining whether services are comparable include the following: the nature and quality of the services provided, the relative benefits of different therapeutic modalities or interventions, geographic location or other aspects of accessibility, the characteristics of the facilities where services are provided, and the characteristics of the individuals who provide the services. Services need not be identical to be comparable, but they must be of the same or similar quality and duration. For example, if a recipient [agency] has made a fact-specific determination that segregating its shelter by sex is necessary to the essential operation of the program, then the shelter provided to male and female clients must be designed to confer substantially equal benefits. These benefits might include a secure and furnished sleeping area, bathroom facilities, kitchen facilities or access to food, case management, social services, and transportation to supportive services. The recipient must make every reasonable effort to ensure that the shelter provided to male and female beneficiaries is comparable in safety, quality, and amenities. The recipient must also make every reasonable effort to ensure that, if male clients are housed off-site, they are integrated into the recipient's other, non-shelter services. If the recipient provides counseling, legal advocacy, or parenting groups in its primary building, then it must make every reasonable effort to arrange for transportation to that building so that the male victim or survivor housed remotely can participate in all of the supportive services that the recipient provides.[9]

The 2013 nondiscrimination provisions motivated some IPV programs to redesign their services, but many others chose not to. Many also claim not to know about the requirements, which is why FORGE always addresses them in trainings and publications.

In addition to the nondiscrimination conditions in the 2013 reauthorization of VAWA, many other local, state, and federal agencies and funders have transgender-specific or LGBTQ nondiscrimination provisions or other specific clauses that protect transgender or LGBTQ people seeking services. Although at the time of this writing some federal agencies have rescinded or changed their protection policies, the following also include protections for transgender individuals: the Family Violence Prevention and Services Act's nondiscrimination requirements for all organizations receiving funds under that act;[10] the US Housing and Urban Development's equal access for transgender people;[11] the US Department of Education's Title IX inclusion of gender identity and expression;[12] the US Equal Employment Opportunity Commission's protection for LGBT workers;[13] and the US Department of Veterans Affairs' guidelines for serving transgender former service members.[14] These are just a few federal-level protections currently in place, in addition to numerous statewide, regional, local, and agency-specific nondiscrimination policies and other transgender-affirming procedures, practices, and proactive inclusion. FORGE discusses all of these nondiscrimination provisions during trainings. Although we are not empowered to "enforce" them, we certainly want agencies to be aware that they are breaking the law if they continue to discriminate.

Reasons to Integrate

Not all shelters providing emergency, temporary, transitional or permanent housing for survivors of intimate partner violence, family violence, sexual abuse, and/or other intimate crimes get some or all of their funding via federal VAWA funds; those who do not are not covered by the nondiscrimination requirement in the 2013 reauthorization. Nevertheless, FORGE believes that best practices call for shelters to provide integrated services that are open to people of all genders. We give our trainees and readers three primary reasons for this recommendation:

avoiding revictimization, minimizing cost, and meeting the increasing need for services for nonbinary survivors.

AVOIDING REVICTIMIZATION

As noted above, there are many reasons why transgender survivors do not attempt to access IPV services. Not requesting victim services because a survivor fears they will not be treated with respect and dignity is a form of revictimization. So are other encounters of transgender people who have experienced IPV and/or sexual assault. Survivors have reported to FORGE incidents such as these: the transmasculine person who was repeatedly called "a rapist" when he asked a rape crisis line for emergency assistance after he was sexually assaulted; the transgender woman who was told that, because she "wasn't a real woman," the IPV women's shelter would not serve her; the nonbinary people who were told they would have to describe the shape of their genitals before agencies could figure out whether or where they would serve them. IPV agencies know well that some of the most important services for survivors include the ability and willingness of providers to listen to and believe survivors. This attention is a healing antidote to the terror, lack of control, and personal erasure that are some of the most damaging parts of being a victim of violence. When survivors fear that a victim service agency will reject them because of their gender (let alone when they actually experience such a rejection), the agency has failed in its mission to provide safety and healing for victims. FORGE believes it is critical for victim service agencies to publicly counter the myth that only some survivors are worth believing and caring for.

MINIMIZING COST

One of the first questions many service providers have asked about the 2013 VAWA nondiscrimination conditions and FAQ is, "Who is going to pay for the necessary changes?" Of particular concern to many providers is the new requirement that transgender survivors and cisgender male survivors be offered "comparable services," a requirement that may be in opposition to the current widespread practice of offering these survivors a few nights' lodging in a hotel rather than admittance to the existing residential shelter that offers longer stays and many more group benefits. There are no new funds to implement the nondiscrimination requirements. Agencies that choose to continue to house transgender and cisgender male survivors in facilities separate from where they serve cisgender female survivors have to come up with new funds or volunteer systems to provide transportation to make sure these survivors can access all of the same services as the rest of their clients. That is why FORGE recommends that shelters strongly consider gender-integrated housing. Adjusting existing female-only shelters to include people of all genders usually costs nothing or very little. Integrated shelter structures that house people of all genders therefore reduce the total cost to agencies and provide, by default, comparable services to all survivors.

MEETING THE NEEDS OF NONBINARY SURVIVORS

If an agency offers sex-segregated services, the VAWA FAQ calls for transgender survivors to be assigned to "the group or service which corresponds to the gender with which the beneficiary identifies." This self-determination method will allow many transgender survivors assignment into the sex-segregated placement that aligns with their gender identity. However, members of the rapidly growing segment of the population that identifies as nonbinary may feel an additional burden or stress if asked to choose between binary options of male or female—neither of which correspond with their gender identity. FORGE offers group services nationally to transgender survivors of sexual assault. We always ask participants to share the pronoun they want us to use when referring to them. In summer 2014, for the first time, the majority of group participants indicated they used a pronoun other than "he" or "she." While this finding does not by itself indicate that these individuals would be uncomfortable in sex-segregated space, it is indicative of the growing population of (predominately young) people who do not identify as either men or women. Since the VAWA FAQ says that agencies offering sex-segregated services must consider those services' "impact on transgender individuals seeking services," the service implications of this growing population of nonbinary individuals deserve serious consideration.

For the above three reasons (among others), FORGE believes the most cost-effective and healing way of implementing VAWA's nondiscrimination provisions is to provide integrated services to all survivors regardless of their assigned sex or gender identity.

Other Service Providers Have Overcome Concerns and Barriers

FORGE has undertaken two major projects to identify the barriers to providing gender-integrated services and respond to those barriers by interviewing service providers who have successfully overcome them. *Gender-Integrated Shelters: Experience and Advice* (available from forge-forward.org as a free download) provides eighty-eight pages of experience and advice from twenty shelters that provide gender-integrated services.[15] Our *Part of the Solution: Gender-Integrated Sexual Assault Support Groups: A Practical Guide for Support Group Facilitators, Therapists, and Decision-Makers* (also available as a free download) similarly outlines concerns potential support group facilitators have and offers responses from those who have successfully run gender-integrated support groups.[16] These documents are aimed at addressing service providers' attitudinal barriers as well as providing practical advice on creating safe and supportive integrated services.

Data Dissemination

FORGE integrates data on transgender victimization (and, sometimes, health disparities) into most of our trainings. The figures we give—including the charts shared previously—often shock attendees because they go against the prevalent view that IPV is perpetrated by men against women. Because of that cognitive dissonance, we know that many people react to these data by refusing to believe it. This is an even greater reason to continue sharing it: it may plant a seed of doubt about the prevailing views of IPV that may blossom later.

FORGE has its own story of how this seed of doubt may work. When FORGE conducted the first national study of transgender survivors of sexual assault in 2004, we were surprised to find that 29 percent of the survivors said they had had one or more female abusers.[17] Fearing that this single statistic could result in the whole study being dismissed as unbelievable, we had to start exploring existing research to try to explain our unexpected finding. As a result, we learned that there actually is a large body of data that shows that rates of IPV and sexual assault are far closer to equal across genders than most people think. We even published an article discussing the many ways in which sexual assault data is skewed to fit the violence against women paradigm.[18]

Case Studies

A detailed case study can be deeply impactful for service providers who may have never put themselves in the position of thinking like a transgender woman, transgender man, or nonbinary person. One of our favorite case studies is Greta.[19] Greta is a fifty-three-year-old woman of transgender experience, and the case study follows her through her first night and day in an intimate partner violence shelter, focusing particularly on the questions and concerns she must navigate in this new environment. The case study is so detailed and personal that service providers frequently tell us they "get" transgender issues much better from Greta's story than they had from more impersonal training strategies.

Videos

For the most part, IPV service providers go into this line of work because they truly care about helping people. One of FORGE's most useful tools for reaching past the violence against women paradigm that tends to invisibilize transgender (and cisgender male) survivors is the inclusion of heart-touching videos. Particularly potent are videos with transgender children, since many people find children more innocent and worthy of care than adults. For that reason, we often use an online "transgender 101" video from the National Center on Transgender Equality, "An Introduction to Transgender People," which features children and parents as well as adult transgender people.[20] Another online child-focused video we love using is even more subtle: "Parents and Transgender Children Read Powerful Affirmations."[21] It has no particular educational content; its impact comes simply from opening hearts. We also particularly like the video that the anti-violence organization 1in6 features on their home page.[22] This video focuses on sexual assault far more than intimate partner violence and does not (explicitly) feature transgender survivors, but it is nevertheless a particularly effective eye-opener for service providers still working out of a violence against women paradigm.

Role-Plays

Role-plays can be a particularly effective training tool for service providers, as they allow service providers to "try out" their responses to new situations in a safe environment. One type of exercise we use asks small groups to come up with five possible responses to a situation, outline the pros and cons of each response, and then choose one to act out for the full group. We also use a version of the "birdcage" exercise in which a survivor of IPV is "caged in" by negative responses from a variety of the people they ask for help.[23] We modify this exercise to make it more trauma-informed by then asking role-play participants to develop and act out *positive* responses to the survivor so that the exercise ends on an empowering note.

Adult Education Principles

Educator Malcolm Knowles, who popularized the theory of adult learning, set out six principles of effective adult education. Adult education should (1) be self-directed/autonomous, (2) utilize knowledge and life experience, (3) be goal-oriented, (4) be relevant, (5) highlight practicality, and (6) encourage collaboration.[24] In keeping with these principles, one of FORGE's favorite training activities is modeled on the World Café method. We place flipcharts around the walls or on the tables, each with a different practical question relevant to that audience. For example, we might reflect on the barriers transgender people have to accessing services and ask questions such as, "In what ways could we tell the transgender community about our services?" and "What policies and forms should we review to make sure they are inclusive of transgender survivors?" Training participants are then encouraged to circulate, read what others have written, and offer their own ideas.

Resource Sharing

FORGE's service model is designed to make as much of an impact on as many people as we possibly can. We secure funding to develop training webinars and publications and then make as many as we possibly can available for free download, findable by anyone with access to a search engine. (Indeed, many of our smaller tip sheets and FAQs are specifically designed to pop up when a service provider conducts an online search for the answer to a specific service question, such as, "How do I safety plan with a transgender client?") To ensure the people we train understand that our materials are always available to help them, we typically highlight many relevant publications during our presentations.

Definitions

The one thing FORGE does *not* do in its trainings is teach the definitions of various gender-related terms. Instead, we teach the "terms paradox": according to this concept, it is critical to know and reflect back the terms someone uses for themselves, but those terms do not tell a service provider what they need to know to provide good services. We elaborate that different people may use different terms for the same type of experience or identity (e.g., *genderqueer* or *nonbinary*), or different people may use identical terms (e.g., *transgender*) but have different experiences (one person may have medically transitioned whereas to another person this term signals that they do not intend to medically transition). We sometimes share a story of once watching a newly trained service provider tell a transgender person they were using the "wrong term" to define themself! We also frequently talk about "master status" and "label of primary potency," both of which refer to the human tendency to attribute everything about a person to only one of their characteristics.[25] In situations involving a transgender person, this can mean assuming someone was abused *because* of their gender identity, without even considering that there may have been other dynamics involved.

Conclusion

Training intimate partner violence service providers so that they can effectively serve transgender survivors is not a simple task. It is not simply an issue of cultural competency training. Transgender survivors break the mold in which most IPV programs are made: helping cisgender women who experience violence from their cisgender male partners. Even transgender women and men can be ineffectively served by service providers, since some providers believe, in part, that maleness and femaleness are rooted solely in biology and/or childhood socialization. Such a service provider may wonder what gender a transgender person "really" is. The violence against women and gender-based violence paradigms also make it very hard for many service providers to recognize and believe survivors who do not present as women, or survivors of any gender identity who had a female or transgender abuser.

The baked-in gender assumptions most intimate partner violence program personnel operate under therefore require a careful approach. FORGE first takes care to avoid setting up an us-and-them dynamic in the training room, instead emphasizing the importance of trauma awareness and empowerment for all. We use adult learning principles and take into account various learning styles in the design of our trainings and publications so that everyone can feel included and valued. We touch on a variety of topics—data, the barriers identified by transgender people to asking for services, the law, evolving understandings of gender identity and sexual orientation among youth—in our trainings, knowing that much of the time we are only planting seeds that may or may not grow later. And we use personal stories—case studies, videos, and role-plays—to sidestep the violence against women paradigm and appeal to providers' heartfelt desire to help people who are in need.

It does not always work, but it works often enough to give us great hope.

Additional Resources

FORGE maintains an extensive free, online archive of resources (at forge-forward.org) designed to guide service providers in delivering respectful and culturally appropriate services to transgender survivors and their loved ones. The majority of our recorded training webinars, reports, guidebooks, and fact sheets focus on working with IPV survivors and cover common issues such as transgender-specific safety planning and power and control tactics, tips from experienced gender-integrated shelters, and how to address and prevent staff and client biases.

NOTES

1. Health and Human Rights Info, n.d.
2. Health and Human Rights Info, n.d.
3. Pennsylvania Coalition Against Domestic Violence, n.d.
4. Centers for Disease Control and Prevention, n.d.
5. munson and Cook-Daniels 2016.
6. Walters, Chen, and Breiding 2013.
7. US Department of Justice 2014.
8. US Department of Justice 2014.
9. US Department of Justice 2014.
10. 45 C.F.R. 1370.5 (2017).
11. Canavan and Ledger 2017.
12. US Department of Education, Office for Civil Rights 2014.
13. US Equal Employment Opportunity Commission, n.d.
14. Cramer 2017.
15. munson and Cook-Daniels 2016.
16. munson and Cook-Daniels 2017.
17. FORGE 2004.
18. Cook-Daniels 1998.
19. FORGE n.d.
20. NCTE 2016.
21. Iris 2017.
22. 1in6 2018.
23. Brandlr and Spangler 2004.
24. Pullagurla 2014.
25. Allport 1979; van den Scott and van den Hoonard 2016.

REFERENCES

1in6. 2018. "Survivors of Sexual Abuse and Assault Reveal an Important Truth." YouTube video, 5:45, April 5, 2018. www.youtube.com/watch?v=2p06x-yumco.

Allport, Gordon W. 1979. *The Nature of Prejudice, Unabridged* (25th Anniversary Edition). Boston: Addison-Wesley Publishing Co.

Brandl, Bonnie, and Deb Spangler. 2004. *Interactive Training Exercises on Abuse in Later Life*. Madison, WI: Wisconsin Coalition Against Domestic Violence. Accessed December 30, 2019. www.communitysolutionsva.org.

Canavan, David, and Fran Ledger. 2017. *Equal Access for Transgender People: Supporting Inclusive Housing and Shelters*. Washington, DC: US Department of Housing and Urban Development. https://safehousingpartnerships.org.

Centers for Disease Control and Prevention. n.d. "Adverse Childhood Experiences (ACEs)." Accessed April 20, 2016. www.cdc.gov.

Cook-Daniels, Loree. 1998. *Female Perpetrators and Male Victims of Sexual Assault: Why They Are so Invisible*. Milwaukee, WI: FORGE. http://forge-forward.org.

Cramer, Tom. 2017. "Transgender Vets, the VA, and Respect." *Veteran's Health Administration*, January 3, 2017. www.va.gov.

FORGE. 2004. Unpublished data from "Sexual Violence in the Transgender Community" survey.

FORGE. 2011. Unpublished data from "Transgender Peoples' Access to Sexual Assault Services" survey.

FORGE. n.d. *Shelter Case Study: Greta*. Milwaukee, WI: FORGE. http://forge-forward.org.

Health and Human Rights Info. n.d. "Selected Links on Gender Based Violence." Accessed July 16, 2018. www.hhri.org.

Iris. 2017. "Parents and Transgender Children Read Powerful Affirmations." YouTube video, 1:58, April 6, 2017. www.youtube.com/watch?v=t9h7jWYJa5w.

James, Sandy E., Jody L. Herman, Susan Rankin, Mara Keisling, Lisa Mottet, and Ma'ayan Anafi. 2016. *The Report of the 2015 US Transgender Survey*. Washington, DC: National Center for Transgender Equality. www.ustranssurvey.org.

munson, michael, and Loree Cook-Daniels. 2016. *Gender-Integrated Shelters: Experiences and Advice*. Milwaukee, WI: FORGE. http://forge-forward.org.

munson, michael, and Loree Cook-Daniels. 2017. *Part of the Solution: Gender-Integrated Sexual Assault Support Groups: A Practical Guide for Support Group Facilitators, Therapists, and Decision-Makers*. Milwaukee, WI: FORGE. http://forge-forward.org.

National Center for Transgender Equality. 2016. "An Introduction to Transgender People." Facebook video, 4:05. www.facebook.com/watch/?v=10153582088701990.

Pennsylvania Coalition Against Domestic Violence. n.d. "Resources about Dismantling Oppression." Accessed July 15, 2018. www.pcadv.org.

Pullagurla, Adyita. 2014. "6 Top Facts about Adult Learning Theory." *eLearning Industry*, April 20, 2016. https://elearningindustry.com.

US Department of Education, Office for Civil Rights. 2014. *Questions and Answers on Title IX and Sexual Violence*. Washington, DC: US Department of Education. www2.ed.gov.

US Department of Justice. 2014. *Frequently Asked Questions: Nondiscrimination Grant Condition in the Violence Against Women Reauthorization Act of 2013*. Washington, DC: US Department of Justice. www.justice.gov.

US Equal Employment Opportunity Commission. n.d. "What You Should Know about EEOC and the Enforcement Protections for LGBT Workers." Accessed April 20, 2016. www.eeoc.gov.

van den Scott, Lisa-Jo K., and Deborah K. van den Hoonard. 2016. "The Origins and Evolution of Everett Hughes's Concept: 'Master Status.'" In Rick Helmes-Hayes and Marco Santoro (Eds.) *The Anthem Companion to Everett Hughes*, pp. 173–192. London: Anthem Press.

Walters, Mikel L., Jieru Chen, and Matthew J. Breiding. 2013. *The National Intimate Partner and Sexual Violence Survey (NISVS): 2010 Findings on Victimization by Sexual Orientation*. Atlanta: National Center for Injury Prevention and Control, Centers for Disease Control and Prevention. www.cdc.gov.

13

Overcoming Barriers to Knowledge Production in Transgender IPV Research

ADAM F. YERKE AND JENNIFER DEFEO

Research is fundamental in the struggle against intimate partner violence (IPV)—it provides an empirical basis for prevention and intervention efforts facilitated by community professionals. However, research has primarily focused on IPV among cisgender, heterosexual individuals, leaving IPV community professionals without guidance for working with people who are lesbian, gay, bisexual, transgender, and/or queer (LGBTQ). In recent years, scholars have increased their study of IPV among LGBTQ populations, with a primary focus on same-gender relationships. Transgender individuals are periodically included in LGBTQ samples, but there are generally too few, if any, participants to make generalizations about transgender intimate partner violence (T-IPV). In addition, scholars rarely concentrate specifically on T-IPV. Consequently, community professionals run the risk of delivering inappropriate services and causing potential harm if they merely rely on the limited cisgender and LGBQ IPV literatures to make assumptions about T-IPV.

This chapter seeks to motivate scholars to respond to the need for quality T-IPV research in order to further inform IPV community professionals and, ultimately, combat and reduce T-IPV. Such scholars must be aware of the unique methodological challenges when conducting T-IPV research, including defining the population, nonprobability and probability sampling with transgender populations, IPV measure diagnostic testing on transgender samples, and inclusivity of distinct T-IPV tactics in IPV survey measures. Unlike with the more extensive and established cisgender IPV literature, the smaller and newer T-IPV literature lacks widespread agreement among scholars on the best practices needed to overcome these methodological challenges. This chapter provides an overview of these issues, and, by drawing on innovative solutions from the T-IPV and broader LGBTQ IPV literature, provides guidance for performing T-IPV research going forward.

Defining the Population

The existing transgender literature, not specific to IPV, includes countless ways to define transgender people. This has proven to be problematic when attempting to compare studies, as well as apply findings to transgender populations at large. Therefore, T-IPV scholars must agree to define the transgender population consistently in order to increase the benefits associated with research. However, this task has become increasingly difficult in recent years because of the vast diversity observed among transgender people. It is generally agreed in a US context that *transgender* people refers to those whose assigned sex at birth differs from their current gender identity. The term is often used as an umbrella term to describe multiple subgroups, including transgender men (i.e., those who identify as men and were not assigned male at birth), transgender women (i.e., those who identify as women and were not assigned female at birth), nonbinary people (i.e., those who do not identify exclusively as men or women), and sometimes also gender nonconforming individuals (i.e., those whose gender expression does not align with stereotypical masculine or feminine gender norms). Additionally, urban and regional planning scholar Petra Doan asserts that the transgender umbrella has essentially "burst wide open," with younger generations of transgender people identifying themselves with new labels all the time.[1] This begs the question of who should be included in the population definition for T-IPV research.

Scholars are advised to be as inclusive as possible when defining the transgender population in research. First, T-IPV research is in its infancy, and more knowledge can be gained by larger numbers of transgender people in research samples. Second, the diversity of transgender people should be represented in population definitions. Lastly, as Doan writes, "if the purpose of counting is to correct the long-standing neglect of the transgender community by trying to gauge the number of people who are subject to fear, discrimination, and potential gender-related violence, then the larger number is justified."[2] In other words, if using more inclusive definitions of transgender populations results in identifying more transgender people in research samples—and if this in turn results in more accurate, generalizable research results that can better improve T-IPV outcomes in the community—then inclusive definitions are warranted.

In addition, it is important to consider that some transgender people previously experienced IPV at a time in their lives when they identified or were perceived as cisgender. There may be inherent value in studying such populations, in part because these particular survivors may already have begun to express gender nonconformity or grapple with their identity, thus enabling transphobia to uniquely shape their experiences with abuse and help seeking. At the same time, researchers who only assess identity at the time of data collection will be unable to determine if participants were pre-transition or did not identify as transgender at the time of abuse, thereby potentially masking key differences in etiologies and outcomes for these two groups. Thus, it is recommended that, in addition to inquiring about identity at the time of data collection, researchers should also ask subjects to report their gender identity at the time of IPV. Then, T-IPV occurrences can be more squarely compared with cisgender IPV.

Population definitions significantly influence research methodology, including development of survey demographic questions. Gender is typically assessed dichotomously (i.e., man or woman), such as with regard to the biennial Crime Survey for England and Wales.[3] However, this system does not allow scholars to determine the number of transgender people in research samples. Therefore, several methods have been developed by researchers to identify transgender people within sample groups, even when the research focus is not specific to transgender populations.

One well-intentioned early approach was to add *transgender* as a third gender option.[4] Unfortunately, this method creates confusion for participants about how to respond based on their identity, and it then leads to inaccurate numbers of transgender people being reported.[5] For instance, based on personal experience, the chapter's first author, who identifies as both a man and as transgender, is often unsure which option to select on surveys. The conundrum is as follows: "Do I select my gender as a man since this resonates with me but then not get counted as transgender? Or do I select my identity as transgender, even though this feels different from my everyday experiences of walking through the world as a man?" In addition, among transgender populations, *transgender* is usually not considered a gender in and of itself, and many people do not claim *transgender* as a self-identity term in any context. For example, a person who identifies as *Two-Spirit* may not feel represented by any of the terms provided (e.g., *man*, *woman*, or *transgender*). As a result, the subject may decide to skip the survey question about gender, choose from among the three options (none of which accurately describes them), or withdraw from the research study altogether. In sum, adding *transgender* as a third option to report gender is a good first step but only a partial solution to identifying transgender people in research samples, and it should not be considered a best practice.[6]

Other research models demonstrate recognition that gender is not as straightforward as three options, and, as a result, researchers should give subjects a definition of "transgender" to encourage transgender subjects to identify themselves accordingly, regardless of where they fall under the transgender umbrella and whether they actively use the word to describe themselves.[7] For example, epidemiologist Kerith Conron and colleagues conducted a study whereby participants were asked in a separate question if they were transgender, as defined by the following: "Some people describe themselves as transgender when they experience a different gender identity from their sex at birth. For example, a person born into a male body, but who feels female or lives as a woman. Do you consider yourself to be transgender?"[8] By asking about transgender status in a survey question distinct from questions about gender identity, this strategy better gauges the number of transgender subjects present in a sample; still, it is restricting for those who identify differently than the researcher's definition.[9] In addition, even for those who do fit under the researcher's definition of being transgender, some may find it oppressive to be forced to check a box for a label (transgender) with which they do not identify or use in their everyday lives.

A more extensive approach is to provide subjects with the opportunity to select from among an extensive list of gender labels, with the option to select as many as apply, as well as an "other" option where the subject can write in their preferred label(s).[10] The US Transgender Survey provides an example of results from this style of gender assessment (table 13.1).[11] Of concern, though, is that this method is limited to terms known by researchers. Given that new gender labels continue to emerge, some subjects will still not find their identities presented on lists of gender labels and, therefore, will be forced to select "other" and write in their preferred label(s).[12] This occurred for 12 percent of the 27,715 transgender respondents to the US Transgender Survey.[13] This approach is useful for transgender-specific samples, such as in T-IPV research. However, when cisgender individuals are also included among research participants, there is a risk that researchers will be unclear about whether to count some subjects as transgender or not, based on their reported gender labels. For instance, those who identify as men or women can be either transgender or cisgender. To determine whether such individuals are transgender would require researchers to inquire about birth-assigned sex in addition to gender identity.

The newest approach to emerge in the transgender literature is use of a two-step process for identifying transgender subjects in research samples.[14] This method requires using two questions, the first to assess a subject's gender identity, and the second to assess a subject's assigned sex at birth. Researchers then identify when a participant's current gender identity differs from the sex they were assigned at birth and count those individuals as transgender.[15] Researchers Charlotte Tate, Jay Ledbetter, and Cris Youssef proved in 2013 that a two-step process is highly effective in identifying transgender participants in a sample, as compared to when only using one question.[16] That said, many of the prior two-step models are limited by the range of identities listed, whether omitting intersex as a birth-assigned sex or omitting several nonbinary gender identities.[17] As a result, subjects may feel offended and marginalized by having their identities excluded by researchers, and ultimately they may be undercounted, pressed to either skip these questions or choose from an incomplete list of answer choices. Therefore, a current best practice is figure 13.1, adapted from physician Madeline Deutsch and colleagues.[18]

Ideally, T-IPV scholars should utilize the revised two-question gender assessment, which includes several options for gender identity, to help further examine IPV among transgender populations. But even other IPV researchers, without specific focus on the transgender population, should employ the revised two-question gender assessment. Doing so will help identify a greater number of transgender participants

TABLE 13.1. US Transgender Survey Gender Identity Terms

Gender Identity Terms	% of respondents
Transgender	65%
Trans	56%
Transwoman (MTF, male to female)	32%
Transman (FTM, female to male)	31%
Nonbinary	31%
Genderqueer	29%
Gender nonconforming or gender variant	27%
Gender fluid/fluid	20%
Androgynous	18%
Transsexual	18%
Agender	14%
Two-Spirit	7%
Bigender	6%
Butch	5%
Crossdresser	5%
Multigender	4%
Third gender	4%
Intersex	3%
Drag performer (king/queen)	2%
AG or aggressive	1%
Stud	1%
Travesti	1%
Bulldagger	<1%
Fa'afafine	<1%
Mahu	<1%
A gender not listed above	12%

Source: James et al. 2016, 44.

among study samples, and this in turn will increase the chances that transgender subsamples will be large enough to provide the statistical power needed to conduct and report T-IPV analyses. This is particularly advisable given that several publications note that collected data on transgender subjects were not reported on due to not having enough transgender participants identified by survey questions.[19] This problem

Figure 13.1. Recommended Two-Question Gender Assessment

QUESTION 1

Which terms best describe your gender identity? (Choose all that apply.)

- o Man
- o Woman
- o Transgender man
- o Transgender woman
- o Nonbinary / Genderqueer / Gender Nonconforming
- o Agender
- o Different gender identity term (please state): _____

QUESTION 2

What sex were you assigned at birth?

- o Male
- o Female
- o Intersex

Note: Adapted from Deutsch et al. 2013.

could be more readily avoided if only researchers took a more proactive approach to oversampling transgender populations and using more transgender-inclusive survey measures.

It is also important to consider the stigma associated with being transgender within the context of defining the population. Because of widespread experiences of discrimination, transgender subjects are often reluctant to disclose their transgender status or history to researchers based on concerns of whether this personal information will be kept private.[20] Scholars can alleviate such fears and encourage research participation by addressing privacy concerns as part of informed consent (e.g., that private information will be kept confidential) and explaining research purposes (e.g., to shed light on T-IPV).

Nonprobability and Probability Sampling with Transgender Populations

Scholars utilize either probability or nonprobability sampling to recruit members from a defined population for research. Probability sampling entails compiling a list of people who meet the criteria of the sampling frame and then randomly selecting individuals to recruit.[21] This method allows scholars to report the chance that an individual from the defined population is included in the research sample. In comparison, when nonprobability sampling techniques are used, researchers cannot calculate the odds that a person from the defined population will be included as part of the research sample. Hence, probability sampling is considered the gold standard because it enables researchers to generalize their findings to a larger population.[22] However, there are several obstacles to performing this type of sampling in T-IPV research.

Probability Sampling

Transgender people are a relatively small portion of the general population, with recent estimates ranging between 0.6 and 3 percent in the United States.[23] Estimates usually include all people under the transgender umbrella, which means the number of individuals in various transgender subgroups (e.g., transgender men, transgender women, people who are nonbinary and/or agender, and gender nonconforming individuals) would be even smaller.[24] Therefore, when IPV studies sampling from the general population are inclusive of transgender participants and use appropriate measures to assess for gender identity (e.g., two-question gender assessment), probability sampling techniques are likely to select few, if any, transgender people to recruit.[25] Even if a huge sample yielded a few transgender participants, the number may be too few to be able to draw any conclusions about the defined population.[26]

An additional barrier to utilizing probability samples of transgender people is the cost and time involved with this methodology.[27] Because transgender people make up such a small proportion of the population, significant resources would be needed to carry out a study that yielded enough transgender participants.[28] For example, the TransPop Study is the first study to employ probability sampling with transgender people.[29] Researchers estimated that successfully recruiting three to five hundred transgender participants would require them to initially reach out to and screen 350,000 people from the general population.[30] Data collection reportedly took place over the course of a year and ended in 2016. Although most scholars do not have the resources to perform this level of research, one more cost-effective way to create probability samples is to include the two-question gender assessment in general population studies of IPV and then oversample transgender participants.

Nonprobability Sampling

To date, T-IPV data have been primarily collected from nonprobability samples in one of two ways. First, transgender subjects have been included in LGBTQ samples for IPV research.[31] However, relative to their cisgender lesbian, gay, bisexual, and queer counterparts, transgender people usually comprise a very small proportion of samples, thus precluding the ability to make any conclusions about T-IPV.[32] For example, in Susan Turell's sample of 499 LGBTQ people, only 1 percent ($n = 7$) identified as transgender.[33] Thus, it would be inappropriate to generalize the findings about LGBTQ IPV from this study to T-IPV. In addition, it is unclear the extent to which transgender subjects were representative of the transgender population as a whole.

The second way nonprobability sampling has been utilized to assess T-IPV is with exclusive samples of transgender subjects.[34] There are several benefits to using transgender-only samples. For instance, there are more opportunities to create interview guides and questionnaires to include T-IPV-specific variables, like questions about experiences of transphobia, internalization of transphobic attitudes, and experiences with unique T-IPV abusive tactics. In addition, researchers have the ability to more easily conduct T-IPV analyses on subsamples (e.g., transgender people who are out or public about being transgender versus those who are not). Much of the current knowledge of T-IPV is drawn from qualitative studies that utilized transgender-only samples, and findings from these high-detail studies have provided direction for subsequent T-IPV research. Ultimately, the use of transgender-specific questions is less common in studies where transgender people represent a small portion of a predominantly cisgender sample, in part because researchers may not wish to burden only a subset of their sample with substantially longer study completion times. Recruiting transgender-only samples enables researchers to center their focus more on transgender issues.

CONVENIENCE AND COMMUNITY VENUE SAMPLING

A primary concern for using nonprobability sampling techniques is that samples are not always representative of the defined populations.[35] Therefore, research findings can only be applied to members of the population who are similar to study participants. In general, people of color, individuals living in rural areas, and lower-income individuals tend to be underrepresented in nonprobability research samples.[36] A review of LGBTQ IPV research reveals that scholars have predominantly utilized convenience samples obtained through LGBTQ organizations or events.[37] Hence, among LGBTQ people, those who are out and live in urban areas where LGBTQ organizations and events are more common tend to be overrepresented in convenience and community venue nonprobability samples.

Since probability sampling is less likely to be utilized in T-IPV research, scholars should anticipate and make efforts to minimize sample biases.[38] Researchers should increase the diversity and representativeness of their samples by actively recruiting members of the population who are less likely to participate.[39] In the case of T-IPV, scholars should target transgender people of color, those living in rural areas, lower-income individuals, and individuals who are not out or open about their transgender status or history.[40] Additionally, snowball sampling can be utilized to recruit transgender people who are less likely to participate, such as by encouraging participants to share recruitment materials with other eligible individuals they know.[41] However, investigators should be cognizant that participants tend to refer people like themselves.[42] Therefore, snowball sampling could just as easily lead to a less diverse sample. By improving the heterogeneity and population representativeness in transgender samples, scholars have greater ability to generalize findings and provide information and tools on T-IPV to community professionals.

Another method for improving the validity of research results is for scholars to avoid sampling from community venues that introduce significant bias.[43] For example, Betty Barrett and Daphne Sheridan point out that research on transgender people's vulnerability to violence is frequently informed by samples of individuals from high-risk environments or who engage in high-risk behaviors, such as sex workers.[44]

Therefore, findings about vulnerability to violence cannot be generalized to transgender people who are not "high-risk."[45] It may not be always feasible for T-IPV scholars to avoid community venues that inject sample bias, particularly given the small size of transgender populations and limits to recruiting individuals who are not out or open about being transgender. But researchers should clarify their reasons for utilizing a certain type of community venue, such as to draw larger numbers of transgender participants who are survivors of IPV. In addition, generalizability limitations should be delineated. For example, to study abuse dynamics experienced by T-IPV survivors, scholars can recruit participants from victim advocacy service agencies. However, applicability of findings should be explained to prevent community professionals from inadvertently providing inappropriate care to individuals not represented in the convenience sample. For instance, results would not apply to survivors who do not seek help.

Another way researchers can improve representativeness of community venue samples is to perform time-space sampling.[46] With this strategy, investigators recruit participants at a venue at randomly selected times throughout the day and week. This approach rests on the assumption that different types of individuals will visit the venue at different times, thus creating a relatively heterogeneous and more representative sample. For instance, T-IPV researchers recruiting from community organizations should recruit during the day and evening throughout the week to give individuals of various socioeconomic and employment statuses the opportunity to participate in the study.[47]

WEB-BASED SAMPLING

The dawn of the internet has been favorable for expanding LGBTQ research.[48] It additionally offers T-IPV scholars the ability to reduce biases associated with convenience and community venue sampling by reaching individuals who live in rural areas, are unaffiliated with transgender or LGBTQ communities, and/or are not out or open about being transgender. Not surprisingly, a primary limitation of web-based sampling is that individuals without internet access are automatically excluded, and therefore their experiences are not represented. In fact, as of 2018, 35 percent of Americans do not have internet access set up in their homes, and 11 percent do not use the internet at all.[49] Furthermore, web-based sampling has been found to result in samples that overrepresent people who are younger, white, and have higher incomes.[50] The US Transgender Survey, which was partly administered online, attempted to reduce such biases by using both passive and active recruitment methods, such as posting online advertisements and conducting face-to-face recruitment.[51] Even more importantly, eligible participants without internet access were provided the opportunity to schedule a time to complete the survey on an agency computer, thus reducing biases introduced by web-based sampling.[52]

Another concern with web-based sampling is that researchers usually lack the technology to know how many eligible people view recruitment materials as opposed to the number of people who agree to participate; therefore, the response rate is unknown.[53] Scholars who attain high response rates can claim strong representativeness of those who view recruitment messages, but, alternatively, reports of low response rates lead to questions about the differences in those who agreed to participate and those who did not.[54] For instance, do participants in a sample differ in a meaningful way from those who opted out of the research? Differences could relate to diversity variables, such as whether someone is out or open about being transgender as well as other issues that result in volunteer bias. In addition, stigma associated with disclosure of information, especially among marginalized groups like transgender people, can preclude research participation. As a result, researchers should attempt to oversample from subgroups less likely to participate.[55] Even more importantly, when concerns about privacy lead to low response rates, such as in the case of participating in a study about T-IPV, researchers can make subject identities anonymous, even to researchers. Web-based sampling can be useful for achieving these objectives, even though the inability to determine response rates is a drawback.[56]

IPV Diagnostic Testing and Survey Measures

Researchers commonly assess IPV among subjects by administering a standardized survey instrument. By far, the most widely used instruments are the Conflict Tactics Scale (CTS) and its revised version, the CTS2.[57] These instruments also have been used in LGBTQ samples, despite not having been validated for such groups.[58] The CTS and CTS2 use gender-neutral language, which, at face value, makes them appropriate for transgender as well as cisgender individuals.[59] However, these measures do not account for differences in IPV in relationships where at least one partner is transgender. For instance, abusive tactics that are unique to T-IPV (e.g., threats of outing) are not assessed. In addition, some CTS2 items imply that all people are men or women (e.g., "My partner explained *his or her* side of a disagreement to me"[60]), thereby erasing the existence of agender, genderqueer, Two-Spirit, and other nonbinary people. Therefore, assessment results can provide an incomplete and inaccurate depiction of IPV for transgender people, given the neglect of T-IPV considerations.[61]

To date, no IPV measures have been diagnostically tested with transgender samples.[62] It would be ideal for researchers to develop a highly reliable and valid survey to study T-IPV. However, given the time, ability, and funding necessary for such an arduous task, this may not be feasible for many investigators. Still, researchers should consider a multitude of factors when assessing T-IPV, whether in the context of creating their own instrument, making adaptations to an existing instrument, or utilizing qualitative methods.

Assessing Relationships

IPV differs from other types of crimes that occur in the context of relationships, such as child abuse, bullying, and sexual abuse by someone who is not an intimate partner. Consequently, it is necessary for researchers to ascertain that the abuse in question occurred within an intimate partner relationship. The CTS and CTS2 address this issue by instructing subjects to only endorse survey items about abuse that transpired during the course of an intimate partnership.[63] This seems relatively straightforward but could be more complicated with transgender people, given the widespread discrimination and victimization they encounter. For instance, in a T-IPV-specific study, Amy Roch, James Morton, and Graham Ritchie found that transgender subjects reported abusive experiences from people other than partners or ex-partners.[64] Subjects recounted incidents where someone who was not a partner forced or tried to force them to engage in sexual activity, including sexual intercourse, viewing pornography, or having sex with others for money.⁶⁵ These types of abusive experiences also can occur in relationships where IPV exists. Consequently, T-IPV researchers need to clearly delineate the type of relationship they seek to assess among subjects. Otherwise, other common abusive experiences may be incorrectly counted as T-IPV.

Assessing for T-IPV also requires investigators to consider variations in how transgender people form and maintain intimate partnerships. Barrett and Sheridan explain, "there is enormous fluidity in the structure and nature of transgender intimate relationships."⁶⁶ This was demonstrated by Greta Bauer and colleagues, who found that 12 percent of 433 transgender subjects endorsed being in an open or polyamorous relationship.⁶⁷ In another study, 9 percent of 321 transgender men reported being in "various relational compositions (i.e., polyamorous relationships)."⁶⁸ With this in mind, T-IPV researchers must be careful to distinguish the types of relationships assessed. For instance, is the focus solely on the primary relationship, if any? What if one of a person's relationships is primarily sexual? Essentially, T-IPV researchers cannot assume that transgender people are only in one relationship at a time, and, as such, there may be multiple relationships at any given time to assess for IPV. Therefore, researchers should first decide whether or not they personally want to include more casual and less-defined relationships as part of their definition of "intimate partner relationship." Then, scholars need to be cognizant of how they define "intimate partner relationship" for research subjects in order to avoid collecting data about relationship situations that do not constitute intimate partnerships but that could still include violence.

Bauer and colleagues additionally reported that sexual orientation is particularly diverse among transgender populations.⁶⁹ For example, in a study of 433 transgender individuals in Ontario, Canada, only 30 percent of subjects identified as heterosexual, and a study of 27,715 transgender people in the US found just 15 percent identified as heterosexual.⁷⁰ Furthermore, transgender people may partner with others within, as well as outside, LGBTQ communities in general and transgender communities in particular. Accordingly, Barrett and Sheridan recommend that "any attempts to create knowledge about transgender people's experiences with IPV must reflect the diversity of configurations in which transgender people choose to love, partner, and/or sexually engage."⁷¹

Assessing Violence

As mentioned earlier, some T-IPV studies with transgender-only samples measure IPV secondary to broader research questions.[72] For instance, in their study of HIV risk, Kristen Clements, Mitchell Katz, and Rani Marx assessed whether subjects had experienced physical abuse in the past twelve months, thus disregarding other types of abuse potentially experienced (e.g., psychological or sexual).[73] This type of study, which assesses broader issues than T-IPV, provides a glimpse into T-IPV, but also leaves many unanswered questions for readers.

In contrast, when IPV is a focal point, particularly in the well-established cisgender IPV literature, researchers utilize many questions to assess various types of IPV under the broader definition of IPV, such as psychological, physical, and sexual abuse. Unfortunately, researchers do not always agree on which types of abusive behaviors and tactics constitute which umbrella types of IPV.[74] Physical abuse is undoubtedly the most studied type of IPV, and as such, researchers have an easier time agreeing on definitions for physical abuse.[75] In contrast, psychological and emotional types of IPV are the "least standardized" and more often include "everything else."[76] While these types of IPV are not always as visible as physical violence, they can be equally, if not more, harmful to survivors. It is especially important for T-IPV scholars to inquire about these types of IPV, as they may be even more common in the context of T-IPV. For instance, Roch, Morton, and Ritchie found that "transphobic emotional abuse" was the most frequently endorsed type of abuse experienced by transgender survivors of IPV (73 percent of the sample).[77] It is additionally worth exploring whether the typical categories and conceptualizations of IPV are valid to utilize when studying T-IPV, considering the original constructions of IPV theory are based on cisnormative and heteronormative understandings of relationships and gender roles.

It makes sense that research investigators are privy to the types of IPV assessed by survey instruments. However, it is necessary that questions posed to participants are framed in a way to avoid stigmatized terms associated with IPV, such as violence, abuse, assault, and batterer.[78] Otherwise, participants are more likely to deny abuse when it exists, thus creating false negatives and leading to underestimates of IPV. Survey questions on the CTS and CTS2 utilize behavioral definitions, which are phrased in such a way to increase the chance that IPV is endorsed when it exists.[79] Instead of asking whether the subject has ever committed or been the victim of physical abuse, the CTS2 asks respondents to assess the frequency of specific behaviors. For example, minor physical abuse is assessed by participants' endorsements of survey items about each of the following behaviors: "threw something at my partner that could hurt, twisted my partner's arm or hair, pushed or shoved my partner, grabbed my partner, and slapped my partner."[80] Subjects also are given the opportunity to endorse whether their partner ever used each of the tactics against them, thus indicating victimization.

An additional way that researchers can "destigmatize the context around IPV" is to include an instruction paragraph at the beginning of a survey.[81] For instance, the CTS2 begins with the following: "No matter how well a couple gets along, there are times when they disagree, get annoyed with the other person, want different things from each other, or just have spats or fights because they are in a bad mood, are tired, or for some other reason. Couples also have many different ways of trying to settle their differences. This is a list of things that might happen when you have differences."[82] Each of these attempts to decrease stigma associated with experiences of IPV contribute to reduction of the social desirability bias in research.

Using behavioral definitions of IPV is not only helpful for decreasing stigma associated with IPV but also for improving IPV measurement validity. Just as researchers often disagree about the behaviors that constitute different types of IPV, subjects' notions of IPV can be even more varied. For example, if subjects were only presented with a question of whether they had been a victim or perpetrator of "physical violence," the likelihood for false positives and false negatives would increase because the types of behaviors the subject had in mind when they responded are unknown. Avoiding these pitfalls, Tyson Reuter and colleagues sought to assess physical, sexual, and verbal abuse in the context of LGBTQ IPV victimization.[83] To assess physical abuse, researchers asked, "Has this partner ever hit, slapped, punched, or hurt you?" With regard to forced sex, researched asked, "Has this partner ever forced you to have vaginal, anal, or oral sex when you did not want to?" Finally, to assess verbal abuse, researchers asked, "Did this partner call you names, insult you, or treat you poorly?"[84] Variables were then dichotomized such that endorsement of the question of physical abuse equated to a positive finding of physical abuse for that participant. As well, endorsement of any of the questions meant a positive finding for IPV in general. This study offers one example of behavioral-specific questions that can be effectively used to assess IPV.

Assessing Perpetration and Victimization

The majority of IPV and T-IPV research has focused on victimization.[85] To date, there is little research that discusses transgender perpetrators of IPV. As a result, it is unclear to what degree transgender perpetrators are different from cisgender perpetrators. Not surprisingly, due in part to IPV-associated stigma and concerns about potential legal consequences, perpetrators are often more difficult to recruit for research and may be more likely to deny or minimize abusive behaviors in studies. It is possible that some transgender abusers are also less likely to self-report perpetration in research due to not wanting to reinforce the false stereotype that transgender people are prone to violence.[86] This is not to say that studying perpetration should be abandoned by T-IPV research efforts. To the contrary, perpetration should be incorporated into studies of T-IPV so that both victimization and perpetration are assessed simultaneously, as is modeled by the CTS and CTS2.

Scholars are advised to utilize the two-question gender assessment, as presented earlier, for all perpetrators and survivors identified in a study. For example, in addition to answering for themselves, a subject should be asked to identify their partner's birth-assigned sex and gender identity at the time of the relationship. It is also recommended that researchers ask subjects, utilizing behavioral definitions, about times they have received as well as committed abuse in relation to each partnership. This will help determine "the directionality of abuse" such as whether the subject was the survivor, perpetrator, or both in the specified relationship, since their role could differ by relationship.[87] Inquiring about perpetration in addition to victimization will add to understanding the complexities at play in T-IPV. As a result, community prevention, intervention, and treatment efforts may be guided by evidence-based knowledge of T-IPV.

T-IPV Distinct Tactics on Survey Measures

As discussed, no IPV measures are available that have been designed for and validated with transgender people. Even though the CTS and CTS2 are sometimes utilized with transgender people in research, these measures were derived from cisgender IPV data.[88] As such, these measures cannot account for any unique manifestations of T-IPV and may distort prevalence rates.[89]

Barrett points out that one popular catalogue of IPV tactics, the power and control wheel, has been revised multiple times to be more inclusive of diverse populations.[90] In one example, Janice Ristock and Norma Timbang go so far as to identify layers of oppression, such as heterosexism and transphobia, which propel the use of power and control tactics against LGBTQ people.[91] More recently, michael munson and Loree Cook-Daniels presented IPV power and control tactics that are specific to transgender people.[92] (See chapter 2 for more on T-IPV tactics.) However, the majority of existing measures of IPV tactics have yet to incorporate IPV tactics specific to transgender populations.

In Roch, Morton, and Ritchie's exemplary report, the authors reveal how researchers can incorporate T-IPV measures in their studies, rather than simply utilizing cisgender IPV measures with transgender people.[93] For instance, in addition to measuring many common psychological, physical, and sexual IPV tactics, this study also assessed transphobic psychological abuse (e.g., whether a subject had ever been made to feel ashamed, guilty, or wrong about their transgender background or identity by a partner, been stopped from being able to express their gender identity through changes in appearance, or had attention drawn to, or focus on, parts of their body that they felt uncomfortable about). Strikingly, 73 percent of the transgender participants endorsed having been the victim of such transphobic behaviors from abusive partners. This makes clear the need to measure tactics unique to T-IPV, rather than only tactics occurring in cisgender abusive relationships.[94]

While there are few similar examples of quantitative studies assessing unique T-IPV tactics, qualitative research offers suggestions for additional T-IPV-specific tactics to study. For instance, Roch, Morton, and Ritchie also performed qualitative interviews with subjects and concluded that there are critical time periods when transgender people are at higher risk of T-IPV victimization, especially transphobic behaviors.[95] The first is when coming out as transgender for the first time to an existing partner, and the second is when revealing plans for gender transition to a partner who is already aware of the person's gender identity but has been in denial about the person's transition needs.[96] Therefore, to understand T-IPV contexts, scholars would be wise to incorporate questions to assess T-IPV in relation to transgender identity development and the coming out process. Roch, Morton, and Ritchie also found from interviews that nonbinary individuals (e.g., those who identify as genderqueer) may be at greater risk of T-IPV because of society's invalidation of nonbinary gender identities.[97] As a result, nonbinary partners may be more likely to receive "dismissive and disrespectful" treatment from their partners within abusive relationships.[98] Accordingly, T-IPV scholars should consider assessing T-IPV tactics distinct to transgender subgroups, such as tactics specific to not only transgender women and men but also tactics specific to nonbinary survivors.

Relatedly, Barrett notes that T-IPV occurs not only in the context of transphobic oppression, but also other intersecting oppressions, like racism, classism, and ableism.[99] Barrett writes, "These structures may exacerbate power inequalities within LGBT relationships and provide perpetrators with additional leverage for exerting power and control over their victims."[100] In turn, researchers Katie Edwards, Kateryna Sylaska, and Angela Neal recommend that T-IPV research explores IPV tactics that may be distinct to intersecting identities and related inequalities.[101] This suggestion is reinforced by findings from the US Transgender Survey, which showed that IPV risk increases for transgender people who experience added layers of oppression beyond transphobia: rates of T-IPV were higher for people of color, undocumented immigrants, people with disabilities, sex workers, and people who had experienced homelessness. Furthermore, victimization was more often reported when subjects were oppressed in multiple ways, such as when a transgender person was simultaneously a sex worker and an undocumented immigrant.[102] All of this is to highlight the fact that not all transgender people are white, middle class, heterosexual, and so forth, but rather they come from diverse backgrounds that may expose them to unique IPV tactics that should be studied within T-IPV research. Ultimately, researchers should be cognizant of transgender people's intersectional identities and how these may influence T-IPV.

Lastly, T-IPV scholars are advised to work in collaboration with transgender communities when they engage in research endeavors, including but not limited to the following: (1) generation of new models to understand T-IPV, (2) development and psychometric testing of IPV measures appropriate for transgender people, and (3) design of strategies for professional prevention and intervention of T-IPV in the community. Researchers Reem Ghandour, Jacquelyn Campbell, and Jacqueline Lloyd report that when diverse populations are the focus of research, "individuals from these communities should be engaged early and often in the development of these tools and models."[103] Researchers may consider the benefits of incorporating an advisory committee including transgender individuals and advocacy groups. For instance, Sandy James and colleagues note that such an advisory committee was used in designing and conducting the US Transgender Survey, with the goal to "increase community engagement in the survey project and raise awareness by connecting with transgender people in communities across the country through a variety of networks."[104] Since the aim of T-IPV research is to produce the most accurate picture of T-IPV, working alongside transgender people can help ensure that the efforts of cisgender and transgender scholars alike are relevant, sensitive to the community's needs, and effective.

Conclusion and Best Practices

The following is a summary of best practices for overcoming barriers to knowledge production in T-IPV research, as detailed throughout this chapter. These are intended to assist scholars in advancing understanding of T-IPV, developing evidence-based strategies for community prevention and intervention, and, ultimately, reducing T-IPV. (See figure 13.2.)

First, population definitions should be as inclusive as possible of the widest possible range of transgender identities, except where research questions focus on a specific transgender subgroup. In addition, the two-question gender assessment should be used routinely to identify transgender subjects and their partners in IPV research, even when the primary research focus is not T-IPV.

Figure 13.2. Recommended Best Practices in T-IPV Research

1. Use clear and inclusive measures of transgender identities.
2. Use sampling designs with enhanced generalizability to diverse transgender populations.
3. Use clear and inclusive measures of T-IPV perpetration and victimization.
4. Collaborate with transgender communities and transgender organizations.

Second, whenever feasible, prevalence rates of T-IPV should be drawn from research that employs probability sampling. When using nonprobability sampling techniques, researchers should work to decrease biases associated with the selected method(s). For instance, scholars can increase diversity and representativeness of transgender samples with added recruitment and oversampling of individuals less likely to participate. Nonprobability samples should additionally be compared with probability samples of transgender populations (e.g., TransPop Study), and generalizability limitations should be delineated in subsequent study reports.

Third, for assessment of T-IPV, scholars should use a clear definition for "intimate partner violence" distinct from other types of violence, and they should measure both victimization and perpetration. In addition, measures should include abusive tactics specific to transgender populations, including tactics specific to transgender subgroups such as abuse shaped by racism, xenophobia, and homophobia. Scholars are encouraged to develop new or adapt old IPV measures accordingly to assess T-IPV, and to validate them with transgender samples. Qualitative research can be vital also in uncovering new forms of T-IPV.

Fourth and lastly, commitment to collaboration with the transgender community in all research endeavors is crucial. By employing community advisory committees, and, when applicable, hiring transgender staff, all researchers should ensure that transgender community members play an active role in the development, implementation, and reporting of research.

NOTES

1 Doan 2016, 103.
2 Doan 2016, 105.
3 Rogers 2017.
4 Meyer and Wilson 2009.
5 Meyer and Wilson 2009.

6 Meyer and Wilson 2009.
7 Landers and Gilsanz 2009; Messinger 2017.
8 Conron et al. 2012, 118.
9 Messinger 2017.
10 Messinger 2017.
11 James et al. 2016.
12 Messinger 2017.
13 James et al. 2016.
14 Deutsch et al. 2013; Reisner et al. 2016, 5.
15 Deutsch et al. 2013; Reisner et al. 2016.
16 Tate, Ledbetter, and Youssef 2013.
17 See Deutsch et al. 2013; Tate, Ledbetter, and Youssef 2013.
18 Deutsch et al. 2013.
19 Messinger 2017.
20 Messinger 2017; Meyer and Wilson 2009.
21 Messinger 2017.
22 Meyer and Wilson 2009.
23 Doan 2016; Flores et al. 2016.
24 Meyer and Wilson 2009.
25 Messinger 2017; Meyer and Wilson 2009.
26 Messinger 2017.
27 Messinger 2017.
28 Messinger 2017.
29 Meyer et al., n.d.
30 Meyer et al., n.d.
31 Yerke and DeFeo 2016.
32 Barrett 2015.
33 Turell 2008.
34 Yerke and DeFeo 2016.
35 Meyer and Wilson 2009.
36 Messinger 2017.
37 Murray and Mobley 2009.
38 Edwards, Sylaska, and Neal 2015; Meyer and Wilson 2009.
39 Edwards, Sylaska, and Neal 2015; Meyer and Wilson 2009.
40 Meyer and Wilson 2009.
41 Meyer and Wilson 2009.
42 Meyer and Wilson 2009.
43 Meyer and Wilson 2009.
44 Barrett and Sheridan 2017.
45 Barrett and Sheridan 2017.
46 Meyer and Wilson 2009.
47 Meyer and Wilson 2009.
48 Meyer and Wilson 2009.

49 Pew Research Center 2019.
50 Meyer and Wilson 2009.
51 James et al. 2016.
52 James et al. 2016.
53 Meyer and Wilson 2009.
54 Messinger 2017.
55 Messinger 2017.
56 Messinger 2017.
57 Barrett 2015; Straus 1979; Straus et al. 1996.
58 Barrett 2015.
59 Messinger 2017.
60 Straus et al. 1996.
61 Barrett 2015.
62 Messinger 2017.
63 Strauss 1979; Straus et al. 1996.
64 Roch, Morton, and Ritchie 2010.
65 Roch, Morton, and Ritchie 2010.
66 Barrett and Sheridan 2017, 143.
67 Bauer et al. 2010.
68 Forshee 2008, 228.
69 Bauer et al. 2010.
70 Bauer et al. 2010; James et al. 2016.
71 Barrett and Sheridan 2017, 144.
72 Yerke and DeFeo 2016.
73 Clements, Katz, and Marx 1999.
74 Messinger 2017.
75 Messinger 2017.
76 Messinger 2017, 39.
77 Roch, Morton, and Ritchie 2010.
78 Messinger 2017.
79 Messinger 2017.
80 Straus et al. 1996, 308.
81 Messinger 2017, 37.
82 Straus et al. 1996, 310.
83 Reuter et al. 2017.
84 Reuter et al. 2017, 103–104.
85 Messinger 2017.
86 Barrett and Sheridan 2017, 145.
87 Messinger 2017, 59.
88 Barrett and Sheridan 2017.
89 Barrett and Sheridan 2017.
90 Barrett 2015.
91 Ristock and Timbang 2005.

92   munson and Cook-Daniels 2013.
93   Roch, Morton, and Ritchie 2010.
94   Roch, Morton, and Ritchie 2010.
95   Roch, Morton, and Ritchie 2010.
96   Roch, Morton, and Ritchie 2010.
97   Roch, Morton, and Ritchie 2010.
98   Roch, Morton, and Ritchie 2010, 19.
99   Barrett 2015.
100 Barrett 2015, 5.
101 Edwards, Sylaska, and Neal 2015.
102 James et al. 2016.
103 Ghandour, Campbell, and Lloyd 2015, 60.
104 James et al. 2016, 27.

REFERENCES

Barrett, Betty J. 2015. "Domestic Violence in the LGBT Community." *Encyclopedia of Social Work* (March): 1–43.

Barrett, Betty Jo., and Daphne Vanessa Sheridan. 2017. "Partner Violence in Transgender Communities: What Helping Professionals Need to Know." *Journal of GLBT Family Studies* 13 (2): 137–162.

Bauer, Greta, M. Boyce, T. Coleman, M. Kaay, K. Scanlon, and R. Travers. 2010. "Who Are Trans People in Ontario? *Trans PULSE E-Bulletin* 1 (1): 1–2.

Brown, Taylor N. T., and Jody L. Herman. 2015. *Intimate Partner Violence and Sexual Abuse among LGBT People: A Review of Existing Research*. Los Angeles: The Williams Institute, UCLA School of Law. http://williamsinstitute.law.ucla.edu.

Clements, Kristen, Mitchell Katz, and Rani Marx. 1999. *The Transgender Community Health Project*. San Francisco: University of California, San Francisco.

Conron, Kerith J., Gunner Scott, Grace S. Stowell, and Stewart Landers. 2012. "Transgender Health in Massachusetts: Results from a Household Probability Sample of Adults." *American Journal of Public Health* 102 (1): 118–122.

Deutsch, Madeline B., Jamison Green, JoAnne Keatley, Gal Mayer, Jennifer Hastings, and Alexandra M. Hall. 2013. "Electronic Medical Records and the Transgender Patient: Recommendations from the World Professional Association for Transgender Health EMR Working Group." *Journal of the American Medical Informatics Association* 20:700–703.

Doan, Petra L. 2016. "To Count or Not to Count: Queering Measurement and the Transgender Community." *Women's Studies Quarterly* 44 (3–4): 89–110.

Edwards, Katie M., and Kateryna M. Sylaska. 2013. "The Perpetration of Intimate Partner Violence among LGBTQ College Youth: The Role of Minority Stress." *Journal of Youth Adolescence* 42 (11): 1721–1731.

Edwards, Katie M., Kateryna M. Sylaska, and Angela M. Neal. 2015. "Intimate Partner Violence among Sexual Minority Populations: A Critical Review of the Literature and Agenda for Future Research." *Psychology of Violence* 5 (2): 112–121.

Flores, Andrew R., Jody L. Herman, Gary J. Gates, and Taylor N. T. Brown. 2016. *How Many Adults Identify as Transgender in the United States?* Los Angeles: The Williams Institute. https://williamsinstitute.law.ucla.edu.

Forshee, Andrew S. 2008. "Transgender Men: A Demographic Snapshot." *Journal of Gay & Lesbian Social Services* 20 (3): 221–236.

Ghandour, Reem M., Jacquelyn C. Campbell, and Jacqueline Lloyd. 2015. "Screening and Counseling for Intimate Partner Violence: A Vision for the Future." *Journal of Women's Health* 24 (1): 57–61.

Hester, Marianne, and Catherine Donovan. 2009. "Researching Domestic Violence in Same-Sex Relationships—A Feminist Epistemological Approach to Survey Development." *Journal of Lesbian Studies* 13 (2): 161–173.

James, Sandy E., Jody L. Herman, Susan Rankin, Mara Keisling, Lisa Mottet, and Ma'ayan Anafi. 2016. *The Report of the 2015 U.S. Transgender Survey*. Washington, DC: National Center for Transgender Equality. www.ustranssurvey.org.

Landers, Stewart, and Paola Gilsanz. 2009. *The Health of Lesbian, Gay, Bisexual, and Transgender (LGBT) Persons in Massachusetts: A Survey of Health Issues Comparing LGBT Persons with Their Heterosexual and Non-transgender Counterparts*. Boston: Massachusetts Department of Public Health. www.masstpc.org.

Langenderfer-Magruder, Lisa, Darren L. Whitfield, N. Eugene Walls, Shanna K. Kattari, and Daniel Ramos. 2014. "Experiences of Intimate Partner Violence and Subsequent Police Reporting among Lesbian, Gay, Bisexual, Transgender, and Queer Adults in Colorado: Comparing Rates of Cisgender and Transgender Victimization." *Journal of Interpersonal Violence* 31 (5): 855–871.

Messinger, Adam M. 2017. *LGBTQ Intimate Partner Violence: Lessons for Policy, Practice, and Research*. Oakland: University of California Press.

Meyer, Ilan H., Walter O. Bockting, Jody L. Herman, and Sari K. Reisner. n.d. TransPop: U.S. Transgender Population Health Survey. Accessed April 15, 2018. www.transpop.org.

Meyer, Ilan H., and Patrick A. Wilson. 2009. "Sampling Lesbian, Gay, and Bisexual Populations." *Journal of Counseling Psychology* 56 (1): 23–31.

munson, michael, and Loree Cook-Daniels. 2013. "Power and Control Tactics Specific to Transgender People." Webinar. http://forge-forward.org.

Murray, Christine E., and A. Keith Mobley. 2009. "Empirical Research about Same-Sex Intimate Partner Violence: A Methodological Review." *Journal of Homosexuality* 56 (3): 361–386.

Pew Research Center. 2019. "Internet/Broadband Fact Sheet." www.pewinternet.org.

Reisner, Sari L., Madeline B. Deutsch, Shalender Bhasin, Walter Bockting, George R. Brown, Jamie Feldman, Rob Garofalo, Baudeqijntje Kreukels, Asa Radix, Jushua D. Safer, Vig Tangpricha, Guy T'Sjoen, and Michael Goodman. 2016. "Advancing Methods for U.S. Transgender Health Research." *Current Opinion in Endocrinology, Diabetes and Obesity* 23 (2): 198–207.

Reuter, Tyson. R., Michael E. Newcomb, Sarah W. Whitton, and Brian Mustanski. 2017. "Intimate Partner Violence Victimization in LGBT Young Adults: Demographic

Differences and Associations with Health Behaviors." *Psychology of Violence* 7 (1): 101–109.

Risser, Jan M. H., Andrea Shelton, Sheryl McCurdy, John Atkinson, Paige Padgett, Bernardo Useche, Brenda Thomas, and Mark Williams. 2005. "Sex, Drugs, Violence, and HIV Status among Male-to-Female Transgender Persons in Houston, Texas." *International Journal of Transgenderism* 8 (2–3): 67–74.

Ristock, Janice, and Norma Timbang. 2005. "Relationship Violence in Lesbian/Gay/Bisexual/Transgender/Queer [LGBTQ] Communities: Moving beyond a Gender-Based Framework." *Violence Against Women Online Resources*. https://vawnet.org.

Roch, Amy, James Morton, and Graham Ritchie. 2010. *Out of Sight, out of Mind? Transgender People's Experiences of Domestic Abuse*. Edinburgh: LGBT Youth Scotland and the Scottish Transgender Alliance. www.scottishtrans.org.

Rogers, Michaela. 2017. "Challenging Cisgenderism through Trans People's Narratives of Domestic Violence and Abuse." *Sexualities*. https://doi.org/10.1177/1363460716681475.

Straus, Murray A. 1979. "Measuring Intrafamily Conflict and Violence: The Conflict Tactics (CT) Scales." *Journal of Marriage and the Family* 41 (1): 75–88.

Straus, Murray A., Sherry L. Hamby, Sue Boney-McCoy, and David B. Sugarman. 1996. "The Revised Conflict Tactics Scale (CTS2): Development and Preliminary Psychometric Data." *Journal of Family Issues* 17 (3): 283–316.

Tate, Charlotte C., Jay N. Ledbetter, and Cris P. Youssef. 2013. "A Two-Question Method for Assessing Gender Categories in the Social and Medical Sciences." *Journal of Sex Research* 50 (8): 767–776.

Turell, Susan. C. 2008. "Seeking Help for Same-Sex Relationship Abuses." *Journal of Gay and Lesbian Social Services* 10 (2): 35–49.

Waters, Emily. 2017. *Lesbian, Gay, Bisexual, Transgender, Queer, and HIV-Affected Intimate Partner Violence in 2016*. New York: National Coalition of Anti-Violence Programs. http://avp.org.

Yerke, Adam F., and Jennifer DeFeo. 2016. "Redefining Intimate Partner Violence beyond the Binary to Include Transgender People." *Journal of Family Violence* 31 (8): 975–979.

14

Working toward Transgender Inclusion in the Movement to Address Intimate Partner Violence

XAVIER L. GUADALUPE-DIAZ AND ADAM M. MESSINGER

Recall Joe's harrowing account of transgender intimate partner violence (T-IPV), detailed in the opening chapter. As a young transgender man early in his transition process, Joe experienced abuse during a particularly vulnerable time in his life. He described, "I was in a really sensitive and kind of unstable place and I was trying to find my footing and . . . it's an ideal time for an abuser to strike."[1] What is more, Joe struggled to identify his experiences as abuse—in part because T-IPV does not conform to societal expectations of what "real" abuse looks like. When he did consider seeking help, he feared others might similarly dismiss his victimization. After enduring months of sexual and identity-based IPV, it was finally with support from an online friend and his mother that change became possible. As Joe explained, "I had to have someone verbally tell me . . . this is what's happening to you. You can't just sit there in denial because you'll get hurt, you'll get even more hurt if that continues. I had to have someone from outside tell me what was going on. I was in denial."[2]

Reemerging time and time again throughout this book's review of the research literature, societal transphobia is directly implicated in the prevalence, dynamics, consequences, and seeming-intractability of T-IPV. Societal marginalization of transgender lives substantially elevates the potency of IPV, further isolating survivors. Differing from the experiences of cisgender people in relationships, the hostile cultural contexts in which transgender people live create distinct susceptibilities to abuse.[3] As Xavier Quinn (chapter 2) and Rayna Momen and Walter DeKeseredy (chapter 4) emphasized, transgender people face a myriad of complicating factors that influence both the dynamics of abuse and the subsequent recovery. These factors include identity-based abuse, the intersections of interpersonal, structural, and institutional forms of violence, transphobic discrimination, cisnormative help-seeking structures, and more. In this concluding chapter, we reflect on the lessons of this book and their implications for future service provision, public policy, and research.

Expanding Assumptions of What IPV Looks Like

Importantly, this book complicates our understanding of what IPV looks like. Eschewing stereotypes in favor of empirical realities represents a vital step toward the development of more targeted, transgender-specific IPV services and policies.

To begin with what must be obvious by now, IPV is not solely a cisgender issue. Although services and policy have historically been oriented toward addressing cisgender IPV, research indicates that T-IPV warrants increased attention.[4] Indeed, the preponderance of evidence in the US and around the world indicates that transgender people experience IPV at rates similar to or greater than those of their cisgender counterparts, with over half of transgender people experiencing IPV in their lifetimes.[5] (See chapter 1 for a review of research on T-IPV prevalence.)

Moreover, while transgender and cisgender people alike experience many of the same forms of IPV, IPV tactics are not always identical in transgender individuals' relationships. In fact, research continues to identify new and potent tactics unique to T-IPV. For instance, abusers of transgender people may manipulate the survivor's identity by exploiting existent cisnormativity and transphobia in society. As Amanda Koontz noted in chapter 3, some of these abusive tactics involve discrediting identity work. The hostile social context that transgender people live in fosters opportunities for abusers to undermine their identities.[6] Abusers of transgender people may redirect or block authentic identity constructions, effectively isolating survivors and eroding their gendered self-concepts. These same hostilities function to keep survivors of T-IPV trapped within cyclical patterns of abuse, with fewer options for escape. (See chapter 4 for an examination of help-seeking barriers facing T-IPV survivors.) For transgender survivors of color, race and migration statuses further complicate the dynamics of abuse, such as when abusers threaten to report an undocumented immigrant survivor to authorities.

(See chapter 6 for more on the unique experiences of T-IPV among immigrants and people of color.)

Research has also begun to challenge traditional assumptions about which types of transgender people are more likely to be abusers versus survivors. Scholars and service providers have long drawn on power-based theoretical models; these envision IPV as emerging when an abuser has greater societal privilege than their partner, privilege that can be leveraged to obtain control in a relationship.[7] Despite the fact that power-based models were developed to explain IPV perpetrated by cisgender men against cisgender women, it is tempting to assume they will apply equally well to T-IPV. There is just one problem: power-based models ignore many abusive relationships that involve one or more transgender people.

Of course, in some instances of T-IPV, abusers do have and do leverage their comparatively greater societal privilege to maintain control over their partners. This can be the case in some relationships between cisgender abusers and transgender survivors, just as it can occur when transgender survivors belong to one or more other marginalized subpopulations. For instance, Xavier Guadalupe-Diaz and Carolyn West (chapter 6) noted that some white abusers who are US citizens leverage their societal privilege to control transgender immigrants and transgender people of color. As researchers Sandy James, Carter Brown, and Isaiah Wilson noted in their analysis of the US Transgender Survey (USTS), "among the most important findings was that many respondents were impacted by the compounding effects of multiple forms of discrimination, and transgender people of color who completed the survey experienced deeper and broader forms of discrimination than white USTS respondents and people in the U.S. population overall."[8] Faced with combinations of racism, xenophobia, classism, and transphobia, transgender people who are immigrants and/or people of color often encounter greater structural disadvantages (e.g., poverty, unemployment, etc.), institutional violence (e.g., police brutality), and various forms of interpersonal violence, which may make them more reliant upon and vulnerable to abusers (see chapter 6).[9] Transgender immigrants in particular may be more likely to stay with abusive partners, fearing that traditional help-seeking avenues (e.g., police, courts, etc.) pose a threat to their citizenship status and may increase their deportation risk.

At the same time, power-based models suffer from a key limitation: they fail to anticipate and help explain abusive relationships in which abusers appear to have less societal privilege than their partners. Quinn (chapter 2), as well as Guadalupe-Diaz and West (chapter 6), caution us to avoid an overly simplistic understanding of IPV as abuse perpetrated by the "haves" of society against the "have-nots." In reality, we are intersectional beings, with varying social locations with respect to our race, class, gender, sexuality, and so forth. Thus, as feminist and critical race theorists have long noted,[10] many individuals—including abusers—are simultaneously privileged and marginalized on different axes of demographic inequality. Moreover, traditional power-based models often overlook the ways in which abusers intentionally leverage their own marginalized status in society to gain control of survivors. For instance, consider Quinn's personal account of his previous IPV victimization, which he detailed in chapter 2. His abuser frequently masked or justified IPV by redirecting attention to the various ways in which the abuser herself was economically and socially marginalized in society.

Consequently, the research literature on T-IPV complicates traditional, cisnormative conceptualizations of who experiences relationship abuse. As is often also true of cisgender IPV, T-IPV does not conform neatly to a single narrative, such as transgender partners always being victims, or transgender identity being the sole factor in shaping the nature of abuse. As service providers, scholars, policymakers, friends, and family, we must discard preconceived notions of who can experience IPV and what abusive tactics look like, and be prepared to challenge abuse wherever it might arise.

Improving Societal Responses to T-IPV

A broader reframing of the role that gender plays in IPV requires that practitioners and policymakers alike challenge the cisnormative, heterosexist assumptions that currently shape many of the resources available to survivors. Transgender survivors contend with regulatory structures that make proper identity documentation difficult to obtain and therefore restrict many formal help-seeking avenues. Many existing policies require cost-prohibitive gender-affirming surgeries, mental health evaluations, legal representation, and more, just to begin the processes of recourse and recovery (see chapters 7 and 10). Legal recourse and interactions with law enforcement can also be hostile at times to transgender survivors, who are often criminalized by the same systems they may need to seek help from (see chapters 9 and 10). Often the ways in which advocates practice prevention and intervention programming are situated within a cisnormative framework (see chapters 8, 11, and 12). Mainstream IPV victim services struggle with providing safe places for transgender survivors that also integrate holistic and inclusive medical and mental health resources.

Throughout the volume, several takeaways construct a viable path toward improving transgender survivors' access to the criminal legal system and social services, while also meeting their medical and mental health needs. Structural responses to IPV typically include the police and courts in the criminal legal system, IPV shelters, and intervention programming, as well as medical and mental health resources. The cisnormative nature, inaccessibility, and oftentimes outright hostility of these structures can hinder efforts to seek help for T-IPV. While some scholars and activists argue against an overreliance on systems that have been historically hostile (e.g., law enforcement), offering harm-reducing solutions for the current structures could provide a way forward for many T-IPV survivors. The proceeding section summarizes some of the major points emphasized by chapter contributors that are necessary to advance how systems, advocates, and practitioners respond to T-IPV.

Police and Courts

Across the spectrum of gender identities, reporting abuse to the police is often among the least sought-after options for survivors of IPV.[11] Kae Greenberg noted in chapter 9 that for transgender people, ongoing patterns of abuse by law enforcement continue a historical legacy of criminalization and oppression. Even so, important changes to law enforcement response could improve access for T-IPV survivors who want to pursue legal recourse. Law enforcement agencies could improve their response by providing officer training that encourages more respectful interactions. Trainings that involve community members could include a basic history of the oppression and criminalization of transgender people in the US, an overview of gender diversity, proper name and pronoun usage, and a description of abusive tactics unique to T-IPV that officers may need to look for during investigations.

For IPV incidents, police are typically required to complete paperwork that requires the use of names that appear on government-issued identification documents. This means that, for transgender survivors, police paperwork often lists their given name either exclusively or above their chosen name. A more transgender-affirming policy would do the reverse: list preferred names either exclusively or above "legal" names. Additionally, a more respectful policing culture would rely less on stereotypes and outdated identity documents—instead, officers should ask transgender people for their name, gender identity, and pronouns. Similarly, police should never perform body searches to "confirm" a transgender person's anatomy (a humiliating and legally dubious action). Furthermore, body searches should be conducted with another officer present, with transgender individuals being given the option to select the gender of the searching officer.

The housing of transgender survivors in police custody should also be improved. Policy should ensure that transgender people in custody have access to the gender-specific or gender-neutral restroom of their choice. Furthermore, the removal of items used for gender expression should be limited. Incarcerated or detained transgender people should be allowed to select which gender-segregated space feels most safe for them, and corrections systems should not disclose their transgender status to others without permission.

Similarly, Leigh Goodmark (chapter 10) made several notable suggestions for court personnel and policies that would foster a more inclusive process for transgender survivors seeking legal recourse. Beyond trainings and education for court personnel, Goodmark noted the ways in which legal documents could better reflect the identities of transgender survivors. Court-issued protective orders should prioritize the use of names that transgender survivors utilize. Transphobic defense tactics like the "trans panic defense" should be dismissed in courtrooms.

While new policy directives and shifts can improve police and courtroom interactions with transgender populations, involving the community through oversight initiatives could provide more substantial feedback. Imagining solutions and alternatives that require minimal or no access to formal judicial or law enforcement assistance may reduce the reliance on a system that has historically revictimized many transgender survivors of IPV.

Shelters, Health Care, and Other Services

Improving responses to T-IPV requires reassessing how survivors access, use, and benefit from a wide range of social and health-care services. Beyond criminal legal recourses, T-IPV survivors may need assistance with transgender-inclusive housing, health care, programming, and intervention strategies. While in many of these areas better training and education are recommended, changes in the structure and design of services are also required.

Brian Tesch's (chapter 8) critique of the origins of IPV shelters reminds us that, by design, the overwhelming majority of IPV shelter services are tailored to the needs of cisgender women. The cisnormative conceptions of gender that often rigidly structure shelter spaces may inherently exclude transgender survivors from feeling safe and welcome. While limited space is an ongoing issue for many shelters, efforts to provide more gender-integrated housing would improve inclusivity for those transgender survivors who do not identify as women (e.g., nonbinary individuals and transgender men) or who prefer separate spaces. Intake paperwork and procedures should also work to include and respect chosen names and pronouns of all survivors.

Momen and DeKeseredy (chapter 4) noted how resilience and coping with violence is complicated for T-IPV survivors, as they face many more barriers to help seeking. Among these barriers are inadequately trained staff, fear of transphobia, and stigmatization. Given these realities, IPV services should strive to improve their competency in understanding and intervening in T-IPV. At the same time, michael munson and Loree Cook-Daniels (chapter 12) stress that cisgender IPV and T-IPV bear core similarities (e.g., power imbalance, controlling behaviors, shame, and fear) and, as such, with minimal additional training service providers used to serving cisgender survivors can and should become prepared to also serve transgender survivors. In this sense, referring transgender survivors out to transgender-specific organizations may not always be necessary, if more mainstream organizations mandated T-IPV-specific trainings for staff. Doing so would also dramatically increase the geographic availability of inclusive services for transgender survivors, particularly in the regions where transgender-focused IPV organizations are not present.

In reflecting on the distinct needs of T-IPV survivors, Shanna Kattari, Héctor Torres, Kim Fountain, and Ing Swenson (chapter 7) noted a lack of transgender-inclusive mental and medical health-care service models. Fear of and actual discrimination on the basis of transgender status keep many transgender survivors from seeking the treatments they need. Transgender-affirming staff, intake procedures, and screenings require that culturally sensitive policies and trainings are provided to ensure respectful and positive interactions with clients. Transgender survivors may be more likely than their cisgender counterparts to require assistance with gender-affirming treatments, the mental health consequences of family rejection, and trauma from multiple sources of conflict, violence, and abuse.

Improving How We Know

Throughout the volume, chapter authors regularly cited the fact that T-IPV research is still developing and emerging as a field. While the literature on IPV among lesbian, gay, bisexual, and queer individuals has expanded significantly in recent years, few of these studies have been fully transgender-inclusive in their efforts to intentionally recruit and survey transgender individuals. Furthermore, owing in part to the small size of transgender populations and the lack of funding for transgender-specific research, the studies that have been conducted on T-IPV often rely on smaller nonprobability samples.

Researching T-IPV is a complex task.[12] First, researchers must grapple with defining the transgender population for the purposes of sampling. In chapter 13, Adam Yerke and Jennifer DeFeo encourage researchers to utilize inclusive definitions that capture more transgender respondents. Importantly, because individuals' understandings of their gender identities can change over time, researchers should include questions that ask about the participant's gender not only at the time of data collection but also at the time they experienced IPV. While there are multiple methods for measuring transgender status—each having their own strengths and limitations—Yerke and DeFeo recommend the two-step process, which entails inquiring about gender identity as well as sex assigned at birth in two separate survey questions. Yerke and DeFeo recommend including a broad range of response categories for each question.

Given the small number of transgender people in many nations, probability samples of the general population rarely include enough transgender individuals to support analyses examining transgender participants, whether collectively or by subgroup. Partially as a result of these challenges, most T-IPV studies utilize nonprobability sampling methods. One common nonprobability technique—convenience sampling at lesbian, gay, bisexual, transgender, and queer (LGBTQ) organizations and community events—can increase the speed of sampling, but it often comes at the expense of the representativeness and generalizability of the data. This is because LGBTQ-centric public spaces may disproportionately overrepresent certain transgender people, such as those who are out or open about being transgender, those who live in urban areas, and those who live in LGBTQ-friendly neighborhoods that can be comparatively homogenous with respect to race, income, and other demographic characteristics. Thus, to diversify their samples, researchers are advised to expand the variety of recruitment sites used for sampling, both in the physical world and, for web-based surveys, on the internet.

Beyond how transgender status is measured, IPV survey questions could be improved by utilizing more gender-neutral language in question phrasing. For example, survey questions that use binary gender pronouns like "he or she" may exclude nonbinary individuals and those who are partnered with them. Commonly used survey instruments like the Conflict Tactics Scale also leave out transgender-specific tactics of abuse.[13] Measures that include transphobic identity abuse tactics can capture a wider range of T-IPV experiences.

Ending T-IPV

As Adam Messinger (chapter 5) notes, theories and data illuminating why T-IPV happens may be the key to reducing its prevalence and impact on survivors. Rebecca Howard, Sharyn Potter, Taylor Flagg, Mary Moynihan, and Zachary Ahmad-Kahloon (chapter 11) remind us that the causes of—and so, too, the solutions to—T-IPV exist at multiple levels of the social ecological model, including the individual, relationship, community, and societal levels. Importantly, as will be reviewed below, even causes that appear at first glance to originate at the individual level tie back to societal-level discrimination. In the end, the contributions in this book repeatedly lead back to one important conclusion: multiple intersecting systems of oppression make transgender people more susceptible to abuse, and therefore it will take a multilevel approach to end T-IPV.

T-IPV Causes at the Relationship, Community, and Societal Levels

At three of the four levels of the social ecological model—relationship, community, and societal—transgender people face a variety of conditions largely beyond their immediate control that either increase their risk of abuse or inhibit their ability to escape it. These conditions include a society which interpersonally and through laws discriminates against transgender people.[14] This discrimination in turn can motivate abusers to similarly devalue their transgender partners,[15] just as it can provide abusers with unique IPV tactics that leverage anti-transgender discrimination to obtain control over their partners.[16] (See chapter 1 for a review of the intersections between interpersonal transphobia, law-based discrimination, and T-IPV.) At the same time, not surprisingly, transphobic discrimination has negatively shaped how potential sources of help view and treat transgender survivors, including some mental and medical health-care providers (see chapter 7), IPV victim shelter staff (see chapter 8), law enforcement (see chapter 9), and other criminal justice system employees such as court and correctional personnel (see chapter 10). Transphobia is common enough that it deters many T-IPV survivors from seeking out a variety of these services (see chapter 4).[17] Being aware of the extent to which transgender people are often isolated from support networks, abusers may be emboldened to initiate and escalate abuse.

T-IPV Causes at the Individual Level

Individual-level causes of T-IPV are often linked to societal discrimination, and thus they require a societal-level solution. To begin, at the individual level, research indicates that survivors and abusers alike often draw upon myths to rationalize T-IPV—such as the myth that IPV is an appropriate tool for validating either a transgender abuser's or survivor's gender identity, or the myth that abuse is a normal response to conflict.[18] The ability to rationalize T-IPV may make it easier for abusers to neutralize potential guilt over initiating and escalating abuse, and, conversely, it may make it harder for survivors to recognize and challenge abuse. (See chapters 2 and 5 for reviews of T-IPV rationalizations.)

Significantly, these T-IPV-condoning attitudes are not innate, inevitable psychological traits. Instead, these attitudes often are rooted in broader societal discrimination. For instance, acceptance of the myth that abuse is a healthy conflict-resolution strategy is often theorized to be caused in part by experiencing family violence, such as child abuse, a theory empirically supported by associations found between T-IPV victimization and family violence exposure.[19] Although discrimination is not the sole cause of family violence exposure, it is undoubtedly one of the causal factors among transgender youth, given that transgender people are estimated to be two to ten times more likely than cisgender people to experience violence by a relative or someone else close to them.[20]

Likewise, the collection of myths that falsely imply that T-IPV can validate one's gender—such as the myths that "real" transgender men should perpetrate IPV, that "real" transgender women want to be abused, and that "real" transgender men cannot be raped because they must always want sex—is reinforced by a culture that constantly questions the legitimacy of the gender identity of transgender people. Consider that all but fifty-one nations deny transgender people the right to change their gender identity on official government documents such as birth certificates and passports,[21] and 49 percent of US transgender individuals who have had an interaction with the police in the last year in which they believed the police knew they were transgender report that the police intentionally used incorrect gender pronouns or titles.[22] Quinn (chapter 2) reflects on the impact of this societal erasure of transgender identities on his own prior experience with abuse: "When my partner denied my gender identity, it was difficult for me to identify it as gaslighting because the rest of the world was consistently creating that same feeling inside me." Indeed, counting on the societal stigma often attached to transgender people who are transitioning, many abusers intentionally attempt to discredit the identity work of their partners as a means of gaining control.[23] (See chapter 3 for more on the discrediting of identity work in T-IPV.) In this sense, T-IPV-condoning attitudes do not arbitrarily emerge in the minds of survivors and perpetrators but rather are indirectly fostered by societal discrimination.

Similarly, societal discrimination may be at least partially responsible for other individual-level covariates of T-IPV victimization identified in research. Studies have linked T-IPV victimization with experiencing bullying, anti-transgender hate crimes or bias incidents, and interpersonal discrimination.[24] As Messinger (chapter 5) reviews, it is theorized that such experiences may heighten one's awareness of societal transphobia, which could in turn decrease self-esteem and trust in potential sources of help and ultimately embolden abusers to initiate and escalate abuse.[25] Of course, each of these risk factors for T-IPV are themselves almost certainly motivated in part by the pervasiveness of transphobia in society.

Other individual-level risk factors for T-IPV victimization—living with HIV, having a disability, having ever engaged in sex work, having been incarcerated, and being an undocumented immigrant[26]—represent characteristics of some transgender people that may increase their emotional and financial reliance on abusers, decrease their faith in sources of help, and, finally, embolden abusers to perpetrate IPV. Again, discrimination is often a contributing cause of many of these risk factors; for example, transphobia in schools and the workplace pushes many transgender people toward underground economies and incarceration. Moreover, societal discrimination against each of these groups (such as discrimination against individuals living with HIV or who have a disability) and criminalization in some cases (such as with respect to undocumented immigrants and sex workers) can depress help-seeking rates—and, in the end, isolate survivors and empower abusers.

Addressing T-IPV at All Levels of the Social Ecological Model

Too often IPV is assumed to be caused predominantly by individual-level factors, and thus it may be tempting to rely solely on solutions that can most directly reduce an individual's risk. This might entail tailoring primary prevention education programs, survivor mental health-care treatments, and court-mandated batterer intervention programs to undermine myths and attitudes condoning T-IPV (see chapters 7 and 11). Likewise, strategies can be employed to decrease the prevalence of common T-IPV risk factors (e.g., implementing safe sex education to decrease rates of HIV, anti-bullying prevention programs to decrease bullying rates, etc.). However, while important steps, this individual-focused approach may be ineffective if societal discrimination—which reinforces individual-level risk factors and which can limit the inclusivity of resources for survivors—is not simultaneously addressed. Moreover, as Guadalupe-Diaz and West emphasize (chapter 6), transgender survivors of IPV often live at the intersections of multiple marginalized identities, and thus it becomes doubly important to champion the human rights of all.

Ending transgender intimate partner violence truly will take a village.

NOTES

1 Guadalupe-Diaz and Anthony 2017, 8.
2 Guadalupe-Diaz 2013.
3 Walker 2015.
4 Messinger 2017.
5 Dank et al. 2014; Griner et al. 2017; Hoxmeier 2016; Hoxmeier and Madlem 2018; James et al. 2016; Landers and Gilsanz 2009; Langenderfer-Magruder et al. 2016; Pitts et al. 2006; Turell 2000; Valentine et al. 2017.
6 Guadalupe-Diaz and Anthony 2017.
7 See Anderson 2005; Dobash and Dobash 2003.
8 James, Brown, and Wilson 2017, 2.
9 de Vries 2015.
10 E.g., Crenshaw 1990; West and Fenstermaker 1995.
11 Guadalupe-Diaz 2016; Kurdyla, Messinger, and Ramirez, 2019.
12 Messinger 2017.
13 Straus 1979; Straus et al. 1996.
14 Ipsos Public Affairs 2018; James et al. 2016; Trans Respect versus Transphobia Worldwide, n.d.
15 E.g., Guadalupe-Diaz and Anthony 2017; Singh and McKleroy 2011.
16 James et al. 2016.
17 Kurdyla, Messinger, and Ramirez 2019; Langenderfer-Magruder et al. 2016; Roch, Morton, and Ritchie 2010.
18 Goodmark 2013; Parsons et al. 2018; White Hughto et al. 2017.
19 Parsons et al. 2018; White Hughto et al. 2017.
20 Browne 2007; Flentje et al. 2016.
21 Trans Respect versus Transphobia Worldwide, n.d.

22 James et al. 2016.
23 Guadalupe-Diaz and Anthony 2017.
24 Brennan et al. 2012; Goldenberg, Jadwin-Cakmak, and Harper 2018; Shipherd et al. 2011; White Hughto et al. 2017.
25 Messinger 2017.
26 Brennan et al. 2012; Goldenberg, Jadwin-Cakmak, and Harper 2018; James et al. 2016.

REFERENCES

Anderson, Kristin L. 2005. "Theorizing Gender in Intimate Partner Violence Research." *Sex Roles* 52 (11–12): 853–865.

Brennan, Julia, Lisa M. Kuhns, Amy K. Johnson, Marvin Belzer, Erin C. Wilson, and Robert Garofalo. 2012. "Syndemic Theory and HIV-Related Risk among Young Transgender Women: The Role of Multiple, Co-occurring Health Problems and Social Marginalization." *American Journal of Public Health* 102 (9): 1751–1757.

Browne, Kath. 2007. *Count Me in Too: LGBT Lives in Brighton & Hove: Initial Findings: Academic Report.* Brighton, England: Kath Brown and Spectrum. www.realadmin.co.uk.

Crenshaw, Kimberle. 1990. "Mapping the Margins: Intersectionality, Identity Politics, and Violence Against Women of Color." *Stanford Law Review* 43 (6): 1241-1299.

Dank, Meredith, Pamela Lachman, Janine M. Zweig, and Jennifer Yahner. 2014. "Dating Violence Experiences of Lesbian, Gay, Bisexual, and Transgender Youth." *Journal of Youth and Adolescence* 43 (5): 846–857.

de Vries, Kylan Mattias. 2015. "Transgender People of Color at the Center: Conceptualizing a New Intersectional Model." *Ethnicities* 15 (1): 3–27.

Dobash, R. Emerson, and Russell P. Dobash. 2003. *Women, Violence and Social Change.* New York: Routledge.

Flentje, Annesa, Armando Leon, Adam Carrico, Debbie Zheng, and James Dilley. 2016. "Mental and Physical Health among Homeless Sexual and Gender Minorities in a Major Urban US City." *Journal of Urban Health* 93 (6): 997–1009.

Goldenberg, Tamar, Laura Jadwin-Cakmak, and Gary W. Harper. 2018. "Intimate Partner Violence among Transgender Youth: Associations with Intrapersonal and Structural Factors." *Violence and Gender* 5 (1): 19–25.

Goodmark, Leigh. 2013. "Transgender People, Intimate Partner Abuse, and the Legal System." *Harvard Civil Rights–Civil Liberties Law Review* 48 (1): 51–104.

Griner, Stacey B., Cheryl A. Vamos, Erika L. Thompson, Rachel Logan, Coralia Vázquez-Otero, and Ellen M. Daley. 2017. "The Intersection of Gender Identity and Violence: Victimization Experienced by Transgender College Students." *Journal of Interpersonal Violence.* https://doi.org/10.1177/0886260517723743.

Guadalupe-Diaz, Xavier L. 2013. "Victims outside the Binary: Transgender Survivors of Intimate Partner Violence." PhD diss., University of Central Florida.

Guadalupe-Diaz, Xavier L. 2016. "Disclosure of Same-sex Intimate Partner Violence to Police Among Lesbians, Gays, and Bisexuals." *Social Currents* 3 (2): 160–171.

Guadalupe-Diaz, Xavier L., and Amanda Koontz Anthony. 2017. "Discrediting Identity Work: Understandings of Intimate Partner Violence by Transgender Survivors." *Deviant Behavior* 38 (1): 1–16.

Hoxmeier, Jill C. 2016. "Sexual Assault and Relationship Abuse Victimization of Transgender Undergraduate Students in a National Sample." *Violence and Gender* 3 (4): 202–207.

Hoxmeier, Jill C., and Melody Madlem. 2018. "Discrimination and Interpersonal Violence: Reported Experiences of Trans* Undergraduate Students." *Violence and Gender* 5 (1): 12–18.

Ipsos Public Affairs. 2018. *Global Attitudes toward Transgender People*. New York: Ipsos Public Affairs. www.ipsos.com.

James, Sandy E., Jody L. Herman, Susan Rankin, Mara Keisling, Lisa Mottet, and Ma'ayan Anafi. 2016. *The Report of the 2015 US Transgender Survey*. Washington, DC: National Center for Transgender Equality. www.ustranssurvey.org.

James, Sandy E., Carter Brown, and Isaiah Wilson. 2017. *2015 U.S. Transgender Survey: Report on the Experiences of Black Respondents*. Washington, DC and Dallas, TX: National Center for Transgender Equality, Black Trans Advocacy, and National Black Justice Coalition. www.ustranssurvey.org.

Kurdyla, Victoria A., Adam M. Messinger, and Milka Ramirez. 2019. "Transgender Intimate Partner Violence and Help-Seeking Patterns." *Journal of Interpersonal Violence*. https://doi.org/10.1177/0886260519880171.

Landers, Stewart, and Paola Gilsanz. 2009. *The Health of Lesbian, Gay, Bisexual, and Transgender (LGBT) Persons in Massachusetts: A Survey of Health Issues Comparing LGBT Persons with Their Heterosexual and Non-transgender Counterparts*. Boston: Massachusetts Department of Public Health. www.masstpc.org.

Langenderfer-Magruder, Lisa, Darren L. Whitfield, N. Eugene Walls, Shanna K. Kattari, and Daniel Ramos. 2016. "Experiences of Intimate Partner Violence and Subsequent Police Reporting Among Lesbian, Gay, Bisexual, Transgender, and Queer Adults in Colorado: Comparing Rates of Cisgender and Transgender Victimization." *Journal of Interpersonal Violence* 31 (5): 855–871.

Messinger, Adam M. 2017. *LGBTQ Intimate Partner Violence: Lessons for Policy, Practice, and Research*. Oakland: University of California Press.

Parsons, Jeffrey T., Nadav Antebi-Gruszka, Brett M. Millar, Demetria Cain, and Sitaji Gurung. 2018. "Syndemic Conditions, HIV Transmission Risk Behavior, and Transactional Sex among Transgender Women." *AIDS and Behavior* 22 (7): 1–12.

Pitts, Marian, Anthony Smith, Anne Mitchell, and Sunil Patel. 2006. *Private Lives: A Report on the Health and Wellbeing of GLBTI Australians*. Melbourne: Australian Research Centre in Sex, Health and Society, La Trobe University. www.glhv.org.au.

Roch, Amy, James Morton, and Graham Ritchie. 2010. *Out of Sight, out of Mind? Transgender People's Experiences of Domestic Abuse*. Edinburgh: LGBT Youth Scotland and the Scottish Transgender Alliance. www.scottishtrans.org.

Shipherd, Jillian C., Shira Maguen, W. Christopher Skidmore, and Sarah M. Abramovitz. 2011. "Potentially Traumatic Events in a Transgender Sample: Frequency and Associated Symptoms." *Traumatology* 17 (2): 56–67.

Singh, Anneliese, and Vel S. McKleroy. 2011. "'Just Getting Out of Bed Is a Revolutionary Act': The Resilience of Transgender People of Color Who Have Survived Traumatic Life Events." *Traumatology* 17 (2): 34–44.

Straus, Murray A. 1979. "Measuring Intrafamily Conflict and Violence: The Conflict Tactics (CT) Scales." *Journal of Marriage and the Family* 41 (1): 75–88.

Straus, Murray A., Sherry L. Hamby, Sue Boney-McCoy, and David B. Sugarman. 1996. "The Revised Conflict Tactics Scale (CTS2): Development and Preliminary Psychometric Data." *Journal of Family Issues* 17 (3): 283–316.

Trans Respect versus Transphobia Worldwide. n.d. "Legal and Social Mapping." July 1, 2018. https://transrespect.org.

Turell, Susan C. 2000. "A Descriptive Analysis of Same-Sex Relationship Violence for a Diverse Sample." *Journal of Family Violence* 15 (3): 281–293.

Valentine, Sarah E., Sarah M. Peitzmeier, Dana S. King, Conall O'Cleirigh, Samantha M. Marquez, Cara Presley, and Jennifer Potter. 2017. "Disparities in Exposure to Intimate Partner Violence among Transgender/Gender Nonconforming and Sexual Minority Primary Care Patients." *LGBT Health* 4 (4): 260–267.

Walker, Julia K. 2015. "Investigating Trans People's Vulnerabilities to Intimate Partner Violence/Abuse." *Partner Abuse* 6 (1): 107–125.

West, Candace, and Sarah Fenstermaker. 1995. "Doing Difference." *Gender & Society* 9 (1): 8–37.

White Hughto, Jaclyn M., John E. Pachankis, Tiara C. Willie, and Sari L. Reisner. 2017. "Victimization and Depressive Symptomology in Transgender Adults: The Mediating Role of Avoidant Coping." *Journal of Counseling Psychology* 64 (1): 41–51.

ABOUT THE EDITORS

Adam M. Messinger, PhD, is Associate Professor of Justice Studies and of Women's and Gender Studies at Northeastern Illinois University, where he researches intimate partner violence in the relationships of lesbian, gay, bisexual, transgender, and queer people (LGBTQ IPV). His most recent book, *LGBTQ Intimate Partner Violence: Lessons for Policy, Practice, and Research*, provides an in-depth look at the last forty years of LGBTQ IPV research, drawing evidence-based tips for future public policy and service provision.

Xavier L. Guadalupe-Diaz, PhD, is Associate Professor of Sociology and Criminology at Framingham State University in Massachusetts. His primary research focuses on various aspects of intimate partner and sexual violence in LGBTQ relationships, including help seeking, campus sexual assault, victimization and identity, emotional abuse, and police disclosure. He is the author of *Transgressed: Intimate Partner Violence in Transgender Lives*.

ABOUT THE CONTRIBUTORS

Zachary Ahmad-Kahloon, MPH, CHES, is Prevention Specialist at the Sexual Harassment and Rape Prevention Program at the University of New Hampshire. He has served on the leadership council of the Campus Advocacy and Prevention Professionals Association, as well as the Advisory Board of the Association of Title IX Administrators. His work focuses on how underserved and marginalized populations are centered in the field of intimate partner violence.

Connie Burk is a principal at the National Anti-Violence Advocacy Initiative, where she works with programs and institutes across the nation seeking to revitalize a survivor-centered, whole-community approach to anti-violence work. For two decades, Burk led the nationally recognized NW Network of Bisexual, Trans, Lesbian & Gay Survivors of Abuse. She is the co-author of the best-selling book *Trauma Stewardship: An Everyday Guide for Caring for Self While Caring for Others*, the author of "Think Re-Think: Accountable Communities" in the book *The Revolution Starts at Home*, and an executive producer of the award-winning documentary *A Lot like You*.

Loree Cook-Daniels, MS, is Policy and Program Director for FORGE. Previous book chapters by Cook-Daniels have appeared in *Transgender and Gender Nonconforming Health and Aging*; *Elder Abuse: Research, Practice and Policy*; and *Addressing the Sexual Rights of Older People: Theory, Policy, and Practice*.

Jennifer DeFeo, PhD, is a clinical psychologist, associate professor, and distinguished professor of psychology. Dr. DeFeo is an active national and international speaker and has presented over two hundred conference presentations on topics such as psychopharmacology, diagnostic and assessment of mental health disorders, neuropsychology, and working with LGBTQ+ populations. Dr. DeFeo presently supervises trainees and interns working with sexual assault and intimate partner violence while also maintaining a private practice, teaching at Mount Saint Mary University in Los Angeles, California, and Oregon State University in Bend, Oregon. Dr. DeFeo is a first lieutenant in the California State Guard and functions as a behavioral health officer.

Walter S. DeKeseredy, PhD, is Anna Deane Carlson Endowed Chair of Social Sciences, Director of the Research Center on Violence, and Professor of Sociology at West Virginia University. He has published more than twenty books and over one hundred scientific journal articles on issues such as violence against women, rural crime and social control, and critical criminological theory.

Taylor Flagg, MA, is Campus and Community Coordinator for uSafeUS at Prevention Innovations Research Center, an internationally recognized research center at the University of New Hampshire dedicated to ending sexual and relationship violence and stalking through the power of effective practitioner and research partnerships. Flagg works to implement uSafeUS, a prevention and response app, at all of the colleges and universities in New Hampshire.

Kim Fountain, PhD, is Chief Operating Officer at Center on Halsted, the Midwest's largest LGBTQ community center. Her formal training is in cultural anthropology, particularly within the field of social suffering. She has worked in the LGBTQ movement for twenty-five years.

Leigh Goodmark, JD, is Professor of Law and Co-Director of the Clinical Law Program at the University of Maryland Carey School of Law, where she directs the Gender Violence Clinic. Professor Goodmark is the author of *Decriminalizing Domestic Violence: A Balanced Policy Approach to Intimate Partner Violence* and *A Troubled Marriage: Domestic Violence and the Legal System*, and the co-editor of *Comparative Perspectives on Gender Violence: Lessons from Efforts Worldwide*.

Kae Greenberg, JD, is Staff Attorney in the Housing Unit of Community Legal Services in Philadelphia, where he provides eviction defense for low-income tenants. Prior to this, Greenberg was an Assistant Defender at the Defender Association of Philadelphia. Throughout his legal career he has attempted to improve services for trans clients, and he currently serves as a member of the Mayor's Commission on LGBT Affairs.

Rebecca Howard, MA, is a former project manager at Prevention Innovations Research Center at the University of New Hampshire, where her research focused on sexual violence prevention among college students. Her previous publications have documented the short- and long-term effects of sexual violence on survivors' education, careers, and mental health.

Shanna K. Kattari, PhD, MEd, CSE, ACS, is Assistant Professor of Social Work and Women's Studies (by courtesy) at the University of Michigan, as well as core faculty at the Center for Sexuality and Health Disparities and director of the Sexuality | Relationships | Gender Research collective. Dr. Kattari's research focuses on barriers and facilitators to affirming care for trans and nonbinary individuals, sexuality across contexts, and disability/ableism/microaggressions, using an intersectional and transdisciplinary approach. She is committed to collaborative, mixed methods, interdisciplinary, and community-engaged research that centers the voices and experiences of marginalized individuals and groups.

Amanda Koontz, PhD, is Associate Professor of Sociology at the University of Central Florida. Her primary areas of interest include social inequalities, culture and consumption, identities, and social psychology. Her current work focuses on narratives and consumption in gendered identity negotiation, understanding connections between identity work and the negotiation of cultural resources, market representations of "authenticity," and art world boundaries. Her articles have appeared in *Journal of Consumer Culture*, the *Sociological Quarterly*, and *Social Currents*.

Rayna E. Momen, MA, is a sociology doctoral student awarded a W. E. B. Du Bois Fellowship at West Virginia University. Momen has several manuscripts forthcoming.

Mary M. Moynihan, PhD, is Adjunct Associate Professor of the Department of Women's and Gender Studies at the University of New Hampshire. Dr. Moynihan is a cofounder and the Prevention and Evaluation Consultant for Prevention Innovations Research Center at the University of New Hampshire. She is also a co-creator of the Bringing in the Bystander Prevention Workshop for Establishing a Community of Responsibility and the Know Your Power Bystander Social Marketing Campaign. In addition, Moynihan co-developed a number of the evidence-based measures of bystander action to prevent sexual violence, intimate partner violence, and stalking and has co-authored a number of peer-reviewed articles focusing on bystander prevention outcomes with college students and members of the United States military.

michael munson is Executive Director of FORGE, a national training and technical assistance organization. Munson's educational background is in psychology, with an emphasis on trauma-informed care and nontraditional healing modalities. His work on violence against transgender and nonbinary individuals stresses the intersectionality between complex components of identity, experience, and societal constructs that can both spur violence and catalyze healing.

Sharyn J. Potter, PhD, MPH, is Professor in the Department of Women's and Gender Studies and co-founder and Executive Director of Research at Prevention Innovations Research Center at the University of New Hampshire. Dr. Potter is a global leader on the social scientific development and evaluation of bystander intervention strategies. Dr. Potter's work focuses on engaging community members to work collaboratively to reduce sexual and relationship violence, stalking, and harassment in high schools, colleges and universities, the United States military, and other workplaces.

Xavier Quinn is a licensed clinical social worker and the manager of the Violence Recovery Program at Fenway Health in Boston, Massachusetts. He has worked with survivors of intimate partner violence for sixteen years and specifically with LGBTQ survivors since 2009. He also is the author of *Open Minds Open Doors: Transforming Domestic Violence Shelters to Include LGBTQ Survivors*.

Ing Swenson, MSW, is a licensed clinical social worker and a certified reciprocal alcohol and drug counselor specializing in working with trans, gender nonconforming, and nonbinary communities. He received his master's in social work at Jane Addams School of Social Work in 2002 and his training in addictions in Seattle, Washington, in 2011. His clinical approach is LGBTQ affirmative, strength based, client centered, harm reduction, informed consent, and trauma informed. He currently works as Director of Behavioral Health at Center on Halsted, the Midwest's largest and most comprehensive LGBTQ community center.

Brian Tesch, MA, is currently working on his PhD in sociology at Mississippi State University. He has previously researched the ways that law enforcement responds to same-sex intimate partner violence (as seen in his 2010 article "Same-Sex Domestic Violence: Why Victims Are More at Risk"), and transgender intimate partner violence (as seen in his 2015 article "Hidden in the Margins: A Qualitative Examination of What Professionals in the Domestic Violence Field Know about Transgender Domestic Violence"). At present, he is studying the ways that the theoretical intersections of transgender theory, queer theory, and feminist theory can be used to analyze, comprehend, and address the social construct of intimate partner violence

Héctor Torres, PsyD, is a social service administrator, educator, and clinical psychologist. His work with the LGBTQ community started in 1996. Since then, Dr. Torres has been involved in the development, implementation, administration, and supervision of several government-funded and foundation-funded projects addressing LGBTQ health issues. He currently works as Chief Program Officer at Center on Halsted, the Midwest's largest and most comprehensive LGBTQ community center.

Carolyn M. West, PhD, is Professor of Clinical Psychology and the Division Chair of Social, Behavioral, and Human Sciences in the School of Interdisciplinary Arts and Sciences at the University of Washington Tacoma. Dr. West is author of more than eighty publications, including the award-winning book *Violence in the Lives of Black Women: Battered, Black, and Blue*.

Adam F. Yerke, PsyD is a licensed psychologist, Associate Professor, and Interim Department Chair for the Clinical Forensic Psychology Program at the Chicago School of Professional Psychology in Southern California. He is an expert on policies concerning transgender people and has published several peer-reviewed journal articles and book chapters on timely topics including transgender people and the armed forces, athletic policies for transgender youth and adults, and intimate partner violence among the transgender population.

INDEX

abuse. *See* intimate partner violence; transgender IPV
African Americans: IPV victimization prevalence among, 137–38, *138*; non-IPV violence and, *141*; police and, 148; stop and frisk related to, 241–42; structural violence and, *142*. *See also* Black women
AIAN. *See* American Indians and Alaskan Natives
altercasting. *See* identity abuse
American Indians and Alaskan Natives (AIAN): IPV victimization prevalence among, *138*, 139; non-IPV violence and, *141*; structural violence and, *142*
ANHPI. *See* Asian Americans, Native Hawaiians, and Pacific Islanders
anti-violence movement: multiple contexts and, x; transgender rights movement and, ix–x. *See also specific organizations*
Asian Americans, Native Hawaiians, and Pacific Islanders (ANHPI): IPV victimization prevalence among, *138*, 139; non-IPV violence and, *141*; structural violence and, *142*

barriers to help seeking. *See* help seeking barriers
bathroom. *See* restrooms
battered women's movement, 203–4
batterer intervention programs (BIPs), 21, 56, 123
Black women: *Battle Cries* and, 153; gay rights movement and, 224; murder and, 134; sex workers and, 270

causes. *See* theories of T-IPV causation
children: ACE study and, 313–14; barriers to escape and, 93; discrimination and, 14; intergenerational transmission of violence theory and, 114; IPV victim shelters and, 209; parental rights and, 117; survival crimes and, 228; threats related to, 19; victim vulnerabilities and, 117; videos supporting, 329
C-IPV. *See* cisgender IPV
cisgender: abuse assumptions related to, 110; barriers to escape and, 93; defined, 3; honour-based violence theory and, 118–19; oriented services, 208–10; police and, 147–49, 231–32
cisgender IPV (C-IPV): causal pathways shared with, 111–17; cisnormative causation and, 110; defined, 5; implications of T-IPV theories and, 123; intergenerational transmission of violence theory and, 113–14; neutralization techniques in, 112; rationalizations by abusers in, 112–13; victim framing and, 112–13; victim vulnerabilities in, 115–17
cisnormative: bias in criminal justice and, 149; causation, 110; defined, 3; limiting T-IPV awareness, 5–6; police and, 4–5, 149; seeking help against, 4–5; shelters, emergence of, 203–4
civil legal system, protective orders and, 260–61

387

coping with T-IPV victimization: conclusions related to, 100–103; cyber abuse and, 102; defined, 92; factors promoting, 99–100; family relationships and, 99; financial resources and, 99–100; help seeking patterns and, 98–99; intersectionality and, 101; overview, 91; pride and, 99; resilience and, 55–56, 92, 98–103; spirituality and, 100
correctional system and detention, 141, 151, 267
court system: charging decisions, 259–60; court clerks, 265; discrimination in, 264–65; lessons related to, 366–68; protective orders, 260–61; trans panic defense in, 265–66; transphobic harassment and, 264–65; transphobic legal strategies, 265–66; undocumented immigrants and, 269–70
covariates of T-IPV victimization. *See* risk factors for T-IPV victimization
cultural abuse. *See* identity abuse
cultural awareness training, 244–45
culturally responsive care: affirmative approach, 187; APA affirming, 177; client-centered, 189–90; core mental health services, 186–90; education supporting, 177–79; in health services, 177–90; mandatory education for, 178–79; multisystem mental health framework, 186; organizational culture improvement, 190; referrals and, 184–85; strengths-based approach, 187; training for, 179; trauma-informed approach, 187–89; victim screening for, 179–84
cyber IPV, 8, 102

dating violence. *See* intimate partner violence; transgender IPV
detention centers, 151. *See also* correctional system and detention

Diagnostic and Statistical Manual of Mental Disorders (*DSM*): gender dysphoria and, 175–76; as transphobic, 176
disabilities, victimization related to, 115
discrediting identity work, 63, 67–68
discrimination: background of, 10–11; barriers to escape and, 93; children and, 14; codified in law, 13; correctional system, 267; in court system, 264–65; education, 14–15; employment, 11–13, 12, 100; family, 12; fear of, 171; financial dependence and, 96–97; global laws related to, 16; good intentions disguising, 174–76; health care, 15, 172–77; in health care admissions and services, 173–74; health care provider competence and, 172–77; health care provider effects of, 176–77; housing, 12, 13; human rights restrictions, 13–17; identity documents and, 14; interpersonal transphobia, 11–13; in IPV victim shelters, 206–7; marriage, 13–14; National Transgender Discrimination Survey, 284; parental rights and, 117; police, 262–64; power, 174–76; prevalence, 12; public accommodations, 12, 13; public restrooms and, 15; right to exist, 16–17; school, 12; T-IPV and, 10–20; T-IPV help seeking and, 19–20; T-IPV motivations and, 17; T-IPV tactics and, 18–19; victimization vulnerability theories and, 121; by victim service resources, 133
disempowerment theory. *See* theories of T-IPV causation
domestic violence. *See* intimate partner violence; transgender IPV
DSM. *See Diagnostic and Statistical Manual of Mental Disorders*

economics: financial abuse and, 51–52; T-IPV impact on, 9–10; victim vulnerabilities and, 117

education: adult, 330; anti-transphobia, 123; culturally responsive care and, 177–79; discrimination, 14–15; IPV victim shelters need for, 212–15; mandatory, 178–79; service provision guidelines for, 177–78; training need in, 179
emotional abuse. *See* psychological IPV
emotional dependence: as barrier to escape, 93, *94*, 97; social network and, 97
employment discrimination, 11–13, *12*, 100

family: discrimination, *12*; intergenerational transmission of violence theory and, 114; prevention and, 290; resilience and, 99; victim vulnerabilities and, 116–17; violence, 134
fear: of being outed, 93, *94*, 96; of incarceration, 230; of police, 226–29; of provider discrimination, 171; of services, 315; of stigmatizing transgender communities, 93, *94*, 97; T-IPV impact on, 10
feminist IPV theory, 203–4
financial abuse. *See* psychological IPV
financial dependence: as barrier to escape, 93, *94*, 96–97; discrimination and, 96–97; homelessness and, 97
FORGE, 183, 243, 312; ACE study and, 313–14; additional resources of, 332–33; adult education trainings by, 330; case studies used by, 329; conclusions, 331–32; cost minimization recommendations of, 326–27; data dissemination by, 328–29; *Gender-Integrated Shelters* advice from, 328; legal provisions training by, 323–25; nonbinary survivors recommendations by, 327; oppression model and, 313; *Part of the Solution* advice from, 328; philosophies of, 313; resource sharing of, 330–31; revictimization avoidance recommendations of, 326; role-plays training by, 330; service integration recommendations of, 325–27; terms paradox training by, 331; training and publications of, 323–31; videos used by, 329
FORGE study: awareness of services and, 316; barriers from provider side in, 320–23, *321*, *322*; barriers from transgender survivor side in, 314–19; cultural competency worries and, 315–16; fear of services and, 315; help seeking making matters worse and, 317–18; men and, 320–21, *321*; reputation of service and, 316; seeking help elsewhere and, 318–19; shame, stigma, embarrassment and, 317; systemic problems and, 319; trust lack and, 318; unwanted/unneeded service, 319; welcome worry and, 315; woman-focused agencies and, 317

gaslighting, xi, 45
Gay-Straight Alliances (GSAs), 295, 298
gender-based violence, terminology nuances, 312
gender dysphoria, 53, 175–76
gender expression: gifts and, 47; manipulating, 46–48
gender identity: court system and, 264–65; neutralization techniques and, 112
Genders and Sexualities Alliances. *See* Gay-Straight Alliances
gender-segregated services, 93, *94*, 96
generic social processes approach, 69–70
Global North and South, 102
GSAs. *See* Gay-Straight Alliances

healing from T-IPV victimization. *See* coping with T-IPV victimization
health care. *See* medical health care services; mental health; mental health care services; public health framework
hegemonic masculinity, shame and, 94–95

help seeking barriers: awareness of victimization, 93–94, *94*; criminal legal system, 259–60; discrimination and, 4–5, 19–20; emotional dependence, 93, *94*, 97; to escape, 93–97, *94*; fear of being outed, 93, *94*, 96; fear of stigmatizing transgender communities, 93, *94*, 97; financial dependence, 93, *94*, 96–97; in FORGE study, 314–23, *321*, *322*; gender-segregated services, 93, *94*, 96; to health care access, 170–72; hegemonic masculinity and, 94–95; help seeking and, 93–97; and identity, race, and immigration, 147–54; intersectionality and, 101; knowledge, 93, *94*, 95–96; to legal remedies, 259–61; overview, 91, 93, 317–18; resources, 95–96; self-blame, 93, *94*, 94–95; shame, 93, *94*, 94–95; transphobia-fueled isolation, 93, *94*, 97

HIV. *See* human immunodeficiency virus

homelessness: financial dependence and, 97; victim vulnerabilities and, 116

homeless shelter, 211

honour-based violence theory. *See* theories of T-IPV causation

hormone therapy: as abuse excuse, 40; honour-based violence theory and, 119

housing discrimination, *12*, 13

human immunodeficiency virus (HIV): causes distinguished from outcomes and, 125; T-IPV impact on, 10; victimization related to, 115

human rights: children and, 14; education and, 14–15; to exist, 16–17; health care and, 15; identity documents and, 14; marriage, 13–14; public restrooms and, 15; restrictions, 13–17; T-IPV tactics and, 18–19

ICE. *See* Immigration Customs Enforcement

identity: Census, US, and, 285; documents, 14; help seeking and, 147–54; social construction and racialization of, 135–37

identity abuse: altercasting and, 67–68, 70–71, 73–81; criminal legal system and, 260; defined, 63; denigration and, 44–45; denying identities as, 45–46; discrediting identity work, 63, 67–68, 81–83; as form of T-IPV, 42, 43–48; forms of, 42, 43–48, 122; gaslighting and, 45; gender expression manipulation in, 46–48; gifts and, 47; implications of T-IPV theories and, 123; maneuverting as, 70–71, 76–81; name choice and, 74; protective orders and, 261; retroverting and, 70–71, 73–76; romantic love narratives and, 63–64, 71–72; stigma power theory and, 122; vulnerabilities and, 18–19

identity work: defined, 62–63; "definition of the situation" and, 67; liminality and, 65; sign-vehicles and, 68

immigrants: asylum policies, 151; conclusions regarding, 154–55; criminality assumptions regarding, 149–50; criminal legal system and, 147–51; deportation threat and, 150; detention centers and, 151; housing instability of, 153; intersectionality theory and, 136–37; migrant statuses and, 150; police and, 147–49; polyvictimization and, 140, 143–46; racialized concept of, 135; shelter services and, 151–54; social construction and, 135; social isolation of, 150–51; victimization prevalence among, 137–39, *138*; violence types experienced by, 134. *See also* undocumented immigrants

immigration: barriers to escape and, 93; help seeking and, 147–54; Sessions and, 144; victimization related to, 115

Immigration Customs Enforcement (ICE): misdeeds of, 143–44; T-POC story related to, 133

incarceration. *See* correctional system and detention
insurance cards, 172
intergenerational transmission of violence theory. *See* theories of T-IPV causation
intersectionality, 101, 136–37
intimate partner violence (IPV): assumptions related to, 110; cisnormative causation and, 110; cycle of abuse, 36, 47; defined, x, 35; disempowerment theory and, 39, 120–21; from distance, 55; dominant culture and, 35–36; Global North and South, 102; healing from, 55–56; hormone therapy and, 40; intersectionality theory and, 136–37; men and, 320–21, *321*; minority stress theory and, 120–21; oppression model of, 312–13; as pattern of behaviors, 37; prevalence, *321, 322*; privilege and, 312–13; rationalizations for, 112–13; rural places and, 101–2; stigma power theory and, 121–22; survivor advocate and, 55–56; tactics of, 35–38; victim vulnerabilities to, 115–17; vulnerability justifying, 39–41; as women's problem, 311. *See also* cisgender IPV; transgender IPV; *specific topics*
isolation abuse. *See* psychological IPV

jails. *See* correctional system and detention
judges, transphobia and, 264. *See also* court system

knowledge, as barrier to escape, 93, *94*, 95–96

Latinx people: IPV victimization prevalence among, *138*, 139; non-IPV violence and, *141*; structural violence and, *142*
law enforcement. *See* police; police directives

lawyers, transphobic strategies of, 265
legal system. *See* civil legal system
legal system reform: barriers to legal remedies, 259–61; conclusions, 271–72; correctional system discrimination and, 267; criminal charges and, 259–60; law enforcement discrimination and, 261–64; marginalized transgender communities and, 267–70; overview, 258; protective orders and, 260–61; recommendations, 271–72; sex workers and, 270; T-POC and, 268; trans panic defense and, 265–66; undocumented immigrants and, 268–70
lesbian, gay, bisexual, transgender, and queer (LGBTQ): bystander interventions and, 299–300; campus climate and, 292–93; community support from, 210–11; disempowerment theory and, 119–21; gay rights movement and, 224; GSAs and, 298; help seeking and, 147; IPV victim shelters, 208, 214–15; isolation abuse and, 49; minority stress theory and, 120–21; National Training and Technical Assistance Center on LGBTQ Cultural Competency, 178; NCAVP and, 258; police and, 148, 237, 244; police competency training, 244; police liaison representing, 237; rural places and, 101–2; sexual assault and, 140; social service organizations, 211–12; victim shelters and, 210–12, 214–17; voter initiatives aimed at, ix; youth survival crimes and, 228
lessons: for all levels of social ecological model, 373–74; on causes, 371; ending T-IPV, 370–74; expanding assumptions, 363–65; improving how we know, 369–70; improving societal responses, 365–69; police and courts, 366–68; shelters, health care, other services, 368–69

LGBTQ. *See* lesbian, gay, bisexual, transgender, and queer
liminality. *See* identity work
love: identity work study and, 70–72; one true love concept, 71; as work project, 71–72. *See also* romantic love narratives

maneuverting. *See* identity abuse
marriage discrimination, 13–14
medical health care services: discrimination, 15, 172–77; help-seeking barriers for, 169–77; organizational culture improvement in, 190; overview, 169, 368–69; referrals and, 184–85; training needed in, 177–79; transgender affirmative approach, 177–90; victim screening in, 179–84
men: IPV and, 320–21, 321; with purses, 249n33. *See also specific topics*
mental health: anti-transphobia education and, 123; bipolar disorder and, 41; T-IPV impact on, 10; vulnerability, 41
mental health care services: client-centered, 189–90; core mental health modalities, 186–90; discrimination, 15, 172–77; help-seeking barriers for, 169–77; multisystem framework in, 186; organizational culture improvement in, 190; overview, 169, 368–69; pathologizing transgender people and, 175–76; referrals and, 184–85; strengths-based approach, 187; training needed in, 177–79; transgender affirmative approach, 177–90; trauma-informed approach to, 187–89; victim screening in, 179–84
minority stress theory: evidence related to, 120; IPV and, 120–21; LGBTQ and, 120–21; strain theory and, 120; transphobia and, 119–21. *See also* theories of T-IPV causation

name choice, 74
National Coalition of Anti-Violence Programs (NCAVP), 140, 258
National Transgender Discrimination Survey, 284
NCAVP. *See* National Coalition of Anti-Violence Programs
neutralization techniques, 112
nonbinary people: and abuse justifications, 44, 54; and affirming terminology during survivor services, 182, 208, 327; defined, 337; and gender-segregated survivor services, 96, 327; and identity document changes, 14, 16; and IPV prevalence, 8–9, 138–139; and police policies, 238; proportion of US population, 341; and research methodology, 340, 342, 348, 354, 370; as transgender subgroup, 3-4
nonprobability sampling: convenience and community venue, 345–46; data collection in, 344; probability sampling compared with, 342–43; web-based, 346–47. *See also* research

oppression model, 312–13
outcomes of T-IPV victimization. *See* risk factors for T-IPV victimization

parasitic abuse, 38–39
parental rights, 117
partner violence. *See* intimate partner violence; transgender IPV
perpetration theories. *See* theories of T-IPV causation
physical IPV: body parts and, 52; as form of T-IPV, 42, 52–53; in health care services, 173; intergenerational transmission of violence theory and, 114; prevalence, 7–9, 9; sleep disruption as, 53; subtle forms of, 53

police: alternatives to, 245; arrest practices and, 149–50, 230, 243–44; best practices and, 238–45; community oversight, 241; community policing, 239–40; criminal legal system and, 147–49; discrimination, 4–5, 147–48, 224–26, 228–29, 260; help seeking barriers and, 147–49, 226–32; institutional violence and, 134, *141*; lessons related to, 245–47, *246*, 366–68; LGBTQ liaison officer, 237, 241; people of color and, 227–28; printed materials, 243; QOL and, 226–27, 248n17; training needed for, 244–45; violence by, 141; walking while trans and, 227, 249n21

police directives: common terms defined in, 234; on frisks, 236; gender classification in, 235–36; introductory statements of, 233–34; localities analyzed, 233; pronoun use, 234–35; on searches, 236–37; for transgender interactions, 232–38; transportation, 237. *See also* police

polyvictimization. *See* violence, non-IPV forms of

power and control wheel, 353

prevention: anti-transphobia education, 123; bias regarding, 281; bystander interventions, 299–300; community-level influences, 292–93; conclusions, 300–301; developing/testing prevention strategies step, 286–87; family and peer support, 290; "Family Violence Prevention and Services Programs Regulations," 178; Green Dot prevention program, 286–87; GSAs and, 295, 298; identifying risk/protective factors step, 286, *287*; individual-level influences, 290; language bias regarding, 281; online interventions, 298–99; primary, 294–300; problem defining step, 285, *285*; public health framework and, 283–88, 294–300; relationship-level influences, 290–92; social ecological model and, 288–94; societal-level influences and, 293–94; steps for, 284–88; strategies using social ecological framework, *296*, *297*; widespread adoption step, 287–88

prisons. *See* correctional system and detention

probability sampling, 342–44. *See also* research

pronoun use: a.k.a., 235, 250n66; police directives on, 234–35

props, 78, 79

protective orders, 260–61

psychological IPV: children, control involving, 19, 117; criminal legal system and, 260; defined, 41–43; financial abuse, 42, 51–52, 117; isolation abuse, 42, 48–50, 116–17; prevalence, 7–9, *9*; verbal abuse, 42

public accommodations discrimination, 12, 13

"Public Health Approach to Violence Prevention" framework (CDC), 284

public health framework: bystander interventions, 299–300; conclusions, 300–301; developing/testing prevention strategies step, 286–87; GSAs and, 295, 298; identifying risk/protective factors step, 286, *287*; online interventions, 298–99; prevention steps within, 284–88; prevention using, 283–88; primary prevention, 294–300; problem defining step, 285, *285*; risk factors and, 283–84; social ecological model and, 288–94; widespread adoption step, 287–88; youth focus, 284–85

quality of life policing (QOL), 226–27, 248n17

race: barriers to escape and, 93; as categorization system, 135; help seeking and, 147–54; polyvictimization and, 140, *141*, *142*, 142–43, 145–46; victim vulnerabilities and, 116. *See also* immigrants; transgender people of color; undocumented immigrants; *specific races*

racialization: defined, 135; intersectionality theory and, 136–37; social construction and, 135–37; of transgender, 135–36

rationalizations of abusers: hormone therapy, 40; mental disorders and, 41; neutralization techniques and, 112; use of, 112–13; victim framing, 112–13

recovering from T-IPV victimization. *See* coping with T-IPV victimization

referrals, 184–85

relationships: assessing, 348–49; family, 99; identity work and, 65–66; lessons related to, 371; monogamous, 64; SV and, 290–92

research: assessing relationships, 348–49; best practices, 355–56, *356*; conclusions, 355–56; convenience and community venue sampling, 345–46; cross-sectional, 111, 125; CTS and CTS2, 347–48, 350–51; inclusive population definitions for, 337–38; interviews, 63; lessons related to, 369–70; longitudinal studies, 111, 124–25; nonprobability sampling, 342–43, 344–47; overview, 336–37; perpetuation and victimization assessment, 352; population defining in, 337–42; power and control wheel, 353; probability sampling in, 342–44; retrospective qualitative studies, 111, 124–25; T-IPV dearth in, 336; T-IPV distinct tactics, 353–55; T-IPV survey measures, 347–55; TransPop Study, 343–44; two-step gender assessment, 340–42, *342*; violence assessment, 350–52; web-based sampling, 346–47

resilience: defined, 92. *See also* coping with T-IPV victimization

restrooms: bathroom bill, 284; discrimination and, 15; school, 292

retroverting. *See* identity abuse

risk factors for T-IPV victimization: child abuse victimization, 114; disability, 115; employment-related, 9–10; family violence victimization, 114; fear, 10; HIV status, 10, 115; incarceration, 115; mental health impact, 10; potential risk factors with mixed evidence, 116–17; sexual risk-taking, 10; sex work, 115; substance use, 10; undocumented immigration status, 115. *See also* theories of T-IPV causation

romantic love narratives: in identity work study, 71–72; retroverting and, 76; self-construction impacted by, 63–64; stability and, 66

rural places, 101–2

screening. *See* victim screening

searches, 236–37

seeking help. *See* help seeking barriers

self-blame: as barrier to escape, 93, *94*, 94–95; hegemonic masculinity and, 94–95; transphobia and, 94

self-harm, as abuse justification, 41

service gap: additional resources addressing, 332–33; adult education addressing, 330; awareness of services and, 316; barriers from provider side of, 320–23, *321*, *322*; barriers from transgender survivor side of, 314–19; case studies addressing, 329; conclusions, 331–32; cost minimization addressing, 326–27; cultural competency worries and, 315–16; data dissemination addressing, 328–29; fear and, 315; FORGE survey of, 314–23;

help seeking making matters worse, 317–18; legal provisions addressing, 323–25; men and, 320–21, *321*; nonbinary survivors recommendations addressing, 327; other federal level agencies addressing, 325; reputation of service and, 316; resource sharing addressing, 330–31; revictimization avoidance addressing, 326; role-plays training addressing, 330; seeking help elsewhere, 318–19; sex-specific/sex-segregated programming addressing, 323–24; shame, stigma, embarrassment and, 317; systemic problems, 319; terms paradox training addressing, 331; trust lack and, 318; unwanted/unneeded service, 319; videos addressing, 329; welcome worry and, 315; woman-focused agencies and, 317

service providers: ACE study and, 313–14; background issues related to, 311–12; FORGE philosophies and, 313; ideology and, 312–14

services, transgender-specific: discrimination by, 133; gender-segregated, 93, *94*, 96; hegemonic masculinity and, 95; reasons to integrate, 325–27. *See also* shelter services; victim shelters, IPV

sexual IPV: boundaries and, 54; bystander interventions, 299–300; community-level influences and, 292–93; conclusions, 300–301; developing/testing prevention strategies step and, 286–87; examples of, 53–54; family and peer support preventing, 290; as form of T-IPV, *42*, 53–55; forms of, 301n2; GSAs and, 295, 298; health and, 282–83; identifying risk and protective factors step, 286, *287*; intergenerational transmission of violence theory and, 114; language bias regarding, 281; LGBTQ and, 140; neutralization techniques, 112; online interventions, 298–99; prevalence, 7–9, *9*, 282; prevention program bias regarding, 281; prevention using public health framework, 283–88; primary prevention, 294–300; problem defining step and, 285, *285*; relationship-level influences and, 290–92; revictimization avoidance and, 326; risk factors and, 283–84; social ecological model and, 288–94; societal impact, 283; societal-level influences and, 293–94; strategies using social ecological framework, *296*, *297*; transgender-specific justifications for, 54–55; White House Task Force to Protect Students from Sexual Assault, 286–87; widespread adoption step and, 287–88; as women's problem, 311

sexual risk-taking, 10

sex workers: legal system reform and, 270; as risk factor for T-IPV, 115; T-IPV prevalence among, 142

shame: as barrier to escape, 93, *94*, 94–95; FORGE study and, 317; hegemonic masculinity and, 94–95; transphobia and, 94

shelter services. *See* victim shelters, IPV

social construction, race and, 135–37

social ecological model: community-level influences, 292–93; individual-level influences, 289–90; lessons for all levels of, 373–74; public health framework and, 288–94; relationship-level influences and, 290–92; societal-level influences, 293–94; strategies, *296*, *297*

social learning theory, 114

social network, emotional dependence and, 97

stigma: fear of stigmatizing transgender communities, 93, *94*, 97; FORGE study and, 317

stigma power theory. *See* theories of T-IPV causation

theories of T-IPV causation: abuser rationalizations and, 39–41, 112–13; disempowerment theory, 39, 119–21; honour-based violence theory, 118–19; implications of T-IPV theories, 122–26; intergenerational transmission of violence theory, 113–14; minority stress theory and, 119–21; neutralization techniques, 112; overview, 110–11; social support network, 116–17; stigma power theory, 121–22; T-IPV and C-IPV shared, 111–17; transphobia-related perpetration theories, 118–21; transphobia-related victimization vulnerability theories, 121–22; unique to T-IPV, 118–22; victim framing, 112–13; victim vulnerabilities, 115–17

T-IPV. *See* transgender IPV

T-POC. *See* transgender people of color

transgender: diversity among, 337; gay rights movement and, 224; as mental illness, 175–76; population size, 8, 26n38; racialization of, 135–36; as survey gender option, 338–39

transgender IPV (T-IPV): categories, 42; causal pathways shared with, 111–17; causal pathways unique to, 118–22; cisnormative causation and, 110; defined, 91; discrimination and, 10–20; emergent literature, 6–7; ending, 370–74; impact, 9–10; implications, 20–21; invisible threat of, 6; motivations related to, 17; overview, 22–24; police assistance and, 4–5; policies excluding, 5; prevalence, 7–9, *9*; seeking help and, 4–5; tactics related to, 18–19. *See also* cyber IPV; identity abuse; intimate partner violence; physical IPV; psychological IPV; sexual IPV; *specific topics*

transgender people of color (T-POC): conclusions regarding, 154–55; criminality assumptions regarding, 149–50; criminal legal system and, 147–51; gay rights movement and, 224; health care services discrimination against, 174; help seeking and, 147–54; housing instability of, 153; ICE story related to, 133; legal system reform and, 268; police and, 147–49; polyvictimization among, 140, *141, 142*, 142–43, 145–46; polyvictimization and T-IPV connected to, 145–46; shelter services and, 151–54; victimization prevalence among, 137–39, *138*; violence types experienced by, 134

transgender rights movement, ix–x

transphobia: barriers to escape and, 93; of court clerks, 265; of court system, 264–66; defined, 3; disempowerment theory and, 119–21; *DSM* and, 176; education to prevent, 123; in health care services, 173; help seeking and, 4–5, 19–20; honour-based violence theory and, 118–19; internalization of, 17; interpersonal, 11–13; in IPV victim shelters, 206–7; isolation abuse and, 50; judges and, 264; lawyers and, 265; as learned, 284; legal strategies and, 265–66; limiting T-IPV awareness, 5–6; minority stress theory and, 119–21; motivations related to, 17; outing threats and, 18; perpetration theories related to, 118–21; police and, 4–5, 147–48; self-blame and shame related to, 94; within shelter services, 152; stigma power theory and, 121–22; T-IPV tactics and, 18–19; victimization vulnerability theories related to, 121–22; as widespread, 284

transsexual, 247n1
Two-Spirit, 339, 348

underground economy. *See* sex workers
undocumented immigrants: court system and, 269–70; legal system reform and, 268–70; Sessions and, 269–70; victimization prevalence among, *138*, 139
United States Transgender Survey (USTS): fear of health provider discrimination, 171; gender labels list in, 339–40, *341*; identity document concerns and, 172; on incarceration, 267; institutional violence and, *141*; out of closet percentages, 18; police and, 229, 250n74; sex workers and, 270; structural violence and, *142*; T-IPV prevalence in, 8; victimization prevalence and, 137–39, *138*; web-based sampling used in, 347
USTS. *See* United States Transgender Survey

VAWA. *See* Violence Against Women Act
verbal abuse. *See* psychological IPV
victim framing, 112–13
victim screening: culturally responsive care and, 179–84; guidance for development of, 183–84; implementing, 181–84; process, 180; protocols, 181; respect for lives in, 182–83; T-IPV unique tactics and, 181–82; transgender-inclusive language in, 182; warning flags and, 180–81
victim shelters, IPV: admission practices, 204–6; alternate housing and support, 210–12; background, 202; children and, 209; cisgender oriented services and, 208–10; community outreach, 215–16; competition for room in, 209; conclusions, 155, 217–18; education and, 212–15; emergence of cisnormative, 203–4; feminist IPV theory and, 203–4; gender identity versus assigned sex and, 206; health issues and, 153–54; help seeking, 151–54; homelessness and, 97; homeless shelter and, 211; hotel/motel options and, 209–10; intake procedures revision, 214; legitimate victim and, 152–53; lessons, 368–69; LGBTQ community support away from, 210–11; LGBTQ social service organizations and, 211–12, 214–15; LGBTQ-specific, 216–17; outreach, 214–15; overview, 202–3; policies review, 214; residents education, 213–14; revictimization avoidance and, 326; self-esteem and, 210; single-gender admission at, 205; staff training, 212–13; transforming, 212–17; transgender people as dangerous myth in, 206; transgender specific victimization and, 215; transphobia within, 152; transphobic discrimination in, 206–7; universal approach in, 208; VAWA and, 5
victim vulnerability: age and, 116; as causal pathway, 115–17; children and, 117; economic resources and, 117; homelessness and, 116; race and, 116; risk factors, 115–16; social support network, 116–17; theories related to, 121–22
violence, non-IPV forms of: within employment, 141; and immigration, 143–45; perpetrated by acquaintances and peer, 134; perpetrated by police, 141; and polyvictimization, 140–46; within prison, 141; within public accommodations, 141; by race and ethnicity, 141–43; within school, 141
Violence Against Women Act (VAWA): cost minimization and, 326–27; expiration of, 5; legal provisions of reauthorized, 323–25; nonbinary survivors and, 327; reauthorization of, x; shelters and, 5; T-POC story related to, 133; transgender people as outside, 311

vulnerability: abuse justified by, 39–41; identity abuse and, 18–19; mental health, 41. *See also* victim vulnerability

walking while trans, 227, 238, 249n21
web-based sampling. *See* research

women: battered women's movement, 203–4; IPV as problem of, 311. *See also* Black women; Violence Against Women Act; *specific topics*
work: employment discrimination, 11–13, 12, 100; financial dependence and, 96–97; isolation abuse and, 49. *See also* identity work